W9-BZJ-041

WITHDRAWN

AN ECONOMIC HISTORY OF THE ENGLISH POOR LAW
1750–1850

AN ECONOMIC HISTORY
OF THE ENGLISH POOR LAW
1750–1850

GEORGE R. BOYER

Cornell University

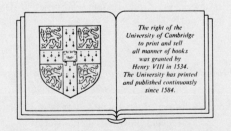

The right of the
University of Cambridge
to print and sell
all manner of books
was granted by
Henry VIII in 1534.
The University has printed
and published continuously
since 1584.

CAMBRIDGE UNIVERSITY PRESS

Cambridge

New York   Port Chester   Melbourne   Sydney

Published by the Press Syndicate of the University of Cambridge
The Pitt Building, Trumpington Street, Cambridge CB2 1RP
40 West 20th Street, New York, NY 10011, USA
10 Stamford Road, Oakleigh, Melbourne 3166, Australia

First published 1990

Printed in the United States of America

Library of Congress Cataloging-in-Publication Data
Boyer, George R.
An economic history of the English Poor Law, 1750–1850 / George R.
Boyer.
p. cm.
Includes bibliographical references.
ISBN 0-521-36479-5
1. Great Britain – Economic conditions – 18th century. 2. Great
Britain – Economic conditions – 19th century. 3. Poor – Great Britain
– History. 4. Poor laws – Great Britain – History. I. Title.
HC254.5.B64   1990
362.5'85'0942 – dc20   89–22365
                                                     CIP

British Library Cataloguing in Publication Data
Boyer, George R.
An economic history of the English Poor Law, 1750–1850.
1. England. Poverty relief, history
I. Title
362.5'8'0942

ISBN 0-521-36479-5 hard covers

For my mother
Louise Coulson Boyer

CONTENTS

ACKNOWLEDGMENTS

This book began in 1981 as a Ph.D. dissertation at the University of Wisconsin and has continued to evolve and expand ever since. I have accumulated many debts in the process of writing the book, and I am happy to be able to thank those people who have generously taken the time to improve it.

My greatest debt is to Jeffrey Williamson, who supervised my dissertation, and who has helped in every stage of the development of this work. Over the past decade Jeff has been my teacher, my critic, and my friend. He has consistently helped me to clarify my thinking and insisted that I find data to support my hypotheses. Without his enthusiasm and encouragement this book would never have been written.

I also owe a major debt to Peter Lindert. Peter played an important role in the early stages of the project, helping me to formulate my ideas and directing me to the data necessary to test them. Since then he has read several versions of almost every chapter of the book and always improved them with his detailed criticisms.

I owe my understanding of implicit contracts theory to two of my colleagues at Cornell, Kenneth Burdett and Randall Wright. Ken taught me contracts theory at the University of Wisconsin, and has continued to give me the benefit of his insights since we both moved to Cornell. Randy offered me invaluable help in revising the model into the form that appears in Chapter 3.

Joel Mokyr (who once called my model of poor relief a "neoclassical soap opera") and Mary MacKinnon read drafts of most of the chapters of the book, and greatly improved them with their criticisms and suggestions. Stanley Engerman and Michael Edelstein read the entire manuscript, and their detailed comments significantly improved the final version of the book.

Several other people have read and criticized drafts of chapters and deserve thanks: Kenneth Snowden, Claudia Goldin, Daniel Baugh, Donald McCloskey, Tim Hatton, Nick Crafts, Nick von Tunzelmann, David Galenson, Paul David, Lars Muus, Roger Avery, Michael Haines, Glen Cain, Henry McMillan, Patricia Dillon, and Carl Dahlman. In addition, I would like to thank my colleagues at the School of Industrial and Labor Relations, especially George Jakubson and Ronald Ehrenberg, for their help and constructive criticism. For their helpful comments, I also thank the participants at the 1982 Cliometrics Conference; the Tenth University of California Conference on Economic History (1986); and the economic history workshops at Northwestern, Chicago, Harvard, Pennsylvania, and Columbia.

For their patient assistance and cooperation in locating books and manuscript sources, I thank the staffs of Olin Library at Cornell; the British Library; the Public Record Office at Kew; and the Essex, Suffolk, Bedford, Cambridge, and Norfolk county record offices. I thank Joshua Schwarz and Phyllis Noonan for their able research assistance. Nancy Williamson at Wisconsin and Eileen Driscoll at Cornell provided invaluable computer programming assistance. Pat Dickerson typed the dissertation, the book manuscript, and every draft in between, and cheerfully put up with my increasingly compulsive behavior during the latter stages of this project. I gratefully acknowledge the assistance and encouragement of my editors at Cambridge University Press: Frank Smith, Janis Bolster, and Nancy Landau.

Financial support for my research was obtained from several sources. A Vilas Travel Grant from the Graduate School of the University of Wisconsin enabled me to spend three months in England during the spring of 1981. The Committee on Research in Economic History of the Economic History Association provided an Arthur H. Cole grant-in-aid that permitted me to spend part of the summer of 1986 doing research in England. The School of Industrial Relations at Cornell provided several small grants to help defray research costs.

While researching this book in England I enjoyed the hospitality of Tim Hatton and the members of the economics department at the University of Essex. Tim generously provided me with lodgings at the Hatton Hotel, and he and his colleagues spent innumerable hours at the Black Buoy, the Rose and Crown, the Horse and Groom, and the Flag passing on to me the famous oral tradition of the economics department (see O. E. Covick, "The Quantity Theory of Drink: A Restatement," *Australian Economic Papers,* December 1974).

I would like to thank the Economic History Association and the editors of *Explorations in Economic History* and the *Journal of Political Economy* for permission to reprint portions of my earlier articles: "An Economic Model of the English Poor Law circa 1780–1834," *Explorations in Economic History* 22 (April 1985): 129–67 (copyright 1985, by Academic Press); "The Old Poor Law and the Agricultural Labor Market in Southern England: An Empirical Analysis," *Journal of Economic History* 46 (March 1986): 113–35 (copyright 1986, by the Economic History Association); "The Poor Law, Migration, and Economic Growth," *Journal of Economic History* 46 (June 1986): 419–30 (copyright 1986, by the Economic History Association); "Malthus Was Right After All: Poor Relief and Birth Rates in Southeastern England," *Journal of Political Economy* 97 (February 1989): 93–114 (copyright 1989, by The University of Chicago).

My friend and companion Janet Millman has offered advice, criticism, research assistance, and encouragement throughout the project. She has suffered through my fixation on this book during the past three years with only a minimum of complaints.

Finally, I thank my mother, Louise Boyer, and my aunts and uncles for their encouragement over the years. When I was young, Muż always found the time to take me to museums and historic sites, and she passed on to me her love of England. For these and so many other reasons, this book is dedicated to her.

Ithaca, New York
January 1990

INTRODUCTION

The English Poor Law dates from 1597, when Parliament passed a law
(39 Elizabeth, c. 3) making it the responsibility of each parish to maintain its poor inhabitants. Four years later Parliament passed another law
(43 Elizabeth, c. 2) clarifying several provisions of the 1597 act. Together, these laws established "the principle of a compulsory assessment
for relief of the poor . . . as an essential portion of [England's] domestic
policy" (Nicholls 1898: I, 187). They also established that poor relief was
to be administered and financed at the parish level. There were no
"fundamentally new idea[s] in the Poor Law Legislation following
1601," but there were definite long-term trends in the administration of
relief, especially with respect to adult able-bodied males (Marshall 1968:
11–12). The two major trends were the shift toward increased generosity
for able-bodied paupers that began around 1750, and the subsequent
decline in generosity that began in 1834 with the passage of the Poor
Law Amendment Act.

This book examines the economic role played by the English Poor
Law during the period 1750 to 1850, the years when relief generosity for
the able-bodied was at its peak. It focuses on the development and
persistence of policies providing relief outside of workhouses to unemployed and underemployed able-bodied laborers, and on the effect of
such policies on the rural labor market. In particular, it provides explanations for the widespread adoption of outdoor relief policies in the 1770s
and 1780s and for the significant differences in the administration of
relief between the southeast of England and the west and north, and it
analyzes the effect of poor relief on wages, profits, birth rates, and
migration.

The issues raised are not new; each of them was debated by contemporary observers of the early-nineteenth-century Poor Law. The writings of
contemporaries and historians who have addressed these issues can be

1

divided into three schools, which I refer to as the traditional, neo-traditional, and revisionist. The traditional analysis of the economics of poor relief is derived largely from the 1834 Report of the Royal Commission to Investigate the Poor Laws. It maintains that the widespread adoption of policies granting outdoor relief to able-bodied paupers was an emergency response to the extremely high food prices of 1795, which caused real wages in rural areas to fall temporarily below subsistence. By guaranteeing workers a minimum level of income, the system of outdoor relief significantly reduced the incentive to work. In the long run, outdoor relief increased unemployment rates, lowered the productivity of workers who remained employed, and caused laborers' wages, farmers' profits, and landlords' rents to decline. Moreover, by artificially reducing the cost of children, the Poor Law increased the rate of population growth, which created an excess supply of labor and thus increased the number of relief recipients in the long run. The traditional literature offers no explanation for the regional concentration of outdoor relief or the persistence of outdoor relief until the passage of the Poor Law Amendment Act in 1834; the system simply is seen as self-perpetuating in nature.

The neo-traditional school includes John and Barbara Hammond, Sidney and Beatrice Webb, Karl Polanyi, and Eric Hobsbawm. These authors disputed the traditional literature's explanation for the widespread adoption of outdoor relief, but they agreed that the payment of outdoor relief to able-bodied males had a significant negative effect on the rural parish economy. Outdoor relief policies were adopted in response to "the collapse of the economic position of the [rural] labourer" in the late eighteenth century, but they proved to be "a wrong and disastrous answer to certain difficult questions" (Hammond and Hammond 1913: 120, 170). The neo-traditional literature maintained that outdoor relief was able to persist into the 1830s only because benefit levels were continuously reduced by parishes from 1815 to 1834.

The revisionist analysis of the Poor Law began in 1963 with the publication of Mark Blaug's classic paper "The Myth of the Old Poor Law and the Making of the New." The work of Blaug (1963; 1964), Daniel Baugh (1975), and Anne Digby (1975; 1978) rejected the hypothesis that outdoor relief had disastrous long-run consequences for the agricultural labor market. To judge the disincentive effects of outdoor relief on labor supply, Blaug (1963: 161–2) estimated benefit–wage ratios for the period from 1795 to 1825, and concluded that the typical relief scale was so modest that it did not offer "an attractive alternative to gainful employment." Baugh (1975: 61) and J. S. Taylor (1969: 295) argued that since rural parishes were "generally small enough to apply any relief system with discretion" (Baugh 1975: 61), the disincentive effects of outdoor relief must have been small. Finally, Blaug (1963: 164–7) and Baugh (1975: 60–3) examined time series of real per capita relief expenditures and concluded, in the words of Blaug, that "there is no evidence whatever of that most popular of all the charges levied at the Old Poor Law: the 'snow-ball effect' of outdoor relief to the able-bodied."

The revisionists also provided explanations for the persistence and regional nature of outdoor relief. Blaug (1963: 171–2) maintained that outdoor relief was used to supplement "substandard" wage rates and to support seasonally and structurally unemployed workers. Seasonal fluctuations in the demand for labor were especially pronounced in grain production, and the southeast was England's major grain-producing region. Digby (1978: 22–3, 105–7) attributed the persistence of outdoor relief to the seasonal nature of arable farming and to the political power of labor-hiring farmers, who used "their position as poor law administrators to pursue a policy with an economical alteration of poor relief and independent income for the labourer."

The contention that outdoor relief increased birth rates also has been challenged by the revisionists. Blaug (1963: 173–4) surveyed the available county-level data and concluded that there was "no persuasive evidence" that outdoor relief caused birth rates to increase. James Huzel (1980: 369–80) tested the hypothesis using parish-level data and found that the payment of child allowances to laborers with large families did not have a significant positive effect on birth rates.

In sum, most of the hypotheses of the traditional literature have been challenged during the past 25 years. How then can I justify another study of the Old Poor Law? The present work can be justified on three grounds. First, some important issues have not been confronted by the revisionists. None of the revisionists attempted to determine when the payment of outdoor relief to able-bodied laborers became widespread. Rather, they accepted the traditional literature's hypothesis that outdoor relief originated in response to the subsistence crises of 1795 and 1800. This suggests either that the reason for the adoption of outdoor relief policies was different from the reason for their persistence, or that seasonal and structural unemployment suddenly became a problem in 1795. Neither conclusion is satisfactory. The revisionists also have not confronted the hypothesis that outdoor relief slowed economic growth by slowing the rate of migration from the agricultural south to the industrial northwest. The use of outdoor relief might have represented an efficient solution to farmers' seasonality problems but at the same time fostered an inefficient allocation of labor across regions.

Second, several aspects of the revisionist analysis are not well developed. For example, Blaug contended that the regional nature of outdoor relief could be explained in part by the seasonality of grain production, but he did not explain why a majority of parishes in the southeast chose outdoor relief policies over other possible methods for dealing with seasonality, such as allotment schemes or yearlong labor contracts. Similarly, while Digby maintained that the use of outdoor relief was "economical" for farmers, she did not determine the precise conditions under which it was in the interest of farmers to lay off workers. The present study develops the revisionist hypotheses into a model of the economic role of poor relief in agricultural parishes.

Third, none of the competing hypotheses concerning the adoption, persistence, and regional nature of outdoor relief has been tested empirically. This study provides such a test. I estimate a three-equation regression model to explain differences in per capita relief expenditures, agricultural laborers' annual earnings, and unemployment rates across 311 rural southern parishes in 1832. The results are used to evaluate explanations of the economic role of outdoor relief. The major data sources used are the 1831 census and the returns to the Rural Queries, a questionnaire distributed to rural parishes in the summer of 1832 by the Royal Poor Law Commission. The returns provide information on the administration of poor relief, wage rates and annual earnings in agriculture, seasonal levels of employment, and the existence of cottage industry and allotments for nearly 1,100 parishes, making them the most important available source of information on the Old Poor Law. However, they have never been fully utilized. That is unfortunate, because the testing of competing hypotheses is necessary in order to determine the economic role of poor relief.

I also provide a test of the hypothesis that child allowances had a positive effect on birth rates. Huzel's (1980) earlier analysis of the effect of child allowances is seriously flawed because it consists of a simple comparison of relief policies and birth rates, without controlling for other possible determinants of fertility. I estimate a regression model to explain differences in birth rates across 213 rural southern parishes in

1826–30. The regression results show that, when other socioeconomic determinants of fertility are accounted for, the use of child allowances did indeed cause birth rates to increase.

The present work is an extension of the revisionist analysis, an attempt to use economic theory to derive additional insights about the development and impact of outdoor relief policies. The rural labor market is analyzed in terms of a tool of modern labor economics: implicit contracts theory. A model of the parish labor market is postulated, which incorporates three important features of the early-nineteenth-century rural economy: the seasonality in the demand for agricultural labor, the general lack of nonagricultural employment opportunities in rural parishes, and the tax system for financing the poor rate that enabled farmers to shift part of their labor costs to non-labor-hiring taxpayers. The model portrays the problem faced by farmers in the early nineteenth century: how to maximize profits subject to the constraint that any implicit contract offered to workers must yield an expected utility large enough to keep the desired number of workers from leaving the parish.

The model contains two somewhat controversial assumptions. First, labor is assumed to be mobile. Although some historians would dispute this assumption, it is supported by recent estimates made by Jeffrey Williamson (1987: 646–7), who found that rural out-migration rates in England from 1816 to 1831 were similar to out-migration rates in developing countries during the 1960s and 1970s. Further evidence of labor mobility, and of the importance of London as a destination of rural southern migrants, is provided by Deane and Cole (1967: 106–15), Wrigley (1967: 45–9), and Schofield (1970: 271–3). The mobility of labor forced southern farmers to take London wage rates (and wage rates in neighboring parishes) into account when determining the value of the labor contracts they offered to farm workers.

Second, I assume that farmers were profit maximizers and workers were utility maximizers. In his Nobel lecture, Theodore Schultz (1980: 649, 644) stated that

poor people [in low-income countries] are no less concerned about improving their lot and that of their children than those of us who have incomparably greater advantages. Nor are they any less competent in obtaining the maximum benefit from their limited resources. . . . Farmers the world over, in dealing with costs, returns, and risks, are calculating economic agents. Within their small, individual, allocative domain they are fine-tuning entrepreneurs, tuning so subtly that many experts fail to recognize how efficient they are.

Similarly, T. S. Ashton (1955: 30) maintained that "those who controlled [agriculture in eighteenth-century England] were no less concerned than iron masters or cotton spinners to maximize their income and properties. . . . Agriculture had its peculiar features. . . . But generally, like other callings, it was ruled by the forces of the market."

However, many historians disagree with Schultz and Ashton. Eric Hobsbawm and George Rudé (1968: 50), writing about the Poor Law, warned that

it is a mistake to apply abstract economic reasoning, however humanitarian, to a situation which cannot be understood except in its context. Speenhamland was not intended to achieve the results which . . . economists have in mind. . . . It was an instinctive escape of country gentlemen into the world they knew best – the self-contained parish dominated by squire and parson.

But surely there is no more justification in dismissing an economic interpretation out of hand than in assuming that any institution that existed must have been rational. Perhaps the Poor Law was both paternalistic *and* profitable to farmers. The proper way to proceed in research is, in the words of Joel Mokyr (1985a: 1), "to employ a priori reasoning to formulate and test hypotheses and then try our best to test these hypotheses." This methodology is adopted in the present study. Hypotheses derived from the implicit contracts model and the traditional literature are tested using both quantitative and qualitative evidence. The results are used to determine the economic role of the Old Poor Law.

The analysis proceeds as follows. Chapter 1 provides the background information needed to understand the role played by policies providing outdoor relief for able-bodied workers. It focuses on three issues: the precise form of outdoor relief payments to able-bodied workers; the timing of the widespread adoption of outdoor relief policies; and the changes in the rural economic environment that occurred during the second half of the eighteenth century. I conclude that the adoption of outdoor relief in the southeast was a response to a decline in family income caused by the decline of cottage industry and laborers' loss of land. Chapter 2 surveys the historiography of the Old Poor Law, from the beginning of the traditional critique of outdoor relief in the late eighteenth century to the development of the revisionist analysis in the 1960s and 1970s.

A theory of the economic role of outdoor relief is developed in Chapter 3. A model of the parish labor market is constructed and solved to determine the conditions under which implicit labor contracts including seasonal layoffs and unemployment insurance (in the form of outdoor relief) were cost-minimizing for farmers. The extent of seasonal fluctuations in labor demand is a key determinant of the nature of the optimal contract. The model therefore provides an explanation for the regional nature of outdoor relief: Contracts including layoffs and outdoor relief were cost-minimizing in grain-producing areas but not in pasture-farming areas. The chapter also contains a discussion of the effect of seasonal migrant labor on the form of grain farmers' cost-minimizing labor contracts.

Chapter 4 provides a test of the hypotheses obtained from the model developed in Chapter 3, as well as several other hypotheses put forward by contemporary critics and historians. A three-equation regression model is estimated, to explain cross-parish variations in 1832 in per capita relief expenditures, agricultural laborers' annual wage income, and the rate of unemployment. The data used in the analysis were obtained from the 1831 census and from the returns to the 1832 Rural Queries. The regression results support several of the hypotheses obtained from the implicit contracts model and reject most of the traditional literature's criticisms of outdoor relief.

Chapters 5 and 6 examine the effect of outdoor relief on birth rates and rural–urban migration. Chapter 5 provides a test of the hypothesis, advanced by Thomas Malthus and adopted by the Royal Poor Law Commission, that the payment of weekly allowances to laborers with large families caused birth rates to increase. I estimate a regression model to explain differences in birth rates across rural southern parishes in 1826–30. The results show that child allowances had a significant positive effect on the birth rate. The widespread adoption of child allowances was a major cause of the increase in birth rates during the first two decades of the nineteenth century.

Chapter 6 offers a test of Arthur Redford's (1964: 93–4) hypothesis that policies providing outdoor relief to able-bodied workers slowed the rate of migration from rural southeast England to the industrial northwest. Assuming that workers' migration decisions were determined largely by the size of rural–urban wage gaps, an estimate of the Poor Law's effect on migration is obtained by determining the extent to which relief payments raised agricultural laborers' incomes above the marginal product of labor, and by comparing this increase to existing wage gaps. I conclude that even if all relief payments to able-bodied workers were in excess of the marginal product of labor, the effect of poor relief on migration was small.

Chapter 7 examines the effect of the New Poor Law on the agricultural labor market. It focuses on three issues: the reasons why the New Poor Law was adopted; the effect of the substitution of the workhouse system for outdoor relief on grain farmers' cost-minimizing labor contracts; and the effect of the abolition of outdoor relief on agricultural laborers' annual income. I conclude that the high cost of indoor relief caused grain farmers either to adopt full employment contracts or, where possible, to evade the 1834 legislation and continue to provide outdoor relief to seasonally unemployed workers. The adoption of the New Poor Law is shown to have had little, if any, effect on farm laborers' income.

The economic role of poor relief in industrial cities is examined in Chapter 8, which presents evidence that textile manufacturers used the Poor Law as an unemployment insurance system. Workers not needed during downturns were laid off or put on short time, enabling manufacturers to shift part of their labor costs to other urban taxpayers. The hypothesis that industrial cities slowed rural–urban migration and perpetuated large rural–urban wage gaps by removing large numbers of nonsettled workers during recessions is tested. I conclude that cities followed a selective removal policy, which should not have reduced the propensity to migrate of able-bodied workers.

1

THE DEVELOPMENT AND ADMINISTRATION OF THE OLD POOR LAW IN RURAL AREAS, 1760–1834

During the last third of the eighteenth century, several changes took place in the administration of poor relief, the most important of which was the widespread provision of relief outside the workhouse to able-bodied laborers who were unemployed or underemployed. The changes in relief methods led to changes in the economic role of the Poor Law in rural parishes. A knowledge of the methods of relief that were adopted, the time when they were adopted, and the changes in the economic environment that brought about their adoption is essential for an evaluation of the economic role played by the Poor Law from 1795 to 1834, the so-called Speenhamland era.

This chapter provides the background necessary for an evaluation of the Old Poor Law. It is divided into three sections. Section 1 describes the methods used to relieve able-bodied laborers from 1780 to 1834. I conclude that the major function of poor relief was the provision of unemployment benefits to seasonally unemployed laborers. Section 2 focuses on the timing of the adoption of policies granting poor relief to able-bodied laborers. The year 1795 was not a watershed in the administration of poor relief; real relief expenditures began increasing rapidly at least 20 years before the famous meeting at Speenhamland, Berkshire. Section 3 discusses two important changes in the rural economic environment that occurred during the second half of the eighteenth century, and presents evidence that these environmental changes caused the sharp increase in real per capita poor relief expenditures. The conclusions concerning the methods of relief used, the timing of their adoption, and the reasons for their adoption are considerably different from those reached by the traditional literature. Whereas the traditional literature viewed the changes in relief methods as exogenous causes of economic dislocation, I view the adoption of outdoor relief as an endogenous response to changes in economic conditions.

9

1. The Administration of Poor Relief

It is possible to identify six methods used by rural parishes to relieve poor able-bodied laborers from 1780 to 1834: allowances-in-aid-of-wages, payments to laborers with large families, payments to seasonally unemployed agricultural laborers, the roundsman system, the labor rate, and the workhouse system. The first five methods are forms of "outdoor" relief, while the workhouse system, which forced relief recipients to enter workhouses, is referred to as "indoor" relief.

Under the allowance system, a laborer (whether employed or unemployed) was guaranteed a minimum weekly income, the level of which was determined by the price of bread and the size of his family. According to the 1834 Report of the Royal Poor Law Commission:

In perhaps a majority of the parishes in which the allowance system prevails, the earnings of the applicant, and, in a few, the earnings of his wife and children, are ascertained, or at least professed or attempted to be ascertained, and only the difference between them and the sum allotted to him by the scale is paid to him by the parish. (Royal Commission 1834: 24)

The most famous allowance scale was that adopted by the Berkshire magistrates who met at Speenhamland on May 6, 1795. The Berkshire scale stipulated that

when the gallon loaf of second flour, weighing 8 lbs. 11 oz. shall cost one shilling, then every poor and industrious man shall have for his own support 3s. weekly, either produced by his own or his family's labour or an allowance from the poor rates, and for the support of his wife and every other of his family 1s. 6d. When the gallon loaf shall cost 1s. 4d., then every poor and industrious man shall have 4s. weekly for his own, and 1s. 10d. for the support of every other of his family. And so in proportion as the price of bread rises or falls (that is to say), 3d. to the man and 1d. to every other of the family, on every penny which the loaf rises above a shilling. (Quoted in Hammond and Hammond 1913: 163)[1]

The allowance scales were, in effect, negative income taxes "with a 100 percent marginal rate of tax on earned income below the minimum" (McCloskey 1973: 434).

The traditional literature maintained that the allowance system was by far the most widespread form of outdoor relief (Hammond and Hammond 1913: 161, 164; Polanyi 1944: 78). It was assumed that most rural parishes in the south and east, in response to the subsistence crisis of

[1] For examples of other allowance scales, see Royal Commission (1834: 21–4).

1795, followed the lead of the Berkshire magistrates, and that allowances remained the major form of relief until 1834.

Recent studies of poor relief at the county or local level do not support this hypothesis. Evidence obtained from parish account books suggests instead that allowance systems were extensively used only during years of exceptionally high food prices, as a substitute for increases in nominal wages. After a study of the records of sixteen Berkshire parishes, Neuman (1972: 102, 107) concluded that although it was "probably true that at one time or another most Berkshire parishes adopted some sort of bread scale as a general guide for relieving their able-bodied poor, . . . evidence suggests these allowances were often of a temporary sort, in response to unusually severe seasons and high prices." A. F. J. Brown (1969: 152) similarly concluded that "from 1795 to 1814, many Essex parishes did thus assist large families for limited periods of very high prices. . . . Generally, when prices fell, allowances were discontinued." My study of parish record books for Essex, Norfolk, and Bedford found that most parishes that adopted allowance systems in 1795, when bread prices were exceptionally high, removed them in 1796 or 1797 when prices declined. The high prices of 1800–1 caused parishes to set up allowance systems again, only to remove them during the summer of 1802. This pattern of instituting bread scales in response to high food prices continued throughout the period up to 1834, although evidence suggests that the number of parishes using the allowance system was never again as high as in 1795 and 1800.[2]

The assumption that allowances-in-aid-of-wages constituted the major form of relief to able-bodied laborers is further refuted by parish responses to questions 24 and 25 of the 1832 Rural Queries and question 1 of an 1824 questionnaire distributed by the Select Committee on Labourers' Wages. Only 41% of the parishes or districts that responded to the 1824 questionnaire admitted paying allowances-in-aid-of-wages (Williams 1981: 151).[3] This led Blaug (1963: 160) to conclude that "fewer parishes practised outdoor relief to the able-bodied in 1824 than in previous years." Blaug's conclusion follows, however, only if one assumes that the allowance system represented the sole form of outdoor relief, which was

[2] My study of surviving parish record books in Essex, Norfolk, and Bedford found that the use of allowance systems occurred primarily during the years 1795, 1796, 1800, and 1801.
[3] The use of allowance systems was particularly widespread in the grain-producing southeast; 50% of the responding southeastern districts admitted paying allowances-in-aid-of-wages (Parl. Papers 1825: XIX).

not the case. The use of allowances-in-aid-of-wages declined sharply from 1824 to 1832. Only 7.5% of the parishes responding to the Rural Queries used allowance systems in 1832 (Williams 1981: 48).[4] Because per capita real relief expenditures in England and Wales increased by 10% from 1824 to 1832, the decline in the use of allowances-in-aid of-wages apparently had little effect on relief expenditures. In the words of Daniel Baugh (1975: 67), after 1815 the allowance system "may have been abandoned, but whatever theoretical significance such an event has, it does not explain the cost of poor relief."

The fact that the allowance system was extensively used only during years of high food prices suggests that it was especially well suited for dealing with harvest failures. This contention is reinforced by evidence that temporary allowance scales were instituted by parishes during periods of high prices before 1795.[5] In the late eighteenth and early nineteenth centuries, southern agricultural laborers' earnings were only slightly above subsistence even during years of moderate food prices (Pollard 1978: 144). A sharp increase in food prices such as occurred in 1795 and 1800 caused laborers' earnings to decline below the subsistence level.[6] To ensure their laborers a subsistence income during harvest crises, farmers had to either raise nominal wage rates, provide food for their laborers, or use poor relief to make up the difference between laborers' income and subsistence. Of these three policies, the use of poor relief was the least expensive to labor-hiring farmers because it enabled them to pass some of the cost of maintaining their laborers on to non-labor-hiring ratepayers. Given that labor-hiring farmers were politically dominant in most southern and eastern parishes, it is not surprising

[4] The share of reporting parishes paying allowances-in-aid-of-wages was as high as 20% in only four counties: Wiltshire, Kent, Worcester, and the East Riding. Fewer than 10% of the reporting parishes in eight southern and eastern counties used the allowance system: Sussex, Essex, Bedford, Berkshire, Huntingdon, Cambridge, Hertford, and Surrey (Blaug 1964: 236–7). Given that relief expenditures per capita were relatively high in each of these eight counties, there would appear to be no positive correlation between the use of allowance systems and total relief expenditures.

[5] For examples of pre-1795 allowance systems, see Section 2 of this chapter.

[6] Evidence that laborers' wages were below the subsistence level in 1795 is given in Appendix A to this chapter. In a recent article, A. K. Sen found that famines are not usually caused by a large overall shortage of food but rather by "a dramatic decline in the exchange rate against labour" which jeopardizes "the ability to survive of the people who live by selling that commodity [i.e., labor]. This is especially so when the people involved are close to the subsistence level already" (Sen 1977: 43, 35; see also Sen 1981). The scenario described by Sen is precisely what happened in southern England in 1795 and 1800.

that a large percentage of rural parishes adopted allowance systems in response to the exceptionally high grain prices of 1795 and 1800.

A second reason why parishes chose to deal with the subsistence crises of 1795 and 1800 by adopting allowance systems rather than raising nominal wage rates has been proposed by several historians. Farmers feared that if they raised wage rates during times of high prices, it would be difficult to reduce them when prices returned to normal levels (Webb and Webb 1927: 173; Hobsbawm and Rudé 1968: 46; Oxley 1974: 110). Several assistant Poor Law commissioners argued in 1834 that parishes had adopted allowance systems during times of high prices because the allowance system was "the only practicable alternative to enforcing by law a definite minimum wage" (Webb and Webb 1927: 173).[7]

It is surprising, however, that allowance systems were used *only* during subsistence crises. If the allowance system represented a cost-minimizing policy for farmers during times of high prices, it should have been cost-minimizing at other times as well. By guaranteeing laborers a minimum level of income, the allowance system enabled farmers to lower the nominal wage rates they paid their laborers, and hence to pass some of their labor costs on to other ratepayers. Although all forms of relief for able-bodied laborers involved some amount of income transfer from non-labor-hiring ratepayers to labor-hiring ratepayers, only the allowance system involved possible subsidization of farmers during peak seasons as well as slack seasons. This may be the key to understanding why the allowance system was used only as an emergency measure. Perhaps a system of relief that involved the subsidization of wage income of fully employed laborers was not politically acceptable either to non-labor-hiring ratepayers or to laborers. Non-labor-hiring ratepayers might have been willing to pay part of the cost of supporting laborers who were unemployed during slack seasons or whose incomes fell below subsistence during harvest crises, but unwilling to pay part of the labor costs of farmers during peak seasons when the entire labor force was employed. One could view the first two categories of relief payments as aiding laborers and the third category as aiding farmers and having no effect on laborers' income.

[7] This suggests that the adoption of allowance systems reduced the responsiveness of nominal wages to fluctuations in living costs. One way to test this hypothesis would be to compare the "stickiness" of nominal wages before and after the development of the allowance system. The scarcity of time-series wage data precludes such a test. However, the wage series presented in Table 1.A1 of Appendix A suggest that wages were sticky in the eighteenth century. Jeffrey Williamson (1982: 41) reaches a similar conclusion.

There are also reasons why farmers might not have wanted to use the allowance system at all times. Many farmers feared that labor productivity would decline if the wage income of fully employed laborers was low enough that it needed to be supplemented by relief payments. The 1834 Rural Queries contain much evidence to support this fear. For example, the parish overseer of Summertown, Oxford, wrote that, because of the allowance system, "with very few exceptions, the labourers are not as industrious as formerly; and notwithstanding the low rate of wages now too generally paid, it costs as much money in the end to have work performed as it did sixteen years ago" (Parl. Papers 1834: XXXII, 380c).[8]

Farmers also might have opposed the allowance system because it created the possibility of some farmers becoming free riders. The problem arose because the allowance system, by guaranteeing laborers a subsistence income, enabled farmers to lower wage rates without affecting their laborers' income. The free-rider problem existed because any farmer who paid wage rates lower than those of the other farmers was in fact having part of his wage bill subsidized by other farmers. Hence, farmers were encouraged to lower wages as much as possible, and any lowering of wages by one farmer would lead other farmers to follow suit rapidly.[9] In the words of Karl Polanyi (1944: 81), the allowance system "should have stopped wage labor altogether. Standard wages should have gradually dropped to zero, thus putting the actual wage bill wholly on the parish." Farmers may have opposed the use of allowance systems except during subsistence crises, therefore, in order to avoid a possible degeneracy of the wage system.

Another form of outdoor relief granted to employed as well as unemployed laborers was child allowances. Eligibility for child allowances was determined by family size. Under the typical policy, only laborers with four or more children under the age of 10 or 12 received aid from the parish. The allowance was generally equal to 1.5s. per week for each child beyond the third. The number of years a laborer received child allowance payments therefore depended on the spacing of births as well as the size of his family.[10]

---

[8] For an interesting, but biased, account of the effect of the allowance system on labor productivity, see Royal Commission (1834: 67–76, 87–97).

[9] The Rural Queries provide evidence that farmers did engage in such practices. For example, see Parl. Papers (1834: XXXIV, 338d; XXXIII, 466c).

[10] For instance, if relief was granted to laborers with four or more children under age 10, a laborer who had four children spaced two years apart would collect relief for four years,

Child allowances were widespread in southern England throughout the early nineteenth century. More than 90% of the southern parishes that responded to the 1824 questionnaire from the Committee on Labourers' Wages admitted having child allowance policies. In 1832 approximately 80% of rural southern parishes used child allowances. Because of the eligibility requirements, it is not possible to determine the percentage of southern agricultural laborers who received child allowances at any point in time, or the average number of years a laborer received child allowances. I would guess that most southern agricultural laborers born between 1775 and 1805 received child allowances at some point in their lives, for anywhere from 1 to 15 years.[11]

What economic role did child allowances perform? If agricultural laborers' wage rates were just high enough to support a wife and two or three children, laborers with larger families would have been forced to go to the parish for support. The child allowance system might have been adopted to standardize this practice. It is also possible that politically powerful farmers saw child allowance policies as a means to reduce real wage rates to a level capable of supporting only a family of four or five. In either case, one should observe lower wage rates in parishes with child allowances than in parishes without them. Malthus and other contemporary observers claimed that child allowances caused the birth rate to increase. Chapter 5 analyzes the effect of child allowances on fertility.

The major function of poor relief in rural parishes from 1795 to 1834 was the payment of unemployment benefits to seasonally unemployed agricultural laborers. The typical relief policy developed to deal with seasonal unemployment was similar to current unemployment insurance policies; laborers unable to find work reported weekly to the parish overseer and were granted a predetermined amount of money, somewhat below the going wage rate.[12] In many parishes, the size of an

while a laborer who had four children spaced two and a half years apart would collect relief for two and a half years.

[11] The administration of child allowance policies varied across parishes. In parishes that relieved laborers with five or more children under age 10, many laborers would have collected allowances for only one or two years. On the other hand, in parishes that relieved laborers with three or more children under age 12, many laborers must have collected relief for more than a decade. A laborer with six children spaced two years apart would collect relief for fourteen years.

[12] It is not possible to determine the typical unemployment benefit–wage ratio in agricultural parishes. Blaug (1963: 161) estimated that the benefit–wage ratio "in the Midlands or Southern counties" was between 0.5 and 0.67 in 1795. He got these ratios by comparing the weekly earnings of a fully employed unmarried agricultural laborer and a family consisting of a laborer, his wife, and one child with the relief benefits they would have

was then divided among all ratepayers in the parish, according to their poor rate assessment. A ratepayer could pay his share of the total either by hiring laborers at the wage rate set by the parish or by paying the amount to the parish overseer as a poor rate. The marginal cost of labor to a ratepayer therefore was equal to zero "up to the amount of labor corresponding to his share of the assessment" (McCloskey 1973: 433). Appendix B reproduces the labor rate adopted by Wisborough Green, Sussex, in November 1832. Using this rate as an example, suppose a ratepayer's share of the parish wage bill was determined to be £20. He could fulfill his assessment by paying £20 to the overseer, by hiring 240 man-days of labor from able-bodied married men, or by any combination of wage payments and poor rates totaling £20. Thus, if a farmer required 200 man-days of labor while the labor rate was in effect, he could deduct this labor cost from his assessment, reducing his poor rate expenditure to £3.33.

Like the previously discussed systems of relief, the labor rate caused a subsidization of labor-hiring farmers by non-labor-hiring ratepayers. Farmers received what was essentially free labor in winter, while family farmers ᴅ tradesmen, who had no need for hired labor, were forced to support a portion of the parish's work force. Commenting on the effects of labor rates, the 1834 Poor Law Report (Royal Commission 1834: 210) concluded: "It may perhaps appear strange, that perpetuating, as they usually do, such serious injury upon the largest portion of the ratepayers, labour-rates should have been so extensively adopted; the explanation is that the large farmers are benefitted, and that in an agricultural parish they command a majority in vestry." Given that labor-hiring farmers required a certain amount of labor in winter, and that the labor rate allowed them to apply their winter wage bill (up to a certain amount) to their poor rate assessment, there is no doubt that labor-hiring farmers were more heavily subsidized by non-labor-hiring ratepayers under the labor rate than under the typical unemployment insurance system. This can be easily demonstrated. Under a labor rate, in winter labor-hiring farmers paid a proportion, e, of the parish's total wage bill (TWB), determined by their share of the parish's poor rate assessment. Under the typical unemployment insurance system, farmers hired a percentage of the parish's work force in winter. The wage bill they paid these laborers (FWB) was not subsidized by the parish. The farmers then paid e percent of the poor relief payments (PRP) to the remaining unemployed laborers in the parish, where PRP equals TWB minus FWB. Thus, the labor-hiring farmers' payments to labor during the winter equaled e(FWB + PRP) under the labor rate and FWB + e(PRP) under the unemployment insurance system. So long as $e < 1$ (that is, there were some non-labor-hiring taxpayers in the parish), the total expenditure on labor by labor-hiring farmers was smaller under the labor rate than under the unemployment insurance system. The converse of this is that non-labor-hiring ratepayers paid more to support parish laborers under a labor rate than they did under an unemployment insurance system, their extra expenditures being equal to $(1 - e) \times$ (FWB).[17]

What effect did the payment of outdoor relief to able-bodied workers have on the supply of labor? McCloskey (1973) maintained that the "100% marginal rate of tax" associated with the allowance system must have produced serious work disincentives. This view was shared by the Poor Law commissioners and many historians, who concluded that the disincentive effects of the allowance system were the cause of the high rates of unemployment that plagued the south and east during the first third of the nineteenth century. Given a 100% marginal tax rate, a family's income was not affected by the number of hours worked over a certain range, since the wage rate was effectively zero, so that one would expect families falling within the relevant range to reduce their supply of labor. The effect of an allowance system with a 100% marginal tax rate on a family's work–leisure decision is depicted in Figure 1.1. The imposition of the allowance system changes the relevant work–income relationship from *TXY* to *TMXY*. If a family's equilibrium income–leisure point before the imposition of the allowance system was either below (e.g., point *B*) or slightly above (e.g., point *A*) the new guaranteed income level, the family's new equilibrium point would be at *M*, which involved no work.[18] In other words, economic theory suggests that the allowance system caused a substantial amount of voluntary unemployment.

The payment of unemployment benefits also had labor supply disincentive effects. It does not follow, however, that either allowances or unemployment benefits magnified the unemployment problem in grain-producing parishes. In blaming outdoor relief for the high levels of unemployment, the traditional literature assumed that parishes were

---

[17] The unpopularity of the labor rate among non-labor-hiring ratepayers can be seen in Appendix D of the 1834 Poor Law Report (Parl. Papers 1834: XXXVIII), which contains statements from small farmers and tradesmen that the adoption of labor rates led to increases in their expenditures on poor relief.

[18] This assumes, of course, that leisure is a normal good. If an individual gained no utility from leisure, all the points on the *MX* line would be optimal.

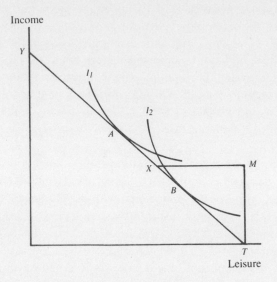

Figure 1.1. The work–leisure decision under the allowance system.

either unwilling or unable to be selective in their granting of relief. Because of the small size of parishes, however, overseers of relief usually knew the employment situation of each labor-hiring farmer and the "industrious" nature of each applicant for relief. Blaug (1963: 130) contends that "two-thirds of the Poor Law authorities in the country were concerned with only a few hundred families and, therefore, might be expected to be familiar with the personal circumstances of relief recipients." The wording of almost all surviving allowance scales indicates that only "industrious" laborers were to be granted relief.[19] Of course, parish overseers might have ignored the wording of allowance scales and granted relief indiscriminately. But so long as the cost of determining a worker's character and economic condition was low (as it must have been in small parishes), it was in every ratepayer's interest to grant relief only to industrious workers.

Sometimes parish resolutions were quite specific regarding the expected behavior of relief recipients. The vestry of Terling parish, Essex, passed a resolution in January 1832 stating that "all parishioners who are assisted by the flour allowance be informed, that upon being known to tipple, to neglect their work, otherwise injure their families, or keep a

[19] Even the 1795 Speenhamland scale used the term "industrious" in describing who should receive relief.

dog without permission of the overseer, they will forfeit this privilege, and be transferred with their families to workhouse discipline, food and clothing" (Essex Record Office: D/P 299/8/5). Moreover, overseers of relief (who were generally labor-hiring farmers) often refused relief to applicants if agricultural employment was available. For example, the parish overseer for Birchanger, Essex, refused to grant further relief to a laborer upon learning that he had been "this day offered work by Mr. J. Linsel at the rate of 6 shillings per week which he absolutely refused" (Essex Record Office: D/P 25/8/2). Assistant Poor Law Commissioner Stuart wrote that "I have seen relief refused to men who it was proved had not used due diligence in seeking for work . . . there being farmers present who could have employed them had they applied to them" (Parl. Papers 1834: XXVIII, 350). Many parishes would not relieve laborers until they had obtained notes from three or more farmers stating that employment was not available.

Another tactic used by parishes to discourage voluntary unemployment consisted of requiring relief recipients to perform work for the parish. A large share of parishes responding to the Rural Queries used unemployed laborers to repair the parish roads.[20] Other parishes simply made up activities to employ the recipient's time. The Poor Law Report of 1834 (Royal Commission 1834: 20) concluded that many parishes

force[d] the applicants to give up a certain portion of their time by confining them in a gravel-pit or in some other enclosure, or directing them to sit at a certain spot and do nothing, or obliging them to attend a roll-call several times in the day, or by any contrivance which shall prevent their leisure from becoming means either of profit or of amusement.

Given these policies to guard against the labor supply disincentive effects of outdoor relief, there is reason to doubt the traditional literature's assertion that outdoor relief policies created large amounts of voluntary unemployment.

The final method for relieving able-bodied workers, the workhouse system, differed from the other methods in that recipients were obliged to enter workhouses in order to obtain relief. The so-called Workhouse Test Act of 1722 empowered parishes to set up workhouses and to deny

---

[20] Question 6 of the Rural Queries asked how unemployed laborers were "maintained in Summer and Winter." Of the 117 parishes from Sussex, Buckingham, and Suffolk (the counties with the highest per capita relief expenditures in 1831) that acknowledged having positive unemployment rates, 67, or 57.3%, responded that unemployed laborers were required to perform work for the parish in order to obtain relief.

relief to anyone who refused to enter them. Data on the extent of workhouses are available for 1803 and 1813–15. In 1803, 26% of the 14,611 "parishes or places" included in the Abstract of Returns Relative to the State of the Poor maintained some of their poor in workhouses. The number of workhouses was approximately the same in 1813–15 (Taylor 1972: 62–3, 76). The responses to the Rural Queries suggest that the extent of workhouses increased sharply from 1815 to 1832. Question 22 asked whether the parish had a workhouse; 60% of the 930 parishes that answered question 22 either had a workhouse in the parish or were associated with a union or hundred workhouse.[21]

There were two major motives behind the adoption of the workhouse system. First, as their name implies, workhouses were to be used to employ the poor. Parishes hoped to make the poor self-sufficient by employing them at "spinning, carding, weaving, knitting, beating and winding various materials" for cloth manufacture (Taylor 1972: 69). Attempts to employ the poor profitably were widespread in the eighteenth century, but they were invariably failures. According to the Webbs (1927: 234), "in many workhouses the produce of sales did not even repay the outlay on materials. . . . From the standpoint of making each pauper earn his own bread the failure of workhouse manufactories was ludicrous in its completeness." As a result, "at workhouse after workhouse the various manufactures that were tried had eventually to be given up" (Webb and Webb 1927: 223).

The second motive behind the adoption of workhouses also was financial. By making the conditions for obtaining relief unpleasant, parishes hoped to deter the poor from applying for, or accepting, relief. As just mentioned, the 1722 act gave parishes the power to withhold relief from persons who refused to enter a workhouse. Parish officials therefore could " 'offer the house' to any persons whom they did not think deserving of [outdoor relief]" (Webb and Webb 1927: 244). So long as the poor considered indoor relief sufficiently unpleasant, some would respond to the "offer of the house" by withdrawing their requests for relief, thereby reducing relief expenditures.

The "workhouse test" offered parishes another means for discouraging

---

[21] The 1722 act allowed parishes to combine for the purpose of setting up workhouses. Similarly, Gilbert's Act (1782) empowered parishes to combine into unions, with joint workhouses. Several of the parishes responding to question 22 stated that they shared a workhouse with other parishes, but had no inmates at present. Thus, the share of parishes that maintained some of their poor in workhouses in 1832 was somewhat less than 60%.

voluntary unemployment, but available evidence suggests that rural parishes were selective in applying the workhouse test to able-bodied male applicants for relief. Because most rural parishes were small enough for overseers to know the "industrious" nature of each applicant for relief, it was unnecessary to use the workhouse test to determine the legitimacy of a worker's request for relief. Overseers could offer indoor relief to those applicants deemed to be voluntarily unemployed, and grant outdoor relief to industrious workers requiring temporary assistance because of seasonal unemployment, sickness, or subsistence crises. It was not practical to relieve seasonally unemployed workers in workhouses, because indoor relief was more expensive than outdoor relief (Oxley 1974: 90; Taylor 1972: 78). Indeed, there is little evidence of unemployed rural workers being forced to enter workhouses from 1780 to 1834. Only two of the southeastern parishes that responded to the Rural Queries admitted granting indoor relief to temporarily unemployed workers. Workhouses were typically inhabited by orphans, single women with dependent children, and the aged and infirm, "in short, . . . all those categories of poor that were sometimes difficult to provide for cheaply through outdoor relief" (Taylor 1972: 65).[22] The relief of temporarily unemployed laborers in workhouses became widespread only after the passage of the Poor Law Amendment Act in 1834.[23]

2. Timing of Changes in Poor Law Administration

Studies of the Poor Law at the county or local level that analyze the pre-1795 administration of relief almost universally conclude, in contrast to the traditional view, that the payment of outdoor relief to able-bodied laborers began before 1795. The Webbs (1927: 170) found evidence that outdoor relief was granted to "able-bodied male adults . . . unable to live by their labour" from the beginning of the eighteenth century. The use of outdoor relief increased throughout the century, with the most pronounced increase occurring after 1760. "There is reason to infer,"

---

[22] Oxley (1974: 91) maintains that forcing temporarily unemployed laborers to enter workhouses "could be positively counter-productive, breaking up the home, disrupting normal life and making it more difficult to start again when work appeared."

[23] The 1834 Poor Law Report recommended that unemployed laborers be relieved only in "well-regulated" workhouses. By 1842 the Poor Law Commission, created by the Poor Law Amendment Act, had issued orders prohibiting the payment of outdoor relief to able-bodied laborers to most rural Poor Law unions. The implementation of the New Poor Law is discussed in Chapter 7.

write the Webbs (1927: 170), "that the decade immediately following the peace of 1763 – when a great expansion of trade and an apparent growth of national prosperity was taking place – was marked also by an unusually great increase in pauperism, especially in the form of Outdoor Relief." Dorothy Marshall (1926: 79) concluded that a "sharp rise [in poor rates] appears to have come between 1760 and 1782, though in most parishes it occurred during the seventies rather than the sixties, owing to the gradual and increasing growth of distress, and thanks to bad harvests."

The increase in outdoor relief took place despite the fact that the 1722 Workhouse Test Act had encouraged parishes to relieve able-bodied paupers in workhouses and to deny relief to anyone refusing to enter a workhouse. Parliament did not sanction the payment of outdoor relief to able-bodied paupers until the passage of Gilbert's Act in 1782.[24] To a large extent, Parliament's actions in 1782 simply legitimized the policies of a large number of parishes that were dissatisfied with the 1722 act (Coats 1960: 46). Scattered cases of parishes using outdoor relief before 1782 can be found in the local studies of poor relief administration. The parish of Tysoe, Warwick, granted outdoor relief to seasonally unemployed laborers as early as 1727, and adopted a roundsman system in 1763 to cope with seasonal unemployment (Ashby 1912: 153–7). Ashby (1912: 157) concluded that "as early as 1770 all the systems and excuses for giving grants to the unemployed poor so much lamented by the Commissioners of 1834, were establishing themselves at Tysoe." Emmison (1933: 50) found examples of the use of roundsman systems in Bedfordshire in 1734, 1758, and 1781. Several Cambridgeshire parishes employed "able-bodied paupers in 'field keeping,' in breaking and sifting gravel, and in carting stones during the middle years of the [eighteenth] century" (Hampson 1934: 187). In Berkshire, "it was common for parish officers to relieve unemployed able-bodied persons . . . since at least the 1770s" (Neuman 1972: 100).

Evidence of the use of outdoor relief becomes more frequent after the passage of Gilbert's Act. Neuman and Hampson found numerous examples of parishes granting outdoor relief to unemployed and underemployed workers in Berkshire and Cambridge, respectively, during the

---

[24] Although the formation of Poor Law unions under Gilbert's Act was voluntary, the act expressly stated that in the unions formed, able-bodied paupers were not to be relieved in workhouses. Rather, unemployed laborers were either to be found employment by the union or granted outdoor relief. The number of parishes directly affected by Gilbert's Act was small. In 1834 there were only 67 Gilbert's Act unions, comprising 924 parishes, approximately 6% of the parishes in England and Wales.

years 1782–95 (Hampson 1934: 189–91; Neuman 1969: 318–19). Moreover, there is evidence that parishes adopted allowances-in-aid-of-wages
during times of high food prices prior to 1795. For example, the hundred
of Whittlesford, Cambridge, decided during a period of high prices in
1783 that "every man who has a family, and behaves himself seemly, be
allowed the price of 5 quartern loaves per week, with 2 quartern loaves
added for each member of his family" (quoted in Hampson 1934: 190).
An assembly of magistrates for the county of Dorset resolved in 1792 to
relieve "any industrious and peaceable poor person . . . with such sum
as shall make up, together with the weekly earnings of him, her, and
their family, a comfortable support for them" (quoted in Neuman 1969:
317). The wording of these resolutions is similar to the wording of allowance policies adopted by parishes in response to the high grain prices in
1795 and 1800. Neuman (1972: 100) concluded that "by 1795 the practice
of supporting the able-bodied with allowances from the parish was com-
monplace in Berkshire." Marshall (1926: 104) went even further, claiming that the allowance system was "at least a century old" by 1795.

Perhaps the above evidence reveals only isolated incidences of the
granting of outdoor relief to able-bodied laborers before 1795, and 1795
was indeed a watershed because a majority of southern and eastern
parishes adopted outdoor relief policies for the first time in that year.
This hypothesis can be tested by examining movements in real per capita
poor relief expenditures over time. If Speenhamland policies were
adopted for the first time in 1795, and if they led to an increase in
pauperism, then a time series of real per capita relief expenditures
(whether at the parish, county, or national level) should show a marked
increase in relief expenditures in 1795 and a continued upward movement throughout the first third of the nineteenth century. Time-series
data for testing the traditional hypothesis are given in Figures 1.2 and
1.3 and Tables 1.1 and 1.2. Figure 1.2 examines the movement of real
poor relief expenditures in five Essex parishes over the period 1760–
1830. None of the parishes has a time series that behaves in such a way
as to provide support for the traditional hypothesis. For example,
Stansted Mountfitchet experienced a substantial increase in relief expenditures in 1795, then a three-year decline to the 1792 level, another
sharp increase through 1804, a decline through 1816, then another sharp
increase. Stapleford Tawney experienced a sharp increase in expenditures in 1796, which was sustained through 1804, followed by a seven-
year period where real expenditures were lower than they had been over

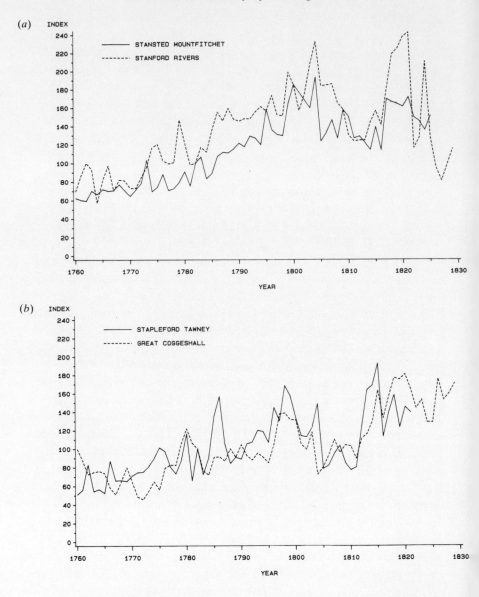

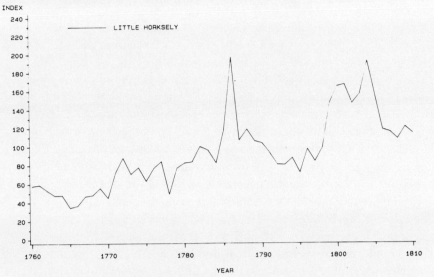

Figure 1.2a–c. Real poor relief expenditures, 1760–1829, for selected parishes. For each parish, 1782 = 100. (*Sources:* Relief expenditure data from Essex Record Office: Stansted Mountfitchet [D/P 109/8/4–5]; Stanford Rivers [D/P 140/8/1–4]; Stapleford Tawney [D/P 141/8/1]; Great Coggeshall [D/P/ 36/8/3–5]; Little Horksely [D/P 307/12/1]. Cost-of-living data from Phelps Brown and Hopkins [1956: 313] and Lindert and Williamson [1983: 11].)

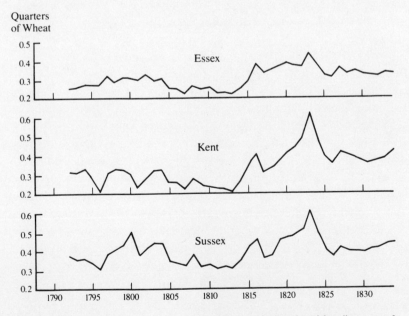

Figure 1.3. Real per capita relief expenditures in agricultural parishes (in terms of wheat). (*Source:* Baugh [1975: 60].)

the period 1785–94. Stanford Rivers's level of expenditures increased sharply in 1799 but returned to the 1785–94 level from 1809 to 1816. Relief expenditures for 1810–13 averaged 19.6% below the 1785–94 level, while the years 1826–9 had the lowest expenditure of a four-year period since the early 1770s. Taken as a whole, the data offer no evidence of a sustained increase in real relief expenditures beginning in 1795. Each parish shows evidence of a substantial increase in expenditures beginning sometime between the late 1770s and the early 1780s. The data suggest that the key to understanding the widespread use of outdoor relief in the early nineteenth century lies in the changes in the economic environment that occurred in rural England during the two decades before 1795.

Figure 1.3 presents movements in real per capita relief expenditures for agricultural parishes in Essex, Kent, and Sussex (three counties with relatively high levels of per capita expenditure) during the years 1792–1834, as constructed by Daniel Baugh (1975: 60). The time series for each county offers little support for the traditional literature's hypothesis that 1795 was a watershed in the history of Poor Law administration. There is no upward trend in real per capita relief expenditures over the period 1792–1814 in any of the counties. Each county did experience a steady upward movement in expenditures from 1813 through 1823, but this was followed by a rapid drop in expenditures in 1824–6 and then a leveling out through 1834 at a level not substantially above the level of 1792–4. The fact that the three time series move almost in unison throughout the period suggests that the major determinant of poor relief expenditures was either parliamentary action or economic conditions. The importance of parliamentary activity can immediately be ruled out because no laws regulating the use of outdoor relief were passed between 1796 and 1834. On the other hand, the timing of movements in relief expenditures can be explained by changes in economic conditions. The years 1815–23 were a time of severe distress in the grain-producing region of England, which included Essex, Kent, and Sussex.[25] The increase in relief expenditures during this period might have been a result of increased unemployment among farm laborers, and the fall in relief expenditures in 1824–6 a result of the return of better times to agriculture. Although many contemporaries and some historians have placed a

---

[25] For a discussion of the postwar agricultural depression in the south and east, see Fussell and Compton (1939).

Table 1.1. *Growth of poor relief expenditures: England and Wales*

Period	Real relief expenditures: annual growth rate (%)	Real per capita relief expenditures: annual growth rate (%)
1748/50–1776	1.79	1.19
1776–1783/5	3.04	2.22
1783/5–1803	2.21	1.12
1803–1818/20	2.84	1.38
1818/20–1832/4	1.10	−0.34
1748/50–1783/5	2.08	1.42
1783/5–1818/20	2.50	1.24
1783/5–1832/4	2.10	0.78

Sources: Relief expenditure data from Parl. Papers (1830–1: XI, 4–5; 1839: XLIV, 4–7). Cost-of-living data from Phelps Brown and Hopkins (1956: 313) and Lindert and Williamson (1983: 11).

large amount of the blame for agriculture's postwar problems on the Poor Law, such an explanation cannot explain why it took 20 years for the adverse effects of outdoor relief on the labor market to appear, or why relief expenditures declined substantially after 1823.

Finally, the hypothesis that 1795 was not a watershed is strongly supported by the limited information available on national poor relief expenditures during the second half of the eighteenth century. Before the annual collection of data on relief expenditures, which began in 1813, expenditure data were collected only for the years ending at Easter 1748–50, 1776, 1783–5, and 1803. Table 1.1 presents evidence on the growth rates of real per capita relief expenditures before and after 1795, obtained from expenditure data for the above years and for the fiscal years (ending March 25) 1818–20 and 1832–4. The average annual rate of increase in real per capita expenditures was higher during the 35-year period from 1748–50 to 1783–5 than during the same-length period from 1783–5 to 1818–20. This result is particularly striking because the payment of outdoor relief to able-bodied laborers was not sanctioned by Parliament until 1782, and nominal relief expenditures were higher in each of fiscal years 1818–20 than in any other year of the Old Poor Law. The rate of growth of expenditures from 1748–50 to 1783–5 looks even more impressive when compared to the entire period of Parliament-

Table 1.2. *Growth of real per capita relief expenditures:*
southeastern counties

County	Annual growth rate (%)		
	1748/50–1783/5	1783/5–1818/20	1783/5–1832/4
Bedford	1.63	1.33	1.44
Buckingham	1.29	1.13	1.20
Cambridge	1.69	1.44	1.43
Essex	1.21	1.33	1.03
Hertford	0.45	1.03	1.00
Huntingdon	2.11	1.50	1.51
Kent	0.89	0.68	0.75
Norfolk	1.85	1.20	1.42
Suffolk	1.12	1.56	1.62
Sussex	1.32	1.24	0.89

Sources: See Table 1.1.

sanctioned relief; the average annual rate of increase in real per capita
expenditures was only 0.78% from 1783–5 to 1832–4.

Outdoor relief was more prevalent in the southeast than in any other
region of England, and per capita relief expenditures were higher in the
southeast than elsewhere throughout the early nineteenth century (Blaug
1963: 178–9; 1964: 236–41). If any region experienced an increase in the
rate of growth of relief expenditures after 1795, it would have been the
southeast. Table 1.2 presents the annual growth rates in real per capita
relief expenditures before and after 1795, for ten rural southeastern counties.[26] Once again there is no evidence that 1795 was a watershed. The
annual rate of increase in real per capita expenditures was higher from
1748–50 to 1783–5 than from 1783–5 to 1818–20 in 7 of the 10 counties,
and higher from 1748–50 to 1783–5 than from 1783–5 to 1832–4 in 8 of 10
counties.

The evidence presented in this section offers strong support for rejecting the traditional hypothesis. The events of 1795 did not lead to a large
sustained increase in relief expenditures. One must look at changes in
the rural economy during the two or three decades before 1795 in order
to understand the long-term increase in poor relief expenditures.

[26] County population data for 1751 to 1801 were obtained from Deane and Cole (1967:
103).

3. Changes in the Economic Environment

In the second half of the eighteenth century, two fundamental changes occurred in the economic environment of the south and east of England: (1) the prolonged increase in wheat prices that began in the early 1760s and lasted through the Napoleonic Wars; and (2) the decline of cottage industry that began as early as 1750 in some areas and spread throughout the southeast by the early nineteenth century.[27] I contend that these changes in the economic environment led to important changes in the implicit labor contract between farmers and agricultural laborers. Before the late eighteenth century, the typical farm worker had three sources of income: a small plot of land for growing food; employment as a day laborer in agriculture during peak seasons; and slack season employment (yearlong for his wife and children) in cottage industry (Laslett 1971: 15–16). The decline of cottage industry reduced or eliminated one source of income, while the rise in wheat prices, by causing an

[27] Three other changes in the economic environment of the south and east during the second half of the eighteenth century and the early nineteenth century have been put forward by historians: the increased specialization of the region in grain production (Snell 1981: 421); the increased use of threshing machines, which eliminated large amounts of winter employment (Hobsbawm and Rudé 1968: 359–63); and the decline in the system of yearly labor contracts (Clapham 1930: 121–2; Hasbach 1908: 176–8; Hobsbawm 1968: 103; Hobsbawm and Rudé 1968: 43–5). I have not included these environmental changes because I contend that each was an endogenous response to either the long-run increase in grain prices or the adoption of outdoor relief for able-bodied laborers. The increased specialization of the rural south and east in grain production was certainly a response to higher grain prices. The use of threshing machines in the south did not begin until the first decade of the nineteenth century (Hobsbawm and Rudé 1968: 359) and so cannot be considered a cause of the long-run increase in relief expenditures during the last quarter of the eighteenth century. Moreover, the existence of outdoor relief must have had an effect on the decision to use threshing machines. In the absence of outdoor relief, farmers would have been forced to maintain laborers whether or not they were employed (in order to secure an adequate peak season labor force), so that the adoption of threshing machines would not have lowered labor costs. With outdoor relief, laborers not needed in early winter because of the adoption of threshing machines would have been partly maintained by non-labor-hiring ratepayers (who contributed to the poor rate). The "shortening of the period of hire" from yearlong contracts to weekly or even daily contracts was probably a response to both the increased cost of food and the development of outdoor relief. Evidence presented by Clapham and Hobsbawm and Rudé suggests that the change took place, to a large extent, between 1795 and 1800, a time of very high food prices. Because laborers hired to yearlong contracts usually received a large share of their income in the form of in-kind payments, farmers hiring them bore the entire burden of inflation. In parishes that adopted allowance systems, however, farmers were able to pass on to the parish some of the cost of maintaining their laborers. Thus, the adoption of weekly labor contracts might have been in response to the high cost of food and the existence of allowance systems during the years from 1795 to 1800.

increase in land values, increased the cost to farmers of providing their laborers with allotments. In response to these environmental changes, a new implicit contract was developed between farmers and laborers that included wage labor in agriculture during peak seasons and a system of poor relief that guaranteed seasonally unemployed laborers a minimum weekly income near the subsistence level. The new form of the implicit labor contract was adopted over other possible methods for dealing with the altered economic environment because it represented the least expensive method available to farmers for securing an adequate supply of peak-season labor.

Between 1740–50 and 1785–95, the price of wheat increased by 76.3%, more than three times the price increase of an unweighted bundle of producer and consumer goods (Deane and Cole 1967: 91). Chambers and Mingay (1966: 111) attributed the long-term rise in wheat prices to "the increase in demand arising from the growth of population, together with a decline in the frequency of good seasons and bountiful harvests." The increased price of wheat led to a sharp increase in the value of arable land, which in turn led to significant changes in the distribution of landholdings in the grain-producing south and east. In areas where the open-field system still existed in 1750, such as East Anglia and the South Midlands, the redistribution of landholdings was accomplished to a large extent by the great waves of enclosures of open fields, commons, and waste that occurred during the 1760s and 1770s and also during the French wars (1793–1815). In grain-producing areas where the arable land had been enclosed before 1750, including much of the southeast, land that had formerly been considered marginal and had been left to the agricultural laborers was now reclaimed by its owners, as high bread prices made it profitable to be brought under cultivation.

What effect did enclosures typically have on day laborers, cottagers, and squatters?[28] Because of the individual nature of enclosure acts the treatment of cottagers and squatters was not uniform across parishes. However, the available data suggest that some generalizations are possi-

[28] The discussion that follows is concerned with the effect of enclosures on laborers in grain-producing areas only. I am not claiming that, in general, enclosures led to the adoption of outdoor relief. Large parts of the north and Midlands that did not specialize in grain production were enclosed after 1750 without resulting in the widespread adoption of outdoor relief. I show later in this section and in Chapter 3 that seasonality in the demand for labor (an important aspect of grain production) was a necessary, but not sufficient, condition for the spread of outdoor relief, and that the decline of laborers' allotments was a major reason why outdoor relief became widespread in the grain-producing south and east.

ble. Cottagers and squatters without legal rights of common, whose use of the commons was purely by custom, seldom received any compensation for their lost land from enclosure commissioners. On the other hand, cottagers who had a legal claim to rights of common invariably received allotments from enclosure acts. Historians of parliamentary enclosure generally agree, however, that despite such awards, owners of common rights were often hurt by enclosures. The problem, according to Chambers and Mingay (1966: 97), was that

the allotment of land given in exchange for common rights was often too small to be of much practical use, being generally far smaller than the three acres or so required to keep a cow. It might also be inconveniently distant from the cottage, and the cost of fencing (which was relatively heavier for small areas) might be too high to be worth while. Probably many cottagers sold such lots to the neighbouring farmers rather than go to the expense of fencing them, and thus peasant ownership at the lowest level declined.

Evidence concerning the effects of enclosures on poor laborers in 69 parishes enclosed between 1760 and 1800 is contained in the *General Report on Enclosures* (1808) prepared by Arthur Young for the Board of Agriculture.[29] Detailed descriptions of the enclosures reveal that laborers were made worse off in 53 of them and better off in 16. For most parishes, the effects of enclosure were similar to that of Letcomb, Berkshire, where the poor could "no longer keep a cow, which before many of them did, and they are therefore now maintained by the parish," or that of Alconbury, Huntingdon, where "many kept cows that have not since: they could not enclose, and sold their allotments, [and were] left without cows or land" (Young 1808: 150, 154). Mantoux (1928: 185) described the report's evidence on the effects of enclosures as being "heart-rending in its monotony."

Some historians have maintained that the loss of commons rights was more than compensated for by increases in wage rates and in "the volume and regularity of employment" that came as a result of enclosure. According to Chambers (1953: 112–3), enclosures created a short-run increase in labor demand for hedging and ditching, and a long-run increase in labor demand by the cultivation of commons and waste, and the adoption of new cropping systems that often followed. However, Snell (1981: 430) found that seasonal fluctuations in the demand for labor became more pronounced in grain-producing areas as a result of

[29] Young obtained information on the effects of these enclosures from interviews with laborers, farmers, and clergy within each parish.

parliamentary enclosures, leading him to question "the capacity of enclosure . . . to provide greater and more regular employment throughout the year for the growing male labour force." Moreover, county-level wage data for 1767 and 1795 suggest that the trend in agricultural laborers' wages was not affected by the extent of parliamentary enclosures before 1793. From 1767 to 1795, real wages declined on average by 18.6% in the southeastern counties where parliamentary enclosure was most prominent before 1793 (Northampton, Oxford, Huntingdon, Buckingham), and by 18.5% in the counties least affected by enclosure (Kent, Essex, Sussex, Suffolk, Hertford).[30] Available wage and employment data therefore do not support the hypothesis that enclosures significantly increased the long-run demand for agricultural labor.[31]

Agricultural laborers residing in parishes enclosed before 1750 were not immune to the effects of rising wheat prices. According to Hobsbawm (1968: 82), the concentration of landholding in response to increased land values "took place in open and enclosed country, among new or old enclosures, through expropriation, forced or voluntary sales." Before the rise in prices, laborers in enclosed parishes were often able to rent allotments to produce a part of their subsistence. As wheat

[30] County-level wage data are given in Appendix A. Data on the extent of enclosure are from Turner (1980: 186–8). Of course, wages were determined by labor supply as well as demand. Population growth is the best available proxy for changes in labor supply. From 1751 to 1801, population increased by 27% in the high-enclosure counties, compared to 40% in the low-enclosure *rural* counties. (I excluded Kent because of its large urban component. Kent's population increased by 88% from 1751 to 1801.) Population data are taken from Deane and Cole (1967: 103). In other words, labor supply increased faster in the low-enclosure counties than in the high-enclosure counties. Although one should not place too much weight on these calculations, they suggest that, before 1795, the demand for labor grew at least as rapidly in areas where enclosures did not take place as in areas where enclosures occurred. One possible explanation for this result is that very little common or waste land was enclosed in grain-producing areas during this period (Turner 1980: 188–9). Thus, the increase in the amount of land under cultivation might have been no larger in high-enclosure counties than in low-enclosure counties.

[31] One further piece of evidence in support of my conclusion is Crafts's (1978: 180–1) finding that, at the county level of aggregation, "the rate of outmigration was . . . positively associated with the proportion of the county enclosed parliamentarily after 1801." On the other hand, Tucker (1975: 244) found a negative relationship "between the level of relief expenditure [1817–21] and the proportion of county land enclosed 1761–1820" in grain-producing regions. This suggests that enclosures did indeed cause an increase in either wage rates or employment opportunities. However, I suspect that Tucker's result is to a large degree spurious, caused by the extremely high per capita relief expenditures in the long-enclosed counties of Sussex, Kent, Essex, and Suffolk. If Tucker had used as his independent variable the share of county land enclosed *as of* 1820, I suspect his results would have been significantly different. Unfortunately, I was unable to obtain data on the share of county land enclosed as of 1820, and therefore could not test my hypothesis.

Table 1.3. *Percentage of parishes renting allotments to laborers*

County	% with no allotments	% with allotments for few laborers	% with allotments for some or most laborers
Essex	75.0	2.3	22.7
Sussex	60.3	22.2	17.5
Kent	66.7	16.7	16.7
Overall	66.4	14.8	18.8

Source: Calculated from answers to question 20 of the Rural Queries (Parl. Papers 1834: XXXI).

prices increased, however, farmers became "very anxious to get the gardens to throw into their fields." Hasbach (1908: 108) concluded that "the cottagers who rented an acre or two of land had to feel the effects of engrossing. Their land was taken away from them and added to the acreage of some large farm; and the farmer's land-hunger was so great that in many places even the cottage-gardens were thrown into the bargain."[32] Unfortunately, there has been little research into the process of engrossment in long-enclosed parishes. Available evidence suggests, however, that by the early nineteenth century laborers in regions enclosed before 1750 had very small cottage gardens and generally were not able to rent allotments. For instance, Arthur Young, the author of agricultural surveys for the long-enclosed counties of Suffolk (1797) and Essex (1807), lamented the general inadequacy of cottage gardens in both counties (1797: 11; 1807: 49).

Data on the extent of laborers' allotments in 1832 can be obtained from question 20 of the Rural Queries, which asked parishes "whether any land let to labourers; if so, the quantity to each, and at what rent." Table 1.3 contains a tabulation of responses to question 20 from parishes located in

---

[32] Of course, engrossment was not a necessary response to increased land prices. If laborers were willing to pay the market price for allotments, and if the price of labor was increasing as rapidly as the price of land, farmers would have had little desire to reclaim their laborers' allotments. However, available evidence suggests that the price of land was increasing faster than the price of labor (Baack and Thomas 1974: 415). It was therefore in the farmers' interests to reclaim, or reduce the size of, laborers' allotments. The desire to reclaim allotments would also be strong if laborers' rental payments were sticky in the face of rising land prices. Because the food produced on allotments was almost always consumed by the laborer's family rather than sold, a reduction in the size of allotments necessarily caused a decline in laborers' incomes, unless consolidation resulted in scale economies.

Essex, Kent, and Sussex, three grain-producing counties almost entirely enclosed before the mid-eighteenth century. I have categorized parishes confirming the existence of allotments into those in which few laborers, some laborers, or most laborers rented allotments. Looking at the combined totals, one-third of the responding parishes mentioned the existence of allotments. However, only 18.8% rented allotments to more than a few laborers, and only 6% of the parishes allowed laborers to rent allotments as large as a quarter acre, the minimum size usually recommended by contemporary proponents of allotment schemes (Barnett 1968: 175).[33]

In grain-producing parishes that contained little common or waste land, increasing grain prices could not have led to significant increases in the amount of land under crops. Laborers' loss of allotments in long-enclosed parishes therefore was almost certainly not compensated for by an increase in agricultural employment. Nor was it compensated for by an increase in wage rates. Real wages in Essex, Kent, and Sussex were lower in 1790–3 (a period of relatively low prices) than in 1767.[34]

In sum, the loss of commons rights or allotments had two important effects on agricultural laborers: (1) It caused a reduction in their annual incomes, and (2) it removed their partial insulation from fluctuations in the price of food. I contend that many laborers' incomes fell below subsistence as a result of their loss of land, forcing them to apply for poor relief. There is ample qualitative evidence of a negative correlation between the existence (and size) of allotments and the level of poor relief expenditures. For instance, data reported by Arthur Young (1808: 164–5) on poor relief expenditures in 51 parishes in Lincolnshire and Rutland reveal a strong negative relationship between the share of laborers in a parish having allotments and the parish's poor rates. In 9 parishes where more than half of the agricultural laborers had allotments and cows, poor rates averaged 3.5d. (pence) per assessed pound, while in 13 parishes where few or none of the laborers had allotments and cows, poor rates averaged 5s. 11d. per pound. There was no doubt in

[33] There are no comparable data on the extent of allotments for any year before 1832. It is therefore not possible to determine the magnitude of the decline in allotments over the period from 1780 to 1832.

[34] Wage data for the early 1790s are scarce. What are available suggest that in Sussex, agricultural laborers' real wages declined by 3% from 1767 to 1793; in Essex, real wages declined by 8% from 1767 to 1790; and in Kent, real wages declined by 9% from 1767 to 1790–2. Nominal wage data for 1767 are from Bowley (1898: 704). Wage data for 1790–3 are from Bowley (1900a: table at end of book); Young (1807: II, 428); and Gilboy (1934: 52).

Young's mind that the correlation between allotments and low poor rates was not simply a coincidence. "It is evident," he wrote, "that the possession of a cottage and about an acre of land, . . . if they do not keep the proprietor in every case from the parish, yet [they] very materially lessen the burthen [of poor relief] in all" (1801: 509). Young's advocacy of allotments as a method for reducing poor rates was echoed by Frederic Eden and David Davies, the authors of two important studies of rural poverty in the 1790s.[35] Allotment schemes became increasingly popular in the wake of the prolonged agricultural depression that began in 1815, and yet the responses to question 20 of the Rural Queries suggest that the majority of southern agricultural laborers did not rent allotments in 1832.[36]

If there was, in fact, a correlation between allotments and low poor rates, why didn't more parishes adopt allotment schemes in order to reduce their relief expenditures? Opposition to allotments seems to have come mainly from labor-hiring farmers, who feared that access to land would reduce the willingness of the poor to serve as day laborers, and who did not want their holdings reduced. Evidence of farmer opposition can be found in the 1834 Poor Law Report. Assistant Commissioners Power and Majendie reported from grain-producing counties that "farmers object very generally to the introduction of allotments." Majendie commented that farmers "are afraid of making labourers independent, and some look with an evil eye to a supposed diminution of their profits by introducing a new class of producers," while Power reported that farmers "are jealous of such deductions from their holdings, . . . and they object to the increased independence of the labourers" (Royal Commission 1834: 183, 185–6). Boys's comments concerning allotments in his 1796 survey of agriculture in Kent reveal that such fears existed long before 1834. He maintained that if laborers were given allotments of two or three acres, they would "entirely support their families without any other labour [and] hence would the most material part of the husbandry labour be lost to the public" (1796: 34–5).

---

[35] Eden (1797: I, xx, xxiii) proposed that agricultural laborers should be given enough land to "maintain a cow or two, together with pigs, poultry, etc.; and enough also to raise potatoes for the annual consumption of the family." Such a policy would "render all the present Paupers of the kingdom easy and comfortable." Davies (1795: 102–3) proposed that each cottager should be allowed "a little land about his dwelling, for keeping a cow, for planting potatoes, for raising flax or hemp."

[36] Between 1795 and 1835, 184 pamphlets proposing allotment schemes were published; 140 of these (76.1%) were published after 1815 (Barnett 1968: 175).

The evidence presented above supports the following conclusions: (1) The long-term increase in wheat prices that lasted roughly from 1760 to 1815 caused a decline in the amount of land available for use by agricultural laborers; (2) the loss of access to land was not adequately compensated for by an increase in wage rates or regularity of employment; and (3) poor relief expenditures were negatively correlated with access to land. In turn, these conclusions reveal a positive relationship between movements in wheat prices and movements in real poor relief expenditures. As the price of wheat, and hence the value of land, increased, grain-producing farmers found it cheaper to include poor relief payments rather than allotments in their implicit contracts with laborers.

The other major change in the economic environment was the decline of cottage industry in the south.[37] The counties most affected by the decline were Norfolk, Suffolk, and Essex, important centers of woollen cloth production in the first half of the eighteenth century. Defoe's *Tour*

[37] I do not offer an explanation for the decline of cottage industry in the south because I do not believe a satisfactory explanation exists. One widely accepted explanation for the decline is E. L. Jones's (1974: 131, 138) hypothesis that "the improvement of agricultural techniques" after 1650 led East Anglia and the south to concentrate on agricultural production, at the expense of cottage industry. Similarly, Joel Mokyr (1976: 139) has demonstrated that "technological progress in agriculture would increase the labor time allocated to agriculture in areas where the change could be applied" and hence would reduce the labor time allocated to cottage industry. These arguments suggest that the decline of cottage industry was an endogenous response to specialization in agriculture. The available empirical evidence does not support this conclusion. Davies (1795: 83) found that the earnings of women and children in agriculture were "insignificant" except during haymaking and harvest. Responses to questions 12 and 13 of the 1832 Rural Queries show that throughout the grain-producing south and east, women and children could not find agricultural employment for 8 to 10 months of the year. The decline of cottage industry clearly was not caused by an increase in the employment of women and children in agriculture. Indeed, Snell (1981: 431) contends that the employment of women in agriculture declined after 1750. Maxine Berg (1985: 125) maintains that "the reasons for the decline of the old cloth centres cannot lie entirely in a comparative advantage for agriculture in the South, because . . . new cottage industries [lacemaking and straw plaiting] developed on the burial mounds of the old." She admits, however, that the new industries "were smaller and poorer than their great predecessor" (1985: 122). In my opinion, the decline of cottage industry in the south was caused by a decline in demand for the goods produced there, as a result of the drying up of foreign markets (precipitated, in part, by the French wars), competition from cottage industry in the north, and, in the later stages of the decline, competition from the expanding factory system in the northwest. Berg (1985: 118–19) blames the decline on "several notable institutional rigidities" including "restrictions on capital," deficiencies of entrepreneurship, and "the polarity of master and man in the South compared to . . . the North. This produced more forceful workers' resistance to mechanization in the South." However, for the purposes of my argument, it is not necessary to determine why cottage industry declined, only the extent of its decline.

Through the Whole Island of Great Britain (1724–6) contained information concerning the prosperity of the East Anglian woollen industry in the 1720s. At the time, the woollen trade was flourishing in Norwich, Colchester, and many of the smaller towns in East Anglia, and Defoe noted that rural villages throughout the region were "employed, and in part maintained, by the spinning of wool" (1724–6: I, 17, 37, 48, 61–2).

By midcentury, however, the Essex woollen trade was in a state of decline. Morant wrote in 1748 that the production of woollens had "removed in a great measure [from Colchester] into the west and northern parts" of England (quoted in Darby 1976: 57). The decline continued throughout the rest of the century; Essex parishes responding to a 1795 inquiry remarked that the woollen trade had been declining for years (Vancouver 1795: 197, 210).

Norwich woollen producers fared somewhat better, achieving their greatest prosperity from 1743 through 1763 (James 1857: 259). However, data on Norwich poor relief expenditures provide evidence of the sharp decline in the production of woollens after 1763 (Lloyd-Prichard 1949: 428, 434; 1951: 371). From 1764 to 1785, real relief expenditures increased by 342%. Real expenditures peaked in 1793 (363% above the 1764 level) and then actually declined somewhat during the Speenhamland era.

The decline of East Anglia's woollen trade caused a sharp decline in wage rates and employment opportunities in cottage industry. Rural parishes in Norfolk, Suffolk, Essex, and parts of Cambridge, Bedford, and Hertford had supplied yarn for Norwich and Colchester manufacturers in the eighteenth century (James 1857: 272; Lloyd-Prichard 1949: 434–5). The effect of Norwich's decline on local cottage industry may be seen in the returns to Arthur Young's 1787 inquiry into the wage rates of spinners; he found that Suffolk spinners were paid significantly less than spinners in any other county (Young 1788: 353).[38]

Contemporary observers also found evidence of declining wages and employment opportunities for wool spinners in Berkshire, Hampshire, Northampton, Oxford, and Wiltshire (Eden 1797: II, 536; III, 796; Prince 1976: 140). After a careful study of data collected by Young and Eden, Pinchbeck (1930: 142–3, 147) concluded that wool spinners'

---

[38] No returns were given for Norfolk wool spinners. Presumably their wage rates were similar to those of Suffolk spinners.

wages throughout the south "were getting steadily lower" in the last quarter of the eighteenth century.[39]

In some areas, the decline of employment in wool spinning was partially offset by increased employment in lacemaking, glovemaking, or straw plaiting. Lacemaking was centered in Bedford, Buckingham, Northampton, and parts of Oxford and Huntingdon; glovemaking in Oxford, Somerset, and Worcester; and straw plaiting in Bedford, Buckingham, and Hertford (Pinchbeck 1930: 202–8, 215–26).[40] But the prosperity of these domestic industries was short-lived. According to Pinchbeck (1930: 208, 221, 224–5), wage rates and employment opportunities began to decline for lacemakers in 1815, for straw plaiters in 1820, and for glovemakers in 1826.[41] Responses to questions 11 through 13 of the Rural Queries, which concerned employment for women and children, reveal that wages in all three domestic industries were quite low by the early 1830s.[42]

In sum, employment opportunities in cottage industry declined throughout most of southern England between 1760 and 1834.[43] This decline had an important effect on family income in agricultural parishes. Cottage industry and agriculture were complementary with respect to labor inputs; laborers not needed in agriculture during slack

[39] Eden and his contemporaries tended to blame the outbreak of war in 1793 for the sharp decline of wool production in the south, but peace in 1815 did not bring a return to prosperity. The Report of the Select Committee on Poor Rate Returns and the Rural Queries of the Royal Poor Law Commission provide evidence of continued stagnation of the wool trade in 1824 and 1832. Of the 184 parishes from East Anglia (Norfolk, Suffolk, Essex, Cambridge) that responded to the Rural Queries, only 20, or 10.9%, acknowledged having cottage industry of any type, and only 4 parishes (all in Norfolk) were still associated with the wool industry.

[40] For evidence on lacemaking in the 1790s, see Eden (1797: II, 4, 8, 24, 27, 28, 29, 536, 544, 548). Similarly, for evidence on straw plaiting, see Eden (1797: II, 2, 6, 275). Responses to question 20 of the Rural Queries suggest that, as of 1832, lacemaking was widespread in Bedford, Buckingham, Huntingdon, Leicester, Northampton, and Oxford; straw plaiting was widespread in Bedford, Buckingham, Essex, and Hertford; and glovemaking was widespread in Oxford, Somerset, and Worcester.

[41] Eden (1797: II, 536) found that in the town of Northampton, lacemakers' wages "have, of late years, much decreased." However, evidence cited by Pinchbeck suggests that this must have been a temporary phenomenon.

[42] For evidence of declining wages in lacemaking, see, for instance, Parl. Papers (1834: XXX, 7a, 31a, 41a, 45a, 332a, 334a, 340a). Evidence of declining wages in straw plaiting can be found in Parl. Papers (1834: XXX, 178a, 217a, 226a). For evidence of declining wages in glovemaking, see Parl. Papers (1834: XXX, 369a, 372a, 382a, 409a, 582a).

[43] Employment opportunities in cottage industry might actually have increased in Bedford, Buckingham, Hertford, and Northampton during the late eighteenth century. However, responses to the Rural Queries show that wage rates and employment opportunities in the lace and straw trades (the most widespread cottage industries in these counties) had declined significantly by the early 1830s (see footnotes 40 and 42).

seasons could be employed in cottage industry. Moreover, cottage industry provided employment for women and children, whose employment possibilities in agriculture declined after 1750 (Snell 1981: 431). The decline of cottage industry meant that laborers who formerly were employed year-round were now unable to find jobs during slack seasons in agriculture, and their wives and children were left jobless for up to 11 months of the year.

Household budgets obtained from Eden and Davies show that in much of the south the typical laborer's family lived close enough to subsistence that it could not have absorbed the loss of income associated with the decline of cottage industry. The decline of employment opportunities in cottage industry therefore must have increased the demand for poor relief. There exists plenty of evidence that earnings from cottage industry and poor relief expenditures were negatively correlated. The major sources of this evidence are: studies of family budgets done by Eden and Davies in the 1790s; parish responses to inquiries from the 1824 Select Committee on Poor Rate Returns; and parish answers to question 11 of the 1832 Rural Queries. Eden (1797: II, 471, 687) blamed the high poor rates of Heckingham, Norfolk, and Melton, Suffolk, on "the high price of provisions, [and] the lowness of wages in spinning."[44] To illustrate the relationship between income from cottage industry and poor relief, Eden cited a typical household budget from Seend, Wiltshire. The weekly income of the family cited totaled 12.5s., including 4.5s. earned by the wife and eldest child by spinning, while weekly expenses amounted to 14s. In order to subsist, the family required 1.5s. per week (£3.9 per year) from the parish. The need for poor relief was a recent phenomenon, however, caused by a decline of approximately 60% in the nominal wages paid to spinners. Before the decline in wages, the earnings of the wife and eldest child had been large enough to keep the family off the parish rolls (Eden 1797: III, 796).[45] Eden's analysis of the relationship between cottage industry and poor relief led him to conclude that "a mixture of agriculture and manufactures, more especially, when the latter are scattered through

---

[44] On the other hand, the relatively low relief expenditure of Dunstable, Bedford, was a result of the "exceedingly great" earnings in straw plaiting during the previous four years (Eden 1797: II, 2).

[45] Davies (1795: 84–6) presented an account of the weekly earnings and expenses of a typical family of seven in 1787. Although the weekly earnings of the wife and eldest daughter from spinning amounted to only 2s. 4d., this income allowed the family to meet its annual expenses without applying to the parish for relief. Without the extra earnings from spinning, the family would have required £4.2 per annum from the parish.

a country, seems to be the most effectual method of keeping the poor in constant employment" (1797: II, 18).

Several parishes that responded to the 1824 parliamentary inquiry blamed the decline of cottage industry for their high level of relief expenditures. For instance, Brinkley, Cambridge, wrote that "the employment of the poor man's family being taken away by machinery in spinning wool, is the sole cause of the alarming increase of the poor rates," and Badwell Ash, Suffolk, responded that "our [poor] rates are increasing, principally owing to our not having any spinning for the women and children" (Parl. Papers 1824: VIa, 25, 21).[46] Similar statements are found in the 1832 Rural Queries. Once again, the most complaints were from East Anglia.[47] However, the responses make it clear that employment in cottage industry was declining throughout the south of England. For instance, the overseer of Claines, Worcester, remarked that the decline of employment for women and children in making gloves was "the principal cause of the increase in the poor rates throughout the greatest part of this county" (Parl. Papers 1834: XXX, 582a). Employment levels and wage rates were also declining for women and children engaged in the lace, straw, silk, button, hosiery, and ribbon trades.[48]

The decline of employment opportunities and wage rates for women and children in cottage industry reduced the earnings of many laborers' families to the point where they were forced to apply to their parish for relief in order to subsist. By eliminating one part of the implicit contract between farmers and laborers, the decline in cottage industry forced farmers to choose between raising agricultural wage rates, increasing the size of laborers' allotments, or granting poor relief to able-bodied laborers, in order to maintain family income at its previous (near subsistence) level. It has already been shown that both real agricultural wage rates and the size of allotments declined during the last third of the eighteenth century. Therefore, the decline of cottage industry, combined with the loss of allotments, must have caused an increase in real per capita poor relief expenditures during the second half of the eighteenth century.

---

[46] See also the responses of Maulden, Bedford; Syston, Leicester; Hollowell, Northampton; and Acton, Stoke Ash, Worlington, Brundish, and Framlingham, Suffolk (Parl. Papers 1824: VIa, 15–29).

[47] See, for instance, Parl. Papers (1834: XXX, 310a, 321a, 460a, 462a; 1834: XXXI, 468b).

[48] For evidence of declining wages in the lace, straw, and glove trades, see footnote 42. Evidence of declining wage rates and employment levels for the other cottage industries can be found in Parl. Papers (1834: XXX, silk, 145a, 169a, 399a, 482a; button making, 140a, 143a; ribbon making, 542a, 546a; hosiery, 283a).

4. Conclusion

The description of the Old Poor Law presented in this chapter differs from that of the traditional literature in three important respects. First, the major function of outdoor relief to able-bodied individuals was the provision of unemployment insurance to seasonally unemployed agricultural laborers. The system of allowances-in-aid-of-wages, considered the most prominent form of relief by the traditional literature, was used extensively only during periods of abnormally high food prices. The disincentive effects of outdoor relief that were stressed by the traditional literature, although likely on theoretical grounds, were of only minor importance in practice, because parish overseers were selective in their granting of relief and recipients were forced to perform work for the parish.

Second, the adoption of policies providing outdoor relief to unemployed or underemployed able-bodied laborers began during the 1760s and 1770s, not abruptly in 1795 as is argued by the traditional literature. No evidence was found to support the hypothesis that the year 1795 represented a watershed in the history of Poor Law administration. Third, the provision of outdoor relief to able-bodied laborers was an endogenous response to changes in the economic environment of the rural south and east. These changes forced labor-hiring farmers to alter the form of their implicit contract with labor. The new form of the implicit contract substituted outdoor relief, and, in particular, unemployment insurance, for allotments and employment in cottage industry.

The above conclusions lay the foundation for a reinterpretation of the economic role played by the Old Poor Law in the rural south from circa 1780 to 1834. An economic model of the Poor Law is developed in Chapter 3. Before turning to the model, however, it is useful to survey previous analyses of the economics of the Poor Law.

Appendix A
Agricultural Laborers' Wages, 1750–1832

The Appendix addresses three issues concerning agricultural laborers' wages: the short-run stickiness of nominal wage rates; the closeness of wages to subsistence; and the trend in real wages from 1750 to 1832. In the text I maintain that nominal wages were sticky in the short run, causing real wages to decline during periods of high food prices, sometimes, as in 1795 or 1800–1, to levels below subsistence. I also maintain that there was a long-run decline in real wages in the second half of the eighteenth century. The data presented here support each of these assertions.

The nominal wage data used in the Appendix are taken mainly from Bowley (1898; 1900a) and Gilboy (1934). Cost-of-living data are from Phelps Brown and Hopkins (1956) and Lindert and Williamson (1983; 1985). Estimates of subsistence were constructed from agricultural laborers' budgets in Eden (1797).

The extent of wage stickiness can be determined by examining time series of daily or weekly wages paid to laborers by individual employers. Few such series exist; four are presented in Table 1.A1, for agricultural laborers in Great Saling, Essex, from 1776 to 1806, Glynde, Sussex (1788–1820), and Leyburn, North Yorkshire (1750–71), and builders' laborers in Maidstone, Kent (1750–99). Although the Maidstone series is not for agricultural laborers, it is for unskilled workers in a town "dominated by agricultural factors" and therefore should be a reasonable proxy for the trend in local agricultural laborers' wages (Gilboy 1934: 51). Each series shows that although nominal wages increased slowly over time in response to long-run increases in the cost of living, wages were not responsive to short-run increases in prices. In each series nominal wages remain constant for several years, despite sharp fluctuations in the cost of living. Glynde farm laborers' wages remained constant from 1798 to 1800 while living costs increased by 51%, and from 1807 to 1812 while prices increased by 39%. Similarly, wages in Great Saling remained constant from 1780 to 1794 despite a 27.6% increase in the cost of living. Sometimes farmers increased nominal wages during periods of rapidly increasing prices, but seldom by enough to keep real wages from falling. From 1794 to 1801, nominal wages increased by 42.9% in Great Saling and by 50% in Glynde, in response to a 66.9% increase in the cost of living.

A decline in real wages need not have elicited the payment of poor relief to employed able-bodied laborers unless wages fell below the subsistence level. Subsistence is difficult to measure, but it can be estimated for 1795–6 from laborers' budgets collected by Frederic Eden (1797). Eden reported earnings and expenditure data for 26 southeastern agricultural laborers' families in 1795–6. The "budgets are for families at the very bottom of the [income] distribution" (Williamson 1985a: 218). The composition of the budgets suggests that they represent rea-

Table 1.A1. *Wages of laborers in four parishes*

	Nominal wages			Real wages		
Year	Maidstone Kent (1750 = 100)	Gt. Saling Essex (1776 = 100)	Leyburn Yorkshire (1750 = 100)	Maidstone Kent (1750 = 100)	Gt. Saling Essex (1776 = 100)	Leyburn Yorkshire (1750 = 100)
1750	100.0		100.0	100.0		100.0
1751	–		100.0	–		102.8
1752	–		100.0	–		98.2
1753	–		100.0	–		100.9
1754	100.0		100.0	95.9		95.9
1755	100.0		100.0	102.1		102.1
1756	100.0		100.0	98.0		98.0
1757	100.0		100.0	80.5		80.5
1758	100.0		100.0	80.7		80.7
1759	100.0		100.0	87.7		87.7
1760	100.0		100.0	91.8		91.8
1761	100.0		100.0	96.1		96.1
1762	100.0		100.0	92.5		92.5
1763	100.0		100.0	90.1		90.1
1764	100.0		100.0	82.7		82.7
1765	100.0		100.0	79.9		79.9
1766	100.0		100.0	79.0		79.0
1767	100.0		100.0	74.7		74.7
1768	100.0		112.5	75.5		85.0
1769	100.0		112.5	82.3		92.6
1770	100.0		112.5	82.6		93.0
1771	100.0		125.0	76.1		95.1
1772	100.0			68.8		
1773	100.0			69.0		
1774	109.4			74.8		
1775	109.4			79.2		
1776	118.8	100.0		87.9	100.0	
1777	118.8	100.0		88.3	100.4	
1778	118.8	100.0		84.9	96.5	
1779	118.8	100.0		92.7	105.4	
1780	121.9	100.0		98.5	109.2	
1781	118.8	100.0		82.8	94.1	
1782	118.8	100.0		82.4	93.7	
1783	118.8	100.0		80.7	91.7	
1784	118.8	100.0		83.1	94.4	
1785	118.8	100.0		87.6	99.6	
1786	118.8	100.0		89.7	102.0	
1787	118.8	100.0		87.4	99.4	

Table 1.A1. *(cont.)*

	Nominal wages			Real wages		
Year	Maidstone Kent (1750 = 100)	Gt. Saling Essex (1776 = 100)	Glynde Sussex (1788 = 100)	Maidstone Kent (1750 = 100)	Gt. Saling Essex (1776 = 100)	Glynde Sussex (1788 = 100)
1788	118.8	100.0	100.0	84.9	96.5	100.0
1789	118.8	100.0	100.0	80.4	91.4	94.8
1790	118.8	100.0	100.0	78.1	88.8	92.1
1791	118.8	100.0	100.0	81.1	92.2	95.6
1792	128.1	100.0	100.0	89.6	94.5	97.9
1793	137.5	100.0	100.0	89.5	87.8	91.1
1794	137.5	100.0	100.0	87.1	85.5	88.7
1795	137.5	114.3	111.1	74.0	83.1	83.7
1796	137.5	121.4	133.3	71.4	85.1	96.9
1797	137.5	–	133.3	82.0	–	111.3
1798	137.5	114.3	133.3	83.2	93.3	112.9
1799	143.8	121.4	133.3	76.5	87.2	99.3
1800		142.9	133.3		77.1	74.6
1801		142.9	150.0		73.3	79.7
1802		142.9	150.0		99.3	108.1
1803		142.9	150.0		101.9	110.9
1804		142.9	133.3		99.7	96.5
1805		142.9	144.4		85.6	89.6
1806		142.9	144.4		89.5	93.8
1807			144.4			99.0
1808			144.4			92.7
1809			144.4			81.7
1810			144.4			77.7
1811			144.4			81.9
1812			144.4			71.0
1813			144.4			72.8
1814			144.4			82.3
1815			144.4			91.7
1816			144.4			87.1
1817			144.4			84.7
1818			144.4			87.0
1819			144.4			91.5
1820			144.4			98.4

Sources: Wage data for Maidstone, Kent, and Leyburn, NorthYorkshire, from Gilboy (1934: 260–1, 150). Wage data for Great Saling, Essex, from Brown (1969: 132). Wage data for Glynde, Sussex, from Parl. Papers (1821: IX, 53). Cost-of-living data from Phelps Brown and Hopkins (1956: 313) and from Lindert and Williamson (1983: 11).

sonable estimates of subsistence. On average, 78% of each family's expenditure was on food, and 64% of food expenditure was on bread and flour.

Assuming that the budgets are close approximations of subsistence, Eden's data suggest that the typical southeastern agricultural laborer's earnings were below subsistence in 1795–6. Of the 26 families for which data were available, 24 (92%) reported expenditures greater than family earnings. Both families that reported earnings greater than expenditures contained only one child. David Davies, the other great social investigator of the 1790s, reached a similar conclusion from his analysis of agricultural laborers' budgets. He maintained that "the present wages of a labouring man constantly employed, together with the usual earnings of his wife, are barely sufficient to maintain in all necessaries . . . the man and his wife with two children" (1795: 24).

I estimate from Eden's data that subsistence for a family of four (six) was 10s.–12s. (12s.–14s.) per week in 1795.[49] The wage data presented in column one of Table 1.A2 show that weekly wages for agricultural laborers were as high as 10s. in only three southeastern counties in 1795: Kent, Surrey, and Sussex. It is not possible to estimate average *family* wages, because the weekly wages of women and children varied sharply both across families and over time within families. Data obtained from Eden suggest that women's earnings were typically less than 2s. per week; the combined earnings of the children varied from 0s. to 5s. per week, depending on the number, age, and sex of the children, and the availability of employment in cottage industry. In sum, Eden's data suggest that a large share of southeastern agricultural laborers (especially those with several children too young to work) had incomes below subsistence in 1795.

Table 1.A2 also contains data on the trend in agricultural laborers' real wages from 1767 to 1832. Laborers in every southeastern county experienced a decline in real wages from 1767 to 1795, varying from 12% to 28%. Moreover, income from allotments and cottage industry, the other major sources of income for agricultural laborers, declined in much of the southeast during the last third of the eighteenth century (see above, Section 3). As a result, the share of agricultural laborers with

---

[49] I assume that the cost of living did not vary much across the southeastern counties. Gilboy (1934: 70, 219) maintained that in the eighteenth century, "the counties in the vicinity of London are characterized by . . . practically the same prices in the essential commodities," and that bread prices were similar throughout England.

Table 1.A2. *Real wages of agricultural laborers, 1767–1832*

County	Nominal wage 1795 s.	Nominal wage 1795 d.	Real wage (1795 = 100) 1767	Real wage (1795 = 100) 1824	Real wage (1795 = 100) 1832
Bedford	7	6	133.5	115.4	149.6
Berkshire	9	0	115.1	99.0	129.9
Buckingham	8	0	138.1	105.0	142.6
Cambridge	8	2	123.9	112.2	144.2
Essex	9	0	118.9	105.5	127.8
Hertford	8	0	129.5	114.5	154.3
Huntingdon	8	6	120.6	95.8	137.5
Kent	10	6	128.2	113.9	139.8
Norfolk	9	0	122.8	103.7	134.0
Northampton	7	6	119.9	108.6	153.3
Oxford	8	6	113.7	96.8	133.1
Southampton	9	0	122.8	96.2	126.7
Suffolk	9	3	118.2	90.8	120.3
Surrey	10	6	118.4	103.5	128.2
Sussex	10	0	117.4	96.7	135.6
Wiltshire	8	4	116.1	91.7	122.3

Sources: Nominal wage data from Bowley (1898: 704; 1900a, table at end of book). Cost-of-living data from Phelps Brown and Hopkins (1956: 313) and Lindert and Williamson (1985: 148).

incomes below subsistence must have significantly increased in the late eighteenth century.

From 1795 to 1824 real wages fluctuated sharply, largely as a result of fluctuations in food prices. Table 1.A1 shows that in both Great Saling and Glynde real wages increased from 1795 to 1798, declined below 1795 levels in 1800–1, then increased in 1802–4 to 21% and 26% above 1795 levels in Great Saling and Glynde, respectively. Real wages in Glynde were above the 1795 level from 1802 to 1808, below the 1795 level from 1809 to 1814, then above again from 1815 through 1820. Wage data for each southeastern county exist for 1824. Table 1.A2 shows that real wages in 1824 were roughly similar to wages in 1795. From 1824 to 1832 real wages increased sharply in every southeastern county. In 1832 real wages were 20% to 54% higher than in 1795, and 21% to 44% higher than in 1824.

The increase in wage rates probably explains the decline in the payment of allowances-in-aid-of-wages from 1824 to 1832. In 1824, 41% of the districts responding to a parliamentary questionnaire reported paying "Wages . . . out of the Poor Rates" to employed laborers, compared with 7% of the parishes responding to the 1832 Rural Queries (Williams 1981: 151). The increase in wage rates and the decline of the allowance system suggest that the share of agricultural laborers with wages below subsistence was relatively small by 1832. On the other hand, the fact that 80% of rural southeastern parishes continued to pay child allowances in 1832 shows that wages were still not high enough for laborers to support large families.

Appendix B
Labor Rate for Wisborough Green

At a meeting held in the vestry-room of the parish at Wisborough Green, in the county of Sussex, this 29th day of November 1832, it was agreed to make a rate for the relief of the poor at 7s. in the pound, and that 4s. in the pound, a part of the said rate, should be expended for the better employment of the poor of this parish, agreeably to the provisions of the Act 2 & 3 Will. IV. c. 96, according to the following resolutions:

The Rev. John Thornton, D.D. in the Chair.

1st. That every rate-payer shall be allowed to work the amount of his or her rate, according to the following scale of wages:

For all boys under 12 years of age ..... 4d. per day
– boys from 12 to 14 ditto .... 5d. –
– boys from 14 to 16 ditto .... 6d. –
– youths from 16 to 18 ditto ...... 10d. –
– youths from 18 to 20 ditto ...... 14d. –
– single men upwards of 20 ditto .. 16d. –
– able-bodied married men .... 20d. –

2d. That every rate-payer shall, at the end of the period agreed on, make a true return of the christian and surname of every man and boy, their place of abode, and wages paid to each man and boy that they may employ; but in no case will higher wages be allowed than from this rate.

3d. That all labourers or servants who shall belong to this parish shall be included in these regulations.

4th. That all the money that shall be collected in lieu of labour shall be applied to the parish fund.

5th. That all the sons of farmers, of the before-mentioned ages, actually employed as labourers by their parents, to be considered similarly situated as other labourers.

6th. That all labourers or servants belonging to this parish shall be included in these resolutions, domestic servants being allowed for according to this scale, only excepting such servants as are liable to the assessed taxes.

7th. That in any case where men, who are not able-bodied labourers, are taken into employment, no greater sum shall be allowed than that which is actually paid.

8th. That this agreement shall take place and be in force from the 3d day of December 1832, to the 14th day of January 1833; and if the before-mentioned rate be not worked out at that time, the money to be paid to the overseer.

9th. That these resolutions be laid before the magistrate at their ensuing petty sessions at Petworth, for their approval and sanction, according to the provisions of the Act of Parliament before-mentioned.

The above resolutions were agreed to at a general vestry duly called.

Source: Parl. Papers (1834: XXXVII, 185).

2

THE OLD POOR LAW IN HISTORICAL PERSPECTIVE

The debate over the economics of the Old Poor Law began before the adoption of the famous relief scale at Speenhamland in 1795 and has continued to the present day. There have been three distinct phases to the debate. The first, which involved the building up of what I shall call the traditional critique of the Old Poor Law, began sometime during the second half of the eighteenth century and culminated in 1834 with the Report of the Royal Commission to Investigate the Poor Laws. The literature during this period focused almost entirely on the supposed disincentive effects on labor supply (and the subsequent effects on wages, profits, rents, and morals) created by the policy of granting outdoor relief to able-bodied laborers. It made no attempt to discern the reasons why the system of outdoor relief had been adopted in the late eighteenth century, or why it had continued to exist for more than 40 years.

The second, or neo-traditional, phase of the debate was ushered in by the publication of John and Barbara Hammond's *The Village Labourer* in 1911, and includes the Webbs' *English Poor Law History* (1927; 1929), and Polanyi's *The Great Transformation* (1944). Rather than simply focusing on the economic effects of outdoor relief, the neo-traditional literature provided explanations for the system's adoption and persistence. The Hammonds, the Webbs, and Polanyi accepted several of the major tenets of the traditional analysis, however, so that their work should be considered extensions of the traditional literature rather than early pieces of revisionism.

A revisionist analysis of the economics of the Old Poor Law began in 1963 with the publication of Mark Blaug's paper "The Myth of the Old Poor Law and the Making of the New." The revisionists rejected the traditional hypothesis that the system of outdoor relief had a disastrous long-run effect on the rural labor market. However, although their cri-

51

tique of the traditional literature is convincing, their analysis of the adoption and persistence of outdoor relief remains curiously underdeveloped.

This chapter presents an analysis of how the Poor Law debate developed over time. It begins by discussing the pre-1834 criticisms of the Poor Law in order to discern the intellectual roots of the Royal Commission's Report. Section 2 presents the 1834 report's arguments in detail and demonstrates how they were rooted in the earlier works of Townsend, Eden, and Malthus. Sections 3 and 4 review the work of the Hammonds, the Webbs, and Polanyi. Section 5 reviews the revisionist interpretation of the Old Poor Law.

1. The Historiography of the Poor Law Before 1834

The first problem faced when trying to survey the historiography of the Old Poor Law is where to begin. Criticism of the granting of outdoor relief to able-bodied laborers began well before the adoption of the Speenhamland bread scale.[1] Probably the most influential attack against relief to able-bodied laborers made before 1795 was Joseph Townsend's *Dissertation on the Poor Laws,* published in 1786.[2]

Townsend believed that any form of poor relief was unnecessary as well as unnatural. He maintained that "hope and fear are the springs of industry. . . . In general it is only hunger which can spur and goad [the poor] on to labour" (1786: 23, 27). The Poor Laws

proceed upon principles which border on absurdity, as professing to accomplish that which, in the very nature and constitution of the world, is impracticable. They say that in England no man, even though by his indolence, improvidence, prodigality, and vice, he may have brought himself to poverty, shall ever suffer from want. In the progress of society, it will be found, that some must want. (1786: 36)

By assuring laborers a subsistence level of income, the Poor Law created insubordination among the poor. "Indeed it is the general complaint of farmers," argued Townsend, "that their men do not work so well as they used to do, when it was reproachful to be relieved by the parish" (1786: 28).

---

[1] The pre-1795 Poor Law debate is discussed by Poynter (1969: 21–44). For an eighteenth-century account of the debate, see Eden (1797: I, 227–410).

[2] Karl Polanyi (1944: 111) wrote that the problem of poor relief "was raised as a broad issue in Townsend's *Dissertation on the Poor Laws* and never ceased to occupy men's minds for another century and a half."

The long-run effects of poor relief were even more serious, since the Poor Law removed the "equilibrium . . . between the numbers of people and the quantity of food" that was maintained by the fear of hunger (1786: 43–4). Thus, the Poor Law sowed "the seeds of misery for the whole community" and would eventually cause "more to die from want, than if poverty had been left to find its proper channel" (1786: 40–1).[3]

In order to "promote industry and economy," Townsend maintained that it was necessary to replace the existing Poor Law with a system in which the relief given to the poor was "limited and precarious" (1786: 62). Although immediate abolition of the Poor Law was not practical, the poor rate "must be gradually reduced in certain proportions annually, the sum to be raised in each parish being fixed and certain" (1786: 63). One consequence of such a policy would be to remove the artificial stimulus to population growth, and thus to once again enable population to "regulate itself by the demand for labour" (1786: 65).

The debate over the Poor Laws was greatly intensified by the subsistence crises of 1795 and 1800. Two important studies of poverty among English laborers were published soon after the 1795 crisis: Frederic Eden's *The State of the Poor* (1797) and David Davies's *The Case of Labourers in Husbandry* (1795). Both works devoted a considerable number of pages to analyzing the effects of the Poor Laws on laborers.

Eden, like Townsend, felt that the Poor Laws were "repugnant to the sound principles of political economy." He maintained that

It is one, and not the least, of the mistaken principles on which a national provision for the relief of the indigent classes of the community is supported, that every individual of the community has not only a claim, but a right, . . . to the active and direct interference of the Legislature, to supply him with employment while able to work, and with a maintenance when incapacitated from labour. [A] legal provision for the Poor . . . checks that emulative spirit of exertion, which the want of the necessaries, or the no less powerful demand for the superfluities, of life, gives birth to: for it assures a man, that, whether he may have been indolent, improvident, prodigal, or vicious, he shall never suffer want. (1797: I, 447–8)

The existing system of poor relief was "the parent of idleness and improvidence" and thus had "a tendency to increase the number of those

---

[3] Townsend here has given a Malthusian argument against the Poor Laws 12 years before the publication of Malthus's *Essay on Population*. Polanyi (1944: 113) commented that "Malthus' population laws might [never] have exerted any appreciable influence on modern society but for the . . . maxims which Townsend deduced . . . and wished to have applied to the reform of the Poor Law."

wanting relief" (1797: I, 481, 450). The policy of providing employment for the poor was doomed to failure, since it would injure persons employed in similar occupations (1797: I, 467). Eden also criticized the recently adopted Berkshire (Speenhamland) bread scale. Under the Berkshire plan, laborers received needed assistance

in the way most prejudicial to their moral interests: they received it as a charity; as the extorted charity of others; and not as a result of their own well exerted industry. . . . Had political regulations not interfered, the demand for labour would have raised its price, not only in a ratio merely adequate to the wants of the labourer, but even beyond it. (1797: I, 583, 582)

To keep relief expenditures from increasing any further, Eden proposed to limit annual expenditures to the average of the previous three or seven years.[4] He also proposed a policy to reduce laborers' dependence on poor relief. There were still thousands of acres of commons and waste in Britain, "which want but to be enclosed and taken care of, to be as rich, and as valuable, as any lands now in tillage" (1797: I, xi). After enclosure, a portion of this land should be given to laborers. If it was

conveniently and judiciously laid out for a garden, and a little croft, enough to maintain a cow or two, together with pigs, poultry, etc.; and enough also to raise potatoes for the annual consumption of the family [it] would be sufficient to render all the present Paupers of the kingdom easy and comfortable, and . . . as independent as it is either possible, or proper, that persons in their sphere of life should be. (1797: I, xx, xxiii)

Davies (1795: 25, 26) agreed with Eden that "the poor-rate is now in part a substitute for wages," and that such a policy "is a great discouragement to the industrious poor, tends to sink their minds into despondency, and to drive them into desperate courses." The "indiscriminate provision [of relief] for all in want," Davies argued, led to a "carelessness about the future" that could be remedied only by drawing a line of separation between the deserving and undeserving poor (1795: 98, 99). Like Eden, Davies maintained that commons and waste lands were Britain's "grand resource[;] their gradual improvement, judiciously conducted, would afford employment and subsistence to multitudes of people" (1795: 81–2). He proposed that each cottager should be allowed "a

---

[4] Eden maintained that "faulty and defective as our Poor System may be in its original construction, and in its modern ramifications, he must be a bold and rash political projector, who should propose to level it to the ground" (1797: I, 470).

little land about his dwelling, for keeping a cow, for planting potatoes, for raising flax or hemp" (1795: 102–3).[5]

Davies disagreed, however, with Eden's explanation for the rapid increase in relief expenditures during the second half of the eighteenth century. Eden (1797: I, 481) argued that the disincentive effects of the existing system of outdoor relief were "the fruitful source of endlessly accumulating expense." Davies maintained that increased relief expenditures were mainly a result of changes in the rural economic environment. The real income of agricultural laborers had declined since 1750, according to Davies, as a result of the general increase in prices of consumer goods, the decline in employment for women and children, and the loss of cottage land through enclosure and engrossment. Thus, "an amazing number of people have been reduced from a comfortable state of partial independence to the precarious condition of hirelings, who, when out of work, must immediately come to their parish" (1795: 57).

Davies's assessment of the economic plight of rural laborers led him to support proposals for putting the poor to work. Parish overseers should find winter employment for adult males, and year-round employment for women and children (1795: 61). If no work could be found for unemployed men, they should "be by law entitled to two-thirds of a day's wages, to be paid out of the poor-rate," for each day's unemployment (1795: 100). Thus, Davies was an early proponent of unemployment insurance. He also proposed that Parliament adopt a minimum wage policy, with the minimum wage payment regulated by the price of bread (1795: 111, 115).

The two great social investigators of the 1790s reached different conclusions regarding the economic role and effects of the Old Poor Law. Eden's hypothesis that the use of outdoor relief had disastrous consequences for labor supply was very mainstream. His criticisms of the Poor Law were similar to those of Townsend, and he was quoted approvingly several times by Malthus. Davies's contention that changes in the economic environment, rather than changes in the administration of relief, were the major cause of increased relief expenditures was ignored by historians for more than 100 years, until John and Barbara Hammond came to his support.

---

[5] Davies believed that the possibility of obtaining an allotment would keep the poor from "vice and beggary." "Hope is a cordial," he wrote, "of which the poor man has especially much need. . . . And the fatal consequence of that policy, which deprives labouring people of the expectation of possessing any property in the soil, must be the extinction of every generous principle in their minds" (1795: 102).

Thomas Malthus was by far the most influential critic of the Poor Law prior to 1834. His interest in the subject followed naturally from his study of the principle of population. The first edition of his *Essay on the Principle of Population,* published in 1798, contained one chapter on the Poor Laws. A significantly more detailed critique of the Poor Laws followed in the greatly expanded second edition of 1803, and this was further expanded and refined in the *Essay*'s succeeding four editions.

Malthus saw the Poor Laws as an ill-conceived governmental attempt to curb the so-called positive check to population. He echoed the sentiments of Townsend and Eden when he wrote that

dependent poverty ought to be held disgraceful. Such a stimulus seems to be absolutely necessary to promote the happiness of the great mass of mankind; and every general attempt to weaken this stimulus, however benevolent its apparent intention, will always defeat its own purpose. (1798: 85)

By guaranteeing parish assistance to able-bodied laborers, the Poor Laws "diminish both the power and the will to save among the common people, and thus . . . weaken one of the strongest incentives to sobriety and industry, and consequently to happiness" (1798: 87). In the long run they "create the poor which they maintain."

Malthus combined the theory of population with the wages-fund doctrine to come up with his indictment of the Poor Law. The Poor Law caused laborers' wage rates to decline in both the short run and the long run. The granting of relief to able-bodied laborers caused wage rates to decline in the short run, since the wages fund determined the total amount of money available for labor, either in the form of wage income or poor relief. "It should be observed in general," wrote Malthus, "that, when a fund for the maintenance of labour is raised by assessment, the greater part of it is not a new capital brought into trade, but an old one, which before was much more profitably employed, turned into a new channel" (1807a: II, 110). Moreover, by basing the amount of a recipient's relief benefit on the size of his family, parishes reduced the cost of having children, which lowered wage rates even further in the long run.[6] The Poor Law's

obvious tendency is to increase population without increasing the food for its support. . . . [A]s the provisions of the country must, in consequence of the increased population, be distributed to every man in smaller proportions, it is

---

[6] A complete account of Malthus's analysis of the effect of outdoor relief on birth rates, and historians' critiques of his analysis, is given in Chapter 5.

evident that the labour of those who are not supported by parish assistance, will purchase a smaller quantity of provisions than before, and consequently, more of them must be driven to ask for support. (1798: 83–4)

Thus, in the long run, "the poor-laws tend in the most marked manner to make the supply of labour exceed the demand for it . . . and thus constantly to increase the poverty and distress of the labouring classes of society" (1817: II, 371).[7]

Malthus's adherence to the wages-fund doctrine led him to criticize parish make-work projects. He argued that it was a "gross error" to suppose "that the funds for the maintenance of labour . . . may be increased at will, and without limit, by a fiat of government, or an assessment of the overseers" (1807a: II, 102). Like Eden, he felt that attempts by parishes to employ the poor in the production of manufactured goods would "throw out of employment many independent workmen, who were before engaged in fabrications of a similar nature" (1807a: II, 108).

Malthus concluded that the distress of the laboring poor was caused by the "absurd" and "arrogant" administration of poor relief, rather than by changes in the economic environment. He attempted to refute the hypothesis that the high levels of relief expenditures during the Napoleonic Wars had been attributable to the high price of food by pointing out in 1817 that "we have seen these necessaries of life experience a great and sudden fall [in price], and yet at the same time a still larger proportion of the population requiring public assistance" (1817: II, 360). Given the cause of distress, the solution was obvious: The granting of relief to able-bodied laborers had to be abolished. Malthus argued that the abolition of poor relief would benefit the poor in the long run. He proposed a plan of gradual abolition in which no child born after a certain date would ever be able to obtain parish relief (1807a: II, 320–4). Moreover, he argued against replacing poor relief with either a guaranteed minimum wage, as proposed by Davies, or an allotment scheme, as proposed by both Eden and Davies. A guaranteed minimum wage would not work because it would not allow the wage rate "to find its natural level," determined by "the relations between the supply of provisions, and the demand for them." It was important for the wage

[7] In a rare agreement with Malthus, David Ricardo (1821: 105–6) wrote that "the clear and direct tendency of the poor laws . . . is not, as the legislature benevolently intended, to amend the condition of the poor, but to deteriorate the condition of both poor and rich; instead of making the poor rich, they are calculated to make the rich poor."

rate to reach its natural level because this "expresses clearly the wants of
the society respecting population" (1807a: II, 89–90). With respect to
allotment schemes, Malthus devoted several pages to criticizing Arthur
Young's plan to grant each rural laborer with three or more children
"half an acre of land for potatoes; and grass enough to feed one or two
cows." According to Malthus, "Young's plan would be incomparably
more powerful in encouraging a population beyond the demand for
labour than our present poor laws" (1807a: II, 376). Malthus blamed the
poverty in Ireland on the ready availability of small allotments of land.
He argued that because of "the facility of obtaining a cabin and potatoes . . . , a population is brought into existence, which is not demanded
by the quantity of capital and employment in the country; and the consequence of which must therefore necessarily be . . . to lower in general
the price of labour" (1807a: II, 374–5). Malthus concluded that it was
best to leave the poor to their own devices, since that would encourage
them to depend on themselves and to practice moral restraint.

The indictment of the Poor Law contained in Malthus's *Essay on
Population* received considerable attention in Parliament during the
post–Napoleonic War period. Between 1817 and 1831, several parliamentary committees were appointed to study the economic effects of the
system of outdoor relief and to consider possible methods for Poor Law
reform. The most important document to come out of these committees
was the 1817 report of the Select Committee of the House of Commons
(Parl. Papers 1817: VI).[8] The report contained little that was new in its
analysis of the Poor Law. Rather, it relied heavily on the arguments of
previous reformers, Malthus in particular.

The report began, in typical fashion, by maintaining that the granting
of outdoor relief to able-bodied laborers instilled bad habits in the working class.[9] It presented evidence that relief expenditures had been con-
tinually increasing since 1776, and argued that this increase was for the
most part "independent of the pressure of any temporary or accidental
circumstances, . . . the rise in the price of provisions and other neces-

---

[8] Poynter (1969: 245) called the 1817 report "the baldest and most dogmatic summary of
the abolitionist case published" in the post–Napoleonic War period.

[9] The report claimed that outdoor relief produced "the unfortunate effect of abating those
exertions on the part of the labouring classes, on which, according to the nature of things,
the happiness and welfare of mankind has been made to rest. By diminishing this natural
impulse by which men are instigated to industry and good conduct, by superseding the
necessity of providing in the season of health and vigour for the wants of sickness and old
age, . . . this system is perpetually encouraging and increasing the amount of misery it
was designed to alleviate" (Parl. Papers 1817: VI, 4).

saries of life," and the increase in population (Parl. Papers 1817: VI, 5). Rather, it was the result of "evils which are inherent in the system." The report predicted that "the amount of the assessment will continue as it has done, to increase till . . . it shall have absorbed the profits of the property on which the rate may have been assessed, producing thereby the neglect and ruin of the land" (Parl. Papers 1817: VI, 8).

Like Eden and Malthus, the report rigidly adhered to the wages-fund doctrine. It maintained that:

what number of persons can be employed in labour, must depend absolutely upon the amount of the [wages] funds, which alone are applicable to the maintenance of labour. In whatever way these funds may be applied or expended, the quantity of labour maintained by them . . . would be very nearly the same. . . . [W]hoever therefore is maintained by the law as a labouring pauper, is maintained only instead of some other individual, who would otherwise have earned by his own industry, the money bestowed on the pauper. (Parl. Papers 1817: VI, 17)

In other words, there existed a one-to-one trade-off between poor relief and wage income, so that governmental make-work projects were always counterproductive. The objective of finding employment for all who required it was "not in the power of any law to fulfill" (Parl. Papers 1817: VI, 17).

Ironically, the 1817 report did not urge that the provision of outdoor relief to able-bodied laborers be immediately abolished, believing this to be impractical at the time. It did suggest, however, that at some time in the future, "under favourable circumstances of the country," the system of outdoor relief should be ended. Abolition would result in an increase in "the natural demand for labour" and would also "have the effect of gradually raising the wages of labour" because it was "the obvious interest of the farmer" to provide each of his workers with "such necessaries of life as may keep his body in full vigour, and his mind gay and cheerful" (Parl. Papers 1817: VI, 18–19).

The major arguments for abolishing the Poor Law, therefore, were laid out 17 years before the appearance of the 1834 Poor Law Report and the passage of the Poor Law Amendment Act. The intellectual roots of the abolitionists' arguments were Townsend's *Dissertation on the Poor Laws,* which argued that relief was unnecessary; the wages-fund doctrine, which was used by Eden and Malthus to argue that relief lowered wage rates; and Malthus's theory of population, which showed that outdoor relief increased the number of paupers in the long run.

2. The Poor Law Report of 1834

The postwar parliamentary committees that were set up to consider various aspects of poor relief made no attempt to abolish or reform the Poor Law. The "impotence" of Parliament was finally ended when the Royal Commission to Investigate the Poor Laws was created by the new Whig government in February 1832. Nine persons were chosen to serve on the commission; by far the two most important members were Nassau Senior, a lawyer and political economist, and Edwin Chadwick, a lawyer and journalist as well as a disciple of Jeremy Bentham.[10]

The first task of the commission was the collection of data on the economic effects of outdoor relief. The commissioners relied on two types of evidence. First, they drew up and distributed two sets of questionnaires, known as the Rural and Town Queries, which were mailed to parishes during the spring of 1832. The commissioners then appointed 26 assistant commissioners to visit parishes throughout England and Wales. The assistant commissioners were directed to ascertain the effects of outdoor relief "on the industry, habits, and character of the labourer, the increase of population, the rate of wages, the profits of farming, the increase or diminution of farming capital, and the rent and improvement of land" (Royal Commission 1833: 417). Those who came upon parishes with a seeming redundancy of population were to determine whether the redundancy was "occasioned either by the want of capital among the farmers, or by the indolence or unskillful habits of the labourers." If the unemployment appeared to be caused by the existence of "more labourers than could be profitably employed at the existing prices of produce, although the labourers were intelligent and industrious, and the farmers wealthy," the assistant commissioners were to ascertain to what extent the redundancy

has been occasioned by the stimulus applied to population by the relief of the able-bodied; and for that purpose inquire into the frequency of marriages where the husband at the time, or shortly before or after the time of the marriage, was in receipt of parish relief, and into the proportion of the number of such marriages to those of independent labourers. (Royal Commission 1833: 418)

In other words, the commissioners assumed that unemployment was caused either by the indolence of labor, as argued by Townsend and

[10] Detailed analyses of the 1834 Poor Law Report can be found in Cowherd (1977: 204–82), Webb and Webb (1929: 1–103), and Poynter (1969: 316–29). See also Williams (1981: 52–8).

Malthus, or by an increase in population caused by the system of out-door relief, as argued by Malthus.

The assistant commissioners' reports were completed by January 1833. The information from these reports, along with information from the Rural and Town Queries, was selectively used in the general report of the Royal Commission (Royal Commission 1834), written almost entirely by Senior and Chadwick, and published in March 1834. Publication of the assistant commissioners' reports and the answers to the Rural and Town Queries followed later in 1834. In all, the report filled 12 volumes of Parliamentary Papers containing thousands of pages. Unfortunately, a large amount of the material contained in the assistant commissioners' reports and the Queries was ignored by Senior and Chadwick, so that the general report's analysis of the use of outdoor relief was little more than a greatly expanded version of the 1817 House of Commons Report on the Poor Law, full of detailed examples of the bad effects of the system of outdoor relief on laborers, landlords, large farmers, small farmers, and tradesmen.

The major conclusion reached by the report was that all forms of outdoor relief produced bad effects and should therefore be abolished. It contended that

out-door relief . . . appears to contain in itself the elements of an almost indefi-nite extension; of an extension, in short, which may ultimately absorb the whole fund out of which it arises. Among the elements of extension are the constantly diminishing reluctance to claim an apparent benefit, the receipt of which im-poses no sacrifice, except a sensation of shame quickly obliterated by habit, even if not prevented by example. (Royal Commission 1834: 44)

The effect of the allowance system, which granted "relief in aid of wages" to privately employed laborers, was to

diminish, we might almost say to destroy, all . . . qualities in the labourer. What motives has the man who . . . knows that his income will be increased by noth-ing but by an increase of his family, and diminished by nothing but by a diminu-tion of his family, that it has no reference to his skill, his honesty, or his diligence – what motive has he to acquire or to preserve any of these merits? Unhappily, the evidence shows, not only that these virtues are rapidly wearing out, but that their place is assumed by the opposite vices. (1834: 68)

These same criticisms were applied to the policy of granting outdoor relief to unemployed laborers, which also was criticized for granting benefits that were as large as the wage rates paid by farmers while requiring only a small amount of work from the recipients (1834: 39). The labor rate and the roundsman system also made laborers indolent.

Under the labour-rate system [and the roundsman system] relief and wages are confounded. The wages partake of relief, and the relief partakes of wages. The labourer is employed, not because he is a good workman, but because he is a parishioner. He receives a certain sum, not because it is the fair value of his labour, but because it is what the vestry has ordered to be paid. Good conduct, diligence, skill, all become valueless. Can it be supposed that they will be preserved? (1834: 219–20)

The labor rate and the roundsman system were further criticized for allowing labor-hiring farmers to pass some of their labor costs to small occupiers, tradespeople, and householders (1834: 197, 210–11). Since Parliament had given sanction to the use of labor rates only two years before 1834, it is surprising that they were criticized so severely in the report.[11]

Unlike earlier critiques of the Poor Laws, the 1834 report gave an explanation for the widespread adoption and persistence of policies granting outdoor relief to able-bodied laborers. Employers supported the use of outdoor relief because it

enables them to dismiss and resume their labourers according to their daily or even hourly want of them, and to reduce wages to the minimum, or even below the minimum of what will support an unmarried man, and to throw upon others the payment of a part . . . of the wages actually received by their labourers. (1834: 59)

Of course, the granting of outdoor relief made laborers indolent and thereby reduced their productivity, so that ultimately "the farmer finds that pauper labour is dear, whatever be its price." However, the decline in labor productivity evolved slowly over time, so the farmer benefited from the use of outdoor relief in the short run (1834: 71). In the long run, "when the apparently cheap labour has become really dear," the farmer "can either quit at the expiration of his lease, or demand on its renewal a diminution of rent" (1834: 73).[12] Whereas leaseholders were thus encouraged to support the allowance system, farmers who owned

---

[11] An entire chapter of the 1834 report was devoted to criticism of the labor rate. Apparently Senior and Chadwick believed that the recent popularity of labor rates made it important to present an especially detailed critique of that method of outdoor relief.

[12] The report concluded that farmers' ability to profit from the use of outdoor relief by reducing their wage bill "accounts for the many instances in our evidence . . . of the indifference of the farmers in some places to poor-law expenditure, and in other places to their positive wish to increase it" (1834: 72).

their land were not. A landowner "may be expected to oppose the introduction of allowance, knowing that for giving up an immediate accession to his income he will be repaid, by preserving the industry and morality of his fellow-parishioners, and by saving his estate from being gradually absorbed by pauperism" (1834: 73). The seeming popularity of the allowance system, therefore, could only be explained by the political dominance of leaseholders in most rural parishes in the south and east.[13]

The report rejected the proposal that outdoor relief be replaced by a policy of supplying laborers with allotments, although the renting of land to laborers by individual farmers was supported. There was no need for parliamentary intervention, since the renting of allotments could be made "beneficial to the lessor as well as to the occupier," and "a practice which is beneficial to both parties, and is known to be so, may be left to the care of their own self-interest" (1834: 193–4). However, although allotments reduced relief expenditures in the short run, the report argued that they would not reduce expenditures in the long run. The amount of land available for allotments "is limited, and the number of applicants is rapidly augmenting, [so that] every year would increase the difficulty of supplying fresh allotments, and diminish their efficiency in reducing the increasing mass of pauperism" (1834: 194).

The most striking feature of the report is that it made no attempt to study the causes of the unemployment that was very much in evidence in the rural south and east. None of the questions in the Rural Queries dealt with the causes of unemployment, and the instructions to the assistant commissioners requested them merely to ascertain whether unemployment was caused by the indolence of laborers or by increases in population brought about by the allowance system. Despite the indifference of the commissioners, many parishes responding to the Rural Queries discussed the causes of their unemployment problems, and several of the assistant commissioners wrote of the economic causes of unemployment, and especially seasonal unemployment, in their reports. This information was ignored by Senior and Chadwick, however, so that the commission's report made no mention of the economic causes of unemployment. Rather, the report maintained that existing unemployment was an artificial creation of the system of outdoor relief. To support this contention, evidence was presented of a decline in unemployment rates in parishes

---

[13] The report does not explain why landowners would allow leaseholders to adopt a system that would cause the parish to be "gradually absorbed by pauperism."

where the use of outdoor relief had been discontinued (1834: 233–7). The report concluded that the unemployment problem "would be rapidly reduced and ultimately disappear" upon the abolition of policies granting outdoor relief to able-bodied laborers (1834: 354).

The report recommended that outdoor relief be replaced by a policy of "less-eligibility," the purpose of which was to lower the utility level of laborers supported by the parish below that of the lowest-paid independent laborers. The report contended that the "most essential of all conditions" imposed on the recipient of relief should be that

his situation on the whole shall not be made really or apparently so eligible as the situation of the independent labourer of the lowest class. . . . [I]n proportion as the condition of any pauper class is elevated above the condition of independent labourers, the condition of the independent class is depressed; their industry is impaired, their employment becomes unsteady, and its remuneration in wages are diminished. Such persons, therefore, are under the strongest inducements to quit the less eligible class of labourers and enter the more eligible class of paupers. . . . Every penny bestowed, that tends to render the condition of the pauper more eligible than that of the independent labourer, is a bounty on indolence and vice. (1834: 228)

In order to achieve less eligibility, the report recommended that, "except as to medical attendance," relief should be granted to able-bodied laborers and their families only in well-regulated workhouses (1834: 262). The elimination of outdoor relief would not only eliminate unemployment, it would also cause laborers to become "more steady and diligent," thereby increasing productivity, which would make "the return to the farmers' capital larger, and the consequent increase of the [wages] fund for the employment of labour enables and induces the capitalist to give better wages" (1834: 329). A graphical representation of the report's hypotheses concerning the effects of Poor Law reform on wage rates and employment is given in Figure 2.1. The report maintained that the elimination of outdoor relief would cause a rightward shift in the supply curve of agricultural labor from S_1 to S_2, and a rightward shift in the demand curve from D_1 to D_2, owing to the increase in labor's productivity, so as to cause both the equilibrium wage rate and the employment of labor to increase.

The Report of the Royal Poor Law Commission is by far the most influential work ever written on the economic effects of the Old Poor Law. Ironically, most of the report's arguments in favor of the abolition of outdoor relief were not original. But the massive amount of evidence

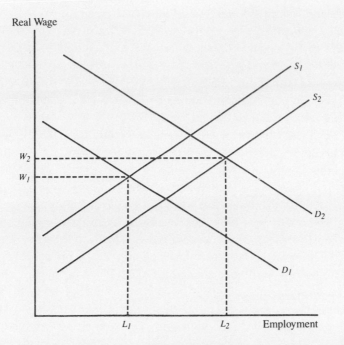

Figure 2.1. The effect of Poor Law reform on real wages and employment: traditional hypothesis.

used to support its arguments, and its air of self-confidence, have made the 1834 report a far more influential work than any of its predecessors. Each study discussed in the remainder of this chapter relied heavily on the information contained in the report.

3. Fabian Interpretations of the Poor Law

The first major interpretive study of the Poor Law to appear after 1834 was John and Barbara Hammond's *The Village Labourer,* published in 1911.[14] This was followed in 1927 and 1929 by a second major study, the

[14] Between 1834 and 1911, the only major study of the Old Poor Law was Sir George Nicholls's two-volume *History of the English Poor Law,* published in 1854 (second edition, 1898). Nicholls was himself an early Poor Law reformer. Appointed overseer of the poor for Southwell, Nottinghamshire, in 1821, he reduced the parish's relief expenditures by 75% in four years, mainly through the abolition of outdoor relief for able-bodied laborers. Nicholls (1898: II, 137) argued that the policy of granting outdoor relief to the able-bodied was responsible for "checking industry, destroying self-reliance, and leading to the pauperization of nearly the entire labouring class." He made no attempt to

seventh and eighth volumes of Sidney and Beatrice Webb's *English Local Government.*[15] Volume seven was devoted to the Poor Law from the 1590s to 1834, and volume eight contained a detailed analysis of the 1834 Poor Law Report. These two works, similar in tone, complemented each other in their analysis of the Poor Law during the Speenhamland era. Together, they form what has been called "the classic Fabian interpretation" of the Poor Law.

Although the analysis of the Poor Law contained in *The Village Labourer* accepted many of the conclusions reached by the 1834 report, the Hammonds argued that the provision of outdoor relief for able-bodied laborers (in their words, the Speenhamland system) was not an exogenous event but rather an endogenous reponse to changing economic conditions in rural areas. Like Davies, the Hammonds argued that the Speenhamland system was adopted to deal with "the collapse of the economic position of the laborer." The collapse was mainly caused by the enclosure movement that began in the 1760s but was brought to a head by the "exceptional scarcity" of 1795 (Hammond and Hammond 1913: 120).

The effect of the enclosure movement was to destroy the economic basis of agricultural laborers' independence. The Hammonds contended that

in an unenclosed village, . . . the normal labourer did not depend on his wages alone. His livelihood was made up from various sources. His firing he took from the waste, he had a cow or a pig wandering on the common pasture, perhaps he raised a little crop on a strip in the common fields. He was not merely a wage earner . . . he received wages as a labourer, but in part he maintained himself as a producer. . . . In an enclosed village at the end of the eighteenth century the position of the agricultural labourer was very different. All his auxiliary resources had been taken from him, and he was now a wage labourer and nothing more. Enclosure had robbed him of the strip that he tilled, of the cow that he kept on the village pasture, of the fuel that he picked up in the woods, and of the turf that he tore from the common. (1913: 106)

determine the reasons why the system of outdoor relief had been adopted, or why it had survived for more than 40 years. His analysis of the economics of outdoor relief was essentially a repeat of the analysis presented in the 1834 Poor Law Report. For this reason, Nicholls's *History* cannot be considered an important contribution to the historiography of the Old Poor Law.

[15] Two other studies published at about the same time as *The Village Labourer* provided analyses of the Old Poor Law: W. Hasbach's *History of the English Agricultural Labourer* (1908: 171–216); and Lord Ernle's *English Farming Past and Present* (1912: 303–31; 431–8). Hasbach and Ernle reached conclusions similar to those of the Hammonds. They maintained that the system of outdoor relief was adopted in response to changing economic conditions; in particular, the enclosure of commons and waste and the decline in real wage rates. Like the Hammonds, they concluded that the use of outdoor relief had disastrous consequences for rural parishes.

In order to compensate the laborer for his losses under enclosure, "it would have been necessary for wage rates to have substantially increased." However, the Hammonds cite evidence that real wages declined during the second half of the eighteenth century (1913: 111). The crisis of 1795 "sharpened the edge of the misery caused by the changes" in the rural economy and revealed that "the labourer's wages no longer sufficed to provide even a bare and comfortless existence. It was necessary then that his wages should be raised, . . . or that the economic resources which formerly supplemented his earnings should in some way be restored, unless he was to be thrown headlong on to the Poor Law" (1913: 123).

The Hammonds go on to discuss four possible remedies for the laborer's plight that were considered in 1795: diet reform, the fixing of a minimum real wage, allotment schemes, and the Speenhamland system. Diet reform proved to be impractical. The minimum wage policy was rejected by farmers because of a fear "that if once wages were raised to meet the rise in prices it would not be easy to reduce them when the famine was over" (1913: 144). Allotment schemes were disliked by two classes in the rural parish, "the large farmer, who did not like saucy labourers, and the shopkeeper, who knew that the more food the labourer raised on his little estate the less would he buy at the village store" (1913: 159). The Speenhamland system was supported by both large farmers and landlords, and therefore was adopted by most rural parishes throughout the south and east in response to the crisis of 1795.

The Hammonds supported the 1834 Poor Law Report's contention that the allowance system was the major form of relief throughout the period from 1795 to 1834. They maintained, however, that the guaranteed income level set by the Berkshire magistrates in 1795 was continuously reduced by parishes from 1815 to 1834. After comparing allowance scales adopted at various times by various parishes, they concluded that laborers' minimum income declined by "as much as a third" between 1795 and 1834 (1913: 184–5).[16] This decline made the laborer's life "wretched and squalid in the extreme" (1913: 186).

[16] The Hammonds reached this conclusion by comparing the 1795 Speenhamland scale with an 1816 Northampton scale, an 1817 Wiltshire scale, 1821 scales from Cambridge and Essex, an 1822 scale from Hampshire, an 1826 Dorset scale, and an 1831 quote by J. R. McCulloch. That is, their conclusion is based on seven scales from seven different counties. They provided no evidence that the scales cited were representative of existing scales in the years in question, or that the decline in generosity of allowances was matched by a decline in generosity of unemployment benefits or other forms of relief. Poor relief expenditure data suggest that generosity could not have declined by nearly as

The Poor Law Report's analysis of the allowance system's effect on laborers was totally accepted by the Hammonds. Speenhamland caused "the destruction of all motives for effort and ambition. . . . All labourers were condemned to live on the brink of starvation, for no effort of will or character could improve their position" (1913: 225). The discussion of Speenhamland's effects was based solely on the anecdotal evidence presented in the 1834 report; no effort was made to analyze the returns to the Rural Queries or the assistant commissioners' reports to determine whether the general report had presented a balanced view of the evidence. Their acceptance of the report's conclusions was based on a preconceived notion of what the effects of the allowance system should have been. The Hammonds wrote that "the effects produced by this system on the recipients of relief were all of them such as might have been anticipated, and in this respect the Report of the Commissioners contained no surprises" (1913: 229).

Although they found the 1834 report to be "a remarkable and searching picture of the general demoralization produced by the Speenhamland system," the Hammonds disagreed with its conclusion that Speenhamland was the major cause of the laborers' economic plight. They wrote:

The Commissioners, in their simple analysis of that system, could not take their eyes off the Speenhamland goblin, and instead of dealing with that system as a wrong and disastrous answer to certain difficult questions, they treated the system itself as the one and original source of all evils. . . . The Commissioners merely isolated the consequences of Speenhamland and treated them as if they were the entire problem, and consequently, though their report served to extinguish that system, it did nothing to rehabilitate the position of the labourer, or to restore the rights and status he had lost. (1913: 232–3)

Thus, although they joined earlier writers in condemning Speenhamland, the Hammonds saw it extending rather than causing the laborers' plight. Unlike other possible remedies to the 1795 crisis, Speenhamland was not designed to promote the independence of the laborers. If either allotment schemes or minimum wage legislation had been adopted in

much as the Hammonds maintain. Real per capita relief expenditures increased by 22% from 1813–17 to 1830–2. (Relief expenditure data are from Blaug [1963: 180], cost-of-living data are from Lindert and Williamson [1985: 148], and population data are from Wrigley and Schofield [1981: 534].) A simultaneous 22% increase in real per capita relief expenditures and 33% decline in relief generosity could take place only with an enormous increase in the share of the population receiving poor relief. There is no evidence that such an increase occurred.

1795, "the position of the agricultural labourer . . . might have been very much better," and there would have been "a very different labouring class in the villages from the helpless proletariat that was created by the enclosures" and allowed to continue by Speenhamland (1913: 232).

Although the Webbs' study of the Poor Law was much more comprehensive than was the Hammonds', the two works reached similar conclusions regarding the origins and effects of the system of outdoor relief. The Webbs' study complemented the Hammonds' work, since the Webbs' prime objective was not to determine the causes and effects of the Poor Law but rather to present a detailed discussion of the changes in the "institutional configuration" of the Poor Law that took place during the eighteenth and early nineteenth centuries.[17] The Webbs' work also is important for presenting the first detailed critique of the 1834 Poor Law Report.

The Webbs were the first historians to point out that outdoor relief to able-bodied laborers became important before 1795. They maintained that "it is clear that from the latter part of the seventeenth century onward, . . . there was, in most parishes, a great deal of Outdoor Relief of those able-bodied male adults who found themselves, for longer or shorter periods, unable to live by their labour" (1927: 170). Moreover, "the amount given to able-bodied men out of employment steadily increased" during the eighteenth century, and "an unusually great increase in pauperism" began in 1763 and continued into the nineteenth century (1927: 170). The Webbs' explanation for the increase in relief expenditures was essentially that of the Hammonds. Expenditures increased as a result of "the transformation of economic organisation brought about by the progress of the Industrial Revolution – coupled with the rapid enclosure of nearly all the remaining common fields and manorial wastes and the gradual diminution of the independent handicraftsmen" (1927: 420–1). Like the Hammonds, they contended that "the high price of food which marked the last decade of the eighteenth century, and which reduced the money wages of the agricultural labourers, . . . did but form the climax of unprecedented economic degradation" (1927: 419).

[17] For a critique of the Webbs' work on the Poor Law, see Williams (1981: 32–4, 21–2). Kidd (1987: 415) contends that the Webbs' history of the Poor Law "is less than it might have been because of the self-imposed limits to scholarship which were a consequence of their political rather than academic priorities." His criticism, however, is directed mainly toward their two volumes on the New Poor Law, published in 1929, which he claims were politically motivated, "produced under [self-imposed] pressure," and full of "short cuts in scholarship" (1987: 408–14).

The first governmental response to the increase in pauperism was the passage of Gilbert's Act in 1782, which signaled "a complete reversion to Outdoor Relief" and away from the workhouse "for all who might be deemed worthy of it" (1927: 417). Gilbert's Act set the stage for the "general adoption of the Allowance System, and especially of the family relief scales" in response to the crisis of 1795 (1927: 418). The allowance system was adopted by most southern parishes because "the farmer in the South of England demonstrated that, . . . at the swollen price of food, . . . he could not possibly afford to pay his labourers a living wage." It was sanctioned by Parliament in 1796 and "continued for a whole generation until it was peremptorily stopped by the Poor Law Commissioners in 1834" (1927: 401). The Webbs accepted the Hammonds' conclusion that the generosity of allowance scales declined sharply from 1795 to 1830 (1927: 182–3).[18]

The Webbs devoted little space to a discussion of the effects of the allowance system on laborers. They simply concluded that when outdoor relief in "the form of small regular sums insufficient for maintenance, and intended to be eked out by casual or underpaid labour . . . became, in any locality, systematised and general, the results were calamitous" (1927: 172). They also criticized the roundsman system and the labor rate. The roundsman system allowed a farmer to pay his workers "as little as he liked, knowing that the balance would be made up by the parish" (1927: 191). Similarly, the labor rate forced "the cottager, the shopkeeper, the innkeeper and the clergyman – and to a lesser extent the occupier of pasture land, as well as the private residents" to bear some of the cost of maintaining the farmers' laborers in winter (1927: 194).

The Webbs' critique of the 1834 Poor Law Report focused on the report's failure to confront the causes of pauperism and on its adoption of the policy of less eligibility. Like the Hammonds, the Webbs accepted the report's analysis of the effect of outdoor relief on the character of laborers. The major problem with the commission's inquiry was that it ignored "the prevalence and cause of destitution." The Webbs contended that

the investigation was far from being impartially or judicially directed and carried out. The active members of the Commission (notably Chadwick), and practically all the Assistant Commissioners, started with an overwhelming intellectual pre-

---

[18] In support of this conclusion, the Webbs cited the same seven allowance scales that the Hammonds cited. Like the Hammonds, they provided no evidence that the scales were representative.

possession, and they made only the very smallest effort to free their investigations and reports from bias. . . . The then existing practice of Poor Relief . . . stood condemned in their mind in advance; with the result that such useful and meritorious features as it possessed were almost entirely ignored. (1929: 85–6)

The commissioners' bias was most pronounced in their support of the principle of less eligibility, and in particular the workhouse system. They collected out of the assistant commissioners' reports "every scrap of fact or argument that pointed to the 'offer of the House' as the only relief for the able-bodied." At the same time, "they excluded from their Report . . . every suggestion or proposal of the Assistant Commissioners that did not emphasise the importance of the panacea in which they had placed their faith. In particular, they had no use at all for suggestions or proposals for preventing – not merely pauperism but – destitution itself" (1929: 70).

The Webbs made two important contributions to the historiography of the Old Poor Law. They were the first historians to point out that outdoor relief to able-bodied laborers became important prior to 1795, and they were the first historians to present a critique of the 1834 Poor Law Report. Their analysis of the Poor Law complemented the Hammonds' work, which had focused on the "collapse of the economic position of the labourer" in the second half of the eighteenth century. Together, these two studies were the beginning of a revisionist view of the Poor Law. However, both the Webbs and the Hammonds accepted the 1834 report's analysis of the effect of outdoor relief on laborers, and both agreed with the report that the use of outdoor relief was, on the whole, a disastrous policy for laborers and farmers. Although they took the first step toward revisionism, their analyses must be considered part of the traditional literature on the Poor Law.

4. Polanyi's Analysis of the Poor Law

Revisionism was taken a step further in 1944 with the publication of Karl Polanyi's *The Great Transformation*, an attempt to discern the political and economic origins of the market economy. The rise and fall of the Speenhamland system plays an important part in the study, for Polanyi believed that Speenhamland was introduced by the rural squirearchy of England in order to prevent the creation of a national labor market and to reinforce "the paternalistic system of labor organization as inherited from the Tudors and Stuarts" (1944: 77–8). By introducing the right to live,

Speenhamland counteracted the effect on labor mobility of the relaxation of the Settlement Law that occurred in 1795.[19] While it became "more attractive for the laborer to wander in search of employment," Speenhamland "made it less imperative for him to do so" (1944: 296).

Polanyi contended that Speenhamland was an endogenous response to changes in rural and urban economic conditions. The agricultural revolution of the eighteenth century caused severe social damage in rural areas. Polanyi wrote that

> both enclosures of the common and consolidations into compact holdings, which accompanied the new great advance in agricultural methods, had a powerfully unsettling effect. The war on cottages, the absorption of cottage gardens and grounds, the confiscation of rights in the common deprived cottage industry of its two mainstays: family earnings and agricultural background. As long as domestic industry was supplemented by the facilities of a garden plot, a scrap of land, or grazing rights, the dependence of the laborer on money earnings was not absolute; . . . and family earnings acted as a kind of unemployment insurance. The rationalization of agriculture inevitably uprooted the laborer and undermined his social security. (1944: 92)

At the same time, the acceleration of industrialization in urban areas created a demand for urban labor, which "caused a rise in rural wages and . . . tended to drain the countryside of its agricultural labor reserve" (1944: 297). These changes in the economic environment created a situation by 1795 in which "agricultural wages were more than the farmer could carry, though less than the laborer could subsist on" (1944: 94).

The Speenhamland system was adopted by the ruling village interest (the squire and the large farmers) to deal with the new economic situation. Polanyi maintained that

> a dam had to be erected to protect the village from the flood of rising wages. Methods had to be found which would protect the rural setting against social

---

[19] The Settlement Act of 1662 empowered parish officials, "by warrant of two Justices, peremptorily to remove any new-comer [to a parish back to his parish of settlement], whether or not he applied for or needed relief, or was immediately likely to do so, unless he could give such security for indemnity of the parish as two Justices should deem sufficient; or unless he either rented land or house let at ten pounds a year or upward" (Webb and Webb 1927: 327). According to Polanyi (1944: 78), the 1662 act "practically bound [the labourer] to his parish." The law was amended in 1795 so that no nonsettled person could be removed from a parish unless he applied to the parish for relief. The Webbs did not share Polanyi's belief that the amendment of the Settlement Law significantly increased labor mobility. The 1795 act "did nothing to protect, from compulsory removal to his place of settlement, anyone who was driven to seek Poor Relief. Yet to be frequently in receipt of Poor Relief was, for forty years between 1795 and 1834 the lot of nearly every farm labourer in southern England" (Webb and Webb 1927: 344).

dislocation, reinforce traditional authority, prevent the draining off of rural labor, and raise agricultural wages without over-burdening the farmer. Such a device was the Speenhamland law. . . . [I]ts social implications met squarely the situation, as it was judged by the ruling village interest – the squire's. (1944: 94)[20]

Polanyi agreed with earlier historians that "the introduction of Speen-hamland was intimately connected with the farmers' fear of rising wages" (1944: 298). However, he was the first historian to argue that fear of rising wages could not explain the continuation of the system for 40 years. Polanyi's major contribution to the Poor Law debate was his recognition that large farmers continued to support the use of Speen-hamland until it was abolished in 1834. This led him to conclude that

the almost unanimous insistence of the farming community in the early thirties on the need for the retention of the allowance system was due not to the fear of rising wages, but to their concern about an adequate supply of readily disposable labor. This latter consideration cannot . . . have been quite absent from their minds at any time, especially not during the long period of exceptional prosper-ity (1792–1813) when the average price of corn was soaring and outstripped by far the rise in the price of labor. Not wages, but labor supply was the permanent underlying concern at the back of Speenhamland. (1944: 298)

Farmers and landlords adopted Speenhamland policies in order to secure "an adequate reserve of labor [, which] was vital to the agricultural indus-try which needed many more hands in spring and October than during the slack winter months" (1944: 297). Speenhamland was adopted over other possible policies because it kept the laboring class dependent on the farmers, unlike allotments, and because it passed some of the farmers' labor costs to the rural middle class, unlike minimum wage policies. Thus, Polanyi was the first historian to argue that Speenhamland had an eco-nomic role other than to keep nominal wage rates from increasing during years of high food prices.

Polanyi did not completely break away from the traditional literature, however. He accepted that the system of allowances-in-aid-of-wages was the major form of relief throughout the period, and that the allowance

[20] Available data do not support Polanyi's contention that urban wages were rapidly in-creasing at the time of Speenhamland's adoption. London was the primary destination for migrants from the rural southeast. Real wages of London building trades' laborers fell by 21% from 1761–5 to 1791–5, increased by 6% from 1791–5 to 1816–20, then increased by 31% from 1816–20 to 1830–4 (Schwarz 1986: 40–1). That is, London wages were declining when Speenhamland policies were adopted; London wages began to increase rapidly at precisely the time that Polanyi claimed rural parishes were reducing relief generosity.

system caused wages to fall below the subsistence level. Moreover, he maintained that, although farmers benefited from Speenhamland in the short run, "in the long run the result was ghastly." Under the allowance system

no laborer had any material interest in satisfying his employer, his income being the same whatever wages he earned. . . . Within a few years the productivity of labor began to sink to that of pauper labor, . . . the intensity of labor, the care and efficiency with which it was performed, . . . became indistinguishable from "boondoggling". . . . Although it took some time till the self-respect of the common man sank to the low point where he preferred poor relief to wages, his wages which were subsidized from the public funds were bound eventually to be bottomless, and to force him upon the rates. Little by little, the people of the countryside were pauperized; the adage "once on the rates, always on the rates" was a true saying. (1944: 79–80)

In response to the decline in labor productivity, rural parishes reduced the guaranteed income level; Polanyi claimed that "between 1815 and 1830, the Speenhamland scale, which was fairly equal all over the country, was reduced by almost one-third (this fall also was practically universal)" (1944: 97).[21] He concluded that "Speenhamland was an unfailing instrument of popular demoralization," and that it "precipitated a social catastrophe" (1944: 98, 99).

Polanyi's *The Great Transformation* is difficult to categorize in terms of Poor Law historiography. His analysis of the reasons for adopting Speenhamland and of its economic role goes far beyond the traditional literature. He was the first historian to point out that farmers' fear of rising wages in 1795 and 1800 cannot account for the continuation of Speenhamland policies for 40 years. On the other hand, he supported the major argument made by the traditional literature, the contention that Speenhamland caused a sharp decline in labor productivity and that it pauperized the countryside. Moreover, his analysis contains many contradictions. One must conclude that since Polanyi accepted the main tenets of the traditional literature, his work should be considered an extension of the traditional view rather than an early piece of revisionism.

Polanyi's analysis of the Speenhamland system has been adopted by

[21] Polanyi cited no evidence to support this statement. His source clearly was either the Hammonds or the Webbs, although neither presented any evidence that relief generosity "was fairly equal all over the country" or that the decline in generosity from 1815 to 1830 "was practically universal." As noted in footnote 16, relief expenditure data suggest that Polanyi's conclusion is incorrect.

some current economic historians, most noticeably Eric Hobsbawm.[22] Hobsbawm and Rudé's book *Captain Swing* (1968), a study of the agrarian riots in southern England in 1830–1, contained a discussion of the Speenhamland system that rejected the revisionist analysis in favor of Polanyi. "It is a mistake," wrote Hobsbawm and Rudé, "to apply abstract economic reasoning . . . to a situation which cannot be understood except in its context" (1968: 50). Like Polanyi, they considered Speenhamland an attempt by landlords and farmers to stop the development of a capitalist labor market. Speenhamland was economically advantageous to agrarian capitalists, but it was also "an instinctive escape of country gentlemen into the world they knew best – the self-contained parish dominated by squire and parson." In the long run, however, Speenhamland

achieved the worst of both worlds. The traditional social order degenerated into a universal pauperism of demoralized men who could not fall below the relief scale whatever they did, who could not rise above it, who had not even the nominal guarantee of a living income since the 'scale' could be – and with the increasing expense of rates was – reduced to as little as the village rich thought fit for a labourer. Agrarian capitalism degenerated into a general lunacy, in which farmers were encouraged to pay as little as they could (since wages would be supplemented by the parish) and . . . labourers, conversely, were encouraged to do as little work as they possibly could, since nothing would get them more than the official minimum of subsistence. (1968: 50–1)

Hobsbawm and Rudé's conclusions are precisely those of Polanyi. In fact, the work of Polanyi and the Hammonds has formed the basis of many of the neo-traditional (and antirevisionist) analyses of the Poor Law that have appeared in recent years.[23]

5. The Revisionist Analysis of the Poor Law

Various parts of the 1834 Poor Law Report's analysis of the system of outdoor relief were found to be incorrect by subsequent historians. The Webbs found that outdoor relief payments to able-bodied laborers became important before 1795. The Hammonds presented evidence that the use of outdoor relief was an endogenous response to changes in the

---

[22] Besides his work with Rudé discussed in the text, see also his *Industry and Empire* (1968: 102–5). Like Polanyi, Hobsbawm (1968: 105) considered Speenhamland to be "a last, inefficient, ill-considered and unsuccessful attempt . . . to maintain a traditional rural order in the face of the market economy."

[23] See, for instance, Thompson (1966: 216–24) and Pollard (1978: 109–10).

rural economic environment that began during the 1760s, and argued that the economic problems of the south and east during the early nineteenth century were mainly a result of changing economic conditions rather than simply an effect of the Speenhamland system. Polanyi pointed out that farmers' fear of rising wage rates could not account for the continuation of outdoor relief until 1834. In combination, these findings amounted to a powerful critique of the traditional literature's analysis of the Poor Law. It was not until 1963, however, that a revisionist analysis appeared, in the form of Mark Blaug's paper "The Myth of the Old Poor Law and the Making of the New."

Blaug's 1963 paper and his 1964 paper, "The Poor Law Report Reexamined," represent an attempt at a thorough refutation of the 1834 Poor Law Report's analysis of the system of outdoor relief for able-bodied laborers. The 1963 paper used theoretical arguments and data on relief expenditures to reassess the system of outdoor relief. The 1964 paper presented a tabulation of the parish responses to several questions from the Rural Queries, and used the results to defend his earlier theoretical arguments. Although several of Blaug's revisionist arguments had been made before, he was the first historian to give a complete, step-by-step critique of the traditional theory, and he was the first to use the Rural Queries extensively to support his analysis empirically.

Blaug's major contentions were as follows:

1. Low wage rates were the reason for the adoption of outdoor relief, rather than an effect of outdoor relief (1963: 161–2; 1964: 242).
2. The use of outdoor relief to supplement wage income led to an increase in labor productivity by repairing "nutritional deficiencies" caused by substandard wage rates (1963: 155; 1964: 242).
3. The scale at which outdoor relief was given was so low that it could not have been "an attractive alternative to gainful employment" (1963: 161–2).
4. The system of allowances-in-aid-of-wages had generally disappeared by 1832 (1964: 231).
5. One of the major reasons for high levels of relief expenditure in the south and east was seasonal unemployment in wheat-producing areas (1963: 171).
6. The decline of local industry in the southeast created a "pool of chronically unemployed labor even during peak seasons" and hence led to increased relief expenditures (1963: 172).

7. The cause of the sharp increase in relief expenditures between 1795 and 1818 was a predominance of bad harvests over good. The decline of expenditures after 1818 was the result of a series of good harvests (1963: 163–4).

Three of Blaug's arguments are extremely important in terms of Poor Law historiography. First, his contention that outdoor relief increased labor productivity and did not appreciably reduce labor supply represented the first suggestion that the Poor Law Report's analysis of the adverse effects of outdoor relief on laborers was incorrect. Blaug admitted that, theoretically, the allowance system reduced laborers' "incentive to supply genuine effort." He maintained, however, that the theoretical argument had to be "severely qualified" when applied to the "low-wage agricultural sector" of an underdeveloped economy (1963: 153–4). The wage income of laborers in rural England was "below the biological minimum" in that their food intake was "not sufficient to permit them to supply their maximum effort per unit of time" (1963: 154). In this situation, "a supplement to wages raises the consumption and hence the energy and productivity of the work force" (1964: 242). Thus, according to Blaug, the use of outdoor relief raised labor productivity rather than reduced it, as the Poor Law Report had argued.[24]

To demonstrate that the labor supply disincentive effects of the allowance system were small, Blaug presented estimates of the typical weekly relief benefits–wage ratio that existed in 1795. Using the original Speenhamland scale, he estimated that a laborer in the Midlands or the south would earn approximately 10s. a week when employed, and 5s. a week relief if he was unemployed. A married laborer with a child could, with his wife, earn 15s. per week; if unemployed, the family would receive 10s. relief. Thus, the benefit–wage ratio varied from 0.5 to 0.67. Blaug concluded that the Speenhamland scale was so modest that it could not have offered "an attractive alternative to gainful employment." Moreover, the guaranteed income level declined by about one-third between

[24] Although this hypothesis is plausible, Blaug did not demonstrate that laborers' wages were in fact low enough to affect productivity adversely. This can be done by estimating "the calorie equivalent of income" and comparing it to "recommended calorie intakes" (Rodgers 1975). If laborers' "calorie income" was below recommended levels, an increase in income could have increased productivity. Wage data and estimates of subsistence levels presented in Appendix A to Chapter 1 suggest that real wages probably were sufficiently low in 1795–6 and 1800–1 for laborers' productivity to be affected by poor relief. It is interesting to note that the allowance system was most widespread in these years.

1795 and 1825, thereby reducing the benefit–wage ratio and hence the incentive for laborers to reduce their labor supply (1963: 162).[25]

Blaug's second contribution to the Poor Law debate was his recognition that poor relief expenditures were highest in wheat-producing counties. He wrote that

> the natural periodicity of arable farming found in the wheat-growing counties threw workers entirely on the parish rates for three or four winter months. Seasonal unemployment was much less of a problem in the West, where no wheat was grown. This might explain why the Speenhamland policy was not adopted in the western counties. . . . There is a striking coincidence, therefore, between the spread of Speenhamland and the production of wheat. . . . [S]easonal unemployment became a social problem in southern agricultural counties which had to be dealt with by public action. (1963: 170–1)

The best solution to the problem of seasonal unemployment, Blaug argued, was a policy of sharing the available winter work among all the parish laborers. This was precisely the effect of the roundsman system and the labor rate; all laborers in the parish were employed at substandard wages, and their income was supplemented by relief payments. By recognizing that seasonal unemployment was a function of crop mix rather than outdoor relief, Blaug was able to conclude that the roundsman system and labor rates were policies for dealing with unemployment rather than causes of unemployment and of laborers' indolence, as argued by the 1834 Poor Law Report.

Blaug's third major contribution to the Poor Law debate was his demonstration, through the tabulation of responses to the Rural Queries, that the allowance system was not the major form of outdoor relief in 1832. Blaug's tabulation revealed that fewer than 10% of the parishes responding to the Rural Queries admitted giving allowances-in-aid-of-wages (1964: 236–7). He concluded that

> from the answers given, it appears that many parishes did at one time make allowances-in-aid-of-wages connected in some way to the cost of living. The Speenhamland system had its greatest vogue during the Napoleonic Wars, but the severe strictures of the Committee Reports on the Poor Laws of 1817 and 1818 and the Select Committee on Labourers' Wages of 1824 would seem to have persuaded most of the poor law vestries to do away with it. (1964: 231)

[25] Blaug presented no new evidence that relief generosity declined over time. To support his statement, he cited the Webbs (1927: 182–3), the Hammonds (1913: 184–5), and E. M. Hampson (1934: 195–6). (Hampson compared the 1795 Speenhamland scale with the 1821 Cambridge scale cited by the Hammonds.) Evidence against Blaug's conclusion is given in footnote 16 to this chapter.

Blaug did not consider whether there might have been any economic reasons for the "abandonment" of the allowance system, nor did he provide an explanation why relief expenditures did not significantly decline after the allowance system was abandoned. Moreover, his assumption that the allowance system was the major form of relief from 1795 to circa 1824, for which he gave no evidence, does not follow from his previous conclusion that one of the major roles of outdoor relief was the provision of unemployment benefits for seasonally unemployed laborers.

Blaug's analysis of the Old Poor Law was at variance with the 1834 Poor Law Report on all major points of contention. Moreover, he supported many of his conclusions with data obtained from the Rural Queries, a survey that the Poor Law Commission had constructed but later ignored. Blaug concluded that

The Old Poor Law, with its use of outdoor relief to assist the underpaid and to relieve the unemployed was, in essence, a device for dealing with the problem of surplus labor in the lagging rural sector of a rapidly expanding but still underdeveloped economy. . . . [I]t was by no means an unenlightened policy. The Poor Law Commissioners thought otherwise and deliberately selected the facts so as to impeach the existing administration on pre-determined lines. Not only did they fail in any way to take account of the special problem of structural unemployment in the countryside, but what evidence they did present consisted of little more than picturesque anecdotes of maladministration. (1963: 176–7)

The revisionist critique of the traditional analysis was strengthened and extended in 1975 by the publication of Daniel Baugh's study of poor relief in Essex, Sussex, and Kent from 1790 to 1834. Baugh constructed time series of real per capita relief expenditures for each county and used them to test the traditional theory that outdoor relief "created dependency, depressed wages, and dampened incentive." His results suggested that the traditional theory was incorrect and that movements in relief expenditures could be explained by changing economic conditions. Unlike Blaug, who argued that the abandonment of the allowance system was a result of pressure from Parliament, Baugh (1975: 67) maintained that changes in relief policies were determined by economic conditions, and that the system of allowances-in-aid-of-wages "was ill-suited to the post-war problem."

Baugh found that the movements in real per capita relief expenditures were quite similar for the three counties. Each county experienced a "fairly steady level of real poor-relief spending from the early 1790s to about 1814," followed by an "upward movement of values after 1813," and a "decline and leveling off of values after 1820" (1975: 56). Baugh used this evidence to form his hypotheses on the system of outdoor relief.

Baugh agreed with Blaug that outdoor relief did not cause a decline in wage rates or have adverse effects on workers' labor supply. He maintained that the data on relief expenditures supported his contention. The fact that real per capita relief expenditures remained steady from 1792 to 1814 implied that "farmworkers' earnings from their labour did not progressively diminish" over the period, "for if they had, the real costs of relief should have risen" (1975: 61). Moreover, "parish allowances probably did not produce a disincentive to labour, even in the short run, because rural parishes were generally small enough to apply any relief system with discretion" (1975: 61).[26] Baugh concluded that "there is no sign of any cumulative economic consequences of relief policy during the war-time years" (1975: 62).

The increase in real per capita relief expenditures after 1814 also was not a consequence of relief policy. Baugh found that there was "little difference . . . between Speenhamland and non-Speenhamland districts in the amount per capita spending changed" from 1814 to 1823 (1975: 63).[27] He maintained that the increase in expenditures was caused by a "fundamental change [in] the conditions of employment and subsistence to which relief measures in south-eastern England responded" (1975: 57). This fundamental change was the postwar agricultural depression that lasted roughly from 1815 to 1824. The low price of wheat during this period reduced farmers' profits and made labor redundant. Relief expenditures increased in response to the increase in unemployment. The depression explained why changes in per capita relief expenditures were so similar between Speenhamland and non-Speenhamland areas.

The major conclusion reached by Baugh was that the policy of outdoor relief "did not matter much at any time, either during or after the war. What mattered was the shape of the poverty problem, and that shape changed" (1975: 67). He was one of the first historians to recognize that the allowance system was extensively used only during harvest crises. Not only was the allowance system "ill-suited to the post-war

---

[26] J. S. Taylor (1969: 295) similarly argued that "there is no reason to assume that most parishes subsidizing wages did so without discriminating on the basis of the number of young children living at home, the health of the family and its economic situation."

[27] Baugh divided each county into Speenhamland and non-Speenhamland districts according to answers given to question 1 of an 1824 survey made by the Select Committee on Labourers' Wages (1975: 62).

problem," it was also incorrect "to suppose that a Speenhamland-type bread scale was the chief method of subsidizing [laborers' incomes] during the wartime period" (1975: 58). Baugh's paper strengthened the revisionist critique of the traditional analysis of the Poor Law by presenting evidence in support of Blaug's hypotheses and by demonstrating that methods of outdoor relief and levels of expenditure were determined by changing economic conditions.

The third important revisionist work was Anne Digby's study of the Poor Law in East Anglia (1975; 1978). Although her work focused on the New Poor Law in Norfolk, it contained an important contribution to the Old Poor Law debate. Digby's analysis of the Poor Law stressed the role played by labor-hiring farmers in the administration of outdoor relief. She maintained that the key to understanding the operation of the Poor Law was that labor-hiring farmers, "who dominated both local government and the administration of poor relief," required a varying number of laborers over the crop cycle. Whereas "there was a tight labor market" at harvest time in the grain-producing southeast, "under-employment existed during most of the farming year" (1978: 22–3). Digby contended that

farmers were ambivalent about the problem of surplus labour since, although they wanted a reserve of labourers to meet peak, seasonal labour demands, they disliked the high level of poor rates that resulted from such under-employment. They were fortunate in being able to resolve this conflict of interest by exploiting their position as poor law administrators to pursue a policy with an economical alteration of poor relief and independent income for the labourer. (1978: 105)

By stressing the political dominance of labor-hiring farmers in rural parishes, Digby gave a more satisfactory explanation for the widespread relief of seasonally unemployed agricultural laborers than had Blaug.

The final important revisionist work is Donald McCloskey's 1973 paper, "New Perspectives on the Old Poor Law."[28] McCloskey used economic theory to discredit the traditional hypothesis that outdoor relief caused a decline in both labor supply and wage rates. To understand the effect of the Poor Law on the labor market, it was necessary to determine whether relief was administered as an income or wage subsidy, and the effect of outdoor relief on the demand for agricultural labor. McCloskey argued that farmers' demand curves for agricultural labor

---

[28] I consider McCloskey's paper to be revisionist, although he is critical of several parts of Blaug's analysis. It is revisionist because McCloskey does not accept the Poor Law Commission's conclusion that outdoor relief had disastrous consequences for the rural labor market.

were not affected by the Poor Law because they were able to pass most of the poor rate on to landlords in the form of lower rental payments (1973: 423–4).[29] He also rejected Blaug's hypothesis that poor relief increased laborers' productivity by improving their diet (1973: 424–7).[30]

McCloskey maintained that outdoor relief was generally administered as an income subsidy. He assumed that the system of allowances-in-aid-of-wages, "a negative income tax with a 100% marginal rate of tax," was the major form of outdoor relief throughout the period.[31] Only the labor rate could be considered "a pure wage subsidy," and it "only became widespread in the last few years of the Old Poor Law" (1973: 433). If the Poor Law was administered as an income subsidy, it reduced the incentive to work by "reducing the utility of the marginal gain from work" (1973: 428). Given the stable demand curve for labor, the reduction of supply necessarily led to an increase in the wage rate. McCloskey's argument is shown in Figure 2.2. If the labor supply curve shifted from S_1 to S_2 while the labor demand curve D_1 remained stable, the wage rate would have increased from W_1 to W_2 and employment would have declined from L_1 to L_2. Thus McCloskey concluded that, "contrary to the opinion of the Poor Law Commissioners, . . . it is impossible, with a constant demand curve, for poor relief to result in both falling wages and falling amounts of labor" (1973: 427).

However, McCloskey did not really prove the commissioners wrong,

[29] McCloskey's assumption that landlords paid their farmers' share of the poor rate is based on the fact that land was an "immobile and fixed factor" whereas farmers "were mobile from one parish or one piece of land to another" (1973: 423). The Poor Law Commissioners also believed that farmers shifted their poor rates to landlords (Royal Commission 1834: 60–2). However, the Webbs (1929: 2–4) and Blaug (1963: 155, 174–5) maintained that "farmers themselves paid a major share" of the poor rate. For a further discussion of this issue, see Chapter 3, Section 3.

[30] Blaug's hypothesis implies that the payment of outdoor relief to able-bodied laborers caused the demand curve for labor to shift out. McCloskey argued that, if the efficiency wage hypothesis is correct, "it may well be that mere self-interest would already have achieved its results. If a better fed worker is more valuable to an employer, one would expect the employer to feed him better" (1973: 425). In any case, "if real wages were too low for the good of farmers and landlords after 1795, it is surely odd that this was not recognized and acted upon in the century before 1795, when real wages were the same or lower" (1973: 425).

[31] McCloskey maintained that "an allowance in support of children is no less an income subsidy and has no less the effect on the supply of labor of such a subsidy than an allowance in support of working members of a family" (1973: 435). The second part of the statement is incorrect. As McCloskey pointed out, the system of allowances-in-aid-of-wages contained a 100% marginal tax rate on earned income. In most parishes, the size of the child allowance paid to laborers was determined solely by the size of their families; it was not affected by changes in laborers' income. Therefore, child allowances affected the supply of labor only through the income effect.

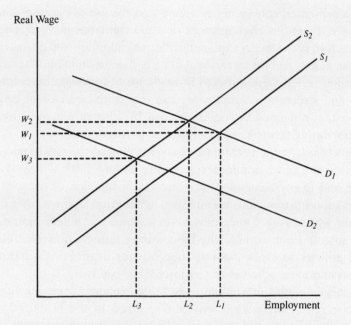

Figure 2.2. The effect of outdoor relief on real wages and employment.

because they did not share his belief that the demand curve for agricultural labor was unaffected by the Poor Law. The commissioners believed that outdoor relief reduced labor productivity and therefore caused the demand curve for labor to shift downward. Given this assumption, it is possible for both the quantity of labor supplied and the wage rate to decline in response to the adoption of outdoor relief. This can be seen in Figure 2.2. If the adoption of outdoor relief caused the labor demand curve to shift from D_1 to D_2 and the labor supply curve to shift from S_1 to S_2, then the new equilibrium involved both a decline in employment (from L_1 to L_3) and a decline in the wage rate (from W_1 to W_3). McCloskey did not address the effect of poor relief on labor productivity and therefore did not refute the commissioners' argument. Still, his paper is valuable for its analysis of the administration of outdoor relief, and in particular for showing that poor relief was an income subsidy.

6. Conclusion

The revisionist analysis of the Old Poor Law amounted to a complete refutation of the analysis given in the 1834 Poor Law Report. Blaug and

Baugh presented convincing evidence that the use of outdoor relief did not have disastrous consequences on the rural labor market. The revisionists also provided an explanation for the adoption and persistence of outdoor relief, and for its regional nature. They maintained that policies of outdoor relief were initiated in response to low wage rates and seasonal and structural unemployment in the south and east of England. The system remained in operation until 1834 because it was supported by labor-hiring farmers, who dominated parish politics.

Unfortunately, the revisionist analysis followed the traditional literature in ignoring economic developments before 1795. Thus, although Blaug and Digby contended that one major function of outdoor relief was to support seasonally unemployed agricultural laborers, they did not explain why seasonal unemployment was not a problem before 1795. They also did not explain why labor-hiring farmers preferred outdoor relief policies to other possible methods for dealing with seasonality, such as allotment schemes or yearlong labor contracts.[32]

To this date, no study has appeared that explains the economic role of outdoor relief, the reason why it developed in the last third of the eighteenth century, and the various forms that it took over time. Chapters 3 and 4 attempt to fill this gap in the historical literature.

[32] Both Blaug and Digby contend that the use of outdoor relief did not reduce farmers' profits, but this is not a sufficient explanation for outdoor relief's persistence. Rather, it is necessary to demonstrate that outdoor relief policies dominated, from the view of labor-hiring farmers, all other feasible methods for dealing with seasonality.

3

AN ECONOMIC MODEL OF THE
ENGLISH POOR LAW

Historians have yet to determine the precise role played by outdoor relief in agricultural parishes. This chapter provides an economic explanation for the adoption and persistence until 1834 of policies granting outdoor relief to able-bodied laborers, and for the regional nature of outdoor relief. I concluded in Chapter 1 that rural parishes adopted outdoor relief in response to the decline of cottage industry and laborers' loss of land in the second half of the eighteenth century. These changes in the economic environment forced farmers to alter their implicit contracts with labor. I show in this chapter that the dominant form of the new implicit contract differed across regions, because of differences in the magnitude of seasonal fluctuations in the demand for labor. In the grain-producing south and east, seasonal layoffs and outdoor relief became integral parts of the labor contract, while in the livestock-farming southwest and north, full-employment contracts were dominant. Labor-hiring farmers were able to choose a profit-maximizing implicit contract because they dominated parish politics.

The chapter is organized as follows: The effect of seasonality on the agricultural labor market is discussed in Section 1. Section 2 presents evidence of the magnitude of seasonal fluctuations in labor demand in early-nineteenth-century England. Section 3 describes how poor relief was financed and offers estimates of the share of the poor rate paid by labor-hiring farmers. A model of profit maximization by farmers is developed in Section 4 and used to demonstrate that implicit labor contracts that included seasonal layoffs and outdoor relief provided the lowest-cost method, to farmers in grain-producing parishes, for securing a peak-season labor force. Section 5 discusses the effect of seasonal migrant labor on the form of the cost-minimizing contract.

The economic analysis in Section 4 is liable to be rough going for nonquantitative historians and other noneconomists. Therefore, I suggest that noneconomists skip part (b) of Section 4. The gist of the argument can be obtained by reading parts (a) and (c), which describe the analysis used in (b) and summarize the results obtained by solving the implicit contracts model. The modeling can be skipped because the results are strongly intuitive; politically dominant farmers were more likely to choose contracts containing seasonal layoffs and unemployment benefits (in the form of outdoor relief) the larger the seasonal fluctuations in the demand for labor (a function of crop mix) and the larger the share of the poor rate paid by non-labor-hiring taxpayers.

1. The Effect of Seasonality on the Rural Labor Market

The working of the rural labor market in nineteenth-century England cannot be understood without taking into account the seasonal character of arable agriculture. The importance of seasonality in determining the nature of implicit and explicit labor contracts has been given considerable attention in the development economics literature. P. K. Bardhan (1979: 479), in particular, has noted that "the competitive wage-equals-marginal productivity theory" of wage determination cannot explain the high levels of seasonal unemployment and relatively sticky wage rates that are observed in the rural sectors of developing countries today.

Seasonal fluctuations in the demand for labor are a product of the "biological nature of agricultural production." Over the crop cycle "there are substantial time periods in which the labor force must be on hand, but technically underemployed. . . . Crops must ripen, animals must mature, and the principal part of the labor cost is the cost of waiting" (Raup 1963: 10). There are generally two periods of peak labor demand in crop production: sowing and harvesting. At these times there is often a shortage of labor, even when women, children, and the aged enter the labor force. Peak-season labor shortages give way to labor surpluses for up to 8 to 10 months of the year.[1] During slack seasons, a large percentage of the work force is either unemployed or underemployed. Seasonally unemployed workers are not surplus labor in the Lewis sense of the term, because their removal from agriculture would

---

[1] For evidence of the extent of seasonal fluctuations in the demand for agricultural labor in currently developing countries, see Oshima (1958: 259–61), Rudra and Biswas (1973: A91–100), Day and Singh (1977: 131–6), Pepelasis and Yotopoulos (1962: 44–5, 130–5), and Hirashima and Muqtada (1986: 42–3, 54–5, 123–8).

cause a reduction in output.[2] They are "in effect . . . supplying the service of availability" (Bauer and Yamey 1957: 32).

The situation is further complicated by the fact that agriculture is dependent on the weather. Changes in rainfall and temperature cause the time of peak labor demand and the quantity of labor demanded to vary from year to year. "Weather dependence not only makes the timing of each individual operation somewhat unpredictable," writes Bardhan (1979: 488), "it also means that when the time comes the job has to be done very quickly, and there are various risks and costs of delay." The uncertainty caused by weather dependence gives farmers a strong incentive to enter into "implicit contracts with laborers for future (i.e., across seasons) commitment of labor" (Bardhan 1980: 93). The form of these implicit contracts varies across regions and over time, but all involve some form of payment to unneeded workers during slack seasons "in return for the workers' assurance of ready availability whenever the need arises." In India, the typical farmer

often supplies the workers with tiny plots of land to cultivate (occasionally at nominal or zero rent) as an income supplement[,] with wage advances long before the crop is harvested, and with other kinds of consumption credit (occasionally at interest rates below what the professional village money lenders would have charged). (Bardhan 1979: 488)

In southeastern England seasonally surplus laborers were laid off and paid poor relief by the parish.

The magnitude of seasonal fluctuations in labor demand is determined by crop mix and technology. Seasonality is more pronounced in arable agriculture than in livestock farming, which involves "a regular daily routine throughout the year." Within arable agriculture the extent of seasonality depends on the crop rotation. Seasonality can be reduced "by planting a variety of crops, calculated to require their chief care at different intervals" (Mujumdar 1961: 66–7). Finally, technological change, such as mechanization of the harvest, can reduce the number of workers

---

[2] W. Arthur Lewis's (1954) two-sector "labor surplus" model of economic development contained an agricultural sector in which "the marginal productivity of labour is negligible, zero, or even negative." Thus, labor could be shifted out of the agricultural sector without reducing agricultural output. Writing about the "doctrine of [agricultural] labor of zero value," Schultz (1964: 53–4) commented that "some writers have let the seasonality of agricultural work confuse them. . . . Agricultural work may be concentrated in a short period, e.g. in wheat growing, and yet the (annual) productivity of this labor may be as large as that of labor in other types of farming that require many more days of work a year."

needed during peak seasons and thus even out the demand for labor over the crop cycle.

The underutilization of labor resulting from seasonality can be alleviated by the existence of complementary nonagricultural employment opportunities. Historically, cottage industry has been widespread in areas with seasonal agriculture.[3] Laborers not needed in agriculture during slack seasons worked at cottage industry. Depending on the wage rate in cottage industry, such an arrangement either reduced or eliminated the payments from farmers (or the parish) to seasonally unemployed laborers. Such payments were reduced even if employment in cottage industry was available only for laborers' wives and children. The prevalence of labor-tying arrangements in agriculture therefore should vary inversely with the availability of nonagricultural employment. The widespread adoption of outdoor relief in late-eighteenth-century England was in part a response to the exogenous decline of employment opportunities in cottage industry.

2. Seasonality in English Agriculture

The extent of seasonality in early-nineteenth-century English agriculture varied enormously across regions because of differences in crop mix. Seasonal fluctuations in labor demand were especially pronounced in the grain-producing south and east. Using data collected by Arthur Young in the 1770s, C. Peter Timmer (1969: 393) calculated that a typical 500-acre farm cropped according to the four-course "Norfolk system" required approximately 70 workers in March and August, but fewer than 25 workers in November, December, January, April, and May. A 500-acre farm that used the traditional three-course system required about 50 workers in August and September, but 20 or fewer workers for seven months of the year.[4] As late as 1867–9, the number of workers employed on grain-producing farms was up to 100% higher in peak seasons than in slack seasons (Collins 1976: 39).

---

[3] See, for example, Oshima (1958: 261), Mendels (1972: 242–3, 254–5; 1982: 77–81), and Mokyr (1976: 241–4).
[4] The differences in labor demand between the three-course and four-course systems were a result of differences in crop mix. Under the three-course system, a typical 500-acre farm was cropped with "120 acres wheat, 120 acres barley, 120 acres fallow, and 140 acres in permanent grass." Under the four-course system, the fallow and permanent grass were replaced by 120 acres of turnips, 120 acres of clover, and 20 acres of permanent grass (Timmer 1969: 386).

Table 3.1. *Unemployment data from the 1832 Rural Queries*

County	Winter unemployment rate (%)		Summer unemployment rate (%)	
	(a)	(b)	(a)	(b)
Bedford	13.9	19.6	7.4	10.3
Buckingham	11.8	19.3	4.6	7.3
Cambridge	11.0	16.1	4.2	5.8
Essex	8.2	17.0	4.3	6.6
Hertford	8.3	15.7	1.2	2.2
Huntingdon	7.7	12.2	1.6	2.8
Kent	9.6	15.2	3.7	5.2
Suffolk	11.9	18.1	8.8	12.1
Surrey	9.0	15.3	3.5	5.9
Sussex	13.8	21.2	5.4	7.8
Average	10.5	17.0	4.5	6.6

Note: The unemployment rates in columns (a) and (b) are defined in the text.
Sources: See text.

Evidence from grain-producing areas shows that substantial amounts of surplus labor during winter months went hand in hand with labor scarcity during planting, haying, and harvest. This evidence comes from three types of sources: responses to the Rural Queries distributed by the Royal Poor Law Commission; testimony before parliamentary commissions dealing with agriculture and the Poor Law; and individual parish record books.

Question 6 of the Rural Queries asked the parish to state the "number of labourers generally out of employment, and how maintained in Summer and Winter." The responses of parishes in grain-producing regions reveal a large amount of seasonal unemployment. Table 3.1 presents estimates of average winter and summer unemployment rates for 10 southeastern counties. The estimates in column (a) give the number of unemployed agricultural laborers divided by the total parish labor force, defined as the number of agricultural laborers, nonagricultural laborers, and adult males employed in handicrafts and retail trade. The estimates in (b) give the unemployment rate in agriculture, that is, the number of unemployed divided by the number of agricultural laborers. Overall, 17.0% of agricultural laborers were unemployed in winter, more than double the summer unemployment rate of 6.6%.

The summer unemployment rates in Table 3.1 do not represent peak-season unemployment rates. The demand for labor was significantly higher at harvest time than in June or July, so that a summer unemployment rate of 6.6% is not inconsistent with full employment at harvest.[5] The Rural Queries did not ask parishes to state the number of laborers unemployed at harvest time. The few parishes that reported the number of laborers unemployed both in summer and at harvest invariably stated that they had a positive level of unemployment in summer but full employment at haying and harvest.[6]

Evidence from the Rural Queries on seasonal wage differentials and on employment of women and children also suggests that most grain-producing parishes experienced full employment during peak seasons.[7] In parishes whose responses to question 6 suggested the existence of year-round unemployment, harvest wages for adult males were often more than double summer wage rates, implying that the extremely elastic labor supply curve of labor-surplus models was not present. The increase in male wage rates took place despite a substantial increase in the work force as women and children joined in the harvest as day laborers.[8] In many parishes haytime and harvest were the only times of the year women and children were employed in agriculture. In other parishes, where women and children were employed weeding, hoeing, or picking stones throughout the summer, their wage rates tended to double at harvest time. Overall, the evidence from the Rural Queries

[5] According to Timmer (1969: 393), a 500-acre farm cropped under the four-course system required 65–70 workers in August, compared to 50 in June and 25 in July.
[6] This conclusion is apparently contradicted by evidence reported by Blaug (1964) that almost 60% of the southern and eastern parishes responding to the Rural Queries "reported the existence of disguised unemployment." He arrived at this conclusion, however, not by consulting the answers to question 6 on the number of workers unemployed but, rather, by comparing "the replies to Question 4: 'Number of labourers sufficient for the proper cultivation of land?' and Question 5: 'Number of agricultural labourers?' " (Blaug 1964: 235). The answers given to the questions concerning employment and wage rates of adult males, women, and children (questions 6, 8, 11, and 12) suggest, however, that the answers to questions 4 and 5 were not made in reference to peak seasons but, rather, gave an estimate of the *average* number of surplus laborers in the parish. Blaug's data therefore should not be used as an estimate of the extent of chronic surplus labor.
[7] This evidence comes from the answers to questions 8 (on adult male wages), 11 (on employment for women and children), and 12 (on wage rates for women and children).
[8] The parish of East Hendred, Berkshire, for example, reported that 16 of 124 laborers (12.8%) were unemployed during the summer. However, the parish also reported that adult male wages more than doubled at harvest, and women joined in the harvest. The weekly income of a male laborer and his wife at harvest time was reported to be 35s., well more than double family earnings during a typical summer week.

suggests that labor was indeed scarce during haytime and harvest in grain-producing areas.[9]

This conclusion is supported by testimony given by local officials who appeared before the numerous parliamentary committees set up between 1816 and 1834 to investigate the depressed rural sector. For instance, James Comely from Hampshire testified before the 1833 Select Committee on Agriculture that whereas "every hand that can be got is employed" at haytime and harvest, laborers were "burthensome to the parish . . . from Christmas till May, when there is little out-of-door work in the fields" (Parl. Papers 1833: V, 187). A Wiltshire farmer testifying before the same committee stated that unemployment was high from "very soon after the harvest . . . till the spring work comes in; . . . from November to March," but there were "no surplus labourers, generally speaking, in the summer" (Parl. Papers 1833: V, 56). Earl Stanhope, appearing before a House of Lords committee in 1831, stated that "some [agricultural] labourers must [be] out of employ during the winter months," but concluded that "in those districts which are entirely agricultural, I do not believe that there is a greater number of persons than could be profitably employed, or than are actually requisite, taking the average of the year" (Parl. Papers 1831: VIII, 212).

The most detailed evidence on seasonal fluctuations in the demand for labor comes from parish record books, and in particular from account books of the overseers of the poor. Although payments to unemployed laborers are lumped together with all other relief payments in most account books, some parishes kept separate accounts of relief payments to unemployed laborers. For example, a weekly account of "surplus labourers' payments" survives for Ampthill, Bedford, for the period April 1826 to March 1830 (Bedford Record Office: P. 30/12/10–12). Quarterly expenditures on relief to unemployed laborers, and the average number of laborers receiving relief payments in summer and winter,

[9] Another part of the 1834 Poor Law Report – Appendix D on the use of labor rates – contains a large amount of evidence on the seasonality of labor demand in agriculture (Parl. Papers 1834: XXXVIII). That the labor rate was designed to deal with seasonal unemployment during the winter months is readily apparent from the information on individual parishes' labor rates. In virtually every parish listed, labor rates went into operation between the last week in November and December 31 and lasted until sometime between the end of March and the end of May. These dates suggest that labor rates usually went into effect right after threshing was completed and stayed in effect until spring planting. The fact that labor rates were not used during the summer months suggests that these parishes did not experience large amounts of unemployment during periods of peak agricultural activity.

Table 3.2. *Quarterly expenditures on surplus laborers, Ampthill parish*

Time period	£.	s.	d.	Average number unemployed per week
June 4–Sept. 2, 1826	14	3	9.5	6.0
Sept. 3–Dec. 2	27	7	10.5	
Dec. 3–Mar. 3, 1827	68	10	2	18.5
Mar. 4–June 2	36	6	8.5	
June 3–Sept. 1	2	2	5	0.8
Sept. 2–Dec. 1	30	18	5.5	
Dec. 2–Mar. 1, 1828	48	5	6	13.1
Mar. 2–May 31	32	4	8	
June 1–Aug. 30	0	0	0	0.0
Aug. 31–Nov. 29	58	17	3.5	
Nov. 30–Feb. 28, 1829	101	5	3	27.3
Mar. 1–May 30	17	19	7	
May 31–Aug. 29	13	12	9	3.9
Aug. 30–Nov. 28	33	6	2	
Nov. 29–Feb. 27, 1830	75	4	2	19.5

Source: Bedford Record Office (P. 30/12/10–12).

are given in Table 3.2. Ampthill's laborers were fully employed every harvest; the number of weeks when no laborers received relief varied from 4 during the summer of 1826 to 13 during the summers of 1827 and 1828. The situation was markedly different during the winter months. For the three-month period from December 1828 through February 1829, an average of 27.3 laborers were relieved each week, 19.4 of whom were relieved for at least 5 of the 6 working days of the week. Unemployment was also a problem during the fall and spring. Thus, although Ampthill experienced full employment throughout the summer, it was plagued by surplus labor for three-quarters of the year.[10]

Besides the evidence on seasonality, two other facets of agriculture are revealed by the Ampthill data: The amount of surplus labor varied from year to year (as can be seen from the levels of winter unemployment); and the time of peak labor demand varied from year to year. Looking at the four years for which data are available, the period of full

[10] For more evidence of seasonality from parish record books, see Boyer (1982: 134–8).

employment ended the last week in August in 1828 and 1829, but ended by mid-August in 1826 and extended two weeks into September in 1827. Full employment existed throughout July and August in 1827 and 1828. In 1826, however, during two weeks in July, 8 and 7 unemployed workers received relief, 4 and 2 for the entire week. During the week ending July 18, 1829, 13 workers received relief, 8 for the entire week.

The Ampthill data illustrate the extent to which the time of peak labor demand and the quantity of labor demanded were determined by the weather. Further evidence of the effect weather had on harvest operations can be seen in data for a Gloucester farm for the years 1830–65 (Jones 1964: 62–3). The length of harvest varied from 23 to 71 days (the average was 34.9 days), while the beginning of harvest varied from July 27 to September 6. John Howlett (1792: 567), a frequent contributor to Arthur Young's *Annals of Agriculture,* concluded that farmers' annual expenditures on labor varied by 25% or more over time as a result of the weather. The expenditure on harvest labor alone could vary by as much as £1 million from one year to the next.[11]

The extent of seasonality in the demand for agricultural labor was significantly different in the pasture-farming west and north than in the south and east. Snell (1981: 423) found that "employment was spread comparatively evenly over the year" for both males and females in pasture-farming areas (see also Jones 1964: 64). Livestock producers experienced increased labor demands during haymaking and calving, but these seasonal peaks were small compared to those associated with grain production, and Snell (1981: 424–5) contends that what seasonality existed affected female more than male employment. Moreover, the effect of weather on the demand for labor was probably smaller in livestock farming than in grain farming. The relative absence of seasonality must have had a significant effect on the form of labor contracts adopted in the west and north. If the major function of outdoor relief was the provision of benefits to seasonally unemployed laborers, such policies should have been more widespread in grain-producing areas than in pasture-farming areas. Evidence that this was indeed the case is given in Section 4.

---

[11] Howlett (1792: 570) estimated that the cost of threshing wheat also varied by up to £1 million from year to year. Because years of large expenditures on harvest labor were also years of large expenditures on threshing, annual expenditures on agricultural labor could vary by as much as £2 million as a result of the weather.

3. The Parish Vestry and the Financing of the Poor Rate

Besides seasonality, two other variables had an important effect on the administration of poor relief, and hence on the economic role played by relief, in agricultural parishes: the political power of labor-hiring farmers, and the share of the poor rate paid by taxpayers who did not hire labor. Poor relief was administered by the parish vestry, which consisted either of all ratepayers within the parish (open vestry) or of 5 to 20 "substantial householders" elected by the ratepayers (select vestry). Ratepayers included all "actual occupiers of lands and houses" who paid taxes into the poor relief fund. A landowner who rented out his land rather than occupying it was generally not rated and hence was not a member of the vestry. The day-to-day administration of relief was handled by the parish overseer, appointed by the vestry usually for a one-year term. In approximately 20% of English parishes a "paid and permanent" assistant overseer was hired by the vestry to assist the annual overseer. The actions of both the overseer and the assistant overseer were controlled by the majority vote of the vestry, so that the vestry "forms, in fact, the ruling authority of the parish" (Royal Commission 1834: 106–7).

The makeup of the parish vestry had a significant effect on relief administration because some ratepayers benefited from the payment of outdoor relief to able-bodied laborers while others clearly did not. A system of outdoor relief that included payments to seasonally unemployed laborers involved the subsidization of labor-hiring farmers by taxpayers who did not hire labor (shopkeepers, artisans, family farmers). It was cheaper for labor-hiring farmers to pay their seasonally redundant workers in poor relief than in wages, because they were not the only parish ratepayers. On the other hand, taxpayers who did not hire labor found it cheaper for labor-hiring farmers to pay the entire cost of maintaining their labor force during slack seasons.

Given the conflicting interests of labor-hiring farmers and non-labor-hiring taxpayers, the widespread use of outdoor relief in the southeast suggests that most parish vestries were controlled by labor-hiring farmers. The reports of the assistant commissioners appointed by the Royal Poor Law Commission support this conclusion. In Suffolk, the administration of relief was "vested, almost exclusively, in those who are the sole employers of labour, [which led them] to pervert it to their own advantage, by making it an instrument for reducing wages, or throwing part of that charge off their own shoulders on others" (quoted in Royal

Commission 1834: 110). The Assistant Commissioner for Huntingdon and Cambridge concluded that "in most agricultural parishes the entire management of the poor is entrusted to those of the farmers who are the principal occupiers of the land, [and who have] no material interest in the reduction" of the poor rates (quoted in Royal Commission 1834: 111–12). The domination of relief administration by labor-hiring farmers was largely a result of "the principle of weighting the right to vote according to the amount of property occupied," introduced by Gilbert's Act in 1782, and extended by the 1818 Parish Vestry Act (Brundage 1978: 7, 10).[12]

Relief expenditures were financed by a tax (poor rate) levied on all parishioners whose annual rateable value exceeded some minimum level – generally £1 or £5. The size of each ratepayer's contribution to the poor rate was determined in most parishes by "the annual value of lands and tenements occupied" (Cannan 1912: 80). Family farmers, shopkeepers, and tradespeople contributed to the fund along with labor-hiring farmers. Thus, farmers who hired (and laid off) agricultural laborers paid only a proportion e $(0 < e \leq 1)$ of the poor rate. The value of e was determined by the distribution of landholdings within the parish.[13] A parish that consisted entirely of labor-hiring farmers and agricultural laborers (who did not contribute to the poor rate) would have a value of e equal to 1, while a parish that contained family farmers and tradespeople as well as labor-hiring farmers would have a value of e less than 1. So long as e was less than unity, labor-hiring farmers were being subsidized by the parish.

Data on the share of the poor rate paid by labor-hiring farmers do not exist, but it can be estimated using data from surviving parish poor rate books. These typically list each ratepayer's name, rateable value of property, and assessed tax. They do not list the ratepayer's occupation. However, if one is willing to make assumptions concerning a person's occupation from the rateable value of his or her property, the data can be used to estimate labor-hiring farmers' share of the poor rate. Labor-hiring farm-

---

[12] The Parish Vestry Act set up the following scale for voting: persons "rated at less than £50, are to have one vote, and 'no more'; persons . . . rated at £50 and upwards, are to be entitled to one vote for every £25 of assessment, up to the limit of 6 votes" (Nicholls 1898: II, 180).

[13] I assume that the value of e was exogenous. However, if labor-hiring farmers dominated relief administration, they might have been able to endogenize e to some extent by underassessing their own lands. For instance, one might suspect that large farmers occupied higher-quality land than did small farmers. If all agricultural land in the parish was assessed at the same value per acre, large farmers' land would be underassessed.

ers were the wealthiest occupiers in most agricultural parishes.[14] Their contribution to the poor rate can be estimated by assuming that all ratepayers with property values larger than some amount x were labor-hiring farmers, and all ratepayers with property values smaller than or equal to x did not hire labor. To distinguish between labor-hiring farmers and "family" farmers, x should be set equal to the typical rateable value of the largest amount of land that could be farmed without hired labor.[15] Estimates of the amount of land a family could farm without hired labor vary from 30 to 50 acres (Clapham 1930: 451; Chambers and Mingay 1966: 133–4).[16] The rateable value of an acre of land was determined by the parish; the typical rateable value seems to have been between 14s. and £1 per acre.[17] The above numbers yield a range of estimates for the maximum rateable value of a family farm of £21 to £50. Table 3.3 contains data on the share of the poor rate paid by taxpayers with rateable property valued at or below £25, £30, and £40, for 62 parishes in Cambridge, Essex, and Suffolk. Assuming these are reasonable values for x, the average share of the poor rate paid by non-labor-hiring taxpayers (labor-hiring farmers) was 17.2–25.2% (74.8–82.8%).

The estimates in Table 3.3 may overstate the effective share of the poor rate paid by labor-hiring farmers. Most farmers were tenants rather than landowners. McCloskey (1973: 423) maintained that because farmers were mobile and land was not, "landlords in a parish with high poor rates . . . would have to charge lower rents to attract farmers with alternative employment for their capital in parishes with low poor rates or elsewhere in the economy."[18] There is evidence in the 1834 Poor Law

[14] Recall that landowners who rented out their land to tenant farmers did not pay poor rates.

[15] Because shopkeepers and tradespeople typically were assessed only on the value of the "lands and tenements" they occupied, their rateable value usually was less than that of the largest family farmers.

[16] The 1851 census contains data on farm size and on the number of hired laborers per farmer. In England and Wales there were 97,800 (82,701) farms of 40 (30) acres or smaller; 91,698 farmers hired no labor. This suggests that the amount of land that could be farmed without hired labor was between 30 and 40 acres.

[17] I was able to locate assessments for only two Essex parishes: Pebmarsh (in 1838), and Little Baddow (in 1827). In Pebmarsh, the total rateable value of 1,978 acres of land was £1,911, or 19.3s. per acre (Essex Record Office: D/P 207/11/6). In Little Baddow, arable land was assessed at 5s.–20s. per acre, depending on its quality; most arable land, however, was assessed at 14s.–20s. per acre. Pasture land was assessed at 14s.–28s. per acre (Essex Record Office: D/P 35/11/3).

[18] On the other hand, Blaug (1963: 175) concluded that "it is far from obvious that rents were in fact reduced when the rates rose. . . . [L]eases of seven to fourteen years were not uncommon, and those must have been very insensitive to increased overhead costs incurred by tenants."

Table 3.3. *Distribution of poor rate assessments*

	Year of rate	% of poor rates collected from valuations less than or equal to		
		£25	£30	£40
Cambridge				
Benwick	1803	28.0	28.0	33.3
Bourn	1833	12.5	14.9	17.9
Cherryhinton	1827	11.1	12.8	12.8
Dry Draton	1830	2.8	4.2	6.0
Fowlmere	1825	25.1	31.5	36.1
Kirtling	1829	7.0	7.0	10.4
Little Abington	1828	15.3	19.1	19.1
Swaffham Bulbeck	1832	10.3	11.8	15.9
Wentworth	1819	31.9	38.1	45.7
Wicken	1813	11.8	14.4	18.7
Witchford	1824	26.6	26.6	36.5
Essex				
Aldham	1832	19.9	22.9	34.8
Ardleigh	1830	10.9	14.1	20.3
Ashdon	1810	15.7	18.0	24.4
Bobbingsworth	1815	19.6	19.6	25.1
Boreham	1811	8.2	8.2	12.5
Broomfield	1830	14.2	15.4	15.4
Castle Hedingham	1820	16.2	18.5	18.5
Copford	1829	15.6	17.6	27.7
Fingringhoe	1821	14.5	14.5	29.0
Great Easton	1830	16.0	19.4	25.5
Great Leighs	1833	20.7	23.7	31.9
Great Oakley	1832	15.5	15.5	18.7
Great Saling	1819	13.4	13.4	18.5
Great Warley	1825	10.2	10.2	11.7
Great Yeldham	1803	13.7	13.7	19.9
High Roothing	1803	19.8	22.6	29.6
Hutton	1826	15.8	15.8	20.9
Layer Breton	1828	15.8	26.4	32.8
Little Baddow	1827	25.0	25.0	28.6
Little Bentley	1832	8.9	15.3	29.0
Little Burstead	1828	9.6	12.2	24.7
Little Coggeshall	1833	17.1	17.1	23.9
Little Tey	1831	44.3	44.3	44.3
Messing	1830	12.7	14.3	23.5

Table 3.3. *(cont.)*

| | Year of rate | % of poor rates collected from valuations less than or equal to | | |
		£25	£30	£40
Pebmarsh	1833	17.7	20.1	23.4
Stondon Massey	1821	7.7	13.4	20.4
Thaxted	1820	20.6	25.5	35.8
Tillingham	1830	15.8	15.8	18.2
Wakes Colne	1830	20.8	24.4	32.2
White Notley	1833	11.4	11.4	20.4
Wormingform	1829	18.5	18.5	24.1
Suffolk				
Benhall	1836	19.3	20.5	20.5
Blaxhall	1833	10.8	10.8	16.9
Boxford	1831	28.2	30.0	37.4
Bredfield	1828	19.3	23.1	27.7
Brome	1833	13.2	16.3	20.6
Chattisham	1826	22.1	22.1	22.1
Cransford	1830	14.3	21.7	30.6
Earl Stonham	1836	20.1	22.1	31.8
Great Bealings	1817	22.1	22.1	31.2
Kenton	1830	11.7	14.6	22.3
Kersey	1829	34.5	36.9	39.7
Peasenhall	1832	16.8	19.9	25.8
Polstead	1835	18.0	19.3	28.4
Redgrave	1829	27.3	29.6	35.2
Saxtead	1835	16.7	22.9	38.0
Sibton	1835	13.2	19.7	24.1
Snape	1833	22.9	22.9	22.9
Thornham Parva	1835	23.1	31.8	41.4
Thwaite	1821	10.6	14.2	14.2
Tunstall	1834	11.2	11.2	13.9

Sources: See text.

Report that farmers were able to shift part of their poor rates to landowners. A Sussex overseer wrote that "poor's-rates are deducted in all calculations for rent, and . . . landlords [rather than farmers] pay them," while a Berkshire overseer commented that "the tenant considers rents and rates as payment for the farm, and one can only increase at the expense of the other" (Royal Commission 1834: 61).

McCloskey's argument holds only if increases in the poor rate raised farmers' production costs. If poor relief was in fact a substitute for wages, then there is no reason why landlords should have agreed to lower rents in response to increased poor rates. Of course, farmers had an incentive to try to convince their landlords that production costs increased with poor rates even if they did not. Such a strategy might have been successful with absentee landlords but probably was not successful with landlords who resided in the parish. Thus, the Poor Law Report's conclusion that "high [poor] rates . . . are a ground for demanding an abatement of rent: high wages are not" hinges on an asymmetry of information between farmers and landlords.

I suspect that farmers were unable to shift any of the poor rate to landlords in a majority of parishes, and that even in parishes where they were successful, they were seldom able to shift more than 25% of their relief expenditures to landlords. Taking account of landlords' contributions lowers labor-hiring farmers' share of the poor rate to perhaps 67–75%.

4. An Economic Model of the Rural Labor Market

a. Introduction to the Model

Were implicit labor contracts containing layoffs and unemployment insurance (in the form of outdoor relief) an efficient method for dealing with the economic environment that existed in agricultural areas from 1780 to 1834? To answer this question, such contracts must be compared with the alternative contracts available to farmers for ensuring the existence of an adequate peak-season labor force. In this section, a simple economic model is used to determine the conditions under which it was efficient for labor-hiring farmers to adopt labor contracts containing outdoor relief provisions.

Farmers anxious to secure a resident peak season labor force had to provide workers with a level of utility at least as large as that which they could have obtained outside the parish. I assume that a rural laborer's "opportunity income" was given by the income of unskilled laborers in the urban sector. To prevent resident laborers from migrating to urban areas, farmers had to offer them an explicit or implicit contract that yielded an expected utility equal to the expected utility of urban unskilled workers minus the utility cost of migration.[19] These contracts differed widely across parishes; the exact form the contract took in a parish depended on the parish's economic and political environment. While all contracts between farmers and laborers included wage labor in agriculture during peak seasons, they differed in their provision of income for laborers during slack seasons. Given the decline of cottage industry, the following four methods for providing laborers with an annual level of utility as large as that of urban unskilled workers (and combinations of these methods) exhaust the feasible set open to farmers:

1. Yearlong labor contracts, with the wage rate either constant for the year or varying with demand, so long as expected utility was at least as high as the necessary minimum level.
2. Wage rates during peak periods high enough to sustain a laborer's family at the minimum level of expected utility for the entire year.
3. Some form of unemployment insurance scheme to provide income to laborers who were unemployed during slack seasons, which could combine with wage labor in agriculture during peak seasons to provide all laborers with an expected utility at least as high as that of urban unskilled workers.
4. Some form of allotment scheme, in which the parish provided land for agricultural laborers on which to grow enough food to be able to reach the minimum level of utility despite slack season unemployment.[20]

[19] During this period migration was hindered by the Settlement Law, which gave parishes the power to "order the removal back to their parish of settlement" any nonsettled persons who applied for relief. The effect of this law, from the standpoint of rural laborers, was to reduce the expected utility of jobs in the urban sector and hence to slow down the rate of migration. However, the quantitative impact of the Settlement Law can easily be exaggerated. Redford (1964: 92) maintained that manufacturers were generally "only too eager to get workmen, [and thus] there was no strong reason why the town authorities should be anxious to check immigration by a harsh use of their power of poor removal" (see also Eden 1797: I, 296–9). Available evidence on removals from manufacturing towns suggests that such places followed selective removal policies, and that the threat of removal had only a small effect on the rural-urban migration of able-bodied laborers (see below, Chapter 8).

[20] Parliament passed laws in 1819 and 1831 empowering parishes to purchase land and rent it, at below market rates, "to any poor and industrious inhabitants . . . to be occupied and cultivated on their own account" (quoted in Nicholls 1898: II, 202). The allotments were meant to be just large enough to occupy "a labourer and his family, during their spare hours"; the optimal size was assumed to be between one-sixteenth and one-quarter of an acre. (See the discussion of allotments in the 1834 Poor Law Report [Royal Commission 1834: 181–94].) However, the responses to question 20 of the Rural Queries, which

Alternatives (3) and (4) differ from (1) and (2) in that workers do not have to rely solely on wage labor in agriculture as their source of income. Also, alternatives (1) and (2) are policies under which the farmers who employ wage laborers pay the entire cost required to keep the laborers from leaving the parish. Under (3) and (4), part of the cost of maintaining workers during the slack season is borne by parishioners who do not hire agricultural labor.[21]

Alternative (4) represented the only policy for dealing with the seasonal demand for labor that gave rural workers employment other than wage labor in agriculture. We have seen, however, that the rise in land values that led to the enclosure movement also made farmers less willing to provide laborers with allotments. The substitution of poor relief for rights to land that occurred throughout the south of England in the late eighteenth century is evidence that grain-producing farmers found it cheaper to include relief payments rather than allotments in their implicit contracts with laborers. Therefore, alternative (4) can be eliminated from further consideration.

In order to demonstrate that outdoor relief was part of the optimal feasible policy for dealing with seasonal fluctuations in labor requirements, it must be shown that an implicit contract between farmers and laborers that contained an unemployment insurance provision and seasonal layoffs dominated all contracts in which the laborers' sole source of income was wage labor in agriculture. The available contract alternatives can be compared using a one-period model of profit maximization by farmers that takes into account seasonal fluctuations in labor requirements. Such a model is developed in part (b). It is similar to the "implicit contracts" models originally developed by Baily (1974), Gordon (1974), and Azariadis (1975) to explain contemporary firms' seemingly anomalous practice of responding to contractions in demand by "laying off unneeded workers and paying unchanged wages to the rest of the work-

concerned the renting of allotments, suggest that the majority of parishes did not adopt allotment schemes. This supports my hypothesis that contracts containing relief payments to seasonally unemployed workers dominated contracts containing allotments.

[21] Private allotment schemes were sometimes established between individual farmers and their laborers. If farmers rented allotments to laborers for less than the market price of land, in lieu of poor relief, they would have borne the entire cost of maintaining agricultural laborers, as in (1) and (2). It is not possible to determine whether parish or private allotment schemes were more extensive during this period. However, parish allotment schemes were clearly less expensive to labor-hiring farmers than private schemes that they initiated. In parishes where labor-hiring farmers were politically dominant, therefore, one would expect to find that existing allotment schemes were financed by the parish.

force" rather than by reducing both employment levels and wage rates (Azariadis 1975: 1183). The model is solved to determine the conditions under which contracts containing seasonal layoffs and outdoor relief were cost-minimizing for labor-hiring farmers.

b. The Model

Suppose that there are t seasons of equal length.[22] Given one unit of land, agricultural technology in season t is described by the production function

$$y_t = f(\ell_t, x_t) \tag{1}$$

where y_t is crop output, ℓ_t is labor input, and x_t is a seasonal factor, a stochastic productivity shock drawn from the cumulative distribution function $F_t(X) = \text{prob}(x_t \leq x)$. Technology varies stochastically across seasons, although peak seasons have a higher mean value of x than slack seasons. The seasonal factor is assumed to be stochastic to take account of the effect of weather on the demand for labor. In any season t, a high value of x_t signifies good weather and a low value of x_t signifies bad weather. The production function is twice differentiable, with $f_1 > 0$ and $f_{11} < 0$. Also, $f_2 > 0$ and $f_{12} > 0$ (that is, higher values of x_t unambiguously index better economic conditions), and $f_1 \rightarrow \infty$ as $\ell \rightarrow 0$. Labor input $\ell_t \equiv n_t h_t$, where n_t is the number of workers and h_t is hours per worker.

A special case of the above model assumes that there are only two seasons, peak and slack, and that x_t varies deterministically across seasons, with $x_p > x_s$.[23] Total output over the year is then the sum of the output in the two seasons; that is

$$y = y_p + y_s = f(\ell_p, x_p) + f(\ell_s, x_s) \tag{2}$$

The population of the parish consists of three types of persons: labor-hiring farmers, non-labor-hiring taxpayers, and laborers. For simplicity, assume that there is only one labor-hiring farmer in the parish and that workers are identical, and normalize the population of workers to 1. The

[22] The model developed here closely follows that of Burdett and Wright (1989a). An earlier published version of this chapter (Boyer 1985) presented a somewhat different model. The conclusions reached here concerning the profit-maximizing form of labor contracts are the same as in the earlier paper.

[23] The assumption that x_t is deterministic says that the demand for labor in season t does not vary from year to year, that is, differences in weather had no effect on the demand for labor.

parish has an outdoor relief policy that enables an unemployed worker with a settlement in the parish to collect a fixed benefit of g.[24] The size of g is determined by the parish vestry.

The farmer has an implicit contract with $N \leq 1$ workers.[25] Given x_t his profit in season t is

$$\pi_t(x_t) = f[n_t(x_t)h_t(x_t), x_t] - n_t(x_t)h_t(x_t)w_t(x_t) \\ - [N - n_t(x_t)]b_t(x_t) - T_t(x_t) \qquad (3)$$

where w_t is the wage rate, b_t is private unemployment insurance (paid by the farmer directly to the laborer), and T_t is the farmer's contribution to the poor rate. Non-labor-hiring taxpayers also contribute to the poor rate, so that the farmer's relief payment in season t is $T_t = e(N - n_t)g$, where e is the farmer's share of the poor rate ($0 < e \leq 1$), and $N - n_t$ is the number of workers on layoff. A worker's income equals his consumption, $c_t = h_t w_t$ or $d_t = g + b_t$. The farmer's profit in season t can be rewritten as

$$\pi_t(x_t) = f[n_t(x_t)h_t(x_t), x_t] - n_t(x_t)c_t(x_t) - [N - n_t(x_t)][d_t(x_t) - s] \quad (4)$$

where $s \equiv (1 - e)g$, the contribution of non-labor-hiring taxpayers to the poor rate, which I will call the poor relief subsidy.

Workers are endowed with one unit of labor time in each season, which they divide between work, h_t, and leisure, $1 - h_t$. The worker's utility is a function of consumption and leisure. The utility function $U(c, 1 - h)$ is twice differentiable, strictly increasing, and strictly concave.[26] Also $U_1 \to \infty$ as $c \to 0$ and $U_2 \to \infty$ as $h \to 1$.

[24] A laborer was entitled to relief only in his parish of settlement. This was usually the parish in which he was born, although a laborer could acquire a settlement in another parish by "being hired for a year to an employer in a particular parish, completing the service of an apprenticeship in a parish, paying parish rates or acting as a parish officer, [or] renting a tenement of the annual value of £10" (Rose 1976: 26). However, it was in a parish's interest not to allow newcomers to obtain settlements, and available evidence suggests that few laborers were able to do so. Eden (1797: III, 743–4) wrote that several parishes in the vicinity of Mollington, Warwickshire, and Oxford imposed a fine on any parishioner "who settles a newcomer by hiring, or otherwise; so that a servant is very seldom hired for the year." The Hammonds (1913: 119) contended that the "practice of hiring servants for fifty-one weeks only was common."

[25] As defined, N represents the share of workers in the parish who are offered contracts by the farmer. If $N = 1$, then n_t can be interpreted as the fraction of workers in the parish who are employed in season t.

[26] The assumption that the utility function is strictly concave says that workers are risk averse, that is, "they are assumed to prefer a constant earnings stream to a fluctuating one," even if the expected earnings from the two streams are the same (Ehrenberg and Smith 1982: 435–6).

Because workers are identical, when layoffs occur they will occur randomly, so that n_t/N is the probability of employment in season t. Each worker under contract derives expected utility in season t of

$$
\begin{aligned}
V_t(x_t) = & \ N^{-1} n_t(x_t) U[c_t(x_t), 1 - h_t(x_t)] \\
& + N^{-1}[N - n_t(x_t)] U[d_t(x_t), 1]
\end{aligned}
\qquad (5)
$$

Let V^* denote the level of utility that a worker could expect if he were to migrate to the urban sector (net of transportation costs, etc.).

The farmer offers N workers an implicit contract

$$
C = C_t(x_t) = [n_t(x_t), h_t(x_t), c_t(x_t), d_t(x_t)]
\qquad (6)
$$

promising an amount of employment, hours per employed worker, consumption while employed and consumption while unemployed in each season as a function of the realized value of x_t.[27]

The farmer's objective is to maximize profit subject to the constraint that any contract offered to workers must yield an expected utility large enough to ensure that at least N workers remain in the parish. Workers' reservation level of expected utility is assumed to be equal to V^*. The farmer's problem can be written as follows

$$
\underset{C,N}{\text{Max }} E\Sigma_t \pi_t(x_t)
$$

subject to

$$
E\Sigma_t V_t(x_t) \geq V^*, \quad N \leq 1, \quad n_t(x_t) \leq N \quad \forall\, t
$$

where E is the expectation operator.

The farmer's problem is solved in the appendix. The nature of the profit-maximizing solution is as follows: Given that workers are risk averse, wage rates and unemployment benefits should be set to equate workers' marginal utility of consumption across seasons, across realizations of the productivity shock within each season, and across employment status. That is,

$$
U_1[c_t(x_t), 1 - h_t(x_t)] = U_1[d_t(x_t), 1] = N/\lambda \quad \forall\, x_t
\qquad (7)
$$

---

[27] The workers who are not offered contracts are assumed to leave the parish, because their expected utility is below V^*. The method used by the farmer to determine how many workers to offer contracts (that is, to determine the size of N) is discussed later in this section.

where λ is the Lagrangian multiplier associated with the constraint $\Sigma_t V_t$ $\geq V^*$. Note that equating marginal utility is not the same as equating total utility, and that unemployed workers could be worse off or better off than their employed colleagues, depending on the specification of the utility function (see Rogerson and Wright 1988).

To establish that a contract containing outdoor relief and seasonal unemployment dominated the alternative labor contracts, it is necessary to show that a profit-maximizing farmer would want to lay off workers during slack seasons, that is, that $n_t(x_t) < N$ for some values of x_t. The conditions under which layoffs occur are obtained from the following equation:

$$f_1[n_t(x_t)h_t(x_t), x_t]h_t(x_t) = c_t(x_t) - d_t(x_t)$$
$$+ s - z_t(x_t) + \theta_t(x_t) \qquad (8)$$

where $z_t(x_t) \equiv \{U[c_t(x_t), 1 - h_t(x_t)] - U[d_t(x_t), 1]\}/U_1[c_t(x_t), 1 - h_t(x_t)]$, the marginal benefit of being employed rather than unemployed, and $\theta_t(x_t)$ is the Lagrangian multiplier associated with the constraint $N - n_t(x_t) \geq 0$. Note that z_t is negative if unemployed workers are better off than employed workers. When $n_t < N$, $\theta_t = 0$ and equation (8) says that the farmer should start laying off workers when the output from the marginal worker, given x_t, equals the cost to the farmer of employing him $[c_t(x_t) - d_t(x_t) + s]$ minus the amount the worker would be willing to pay not to be laid off, $z_t(x_t)$. In other words, layoffs will occur during season t if, for some $n_t(x_t) < N$

$$f_1[n_t(x_t)h_t(x_t), x_t]h_t(x_t) < c_t(x_t) - d_t(x_t) + s - z_t(x_t) \qquad (9)$$

Burdett and Wright (1989a) show that for any layoff regime wages, hours per worker, and payments to unemployed workers are independent of the value of x. Thus the right-hand side of inequality (9) is a constant.

For a given level of the poor relief subsidy, s, the number of layoffs will be determined by the extent of seasonal fluctuations in the demand for labor. Because seasonality was significantly more pronounced in the grain-producing south and east of England than in the pasture-farming west and north, the extent of seasonal layoffs should have differed markedly across regions. In grain-producing areas the sharp fluctuations in labor demand suggest that, if all N workers under contract were employed during the winter, the marginal product of labor would have been approximately equal to zero under normal weather conditions. Farmers therefore were able to reduce costs by laying off workers and having them collect poor relief during the winter.[28] Timmer's (1969) calculation of the monthly labor requirements of grain-producing farms suggests that farmers might have found it profitable to employ fewer than N workers (that is, to lay off workers) in as many as eight months of the year, although the number of layoffs would have been small during some months. In pasture-farming areas, the slight seasonal fluctuations in labor requirements suggest that under normal weather conditions, farmers would have found it profitable to lay off workers for only short periods during the year, if at all. Bad weather could lower workers' productivity by enough to prompt layoffs during some years, but on average, pasture-farming areas should have achieved full employment. In sum, the model predicts that labor contracts containing seasonal layoffs and outdoor relief for unemployed laborers dominated full employment labor contracts in the south and east, while full employment contracts were dominant in the west and north.

Besides seasonality, the other important determinant of the number of layoffs is the size of the poor relief subsidy, $s \equiv (1 - e)g$. It will be recalled that s measures the contribution of non-labor-hiring taxpayers to the poor rate. The larger the poor relief subsidy, the lower the cost to farmers of laying off workers. For any given season, there exists a critical value of s, s^*, so that if $s \geq s^*$, farmers will choose to lay off workers. The value of s^* differs across seasons; during the harvest season s^* is so high that layoffs occur only for very low values of x (that is, extremely bad weather). During other seasons, however, farmers' decisions concerning how many, if any, workers to lay off were affected by the size of the poor relief subsidy (see Burdett and Wright 1989a).

The poor relief subsidy is made up of two parts: the share of the poor rate paid by taxpayers who did not hire labor $(1 - e)$, and the size of an unemployed worker's public relief benefit, g. For a given value of g,

---

[28] To the extent that agricultural labor involved farm-specific training, it was in farmers' interests to employ the same workers year after year. Although there were no formal mechanisms to ensure that farmers would be able to hire back, in peak seasons, the workers they laid off in slack seasons, there is some evidence that farmers employed the same laborers from year to year. Assistant Poor Law Commissioner Alfred Power wrote that the system of outdoor relief "gives an undue facility to the employers for the hiring and dismissal of labour; . . . since the labourer may be dismissed at any time without the risk of his being driven out of reach by the necessity of meeting with another employer, finding as he does upon the spot an involuntary paymaster in the parish, who is always willing to render him back at the most convenient season to the private employer" (Parl. Papers 1835: XXXV, 141). If workers were homogeneous except for their farm-specific training, farmers should have made informal agreements among themselves not to hire each other's laborers.

seasonal layoffs were more likely to occur the larger the share of the poor rate paid by non-labor-hiring taxpayers. The value of e was determined by the distribution of property holdings in the parish and was therefore largely insulated from parish politics. Because parish authorities determined property assessments, however, the political makeup of the parish could potentially have affected the value of e. If those in power tended to underassess their own property, then, for a given distribution of property, e would have been smaller in parishes dominated by labor-hiring farmers than in parishes dominated by taxpayers who did not hire labor.

The size of poor relief benefits was determined by the parish vestry. Recall that unemployed workers received income d_t, which consisted of private (severance) payments from farmers to workers, b_t, and public relief benefits. It was clearly in the interest of labor-hiring farmers to substitute public for private relief, since public relief was partly paid for by non-labor-hiring taxpayers. Where labor-hiring farmers dominated parish vestries, therefore, unemployed workers should have received only poor relief. Conversely, where vestries were controlled by taxpayers who did not hire labor, poor relief benefits might have been set below the efficient level of d_t (determined from equation (7)), forcing farmers to offer private relief payments to workers they laid off during slack seasons.[29] Because the level of public relief benefits was set by the parish vestry, the size of the poor relief subsidy and, therefore, the number of layoffs were partly determined by the political makeup of the parish. For any given values of e and x_t, the number of layoffs should have been larger in parishes dominated by labor-hiring farmers than in parishes dominated by taxpayers who did not hire labor.

The model shows that layoffs should never occur if $s = 0$. This result may appear surprising at first, but it has an intuitive explanation. Consider an allocation of labor hours in which there is less than full employment, which yields an expected utility V' for each worker and a profit π' for the farmer. Suppose this allocation of labor hours is replaced by a new allocation in which all workers are employed, and hours per worker are reduced by enough to equate total labor hours across the two allocations. If $s = 0$ and the total man-hours worked are the same, the farmer's profits are the same for both allocations, and he should be indifferent

---

[29] Private relief benefits typically took the form of allotments of land or potato ground offered by farmers to their workers at zero or below-market rent.

between them.[30] However, because workers are risk averse, they prefer the new allocation of labor, which assures them employment, despite the fact that the expected income from the two contracts is the same. Thus, full-employment contracts are always dominant if $s = 0$, that is, if labor-hiring farmers are the only parish taxpayers ($e = 1$) or poor relief is not given to able-bodied workers ($g = 0$).

One other result obtained from the model should be mentioned. Recall that the farmer is assumed to enter into an agreement (implicit contract) with N workers, where N does not necessarily equal all the workers in the parish (that is, $N \leq 1$). The size of N is determined by the following equation

$$E\Sigma_i\{f_1[n_t(x_t)h_t(x_t),x_t]h_t(x_t) - c_t(x_t) + [1 - n_t(x_t)/N]z_t(x_t)\} - \gamma = 0$$

where γ is the Lagrangian multiplier associated with the constraint $N \leq 1$. When $N < 1$, $\gamma = 0$, and the optimal number of workers under contract is determined by equating the average output from the marginal worker to the average cost of hiring him, which is his consumption net of the amount he is willing to pay not to be laid off times the probability of layoff.[31] All workers in the parish will be under contract if the average output from the marginal worker is sufficiently high.

If $N < 1$, the parish contained more able-bodied workers than it needed. By law the parish was under an obligation to offer poor relief to all persons unable to provide for themselves. But it was not necessary to provide all persons with outdoor relief. It was in the ratepayers' interest to force chronically unemployed workers either to perform onerous tasks or to enter a workhouse in order to obtain relief. The purpose of such tactics was to ensure that the expected utility of redundant workers was less than V^*, and thus to cause them to leave the parish. In this way the parish vestry was able to maintain the resident work force at approximately the number of workers needed by labor-hiring farmers.

Up to this point I have assumed that cottage industry did not exist in the parish. However, although wage rates and employment opportuni-

[30] If $s > 0$, the farmer's profits are larger under the original allocation of labor time, because workers on layoff are supported in part by non-labor-hiring taxpayers.

[31] Burdett and Wright (1989b) show that the number of workers under contract is negatively related to the value of a firm's experience-rating factor, which is essentially the same as e in my model. That is, the firm's long-run demand for labor is affected by the marginal tax cost of layoffs. In terms of my model, an increase in the share of the poor rate paid by non-labor-hiring taxpayers would increase the number of workers the farmer offered a contract, N.

ties in cottage industry declined sharply after 1780, women and children were still employed at straw plaiting, lacemaking, and the like, in parts of the rural south in 1832.[32] Cottage industry can be incorporated into the model by including the utility obtained from such employment, $V(H)$, in the workers' utility constraint faced by the farmer, as follows

$$E\Sigma_t V_t(x_t) \geq V^* - V(H)$$

The existence of nonagricultural employment opportunities for women and children reduced the utility value of the implicit contract farmers had to offer their workers to keep them from leaving the parish. Agricultural wage rates or relief benefits should have been lower in parishes with cottage industry than in parishes without cottage industry, other things equal.

c. Summary of the Model's Results

The model developed in this section shows that implicit contracts containing seasonal layoffs and poor relief payments to unemployed workers were cost-minimizing for labor-hiring farmers only under certain conditions. The major determinants of the form of farmers' profit-maximizing labor contracts were the extent of seasonal fluctuations in the demand for labor (a function of crop mix), the share of the poor rate paid by non-labor-hiring taxpayers, and the political makeup of the parish. In grain-producing areas, where the demand for labor fluctuated sharply over the crop cycle, farmers minimized labor costs by laying off unneeded workers during slack seasons and having them collect poor relief. Full-employment contracts were cost-minimizing in pasture-farming areas, where the demand for labor was spread relatively evenly over the year.

For any given crop mix, the larger the contribution of non-labor-hiring taxpayers to the poor rate, the lower the cost to farmers of laying off workers and the larger the number of layoffs. The contribution of non-labor-hiring taxpayers was determined by the distribution of property holdings in the parish and by the size of relief benefits paid to unemployed workers. The latter was set by the parish vestry and therefore was affected by the political makeup of the parish.

County-level data on per capita relief expenditures and information

[32] See Chapter 1, Section 3.

on regional variations in the length of labor contracts suggest that, on average, labor-hiring farmers responded in a cost-minimizing manner to the economic environment. Explicit yearlong labor contracts remained widespread in pasture-farming areas throughout the Speenhamland era, while weekly (or even daily) contracts became predominant in the south and east during the last few decades of the eighteenth century (Hasbach 1908: 176–8, 262–3, 329; Hobsbawm and Rudé 1968: 40, 43–4). The absence of yearlong contracts in grain-producing areas suggests that farmers were indeed laying off laborers during certain seasons.

There is also a strong positive correlation, at the county level of aggregation, between per capita poor relief expenditures and the importance of grain production.[33] Figure 3.1 presents county-level data on per capita relief expenditures in 1831. There is a clear regional aspect to the level of per capita expenditures, which were significantly higher in the southeast than in the west or north. County-level data on the share of farm land recorded as arable and on the ratio of arable to pasture land in 1836 are given in Figure 3.2. The land-use estimates were constructed by Kain (1986) from the tithe surveys conducted under the Tithe Commutation Act of 1836.[34] The data show the importance of arable farming in the southeast and pasture farming in the west.

The positive relationship between per capita relief expenditures and arable agriculture can be seen by combining the data from Figures 3.1 and 3.2. In the 12 counties with more than 50% of their farm land recorded as arable, per capita relief expenditures averaged 14.9s. per annum in 1831. In the 12 counties with 35–50% of their farm land arable, per capita relief expenditures averaged 11.4s. per annum. Finally, in the 11 counties with less than 35% of their farm land arable, per capita relief expenditures averaged 7.5s. per annum. In 1821, per capita relief expenditures averaged 16.1s., 13.6s., and 9.2s. in counties with more than 50%, 35–50%, and less than 35% of their farm land arable. I also grouped counties according to the ratio of arable to pasture land. In the 12 counties where the ratio of arable to pasture land was greater than 1.8, per capita relief expenditures averaged 15.2s. in 1831. In the 11 counties where the ratio was between 0.8 and 1.8, per capita relief

---

[33] This correlation was first pointed out by Blaug (1963: 171), who noted a "striking coincidence . . . between the spread of Speenhamland and the production of wheat."

[34] Kain was able to construct land-use estimates for only 35 English counties (including Monmouth) from the 1836 tithe surveys. Land-use estimates are not available for Middlesex, Northampton, Leicester, Nottingham, Westmorland, and Cumberland.

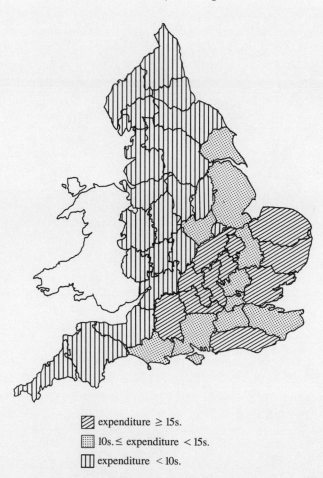

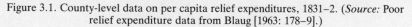 expenditure ≥ 15s.

☷ 10s. ≤ expenditure < 15s.

▥ expenditure < 10s.

Figure 3.1. County-level data on per capita relief expenditures, 1831–2. (*Source:* Poor relief expenditure data from Blaug [1963: 178–9].)

expenditures averaged 10.6s. per annum. In the 12 counties where the ratio was less than 0.8, per capita relief expenditures averaged 8.2s. per annum.[35]

[35] The relief expenditure data used in these calculations cover all forms of parish poor relief, not just outdoor relief to able-bodied laborers. However, there is no reason to believe that the differential in per capita relief expenditures between "corn and grazing counties" would decline if the calculations were performed using only data on relief expenditures for able-bodied laborers.

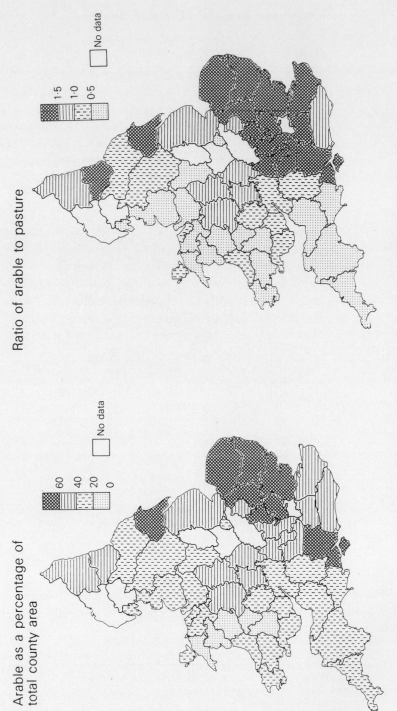

Arable as a percentage of
total county area

Ratio of arable to pasture

Figure 3.2. County-level data on crop mix, 1836. (*Source:* Kain [1986: 462].)

5. The Effect of Migrant Labor on the Rural Labor Market

The model developed in Section 4 assumed that farmers only employed workers who resided in the parish during the entire year. But profit-maximizing farmers might have preferred to reduce the resident labor force and hire migrant labor at harvest time rather than to maintain a resident labor force large enough to meet peak-season labor requirements. The attractiveness of the former policy depended on the elasticity of the supply curve of migrant labor and on the seasonal distribution of labor requirements in agriculture.

Consider first the demand for migrant labor. The ability of farmers to profit from an elastic supply of migrant labor depended on their farms' crop mix, which determined the seasonal distribution of their labor requirements. In the pastoral-farming west and north, the demand for labor was fairly steady across seasons and there was little need for migrant labor. The grain-producing south and east experienced large seasonal fluctuations in demand for labor and therefore would appear to have been amenable to migrant labor. Within the south and east, however, the demand for migrant labor varied across parishes, according to the precise crop rotation in use. Figure 3.3 shows the monthly labor requirements of two typical 500-acre farms, as calculated by C. Peter Timmer (1969). The "old" farm is cropped according to the traditional three-course rotation, with "120 acres wheat, 120 acres barley, 120 acres fallow, and 140 acres in permanent grass" (Timmer 1969: 386). The "new" farm is cropped according to the four-course "Norfolk" system, in

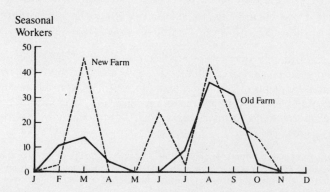

Figure 3.3. Monthly labor requirements of two 500-acre farms. (*Source:* Timmer [1969: 394].)

which the 260 acres of fallow and permanent grass are replaced by 120 acres of turnips, 120 acres of clover, and 20 acres of permanent grass.

The transition from the three-course system of cultivation to the four-course system began on the well-drained, thin, and infertile soils of "the home counties, East Anglia, and much of Southern England" during the late seventeenth century (Chambers and Mingay 1966: 59). The number of southern and eastern farms practicing the Norfolk system substantially increased during the eighteenth century, although the traditional three-course technique continued to be used in areas that received large amounts of rainfall or had soils unamenable to the new rotation.[36]

The adoption of the Norfolk system had an important effect on the seasonal distribution of labor requirements. As seen in Figure 3.3, the cultivation of turnips on the new farm led to two new peak periods of labor demand, in March and June. The increased demand for labor during the early spring made the new farm much less amenable to the use of seasonal migrant labor than was the old farm. A farm practicing the Norfolk system required as many laborers in March as it did in August, but migrant labor generally was available only during the summer. Thus, a farmer whose crop mix corresponded to that of the new farm would require a resident labor force as large as his harvest labor force.

Farmers using the Norfolk system had the option of using migrant labor instead of resident labor at harvest time, but any reduction in resident laborers' harvest earnings had to be made up either in poor relief or in higher wages during other seasons, in order to maintain workers' expected utility at its reservation level. So long as farmers could not use migrant labor to reduce the number of workers under contract, it was cheaper to use resident labor rather than migrant labor at harvest time. According to E. J. T. Collins (1976: 56)

As a general rule outsiders were not taken on until all local labour was fully employed and custom decreed that first refusal of casual work was given to the wives and dependents of permanent workers. Farmers were anyhow mindful of the connexion between earnings in summer and poor relief in winter, and, thus cautioned, were loath to interfere in what were commonly regarded as the "rights of labor."

[36] According to Chambers and Mingay (1966: 58), "the difficulty of growing roots and the new legumes and grasses on . . . the wet and cold clays provided a serious and persistent obstacle to agricultural progress in the midland clay triangle and other districts of similar soils. . . . Of necessity, two crops and a fallow remained the basic rotation on them . . . until cheap under-drainage came in towards the middle of the nineteenth century."

The situation was very different for the farmer whose crop mix corresponded to that of the old farm. The only major peak period of labor demand on the old farm occurred at harvest time, when migrant labor was available. Given an elastic supply of migrant labor, a farmer practicing the traditional three-course rotation could minimize costs by having a resident labor force large enough to meet labor requirements on the farm for all months except August and September, and hiring migrant labor during the peak season. The substitution of migrant labor for resident labor reduced costs because the farmer did not have to support migrant workers during slack seasons.[37]

Farmers' use of migrant labor was determined by its availability as well as by crop mix. There were two broad sources of seasonal migrant labor: workers from nonagricultural (often urban) occupations who participated in the harvest in nearby agricultural areas; and agricultural workers from other regions where the harvest occurred at different times. The first source of migrant labor declined in importance during the early nineteenth century as a result of "the decay of rural industry . . . and new work rhythms [of factory employment] which precluded the allocation of labour-time between field and workshop" (Collins 1976: 40). The Kent hops fields continued to attract London workers at harvest time, but much of the grain-producing southeast was too far from London, and other cities, to attract harvest labor.

The second, and more important, source of migrant labor was the agricultural sector of the " 'Celtic fringe' – the Scottish Highlands, the Welsh hill country, and above all, western Ireland" (Collins 1976: 45). There is evidence of Scottish and Irish harvesters in southern England in the late eighteenth century. Their numbers declined during the French wars (1793–1815) because of agricultural prosperity in Scotland and Ireland, then increased sharply after the Irish famine of 1822 (Redford 1964: 142). Large-scale Irish migration into the southeast began in the late 1820s (Kerr 1942–3: 373).

The "vast influx" of Irish labor was largely a result of agricultural depression in Ireland and of the introduction of cheap steamship service between Ireland and Britain. The pattern of migration was determined by

---

[37] This conclusion assumes that resident workers made redundant by migrant labor left the parish. If they remained, the parish was obliged to pay them poor relief, which increased the cost of using migrant labor. However, the parish could make the conditions for obtaining relief onerous enough to convince redundant workers to leave the parish, by forcing them to enter a workhouse or to perform manual labor.

the seasonal labor requirements of both origin and destination. Laborers left Ireland after planting their potato crops and "returned in time for the potato-digging," so that they were in England from May through August (Redford 1964: 147). In England they "took two or even three harvests a season [by] exploiting the different harvest timings of upland and low-land, north and south, clay land and light land" (Collins 1969a: 77).

What effect did the availability of seasonal migrant labor have on the form of farmers' cost-minimizing implicit labor contracts? The model developed in Section 4 shows that farmers should lay off workers during season t if the marginal product of labor at full employment ($n_t = N$) was sufficiently small. Migrant labor affects the form of the cost-minimizing contract by reducing the number of workers the farmer offers an implicit contract, N. A decline in N raises the marginal product of labor at full employment in each season (because $f_{11} < 0$), and therefore reduces the number of layoffs. Under certain conditions the availability of migrant labor will reduce N by enough to eliminate seasonal layoffs altogether, and therefore change the form of the cost-minimizing labor contract. This will occur if the demand for labor is relatively constant across all seasons except harvest.

The data in Figure 3.3 can be used to estimate the effect of migrant labor on farmers' implicit contracts in parishes that practiced the three-course system of agriculture. An elastic supply of migrant labor enabled a farmer to reduce the number of workers under contract by up to 40%.[38] The reduction in N reduced the number of months in which farmers would have laid off workers from perhaps 10 to between 1 and 5.

One must be careful, however, not to overstate the role played by migrant labor. The actual decline in the number of workers under contract was probably smaller than the data in Figure 3.3 suggest, because there was added uncertainty (for farmers) associated with the use of migrant labor. In particular, a farmer could not be sure that migrant labor would be available when it was needed. To reduce uncertainty, farmers entered into implicit contracts with migrant workers to ensure their return. A contemporary wrote that Irish harvesters "mostly resort

---

[38] Timmer's (1969: 393) calculations show that a 500-acre farm cropped under the three-course system required approximately 50 workers in August and September, but no more than 30 in any other month. If migrant labor was available in August and September, the farmer could have reduced the number of laborers under contract by 20, a decline of 40%.

year after year to the same districts, where they become known; and the English farmer not infrequently engages during the current harvest the labourers who are to come . . . to assist him in getting in his crops in the next" (quoted in Redford 1964: 147–8). But it is not clear how farmers enforced such agreements. The effect of weather on the timing of peak labor demand posed special problems. The key to success of the migrant labor system was that the timing of the harvest varied across areas, but the usual harvest pattern could be disrupted by the weather. According to Collins (1976: 42), "shortages of migrant labour were most apt to develop at harvest time when, following a spell of hot, dry weather, the corn matured simultaneously over whole large areas, thereby interrupting the smooth flow of labour between the earlier and later ripening districts." From 1790 to 1814, "dry (quick-ripening) summers" caused harvest labor shortages in 14 years. Quick-ripening harvests also occurred in 1819, 1822, and 1825 (Collins 1976: 42). Farmers anxious to reduce this uncertainty would have retained under contract a resident labor force larger than that necessary to meet labor requirements on the farm for all seasons except harvest.[39]

Finally, one can speculate as to the effect of changes in the supply and demand of migrant labor on the use of outdoor relief. England experienced a scarcity of harvest labor during the period 1790–1815, caused in part by a decline in the number of Scottish and Irish harvesters (Collins 1969a: 67; Redford 1964: 142). Farmers might have responded to the decline in migrant labor by making labor-tying agreements (in the form of implicit contracts with unemployment insurance provisions) with resident laborers. Also, the widespread adoption of the four-course system in the eighteenth century reduced the potential benefit of migrant labor by making March a period of peak labor demand. The increased use of resident labor increased the demand for implicit contracts containing seasonal layoffs and poor relief. Changes in the supply and demand of migrant labor therefore reinforced the effect of declines in cottage industry and land allotments on the demand for outdoor relief. On the other hand, the "vast influx" of Irish harvesters into the southeast in the late 1820s reduced the need for outdoor relief, at least in areas where the three-course system remained.

[39] The number of "extra" workers under contract was determined by the probability of a labor shortage occurring at harvest times the expected cost to the farmer of a labor shortage, and by the cost to the farmer of maintaining resident workers under contract.

6. Conclusion

This chapter offers an explanation of the economic role played by outdoor relief in early-nineteenth-century agricultural parishes. I have used a tool of modern labor economics, implicit contracts theory, to demonstrate that the adoption of outdoor relief was a rational (that is, profit-maximizing) response by grain-producing farmers to the economic environment they faced. The model provides an economic explanation for the regional nature of outdoor relief: Contracts containing seasonal layoffs and outdoor relief were cost-minimizing only in areas where the demand for labor varied significantly over the crop cycle. In areas where seasonality was not pronounced, such as the pasture-farming west of England, full-employment contracts were cost-minimizing.

I am not claiming that the system of outdoor relief was efficient from society's standpoint. There were social costs associated with the use of outdoor relief. The payment of outdoor relief to unemployed laborers might have reduced migration from agriculture to labor-scarce industrial areas. (An analysis of the effect of outdoor relief on rural–urban migration is given in Chapter 6.) Moreover, the system of outdoor relief reduced agricultural output in slack seasons. Because unemployed workers were partly supported by non-labor-hiring taxpayers, farmers' cost-minimizing strategy in slack seasons involved laying off workers whose marginal product of labor was positive. The larger the contribution of taxpayers who did not hire labor to the poor rate, the larger the optimal number of layoffs, and therefore the larger the reduction in slack-season output. In this regard the system of outdoor relief was similar to the current unemployment insurance system in the United States, in which the "subsidy element" created by firms' incomplete experience rating imposes "an efficiency loss by distorting the behavior of firms to lay off too many workers when demand falls rather than cutting prices or building inventories" (Feldstein 1978: 844–5). However, from the view of politically dominant labor-hiring farmers, it was efficient because it represented the lowest-cost method for securing an adequate peak-season labor force.

Although the analysis has focused on the response of rural English parishes to the breakdown of their preindustrial economy, it has broader implications. A. K. Sen (1977: 56) has suggested that one of the stylized facts of economic development is the existence of "an intermediate phase of development in which the dependence [of rural laborers] on the market increases sharply (given the breakdown of the traditional peasant economy) and in which guaranteed entitlements in the form of social security benefits have yet to emerge." The method for analyzing the English Poor Law developed here could also be applied to the study of rural labor contracts in other countries during their period of industrialization. I suspect that the result of such research will be to confirm the hypothesis that many of the apparent imperfections in rural labor markets are in fact rational "institutional response[s] to the presence of seasonal peaks of labour requirements" (Bardhan 1977: 1108).

Appendix

The farmer's problem can be written as follows

$$\text{Max } E\Sigma_t\pi_t(x_t)$$
$$C, N$$

subject to

$$E\Sigma_tV_t(x_t) \geq V^*, \quad N \leq 1, \quad n_t(x_t) \leq N \quad \forall\, t$$

The variables are defined in Table 3.A1. To characterize equilibrium contracts, form the Lagrangian

$$
\begin{aligned}
L = E\Sigma_t\{&f[n_t(x_t)h_t(x_t), x_t] - n_t(x_t)c_t(x_t) - [N - n_t(x_t)][d_t(x_t) - s] \\
&+ \lambda N^{-1}n_t(x_t)U[c_t(x_t), 1-h_t(x_t)] + \lambda N^{-1}[N - n_t(x_t)]U[d_t(x_t), \\
&1] + \gamma(1 - N) + \theta_t(x_t)[N - n_t(x_t)] - \lambda V^*\}
\end{aligned}
$$

where λ, γ, and θ are the Lagrangian multipliers corresponding to the three constraints. The first order conditions are as follows: in each season t, for each value of x, the contract satisfies

$$
\begin{aligned}
L_{n(x)} = &f_1[n_t(x_t)h_t(x_t), x_t]h_t(x_t) - c_t(x_t) + d_t(x_t) - s + \\
&\lambda N^{-1}\{U[c_t(x_t), 1 - h_t(x_t)] - U[d_t(x_t), 1]\} - \theta_t = 0 \quad (1.1)
\end{aligned}
$$

$$
\begin{aligned}
L_{h(x)} = &f_1[n_t(x_t)h_t(x_t), x_t]n_t(x_t) - \lambda N^{-1}n_t(x_t)U_2[c_t(x_t), \\
&1 - h_t(x_t)] = 0 \quad\quad\quad\quad\quad\quad\quad\quad\quad\quad\quad\quad\quad (1.2)
\end{aligned}
$$

$$L_{c(x)} = -n_t(x_t) + \lambda N^{-1}n_t(x_t)U_1[c_t(x_t), 1 - h_t(x_t)] = 0 \quad (1.3)$$

$$L_{d(x)} = -[N - n_t(x_t)] + \lambda N^{-1}[N - n_t(x_t)]U_1[d_t(x_t), 1] = 0 \quad (1.4)$$

$$
\begin{aligned}
L_N = E\Sigma_t\{&-d_t(x_t) + s -\lambda N^{-2}n_t(x_t)U[c_t(x_t), 1 - h_t(x_t)] + \\
&\lambda N^{-2}n_t(x_t)U[d_t(x_t), 1] + \theta_t(x_t) - \gamma\} = 0 \quad\quad (1.5)
\end{aligned}
$$

and the equality $E\Sigma_t V_t = V^*$, plus the conditions $n_t(x_t) \leq N$, $n_t(x_t) < N \Rightarrow$ $\theta_t(x_t) = 0$ and $N \leq 1$, $N < 1 \Rightarrow \gamma = 0$.

Combining first order conditions (1.3) and (1.4) yields the efficient risk-sharing conditions

$$U_1[c_t(x_t), 1 - h_t(x_t)] = U_1[d_t(x_t), 1] = N/\lambda \quad \forall x_t \tag{2}$$

which equate workers' marginal utility of consumption across seasons, across realizations of the productivity shock within each season, and across employment status. Combining (2) with (1.2) yields the condition determining hours per worker

$$f_1[n_t(x_t)h_t(x_t), x_t] = \mu_t(x_t) \quad \forall t \tag{3}$$

where $\mu_t(x_t) \equiv U_2[c_t(x_t), 1 - h_t(x_t)]/U_1[c_t(x_t), 1 - h_t(x_t)]$ is the marginal rate of substitution for employed workers.

The conditions under which layoffs occur are obtained from first order condition (1.1). The farmer will lay off workers during season t if, for some $n_t(x_t) < N$

$$f_1[n_t(x_t)h_t(x_t), x_t]h_t(x_t) < c_t(x_t) - d_t(x_t) + s - z_t(x_t) \tag{4}$$

where $z_t(x_t) \equiv \{U[c_t(x_t), 1 - h_t(x_t)] - U[d_t(x_t), 1]\}/U_1[c_t(x_t), 1 - h_t(x_t)]$, the marginal benefit of being employed rather than unemployed. Equation (4) says that the farmer should lay off workers if the output from the marginal worker, given x_t, is less than the cost of employing him ($c_t - d_t + s$) minus the amount the worker would be willing to pay not to be laid off, z_t.

Finally, the number of workers under contract, N ($N \leq 1$), is obtained from condition (1.5), which can be rewritten as

$$\begin{aligned} E\Sigma_t\{f_1[n_t(x_t)h_t(x_t), x_t]h_t(x_t) - c_t(x_t) \\ + [1 - n_t(x_t)/N]z_t(x_t)\} - \gamma = 0 \end{aligned} \tag{5}$$

When $N < 1$, $\gamma = 0$ and (5) determines the number of workers under contract by equating the average output from an employed worker to the average cost, which is his consumption net of the amount he is willing to pay not to be laid off times the probability of layoff.

Table 3.A1. *Definition of variables*

C	=	the implicit contract offered to workers
N	=	the number of workers offered an implicit contract
E	=	the expectation operator
π_t	=	farmer's profit in season t
x_t	=	seasonal factor, a stochastic productivity shock
V_t	=	worker's expected utility in season t
V^*	=	worker's reservation level of expected utility
n_t	=	number of workers employed in season t
h_t	=	hours per worker in season t
c_t	=	worker's consumption (income) when employed in season t
d_t	=	worker's consumption (income) when unemployed
s	=	the poor relief subsidy, the contribution of non-labor-hiring taxpayers to the poor rate
$f[\cdot]$	=	production function in agriculture
$U[\cdot]$	=	worker's utility function

4

THE OLD POOR LAW AND THE AGRICULTURAL LABOR MARKET IN SOUTHERN ENGLAND: AN EMPIRICAL ANALYSIS

From the passage of Gilbert's Act in 1782 to the adoption of the Poor Law Amendment Act in 1834, real per capita relief expenditures increased at a rate of nearly 1% per annum. Several explanations have been offered for the rapid increase in expenditures: the disincentive effects of generous relief benefits, laborers' loss of land through enclosures and engrossment, the decline of employment opportunities for women and children in cottage industry, a reduction in wage rates for agricultural laborers.

To date, however, none of these explanations has been tested empirically. In view of the general paucity of time-series data, this is perhaps not surprising. But there is a gold mine of cross-sectional parish-level information concerning the administration of poor relief, and agricultural labor markets in general, that to this date has been underutilized. I refer to the Rural Queries, the questionnaire mailed to rural parishes throughout England in 1832 by the Royal Poor Law Commission, and answered by approximately 1,100 parishes. Throughout this period, the level of per capita relief expenditures differed significantly across counties, and across parishes within counties. Presumably, the same explanations given for the long-term increase in relief expenditures can be used to account for cross-parish variations in expenditures. By combining information from the Rural Queries with occupational data from the 1831 census, it is possible to test most of the hypotheses that have been put forth to explain variations in relief expenditures across parishes.[1]

---

[1] To date, the only attempt to determine the causes of cross-sectional variations in per capita relief expenditures during this period has been by G. S. L. Tucker (1975). Tucker's analysis is at the county level of aggregation, whereas poor relief was administered by the parish. Because relief administration and economic conditions were not uniform across parishes within a particular county, his analysis has serious shortcomings. Moreover, Tucker did not make use of the Rural Queries and thus was unable to test several

This chapter provides one such test. Data from a sample of southern parishes that responded to the Rural Queries are used to estimate a three-equation model to explain cross-parish variations in per capita relief expenditures, agricultural laborers' annual wage income, and the rate of unemployment. The results are used to evaluate existing explanations for the long-term increase in relief expenditures.

1. Explanations for the Long-Term Increase and Regional Variations in Relief Expenditures

Most contemporary critics of the Old Poor Law concluded that the rapid increase in per capita relief expenditures during the first third of the nineteenth century was caused almost entirely by the widespread adoption of outdoor relief during the subsistence crises of 1795 and 1800. For example, Malthus (1798: 83–7) maintained that the Poor Law diminished workers' "incentive to sobriety and industry" and thus "create the poor which they maintain," and Ricardo (1821: 106) wrote that "whilst the present laws are in force, it is quite in the natural order of things that the fund for the maintenance of the poor should progressively increase till it has absorbed all the net revenue of the country." The 1834 Poor Law Report (Royal Commission 1834: 233–7, 68–70, 59) concluded that outdoor relief created voluntary unemployment, and enabled labor-hiring farmers to substitute relief payments for wages as compensation for their workers. Because of their focus on the disincentive effects of outdoor relief, neither the Poor Law commissioners nor the other contemporary critics of the administration of relief were able to explain the regional variations in per capita relief expenditures. The commissioners concluded simply that "the abuses of the Poor Laws" were generally confined to the south of England.

Frederic Eden (1797) and David Davies (1795) found evidence that the increase in relief expenditures was caused, at least in part, by changes in the economic environment during the second half of the

prominent hypotheses concerning the causes of cross-sectional variations in relief expenditures. He regressed average annual per capita relief expenditures in 1817–21 on the nominal weekly wage of agricultural laborers in 1824, the share of families "chiefly employed in agriculture" in 1821, the percentage of land enclosed by Act of Parliament from 1761 to 1820, the "fertility ratio" in 1821, and the share of the population aged 60 and over in 1821. He used annual relief expenditure data collected by Parliament, wage data from Bowley (1898), and enclosure data from Gonner (1912). All other data were obtained from the 1821 census.

eighteenth century, in particular, the decline in employment for women and children (due mainly to the collapse of cottage industry in the south), and the loss of cottage land through enclosures and engrossments. Both Eden and Davies presented evidence of a negative correlation between earnings in cottage industry and poor relief expenditures (Davies 1795: 84–6; Eden 1797: II, 2, 471, 687; III, 796). They also believed that granting allotments of land to poor laborers would significantly reduce their dependence on poor relief (Davies 1795: 102–3; Eden 1797: I, xx). Many others shared this belief. The most vocal advocate of allotments was Arthur Young, who maintained that "the possession of a cottage and about an acre of land, . . . if they do not keep the proprietor in every case from the parish, yet [they] very materially lessen the burden [of poor relief] in all" (1801: 509).

Karl Polanyi (1944) maintained that the adoption of outdoor relief was a response by rural parishes to the increased demand for labor in urban areas. Polanyi saw outdoor relief as part of a relatively inexpensive method for farmers to secure "an adequate reserve of labor" for peak seasons, because it enabled them to pass some of their labor costs on to the "rural middle class" (1944: 297–8). However, Polanyi ignored the evidence of regional variations in relief expenditures, maintaining that outdoor relief "became the law of the land over most of the countryside" (1944: 78).

Mark Blaug (1963: 161–2) maintained that rural parishes adopted outdoor relief in order to supplement wage rates that were precariously close to the subsistence level. Blaug provided an explanation for regional variations in per capita relief expenditures. Relief expenditures were relatively high in the south and east, first, because seasonality in the demand for agricultural labor was especially pronounced in grain production, and the southeast was the major grain-producing region of Britain. Second, fixed-income annual labor contracts were common in the north, whereas in the south labor was hired by the week or even by the day. Third, southern rural areas suffered from "disguised unemployment" caused by the decline of cottage industry after 1800 and the "relative immobility of rural labor" (1963: 170–2).

Anne Digby (1975; 1978) expanded on Blaug's contention that relief expenditures were positively correlated with the extent of seasonality in labor demand. She found that labor-hiring farmers dominated parish government in rural Norfolk, and that they responded to the seasonal nature of grain production by "exploiting their position as poor law administrators to pursue a policy with an economical alteration of poor relief and independent income for the labourer" (1978: 105).

In Chapter 1, I argued that the major function of outdoor relief was to provide unemployment benefits for seasonally unemployed agricultural laborers. The decline of cottage industry, and the loss of land from enclosures and engrossment, magnified the problem of seasonality in grain-producing areas. To maintain their laborers' income at its previous level, farmers anxious to secure an adequate peak-season labor force either had to raise agricultural wage rates or agree to grant poor relief to workers not needed during the winter months.

The model developed in Chapter 3 showed that contracts containing outdoor relief and layoffs dominated alternative contracts in areas where the demand for labor fluctuated sharply over the crop cycle, while yearlong wage contracts were dominant in areas where the demand for labor remained fairly steady throughout the year. One should find, therefore, that per capita relief expenditures were higher in grain-producing areas than in pasture-farming areas. Moreover, the value of the compensation package, in terms of utility, that labor-hiring farmers had to offer in order to retain their workers was found to be negatively related to the cost of migrating from the parish to an urban industrial area. Assuming that cost of migration can be proxied by distance, wage rates or relief expenditures should have been lower the farther a parish was from an urban labor market.

Employment opportunities for women and children in cottage industry or allotments of land reduced the value of the compensation package farmers had to offer their workers. In response to these other income sources, poor relief expenditures might have declined, as Davies, Eden, and Young maintained. It is also possible, however, that labor-hiring farmers responded to such advantages by cutting wage rates for adult male agricultural laborers rather than by reducing relief expenditures. The small size of rural parishes suggests that it was not difficult for farmers to agree to do so.[2]

[2] For the sample of southern agricultural parishes used in the empirical analysis here, the average number of labor-hiring farmers per parish was 16 in 1831. Because part of the poor rate was paid by taxpayers who did not hire labor, it was in every labor-hiring farmer's interest to respond to other income sources by reducing wages rather than relief expenditures. Of course, non-labor-hiring taxpayers had an incentive to reduce relief expenditures, so the extent to which farmers were able to reduce wages depended on their political power in the parish. The regression results in Tables 4.5 and 4.6 show that the existence of other income sources reduced both wages and relief expenditures. Note that I am assuming that workers made decisions concerning migration based on their total

Of course, the extent to which farmers were able to respond to the existence of allotments or cottage industry by cutting wages rather than relief expenditures depended on the extent of their political power. Because this varied across parishes, there is no reason to believe that all parishes reacted in the same way to, say, the existence of cottage industry. Rather, I predict that labor-hiring farmers were more likely to reduce wage rates the more dominant they were in parish politics.

This summary of the literature on the economic role of poor relief has revealed several testable hypotheses concerning the causes of the rapid increase in relief expenditures from 1780 to 1834, and of regional variations in relief expenditures. The lack of time-series data makes it impossible to test directly the hypotheses concerning the long-term increase in relief expenditures. Most of the hypotheses can be tested indirectly, however, by a cross-sectional regression to explain variations in relief expenditures across parishes. For instance, if the long-term rise in per capita relief expenditures was indeed related to the decline in employment opportunities for women and children in cottage industry, it should be the case that at any point in time parishes with employment opportunities in cottage industry had lower per capita relief expenditures than parishes without cottage industry, other things equal.

There are possible problems with using cross-sectional data to infer time-series explanations. Such a procedure is valid only if the same model is correct for both the time series and the cross section; that is, the same variables that explain cross-sectional differences in relief expenditures also explain differences in relief expenditures over time. In my opinion, this condition is met here. Historians and contemporary observers hypothesized that the long-term increase in relief expenditures was caused by a decline in agricultural wage rates, laborers' loss of land, the decline in cottage industry, increased specialization in grain production, increased local political power of labor-hiring farmers, or increased generosity of outdoor relief. Differences in relief expenditures across parishes should be explained by precisely the same variables.

A more specific problem concerns inferences drawn from the coefficients of dummy (yes/no) variables, several of which are included in the cross-sectional analysis. Because dummy variables measure the occur-

compensation package rather than simply on their wage income in agriculture. In other words, I claim it was not necessary to pay workers their marginal product *in wages*. It follows that a worker receiving poor relief should be indifferent between a reduction in wage income or in relief benefits in response to an increase in his wife's earnings in cottage industry, or in the size of his allotment.

rence of a phenomenon rather than its magnitude, one cannot always make meaningful time-series inferences from their cross-sectional coefficients. The problem is best shown by an example. The cross-sectional analysis below includes a dummy variable equal to 1 if laborers had allotments of land. The typical allotment in 1832 was perhaps one-eighth acre, while the typical amount of land lost by laborers through enclosures or engrossment was much larger, perhaps one to three acres. The coefficient from the cross-sectional regression therefore will significantly understate the long-term effect of laborers' loss of land on per capita relief expenditures. Although the problem is most serious for allotments, it also might exist for the dummy variables for cottage industry and the use of allowances-in-aid-of-wages.[3]

The above hypotheses imply that a single-equation model is inadequate to explain cross-parish variations in relief expenditures. Historians and contemporary critics of the Old Poor Law considered wage rates and unemployment rates to be determinants of relief expenditures, but they also assumed that relief expenditures lowered wage rates and increased unemployment rates. Moreover, the model developed in Chapter 3 assumed that labor-hiring farmers had three choice variables: the wage income of employed laborers, the employment level during non-peak seasons, and the level of weekly benefits for unemployed workers.

2. Data

The major data source used in the analysis is the returns to the Rural Queries, an "elaborate" questionnaire distributed among rural parishes in the summer of 1832 by the Royal Poor Law Commission, and printed as Appendix B of the 1834 Poor Law Report. The Rural Queries contained 58 questions relating to the administration of poor relief, wage rates and employment opportunities for adult males, females, and children, seasonal levels of unemployment, the existence of cottage gardens and allotments for laborers, and the productivity of the labor force. It is

---

[3] Earnings from cottage industry were very low in 1832. If the decline in earnings from cottage industry from 1750 to 1832 was larger than the typical family's earnings from cottage industry in 1832, then the coefficient from the cross-sectional regression will understate the effect that the long-term decline of cottage industry had on relief expenditures. The Hammonds and several later historians maintained that the generosity of allowances-in-aid-of-wages declined by up to 33% from 1795 to 1832. I argued in Chapter 2 that the evidence in support of this claim is very weak. However, if the Hammonds are correct then the coefficient of the variable SUBSIDY will understate the effect of the adoption of allowances-in-aid-of-wages after 1795 on unemployment rates, wages, and per capita relief expenditures.

not clear how many parishes received the questionnaire, but approximately 1,100 responses were returned to the Poor Law Commission, representing about 10% of the rural parishes in England.

The returns have never been fully utilized. Historians of the Old Poor Law have used them almost exclusively as a source of critical comments from local officials concerning the adverse effects of outdoor relief. The apparent reason for the neglect is the "unmanageable nature" of the data, which filled five volumes of Parliamentary Papers, each about a thousand pages in length. The Poor Law Commission itself was overwhelmed by the returns.[4] The first and only attempt to analyze the returns was made by Blaug (1964), who tabulated at the county level of aggregation the answers to several questions dealing with the existence of various policies of outdoor relief. Blaug's tabulation provides important information concerning differences in the administration of outdoor relief across counties, but it does not pretend to be a thorough statistical analysis of the returns.

My data set consists of a sample of 311 parishes from the 20 counties lying south of a line between the Severn and the Wash.[5] I chose to use only southern parishes for two reasons. First, outdoor relief was used most extensively in the south, and the Poor Law Commission and most historians focused their analyses on southern counties. Second, there are reasons to believe that the responses of many northern parishes are not reliable. The Rural Queries were drawn up with southern agricultural parishes in mind, although they were mailed to parishes throughout England. Many of the northern parishes that responded were close to

---

[4] In the introduction to the 1834 Poor Law Report (Royal Commission 1834: 2–3), the commissioners wrote: "The number and the variety of the persons by whom [returns to the circulated queries] were furnished made us consider them the most valuable part of our evidence. But the same causes made their bulk so great as to be a serious problem to their publication in full. It appeared that this objection might be diminished, if an abstract could be made containing their substance in fewer words, and we directed such an abstract to be prepared. On making the attempt, however, it appeared that not much could be saved in length without incurring the risk of occasional suppression or misrepresentation. Another plan would have been to make a selection, and leave out altogether those returns which appeared to us of no value. . . . But on a question of such importance as Poor Law Amendment, we were unwilling to incur the responsibility of selection." Rather than attempt to analyze the data, the commissioners simply printed all the returns as Appendix B of the report.

[5] In an earlier published version of this chapter (Boyer 1986a) I included 21 counties in my data set. The substitution of previously unavailable crop-mix data from the 1836 tithe surveys for the 1866 data used in the earlier paper forced me to exclude Northamptonshire, for which 1836 data were not available. The 1836 data are preferable to the 1866 data, given the changes in the price of grain relative to livestock from 1832 to 1866.

industrial cities and contained large numbers of handloom weavers and other nonagricultural laborers. They appear to have responded to questions concerning agricultural laborers with information on the poorest laborers in their parish, generally handloom weavers. Thus, empirical models designed to explain variations in relief expenditures across agricultural parishes might not perform well on the northern data.

A total of 704 southern parishes responded to the Rural Queries. The sample of 311 parishes was chosen on the basis of the completeness of their returns. All parishes that responded to each of a selected subset of questions deemed necessary for the statistical analysis were included in the sample. The sample therefore is not random. It will be biased if parishes that supplied relatively complete returns were systematically different from parishes that did not. The direction of any possible bias is not obvious. Perhaps parishes in which outdoor relief played an important role tended to supply more complete returns than parishes that offered little support to able-bodied laborers. For instance, if some parishes without child allowances or labor rates simply did not answer the questions about those policies, then the sample would overstate the share of parishes with child allowances or labor rates. On the other hand, if parishes feared how the Poor Law Commission was going to use the returns, those with generous outdoor relief policies might have tried to hide their generosity from the commission by not answering certain questions. In that case, the sample probably would understate the share of parishes with child allowances.

Some indications of the representativeness of the sample are given in Appendix B to this chapter. For several variables included in the analysis, I compared the means for the parishes in the sample with the means for those parishes not in the sample for which data were available. As can be seen in Appendix B, the two sets of parishes are remarkably similar. Per capita poor relief expenditures averaged 18.0s. for the 311 parishes in the sample. Of the remaining 393 parishes, 378 supplied data on relief expenditures; their average per capita expenditure was 18.2s. Real annual income averaged £29.6 for the parishes in the sample and £29.5 for those not included. The extent of cottage industry, allotments, workhouses, child allowance policies, and labor rates also were similar between the two sets of parishes.

The low number of responses to the question on unemployment presents a possible problem. Only 57 of the 393 parishes not in the sample reported unemployment data. Perhaps parishes with high unemployment rates tended not to supply unemployment data. I suspect, however, that the reason for the low response rate was simply that many respondents did not know the level of unemployment in their parishes. The fact that the two sets of parishes are otherwise so similar suggests that their unemployment rates probably were not systematically different. In sum, there are no indications that the sample used here is unrepresentative.

There are several problems associated with using the returns. First, the poor wording of some of the questions led to vague and sometimes uninterpretable responses. This is especially unfortunate in the case of question 23, which asks: "What number of individuals received relief last week, not being in the workhouse?" Parishes answered this question in several ways. In rare cases the answer is stated in the form "We have X number of men, women, and children on relief." The usual response simply states the number of recipients, without stating explicitly what the number entails. In such cases it is not possible to tell whether the answer relates to the number of able-bodied heads of households on relief, the number of able-bodied heads and their wives and children, or the number of able-bodied heads, widows, and old and infirm people receiving outdoor relief. Equally seriously, question 23 asks how many people received outdoor relief "last week." Because the parishes returned the queries over a four-month period, from September 1832 to January 1833, it is never clear when in the seasonal cycle the parish responded. Thus, the returns do not yield reliable information on the number of people on relief, and it is therefore not possible to measure the incidence of relief (relief recipients/population) or the average generosity of relief (relief expenditures/recipients). The only reliable measure of relief expenditures available at the parish level is expenditures per capita. Although this variable fails to distinguish between incidence and generosity, it has been used by virtually all students of the matter as a proxy for either or both.

The vagueness of parish responses to other questions made it possible to categorize their answers only as "yes" or "no." For instance, question 20 asked: "Whether any land let to labourers; if so, the quantity to each, and at what rent?" A large number of parishes responded that laborers rented allotments, but did not give the size of the allotments, the rent paid, or the size of the parish rent subsidy, if any. It was therefore possible only to determine the presence or absence of rented allotments. Similar responses were obtained from questions dealing with the use of allowances-in-aid-of-wages, child allowances, labor rates, and roundsmen systems, and the existence of cottage industry.[6] The information from these questions could be introduced into the regression analysis only in the form of dummy (yes/no) variables.

It was necessary to construct estimates of laborers' annual earnings for parishes that reported wage data but not earnings data. For each county, the relationship between wage rates and annual earnings was determined for those parishes that returned both. This information was then used to estimate annual earnings in those parishes that reported only wage rates. A detailed description of how the earnings estimates were constructed is given in Appendix A at the end of this chapter.[7]

The other major source of data was the 1831 census, in particular the occupational enumeration. The census reported the number of males 20 years of age and older for each parish, and the number belonging to each of nine occupational categories. I used five of the categories in constructing variables: farmers employing laborers; farmers not employing laborers (that is, family farmers); laborers employed in agriculture; persons employed in handicrafts and retail trade; and nonagricultural laborers. These data were used to estimate unemployment rates, specialization in agriculture, and the proportion of parish taxpayers who were labor-hiring farmers.

County averages for some of the variables included in the regression analysis are given in Table 4.1. The extent of cottage industry and allotments varied enormously across counties. Cottage industry was prominent in the midland counties of Bedford, Buckingham, and Oxford, and almost nonexistent in Kent, Sussex, and much of East Anglia. Allotments were abundant in the southwest, and scarce in areas close to London. Unemployment rates, as one would suspect, were high in many (but not all) grain-producing counties and low in the pasture-farming southwest. Winter unemployment rates tended to be significantly higher than summer unemployment rates. Both per capita relief expenditures

---

[6] A large share of the parishes with child allowances noted the number of children at which allowances began. This information is used in the analysis of birth rates in Chapter 5.

[7] The estimates of earnings obtained from this procedure are very similar to those constructed by Arthur Bowley (1898) from the same data source. Column 6 of his table on pages 704–7 presents estimates of agricultural laborers' average "total annual earnings [in 1832] divided by 52" for each English county. (Bowley claims the wage data are for 1833, but in fact the Rural Queries were distributed in the summer of 1832 and returned to the commissioners by January 1833 [Royal Commission 1834: 2].) My estimates of agricultural laborers' earnings are within 5% of Bowley's for 18 of the 20 counties included in my sample. The only exceptions are Buckingham, where my estimate is 7.6% larger than his, and Dorset, where my estimate is 12.6% larger than his.

Table 4.1. *County averages: selected variables*

	Per capita relief expenditures 1831 (s.,d.)	Average annual unemployment rate (%)	Average summer unemployment rate (%)	Average winter unemployment rate (%)	Agricultural laborers		% of parishes		% of county land devoted to arable farming
					Reported annual income (in £)	Expected annual income (in £)	With cottage industry	Granting allotments	
Sussex	19.4	9.6	5.4	13.8	31.78	28.73	1.2	39.7	43.8
Buckingham	18.7	8.3	4.6	11.8	29.39	26.95	71.4	19.2	55.8
Suffolk	18.4	10.3	8.8	11.9	28.99	26.00	7.8	32.5	70.3
Essex	17.2	6.4	4.3	8.2	28.29	26.48	24.5	25.0	72.4
Bedford	16.11	10.8	7.4	13.9	28.60	25.50	100.0	80.0	60.1
Oxford	16.11	9.8	6.8	12.8	27.75	25.03	44.8	73.7	55.8
Wiltshire	16.9	10.5	4.5	15.9	24.86	22.25	20.7	82.6	35.1
Berkshire	15.9	5.6	3.0	8.1	28.92	27.30	20.0	40.7	58.5
Norfolk	15.4	9.0	6.0	12.0	31.07	28.27	12.5	40.0	63.8
Huntingdon	15.3	4.7	1.6	7.7	30.81	29.36	15.4	30.0	49.8
Kent	14.5	6.8	3.7	9.6	34.61	32.26	1.9	33.3	48.5
Southampton	13.10	7.2	4.2	10.0	29.04	26.95	10.5	65.2	64.3
Cambridge	13.8	7.7	4.2	11.0	28.36	26.18	4.7	59.4	70.1
Hertford	13.2	4.8	1.2	8.3	29.82	28.39	50.0	25.0	66.6
Dorset	11.5	5.4	0.0	10.9	25.40	24.03	62.5	100.0	21.5
Surrey	10.11	6.3	3.5	9.0	33.56	31.45	13.8	22.2	48.8
Devon	9.0	4.9	2.6	6.4	24.55	23.35	24.1	75.0	22.5
Somerset	8.10	3.8	3.7	3.8	21.27	20.70	44.0	68.4	24.4
Gloucester	8.8	4.8	2.9	6.4	24.32	23.15	22.2	61.9	32.0
Cornwall	6.8	3.0	1.2	4.7	22.88	22.19	23.3	56.0	23.8

Sources: Data on per capita relief expenditures were obtained from Blaug (1963: 178–9). Data on the extent of arable farming were obtained from Kain (1986). All others were calculated from answers to the Rural Queries (Parl. Papers 1834: XXX–XXXII).

and the annual earnings of agricultural laborers declined as one moved farther from London, suggesting that the labor market in southern England was well integrated by 1832.

3. Estimation of the Three-Equation Model

The model to be estimated consists of three equations, to explain cross-parish variations in per capita relief expenditures, annual income of agricultural laborers, and annual unemployment rates. Two specifications of the model are estimated. The first is a three-equation reduced form. The specification of a reduced form model is based on the supposition that labor-hiring farmers dominated local parish politics and thus were able to choose relief expenditures, wage income, and the level of unemployment to maximize profits. Estimates obtained from the reduced form yield predictions of how changes in economic and demographic conditions affected labor-hiring farmers' choices concerning relief expenditures, wage income, and unemployment rates, and thus aid in explaining the long-term increase in relief expenditures. The reduced form model regresses per capita relief expenditures, annual wage income, and annual unemployment rates on all the allegedly exogenous variables, CINDUSTRY through WEALTH, in Table 4.2. The expected impact of each exogenous variable is given in Table 4.3.

The reduced form model does not test the hypothesis of contemporary observers that the long-term increase in per capita relief expenditures was a result of interactions among relief expenditures, wage rates, layoffs, and voluntary unemployment. To test this hypothesis, a three-equation simultaneous system should be estimated, in which wage income and the unemployment rate are assumed to be determinants of per capita relief expenditures, but also to be determined in part by the level of relief expenditures. Unfortunately, because per capita relief expenditure is generosity of relief times incidence, and incidence of relief is obviously correlated with the unemployment rate, it is not possible to determine the effect of relief generosity on unemployment. Per capita relief expenditures could have a positive effect on the rate of unemployment even if generosity of relief had no effect on unemployment.[8]

The hypothesis that relief expenditures and laborers' wage income

---

[8] Although the effect of relief generosity on the rate of unemployment cannot be estimated, two explanatory variables included in the unemployment equation should yield some information on the effect of outdoor relief on unemployment, namely, WORKHOUSE and SUBSIDY.

Table 4.2. *Variable definitions*

RELIEF	=	per capita relief expenditures of parish
INCOME	=	expected annual income of adult male agricultural laborers
UNEMPLOYMENT	=	annual unemployment rate
CINDUSTRY	=	dummy variable equal to 1 if cottage industry exists in the parish
ALLOTMENTS	=	dummy variable equal to 1 if laborers have allotments of farm land
LONDON	=	distance from London
FARMERS	=	ratio of labor-hiring farmers to total number of parish taxpayers
WORKHOUSE	=	dummy variable equal to 1 if parish has a workhouse
CHILDALLOW	=	dummy variable equal to 1 if parish pays child allowances
SUBSIDY	=	dummy variable equal to 1 if parish subsidizes wage rates of privately employed laborers
LABORRATE	=	dummy variable equal to 1 if parish uses a labor rate
ROUNDSMEN	=	dummy variable equal to 1 if parish uses a roundsmen system
GRAIN	=	estimated percent of parish's adult males employed in grain production
DENSITY	=	density of population in parish
WEALTH	=	per capita value of real property in parish

were interrelated was tested by estimating the determinants of relief and wage income as a simultaneous system. The specific form of the model is

$$
\begin{aligned}
\text{RELIEF} = {} & b_0 + b_1\text{CINDUSTRY} + b_2\text{ALLOTMENTS} + \\
& b_3\text{LONDON} + b_4\text{FARMERS} + b_5\text{WEALTH} + \\
& b_6\text{WORKHOUSE} + b_7\text{UNEMPLOYMENT} + \\
& b_8\text{INCOME} \quad\quad\quad\quad\quad\quad\quad\quad\quad\quad\quad\quad (1)
\end{aligned}
$$

$$
\begin{aligned}
\text{INCOME} = {} & a_0 + a_1\text{CINDUSTRY} + a_2\text{ALLOTMENTS} + \\
& a_3\text{LONDON} + a_4\text{CHILDALLOW} + \\
& a_5\text{SUBSIDY} + a_6\text{LABORRATE} + \\
& a_7\text{ROUNDSMEN} + a_8\text{DENSITY} + \\
& a_9\text{RELIEF} \quad\quad\quad\quad\quad\quad\quad\quad\quad\quad\quad\quad (2)
\end{aligned}
$$

The expected impact of each explanatory variable is given in Table 4.4. The reasoning behind the expectations given in Tables 4.3 and 4.4

Table 4.3. *Expected and actual impact of explanatory variables:*
reduced form model (summary table)

	Dependent variable: Per capita relief expenditures		Dependent variable: Annual male income		Dependent variable: Unemployment rate	
	Expected	Actual	Expected	Actual	Expected	Actual
CINDUSTRY	−	0	−	−	+	0
ALLOTMENTS	−	0	−	−	+	+
LONDON	−	−	−	−	+	−
FARMERS	+	+	−	0	+	+
DENSITY	+	0	−	−	+	0
CHILDALLOW	+	+	−	−	+	+
SUBSIDY	+	0	−	0	+	0
WORKHOUSE	?	0	?	0	−	0
ROUNDSMEN	+	0	−	0	?	+
LABORRATE	+	0	−	0	−	0
GRAIN	+	+	−	0	+	+
WEALTH	+	0	+	0	−	−

Table 4.4. *Expected and actual impact of explanatory variables:*
simultaneous equations model (summary table)

	Dependent variable: Per capita relief expenditures		Dependent variable: Annual male income	
	Expected	Actual	Expected	Actual
CINDUSTRY	−	−	−	−
ALLOTMENTS	−	0	−	−
LONDON	−	−	−	−
FARMERS	+	−		
DENSITY			−	−
CHILDALLOW			−	0
SUBSIDY			−	0
WORKHOUSE	+	0		
ROUNDSMEN			−	0
LABORRATE			−	0
WEALTH	+	0		
UNEMPLOYMENT	+	+		
INCOME	−	0		
RELIEF			−	−

should be briefly noted. Per capita relief expenditures are expected to be determined, first of all, by the existence and magnitude of alternative income sources, namely, employment opportunities in cottage industry, the existence of allotments, and the expected wage income of agricultural laborers. Distance from London is a proxy for cost of migration.[9] As the cost of migration increased, the cost of securing an adequate peak-season labor force declined, which should have caused a reduction in relief expenditures.[10] The variable FARMERS tests whether, as the political power of labor-hiring farmers (estimated by the ratio of labor-hiring farmers to total taxpayers) increased, they were able to pass more of the cost of maintaining their workers on to the parish. A parish's per capita property wealth might be a determinant of its relief generosity, and thus is expected to have a positive effect on relief expenditures. The variable GRAIN is a proxy for seasonality in the demand for labor. An increase in seasonality should have increased the winter unemployment rate and, therefore, per capita relief expenditures. The rate of unemployment is included as an explanatory variable in the simultaneous equa-

[9] By using distance from London as a proxy for the cost of migration, I am assuming that London was the destination for all potential migrants from the agricultural south. The assumption may be incorrect for rural areas close to other southern cities. During the period 1801–31, the combined populations of Bath, Brighton, Bristol, Norwich, Plymouth, Portsmouth, and Southampton increased by 174,000. However, over the same period the population of London increased by 790,000 (Mitchell and Deane 1962: 19, 24–7). Deane and Cole (1967: 115) found that all southern counties outside the London area experienced net out-migration from 1801 to 1831, while London experienced heavy in-migration. Thus the attraction of, say, Bristol was not strong enough to keep Gloucester from losing workers to London. Moreover, Redford (1964: 63–6), Hunt (1973: 282–4), and Pollard (1978: 107–8) agree that there was very little migration from the rural south to the industrial cities of the northwest during this period, which suggests that London was indeed the major destination of southern migrants. Hunt (1973: 281–2) concludes that "a large part of the southern labor force appears to have operated in a particularly restricted market. They moved overwhelmingly in one direction – towards London."

[10] A negative correlation between distance from London and relief expenditures or wage income might be explained by regional differences in the cost of living rather than by my hypothesized cost-of-migration effect. In other words, real wage income and per capita relief expenditures might not have varied inversely with distance from London even though nominal wage income and relief expenditures did. Unfortunately, there are little available data with which to test this hypothesis. The only attempt to measure regional variations in the cost of living has been by N. F. R. Crafts (1982) for the year 1843. He found that although the cost of living was indeed higher in London than in the rural south, there was no evidence of an inverse relationship between cost of living and distance from London (1982: 62). One can question this result, since Crafts assumes that rural rents were equal throughout England (1982: 61). However, his assumption is supported by evidence cited in Hunt (1973: 79–80). In order to take account of the regional cost-of-living differences found by Crafts, I deflated nominal wage income and per capita relief expenditures using his "rural perspective" southern agricultural price index (1982: 62).

tions model, and GRAIN is omitted.[11] Finally, WORKHOUSE is included to test the contention, often heard before parliamentary committees, that indoor relief was more expensive than outdoor relief.[12]

Equation (2) tests the extent to which alternative sources of income, various forms of outdoor relief, distance from urban labor markets, and surplus labor affected laborers' expected annual income. The variables CINDUSTRY and ALLOTMENTS test whether labor-hiring farmers responded to the existence of alternative (non-relief) sources of family income by reducing wage rates. Per capita relief expenditure was included in the simultaneous equations model to test whether poor relief was a substitute for wage income. The cost-of-migration hypothesis suggests that wage income, as well as relief expenditures, should be negatively related to distance from London. Density is a proxy for "population pressure on the land" (Mokyr 1985a: 45–6). The higher the density, the lower the land–labor ratio and, given diminishing returns, the lower the marginal product of labor. Density therefore is expected to be negatively related to wage income.

The remaining four variables represent specific forms of outdoor relief, each of which is expected to have a negative effect on wage income. The existence of child allowances for laborers with large families should have enabled farmers to reduce their wage payments to a level just high enough to support a family of four or five. Allowances-in-aid-of-wages, labor rates, and roundsmen systems all involved parish subsidization of farmers who employed laborers, and thus should have caused market wage rates to decline.

A parish's unemployment rate should be determined by its crop mix, its degree of population pressure, its relief policies, and the availability of alternative income sources. The more a parish specialized in the production of grain, the higher its unemployment rate should have been, because of the highly seasonal nature of labor requirements in grain production. The higher the degree of population pressure (that is, the lower the land–labor ratio), the more seasonally redundant laborers there will be for any given crop mix. Density, the proxy for population pressure, should therefore be positively related to unemployment.

[11] GRAIN is omitted because it should affect relief expenditures only through its effect on the unemployment rate.

[12] Of course, the recipients of poor relief included widows and old, sick, or infirm persons as well as able-bodied laborers and their families. Thus cross-parish variations in per capita relief expenditures could be caused in part by differences in the proportion of widows, and so on, in the parishes' populations. Unfortunately, lack of data have made it impossible to control for such differences.

The existence of a workhouse enabled parishes to threaten unemployed workers with indoor relief and thus should have reduced voluntary (and total) unemployment. Payment of allowances-in-aid-of-wages (the so-called Speenhamland system) might have created serious work disincentive effects; the variable SUBSIDY tests whether Speenhamland policies caused an increase in the rate of unemployment. The political power of labor-hiring farmers is expected to have a positive effect on seasonal layoffs and thus on the unemployment rate. The existence of alternative income sources in the form of cottage industry and allotments might have increased the willingness of farmers to lay off workers during slack seasons.[13] Both labor rates and roundsmen systems reduced the cost of employing workers during the winter months and therefore should have a negative effect on unemployment rates. However, the administration of roundsmen systems often encouraged farmers to increase layoffs in order to rehire the same workers at reduced wage costs. Depending on how respondents to the Rural Queries defined unemployment, unemployment rates might have increased under the roundsmen system.

4. Regression Results

The results obtained from estimating the reduced form and simultaneous equations models are given in Tables 4.5 and 4.6, and summarized in Tables 4.3 and 4.4. Several of the hypotheses discussed above are borne out by the data.

Cottage industry and allotments had a significant effect on agricultural labor markets, though not necessarily the effect predicted by Eden and Davies. Employment opportunities for women and children in cottage industry had a negative effect on per capita relief expenditures, but allotments did not.[14] Per capita relief expenditures were 1.7s.–3.4s.

---

[13] Alternatively, agricultural laborers might have voluntarily reduced their labor supply in response to the existence of cottage industry or allotments. See footnote 15, below.

[14] The insignificant effect of allotments in the regression does not necessarily mean that Young, Eden, Davies, and other contemporary observers were wrong in maintaining that providing the poor with allotments would reduce their dependence on poor relief. Young (1801) claimed that one-acre allotments would "very materially lessen" relief expenditures. Most contemporary proponents of allotment schemes recommended that allotments be at least a quarter acre in size (Barnett 1968: 175). The responses to question 20 of the Rural Queries suggest that the typical allotment in 1832 was one-eighth acre or smaller. Moreover, in many parishes with allotments only a small share of the laborers actually possessed land (Barnett 1968: 172). If parishes had provided allotments of a quarter acre or larger to all laborers who wanted them, allotments might have had a significant negative effect on relief expenditures.

Table 4.5. Regression results: Reduced form model

	Dependent variable: Per capita relief expenditures			Dependent variable: Annual male income			Dependent variable: Unemployment rate		
	$\hat{\beta}$	t Statistic	Prob > |t|	$\hat{\alpha}$	t Statistic	Prob > |t|	$\hat{\gamma}$	t Statistic	Prob > |t|
CONSTANT	11.20	4.92	0.0001	35.67	26.54	0.0001	0.17	0.07	0.942
CINDUSTRY	-1.70	1.75	0.082	-2.83	4.93	0.0001	1.01	1.02	0.308
ALLOTMENTS	0.10	0.13	0.899	-0.85	1.82	0.070	2.19	2.70	0.007
LONDON	-0.04	3.85	0.0001	-0.06	9.57	0.0001	-0.02	1.40	0.164
FARMERS	5.30	2.46	0.015	1.99	1.56	0.119	3.80	1.72	0.086
WEALTH	-0.30	1.64	0.103	0.07	0.67	0.503	-0.50	2.67	0.008
DENSITY	-0.55	1.11	0.268	-0.65	2.21	0.028	0.42	0.83	0.406
CHILDALLOW	5.52	5.31	0.0001	-1.36	2.21	0.028	3.17	2.98	0.003
SUBSIDY	-0.11	0.11	0.912	-0.40	0.67	0.503	1.62	1.58	0.114
GRAIN	0.29	3.11	0.002	-0.09	1.67	0.097	0.28	2.91	0.004
WORKHOUSE	1.24	1.41	0.158	0.70	1.36	0.175	1.23	1.38	0.170
ROUNDSMEN	1.10	0.88	0.381	0.49	0.66	0.508	2.00	1.57	0.119
LABORRATE	1.24	1.30	0.195	0.004	0.01	0.994	0.81	0.83	0.408
R^2	0.304			0.363			0.168		
N	311			311			311		

Table 4.6. *Regression results: Simultaneous equations model*

	Dependent variable: Per capita relief expenditures			Dependent variable: Annual male income		
	$\hat{b}$	t Statistic	Prob $> |t|$	$\hat{a}$	t Statistic	Prob $> |t|$
CONSTANT	32.75	1.51	0.133	38.91	24.14	0.0001
CINDUSTRY	−3.40	1.79	0.075	−3.30	5.36	0.0001
ALLOTMENTS	−0.85	0.95	0.342	−0.88	1.78	0.076
LONDON	−0.08	2.12	0.035	−0.07	9.28	0.0001
FARMERS	8.39	3.29	0.001			
WEALTH	−0.002	0.01	0.993			
DENSITY				−0.86	2.80	0.006
CHILDALLOW				−0.19	0.24	0.810
SUBSIDY				−0.39	0.64	0.523
WORKHOUSE	0.75	0.70	0.484			
ROUNDSMEN				0.91	1.17	0.244
LABORRATE				0.16	0.26	0.793
UNEMPLOYMENT	0.34	3.48	0.001			
INCOME	−0.49	−0.75	0.454			
RELIEF				−0.19	2.33	0.020

lower in parishes with cottage industry than in parishes without cottage industry. Both cottage industry and allotments had a negative effect on agricultural laborers' earnings. On average, laborers' annual wage income was £2.8–£3.3 lower in parishes with employment opportunities in cottage industry than in parishes without cottage industry. The existence of allotments caused a reduction of £0.9 in laborers' income, other things equal. Unemployment rates were higher in parishes with allotments, suggesting that farmers increased their use of layoffs where laborers' families had other sources of income.[15] Together these results offer strong support for the hypothesis that politically dominant farmers made use of cottage industry and allotments to reduce their wage bill.

[15] As mentioned in footnote 13, there is another possible interpretation for the positive effect of allotments on the unemployment rate. Alternative sources of income might have caused agricultural laborers to reduce their labor supply voluntarily. We can distinguish between these two hypotheses by determining the effect of allotments (and cottage industry) on weekly wage rates. A reduction in labor supply in response to other sources of income should have caused agricultural wage rates to increase. However, estimation of both models using agricultural laborers' summer wage rates instead of annual earnings yields the opposite result; weekly wage rates were lower in parishes containing cottage industry and allotments, other things equal. This result supports my hypothesis that labor-hiring farmers increased seasonal layoffs in response to alternative sources of income for laborers' families.

Distance from London had a negative effect on agricultural laborers' earnings and on per capita relief expenditures. A 10% increase in distance from London resulted in a 1.5–2.9% reduction in relief expenditures and a 1.3–1.4% reduction in wage income. The importance of distance supports the hypothesis that the cost of migration affected the utility value of agricultural laborers' implicit labor contracts, and suggests that the southern labor market was well integrated by the early nineteenth century.

Population pressure on the land, as proxied by density, had a negative effect on laborers' earnings, but the effect was quantitatively small. A 10% increase in density resulted in a 0.1% decline in earnings. Surprisingly, density did not have a significant effect on unemployment.

Specialization in grain had a positive effect on both the rate of unemployment and per capita relief expenditure in the reduced form model. The elasticities associated with specialization in grain are large. A 10% increase in the share of land devoted to grain resulted in a 5.0% increase in the unemployment rate and a 2.1% increase in relief expenditures. In the simultaneous equations model, the elasticity of relief expenditures with respect to the unemployment rate is 0.14. The provision of unemployment insurance was indeed a major function of outdoor relief, and the unemployment rate was determined, in part, by crop mix.

The political power of labor-hiring farmers had a positive effect on per capita relief expenditures and the rate of unemployment. A 10% increase in the proportion of parish taxpayers who were labor-hiring farmers resulted in a 1.8% increase in the unemployment rate, and a 1.1–1.7% increase in per capita relief expenditures. These results support my contention that labor-hiring farmers used their political power to increase their subsidization by other local taxpayers.

Evidence is mixed concerning the hypothesis that relief expenditures and agricultural laborers' wage income were interrelated. Per capita relief expenditures had a negative effect on laborers' annual earnings in the simultaneous equations model. A 10% increase in relief expenditures resulted in a 1.2% decrease in annual earnings. The payment of child allowances had a negative effect on laborers' earnings in the reduced form model.[16] On average, agricultural laborers in parishes granting child al-

[16] Child allowances also had a positive effect on per capita relief expenditures in the reduced form model. Parishes that granted relief to laborers "on account of their families" spent on average 5.5s. more per capita on relief than parishes without child allowances, other things equal. The mean level of per capita relief expenditures for the sample was 18.0s.

lowances received an annual wage income £1.4 below that of laborers in parishes without child allowances.[17] The above results suggest that, to some extent, the Poor Laws did indeed "create the poor which they maintain." On the other hand, the use of allowances-in-aid-of-wages did not affect either relief expenditures or earnings. Moreover, the annual earnings of agricultural laborers had no effect on per capita relief expenditures. Thus, the widely accepted hypothesis that outdoor relief was used to supplement "substandard" wage income is not supported by the data.

Finally, there is little support for the hypothesis that outdoor relief caused an increase in voluntary unemployment. Neither the payment of allowances-in-aid-of-wages nor the existence of workhouses had a statistically significant effect on the unemployment rate. Thus, although it was not possible to estimate directly the effect of relief generosity on unemployment, the above results provide tentative support for the revisionist hypothesis that rural parishes were selective in their granting of relief to able-bodied laborers.

5. Implications for the Long-Term Increase in Relief Expenditures

The evidence does not support the Royal Poor Law Commission's hypothesis that regional variations in per capita relief expenditures were caused simply by "the abuses of the Poor Laws" by parishes in southeastern England. Conversely, several revisionist hypotheses are confirmed by the data. Crop mix, income from cottage industry, and the political power of labor-hiring farmers were important determinants of per capita relief expenditures. Surprisingly, the hypothesis that poor relief was used to supplement "substandard" wages was not supported by the data. Arthur Young's observation in the 1770s that agricultural wage rates varied inversely with distance from London was found to hold also for 1832. Per capita relief expenditures also varied inversely with distance from London. Together, the results support my hypothesis that farmers anxious to secure an adequate peak season labor force were able to reduce the utility value of their workers' implicit labor contracts as the cost of migration to London increased.

---

[17] The mean expected annual income for the sample of parishes was £29.6. None of the other three specific forms of outdoor relief (namely, allowances-in-aid-of-wages, roundsmen system, labor rate) had a significant effect on either wage income or per capita relief expenditures.

What insights do the above results yield concerning the rapid increase in per capita relief expenditures after 1750? For one thing, they enable us to reject the contemporary notion that the increase in relief expenditures was caused almost exclusively by the lax administration of outdoor relief, and its effects on wage rates, laborers' productivity, and voluntary unemployment. The payment of allowances-in-aid-of-wages did not increase unemployment rates or per capita relief expenditures, or reduce laborers' earnings. The existence of workhouses did not reduce unemployment rates. Moreover, although relief expenditures had a negative effect on agricultural laborers' earnings, as the Poor Law Report maintained, earnings did not have a significant effect on relief expenditures. But the major reason for rejecting the contemporary analysis is simply that other factors ignored by the Poor Law Commissioners, such as cottage industry and the extent of seasonal unemployment, were important determinants of per capita relief expenditures.

The results also appear to reject the hypothesis that relief expenditures increased in response to the decline in laborers' landholdings caused by enclosures and other forms of engrossment. However, I noted in Section 1 that, because of the small size of allotments in 1832, the coefficient from the cross-sectional analysis understates the long-term effect of laborers' loss of land. One cannot therefore ascertain the effect of the decline in laborers' landholdings on per capita relief expenditures from the cross-sectional analysis.

On the positive side, the regression results offer support for several revisionist hypotheses. Long-term changes in crop mix, employment opportunities or wage rates in cottage industry, the local political power of labor-hiring farmers, urban wage rates, or cost of migration to London could have caused relief expenditures to increase.

Parishes in the southeast of England responded to the long-term rise in grain prices from 1760 to 1815 by increasing their specialization in grain production (Snell 1981: 421–2). Because of the highly seasonal labor demands of grain production, the change in crop mix must have exacerbated the problem of seasonal unemployment. Indeed, Snell (1981: 411) found that the seasonal distribution of male unemployment became more pronounced over the period. The increased specialization in grain was certainly an important factor in the increase in per capita relief expenditures after 1760.

The political power of labor-hiring farmers increased in southern parishes after 1760, as a result of changes in the economic and legal environment. The "long-term . . . consolidation of farms into larger and more efficient units" that had begun in the seventeenth century was encouraged by the wave of enclosures between 1760 and 1815 (Chambers and Mingay 1966: 92). The consequent decline in the number of small landholders increased the political power of labor-hiring farmers. The passage of Gilbert's Act (1782) introduced "the principle of weighting the right to vote according to the amount of property occupied." This principle was extended by the 1818 Parish Vestry Act, which allowed ratepayers up to six votes in vestry, depending on their poor rate assessment (Brundage 1978: 7, 10). Because labor-hiring farmers were generally the largest property holders in rural parishes, their political power was significantly increased in parishes that adopted either of these acts. The cross-sectional evidence suggests that farmers used their increased political power to increase relief expenditures and therefore to pass more of their labor costs on to non-labor-hiring ratepayers.

However, the most important cause of the increase in relief expenditures probably was the combination of: (1) the decline in employment opportunities and wage rates for women and children in cottage industry, and (2) the rapid increase in London wage rates. From 1795 to 1832, real wage rates of London builders' laborers increased by 44%.[18] During the same period, the weekly earnings of an agricultural laborer's wife and children in cottage industry declined from perhaps 2s.–5s. to 0s.– 3s.[19] The decline in cottage industry was most pronounced in East Anglia, but the responses to question 11 of the Rural Queries show that employment in cottage industry was declining throughout the south. The conclusion here that the southern labor market was well integrated in the early nineteenth century suggests that, in response to the decline in cottage industry and the increase in London wage rates, farmers anxious to secure an adequate peak-season labor force had to increase laborers' wage rates or relief expenditures. The average weekly wage of southern agricultural laborers increased from 8.8s. in 1795 to 10.6s. in 1832, which was barely enough to offset the decline in earnings from cottage indus-

[18] Nominal wage data for London laborers were obtained from Schwarz (1986: 37–8). Cost-of-living data were obtained from Lindert and Williamson (1985: 148–9).
[19] Estimates of the weekly earnings of women and children in cottage industry in 1795 were obtained from Eden (1797). Estimates of weekly earnings in 1832 were obtained from the responses to question 11 of the Rural Queries (Parl. Papers 1834: XXX). Question 11 also contains evidence that by 1832 cottage industry had completely disappeared from some areas in which it had flourished in the late eighteenth century. For a discussion of the long-term decline in wage rates and employment opportunities in cottage industry see Chapter 1, Section 3, and Pinchbeck (1930: 138–45, 208, 220–1, 225).

try.[20] At best, the typical family's earnings increased by 1s. per week, from, say, 11.5s. to 12.5s. In real terms, family earnings increased by a maximum of 22%, approximately one-half of the increase in London wage rates. In some counties, such as Essex and Suffolk, real family earnings remained roughly constant from 1795 to 1832. The slow growth of rural earnings relative to London earnings suggests that farmers responded to the increase in London wages, and thus the increase in their workers' reservation utility, by increasing relief expenditures as well as rural wages. This is precisely the response that the model developed in Chapter 3 would have predicted. By increasing relief expenditures, farmers shifted part of the increase in their labor costs on to non-labor-hiring taxpayers.

On the other hand, increases in London wage rates cannot explain the widespread adoption of outdoor relief during the 1770s and 1780s. Wages of London laborers and agricultural laborers moved closely together during these decades. From 1767 to 1795, real wages of London builders' laborers declined by 16%, while real wages of southeastern agricultural laborers declined, on average, by 18%.[21] However, as a result of the sharp decline in earnings from cottage industry and rural laborers' loss of land in the last third of the eighteenth century, the decline in total family income was much larger for agricultural laborers than for London laborers. Rural parishes increased poor relief expenditures in response to the relative decline in agricultural laborers' income.

6. Conclusion

The empirical analysis has shown that variations in per capita relief expenditures across parishes were largely a result of differences in their economic and political environment. Changes in these same economic and political factors appear to have been a major cause of the rapid increase in relief expenditures from 1750 to 1834. The results offer strong support for the revisionist analysis of the economic role of the Old Poor Law begun by Blaug. They contrast sharply with the analysis contained in the 1834 Report of the Royal Poor Law Commission. This is ironic, since the data used here were collected by the Poor Law Commission.

---

[20] Wage data are from Bowley (1898: 704). The average is for the 16 counties included in Table 1.A2 of Appendix A to Chapter 1.

[21] Nominal wages of London laborers and agricultural laborers increased by 17% and 13%, respectively, from 1767 to 1795. Data were obtained from Schwarz (1986: 37–40) and Appendix A to Chapter 1.

Why did the commission choose to ignore the Rural Queries, except as a source of critical comments from local officials concerning the administration of outdoor relief? Perhaps their neglect was caused by the "unmanageable nature" of the data. The uses that the commissioners could have made of the data were limited, of course, but they could have tabulated the answers to the questions, as Blaug (1964) did. A tabulation would have revealed that the system of allowances-in-aid-of-wages, rather than being the major form of outdoor relief, was in fact used by fewer than 10% of the responding parishes, and that fewer than 1% of the parishes granting child allowances began relief at the birth of the first or second child. In addition, an analysis of the responses to question 6 (on unemployment) together with the information on labor rates in Appendix D of the 1834 Poor Law Report would have revealed that rural unemployment was largely a seasonal phenomenon. This information might have led the commissioners to reach a different conclusion about the economic effects of outdoor relief.

It is also possible that the commissioners neglected the returns because they had already concluded that the administration of outdoor relief was to blame for the long-term increase in relief expenditures. The Webbs (1929: 85–6) maintained that the commission's "investigation [of the Poor Law] was far from being impartially or judicially directed and carried out." Their hypothesis would appear to be supported by the 1834 report's selective use of information from the Rural Queries. Whatever the cause, the upshot was unfortunate, since the Poor Law Commission's report continues to influence attitudes toward social welfare.

Appendix A
Data Sources

The sources of the data utilized in the empirical analysis are listed below. Shortened names of variables are in parentheses.

Per Capita Relief Expenditures (RELIEF): Relief expenditures in 1831 (measured in shillings) divided by population in 1831. All data were obtained from the Rural Queries.

Unemployment Rate (UNEMPLOYMENT): Data on unemployment were obtained from question 6 of the Rural Queries: "Number of Labourers generally out of employment, and how maintained in summer and winter?" The unemployment rate was constructed by taking a simple average of the summer and winter unemployment levels (assuming the winter unemployment level to be relevant for one half of the year and the summer unemployment level for one half) and dividing by an estimate of the total number of wage laborers in the parish. The latter was assumed to consist of the number of agricultural laborers, nonagricultural laborers, and adult males employed in handicrafts and retail trade, as given in the 1831 census.

Laborers' Annual Wage Income (INCOME): Data were obtained from the Rural Queries, questions 8 (weekly wages for adult males), and 10 (annual income for adult males). Problems arose because question 10 had a relatively low response rate. Fortunately, the response rate to question 8 was nearly 100%. I constructed estimates of annual wage income for those parishes that did not answer question 10 in the following way.

First, the data were divided up by counties. Second, for those parishes in each county that had data on male summer wage rates, winter wage rates, and annual earnings, Y_{ij}, an estimate of annual income, Z_{ij}, was constructed:

$$Z_{ij} = 26W_{s_{ij}} + 26W_{w_{ij}} \tag{1}$$

where

W_s = summer wage
W_w = winter wage
i = parish, $i = 1, n$ n = number of parishes in county
j = county, $j = 1, 20$

A ratio R_{ij} was then defined as

$$R_{ij} = Z_{ij}/Y_{ij} \tag{2}$$

Each county's ratio was thus

$$R_j = \Sigma_i R_{ij}/n \tag{3}$$

Third, each county's ratio, R_j, was used to construct estimates of annual earnings, Y_{ij}, for those parishes that reported wage rates but not earnings data.

$$Y_{ij} = [26W_{s_{ij}} + 26W_{w_{ij}}]/R_j \quad \text{or} \quad Y_{ij} = Z_{ij}/R_j \tag{4}$$

The calculated R_j for each county was approximately equal to 1.0. This suggests that neither harvest wages nor unemployment probabilities were taken into account in the estimates of male income given by parish overseers in question 10.

Cottage Industry (CINDUSTRY): Dummy variable equal to 1 if some form of cottage industry existed in the parish. Information on the existence of cottage industry was obtained from question 11 of the Rural Queries: "Have you any and what Employment for Women and Children?"

Allotments: Dummy variable equal to 1 if laborers rented land on which to grow food. Information on the existence of allotments was obtained from question 20 of the Rural Queries: "Whether any land let to labourers; if so, the Quantity to each, and at what Rent?"

Distance from London (LONDON): Distance from the center of each county to London. Distance was measured at the county level because of the difficulty of locating individual parishes within counties.

Political Power of Labor-Hiring Farmers (FARMERS): The variable measures the percentage of parish ratepayers who were labor-hiring farmers. The number of labor-hiring farmers is given in the 1831 census. The number of parish ratepayers was estimated by assuming that all adult males not designated by the 1831 census as agricultural laborers, nonagricultural laborers, or persons employed in handicrafts or retail trade owned enough property to be taxed.

Density: Density is measured as population per acre. Population data were obtained from the Rural Queries. Data on parish acreage were obtained from the 1831 census.

Child Allowances, Employed Laborers Receiving Relief (CHILD-ALLOW, SUBSIDY): CHILDALLOW is a dummy variable equal to 1 if the parish had a system of child allowances. SUBSIDY is a dummy variable equal to 1 if laborers received relief payments while privately employed (i.e., allowances-in-aid-of-wages). Information on the existence of both practices was obtained from question 24 of the Rural Queries: "Have you any, and how many, able-bodied labourers in the employment of individuals receiving allowance or regular relief from your parish on their own account, or on that of their families?"

Specialization in Grain Production (GRAIN): An estimate of the extent of grain production in the parish was obtained by calculating the percentage of a parish's adult males who were employed in agriculture (using data from the 1831 census) and multiplying this figure by the relevant *county's* share of agricultural land devoted to grain crops (wheat, barley, oats) in 1836. County-level data on crop mix were obtained from Roger Kain (1986), who estimated land use and crop acreage for 35 of 42

English counties using data from the tithe surveys carried out under the 1836 Tithe Commutation Act. For a discussion of the tithe survey data, see Kain (1986: 1–25) and Kain and Prince (1985).

Workhouse: Dummy variable equal to 1 if the parish contained a workhouse. Data obtained from question 22 of the Rural Queries: "Have you a workhouse?"

Roundsmen System (ROUNDSMEN): Dummy variable equal to 1 if the parish used a roundsmen system. Data obtained from question 27 of the Rural Queries: "Whether the system of roundsmen is practiced, or has been practiced?"

Labor Rate (LABORRATE): Dummy variable equal to 1 if the parish used a labor rate. Data obtained from question 28 of the Rural Queries: "Whether labourers are apportioned amongst the occupiers according to the extent of occupation, acreage rent, or number of horses employed?"

Per Capita Property Value (WEALTH): Per capita value of real property in parish. Data on real property value in 1815 obtained from the 1831 census.

Appendix B
Representativeness of Sample

	Parishes in sample		Parishes not in sample	
	Number of observations	Mean	Number of observations	Mean
RELIEF	311	18.0s.	378	18.2s.
INCOME	311	£29.6	325	£29.5
UNEMPLOYMENT	311	7.4%	57	6.4%
GRAIN	311	13.3%	362	12.2%
CINDUSTRY	311	23.2%	329	22.5%
ALLOTMENTS	311	47.6%	230	44.3%
FARMERS	311	35.9%	355	32.7%
CHILDALLOW	311	81.7%	295	86.4%
LABORRATE	311	23.2%	226	21.2%
ROUNDSMEN	311	12.2%	228	9.2%
WORKHOUSE	311	64.6%	234	59.8%

Source: Calculated by author from the Rural Queries (Parl. Papers 1834: XXX–XXXI).

5

THE EFFECT OF POOR RELIEF ON BIRTH RATES IN SOUTHEASTERN ENGLAND

One of the most often heard contemporary criticisms of the Old Poor Law was that the granting of outdoor relief to able-bodied laborers promoted population growth. The aspect of outdoor relief that supposedly had the strongest effect on the rate of population growth was the payment of child allowances to laborers with large families. Like most parts of the traditional critique of the Old Poor Law, the hypothesis that child allowances caused population to increase has been challenged by revisionist historians. In particular, two papers by James Huzel (1969; 1980) have led Joel Mokyr (1985b: 11) to conclude that "the demographic argument against [the Poor Law] has been effectively demolished." The judgment is premature. This chapter uses Huzel's data source to demonstrate that, when other socioeconomic determinants of fertility are accounted for, the payment of child allowances did indeed cause an increase in birth rates. Malthus was right.

The chapter will proceed as follows: Section 1 reviews the historical debate over the role of poor relief in promoting population growth. The administration of child allowance policies, and the economic value of child allowances to agricultural laborers, are discussed in Section 2. A cross-sectional model to explain variations in birth rates across southeastern parishes for 1826–30 is developed in Section 3 and estimated in Section 4. Section 5 tests whether child allowance policies were an endogenous response to changing demographic patterns. Some implications for the role played by poor relief in the fertility increase of the early nineteenth century are given in Section 6.

1. The Historical Debate

Thomas Malthus was by far the most influential contemporary critic of the Old Poor Law. According to Malthus, the Poor Law undermined the

150

"preventive check" to population growth (late marriage and abstention) by artificially reducing the cost of having children. Under the system of child allowances, there was no reason for laborers "to put any sort of restraint upon their inclinations, or exercise any degree of prudence in the affair of marriage; because the parish is bound to provide for all that are born" (1817: II, 372). Indeed, poor relief was administered in such a way as to "afford a direct, constant and systematical encouragement to marriage" (1817: III, 138). Malthus concluded that, in the long run, the administration of poor relief would create an excess supply of labor and thus, ironically, "increase the poverty and distress of the labouring classes of society" (1817: II, 371).

The 1834 Report of the Royal Poor Law Commission included the Malthusian argument as one of its many criticisms of the administration of outdoor relief. The report maintained that although the typical unmarried laborer earned a wage close to subsistence, "he has only to marry, and it increases." Moreover, his income increased "on the birth of every child [so that] if his family is numerous, the parish becomes his principal paymaster" (Royal Commission 1834: 57). Evidence from several parishes was presented to demonstrate that the effect of such allowances was to "encourage early and improvident marriages, with their consequent evils" (1834: 24–31).

Early attempts to test the Malthusian hypothesis empirically reached conflicting conclusions. Griffith (1926) and Blackmore and Mellonie (1927–8) found that poor relief had no effect on birth rates over the period 1801–31, while Krause (1958: 68) concluded that "the Poor Laws were clearly associated with high fertility" in the period 1817–21. However, as Huzel (1969: 437–44) has pointed out, the empirical analysis of each of these studies is seriously flawed, because: (1) they used county-level data, whereas poor relief was administered by the parish; (2) they somewhat arbitrarily classified counties as either allowance counties or nonallowance counties; and (3) they consisted of simple comparisons of birth rates across allowance and nonallowance counties, ignoring all other socioeconomic determinants of fertility.

The revisionist literature has, until recently, paid little attention to the demographic impact of poor relief. Blaug (1963) quickly disposed of the Malthusian hypothesis in his reinterpretation of the economic effects of the Old Poor Law. While admitting that "most of the Speenhamland counties had fertility ratios above the national average" in the early nineteenth century, he concluded that there was "no persuasive evidence" that outdoor relief caused birth rates to increase (1963: 173–4). On the other hand, he suggested that generous relief might have caused the infant mortality rate to decline (1963: 174). Marshall (1968: 38–43) compared county-level data on the administration of poor relief tabulated by Blaug (1964) with rates of population growth and concluded that there was no support for the Malthusian hypothesis. However, his analysis is flawed in ways similar to the earlier papers by Griffith, Blackmore and Mellonie, and Krause.

The latest and most careful empirical analysis of the Malthusian hypothesis was carried out by Huzel (1980). Unlike earlier historians, Huzel used parish-level data to test whether the payment of allowances-in-aid-of-wages or child allowances "led directly to higher birth- and marriage-rates and in turn to population increase" (1980: 369). Huzel provided three tests of the Malthusian hypothesis. First, he determined the "impact of the abolition of the allowance system" on birth, marriage, and infant mortality rates for 22 parishes (1980: 369–75). Second, he made a demographic comparison of 11 Kent parishes that paid both allowances-in-aid-of-wages and child allowances with 18 Kent parishes that used neither relief system (1980: 375–8). Finally, he compared demographic indices for 49 Kent parishes divided "into five categories in regard to the payment of child allowances" (1980: 379–80).

Each test yielded the same result. The payment of child allowances and allowances-in-aid-of-wages did not have a significant positive effect on birth or marriage rates, or a negative effect on infant mortality rates. Indeed, Huzel's results suggest that the Malthusian hypothesis should "be turned on its head"; the allowance system appears to have been associated with relatively low birth and marriage rates and high infant mortality rates (1980: 380).

However, there are problems with each of Huzel's tests. The second and third tests, which compare demographic variables across Kent parishes, are open to one of the criticisms used by Huzel against earlier empirical studies, namely, that they consist of simple comparisons of relief policies and birth, marriage, and infant mortality rates, without controlling for other possible determinants of these demographic variables. Huzel has failed to isolate the effect of allowances on birth rates and therefore has not offered a proper test of the Malthusian model.

His first test gets around this problem to some extent by examining changes in demographic indices within parishes after they abolished the allowance system. However, his finding that birth and marriage rates increased and infant mortality rates decreased in a majority of parishes after abolition raises several questions, none of which Huzel confronts. Why did these parishes abolish allowances to able-bodied laborers? Why did the payment of allowances cause birth and marriage rates to decline?

One possible explanation for Huzel's results is that the parishes stopped paying allowances because they were no longer needed. An increase in nominal wages in agriculture or cottage industry, a decline in food prices, or the introduction of allotments might have raised laborers' real incomes by enough to make allowances unnecessary. The increase in income also would have stimulated marriage rates and birth rates.[1] As before, Huzel's simple comparison of demographic variables with relief policies makes it impossible to determine the cause of the postallowance increase in birth and marriage rates.

2. The Economic Value of Child Allowances

Child allowances were one of the most widespread forms of poor relief granted to able-bodied laborers in the early nineteenth century. Estimates of the extent of child allowance policies can be obtained for 1824 and 1832 from data collected by the Committee on Labourers' Wages and the Royal Poor Law Commission.[2] Approximately 75% of rural parishes granted child allowances in 1824, while only 50% did so in 1832. Child allowances were particularly widespread in the grain-producing southeast. More than 90% of southeastern parishes used child allowances in 1824, declining to 80% in 1832.

The administration of child allowance policies differed across parishes. In 1832, 36% of southeastern parishes granting child allowances gave relief to families with three children under the age of 10 or 12, 43%

---

[1] The hypothesis that the abolition of allowances coincided with an increase in laborers' income cannot be tested, because data on movements in income are not available for most of the 22 parishes in Huzel's sample. What evidence is available, however, tends to support my hypothesis. Assistant Poor Law Commissioner Majendie reported that after the abolition of allowances in Westerham, Kent, in 1825 the laborers were "better clothed and fed than they were before" (Parl. Papers 1834: XXVIII, 208). In Farthinghoe, Northampton, child allowances were gradually reduced beginning in 1827 and "discontinued altogether" in 1829. From 1826 to 1829 wages increased from 6s. to 10s., and land allotments and clothing clubs were introduced. Together, these changes made "the condition of even the largest families better than it was under the old [allowance] system" (Parl. Papers 1834: XXVIII, 408–9).

[2] Data for 1824 were obtained from the responses to question 2 of a survey distributed by the Select Committee on Labourers' Wages (Parl. Papers 1825: XIX). Data for 1832 were obtained from the responses to question 24 of the Rural Queries, distributed by the Royal Poor Law Commission (Parl. Papers 1834: XXXI).

began relief upon the birth of a fourth child, and 21% began relief at five or more children. The number of years a laborer received relief depended on the spacing of births as well as the size of his family. If a parish granted relief to laborers with three children under age 10, a laborer with three children born two years apart would receive an allowance for six years, while a laborer with three children spaced three years apart would receive an allowance for four years.

The allowance was generally equal to 1.5s. per week (£3.9 per year) for each child at and beyond the number at which relief began.[3] In other words, a parish that began relief at three children under age 10 would pay 3s. per week to families with four children under age 10 and 4.5s. to families with five children. Annual earnings for an agricultural worker were approximately £28 in 1832; thus, a laborer's annual income increased by roughly 14% for each child granted an allowance.[4]

The effect of child allowances on fertility depended on the administration of relief and the spacing of births. Suppose that laborers were given a weekly allowance of 1.5s. as long as they had three children under age 10. If births were spaced two and a half years apart, a laborer would receive £3.9 a year for five years upon the birth of a third child. Assuming a 5% discount rate, the present value of the child allowance was equal to £17.7, or 63% of the annual earnings of an agricultural laborer.[5] If allowance payments were continued as long as a laborer had three children under age 12, the present value of the child allowance to a laborer with three children spaced two and a half years apart was £23.7, or 85% of his annual earnings.[6] The laborer would receive a similar benefit for each child beyond the third.[7]

[3] In the counties of Sussex, Kent, Essex, and Norfolk weekly benefits were equal to 1.5s. in 63% of the responding parishes, 1s. in 22%, and 2s. in 11%.
[4] Jeffrey Williamson (1982: 48) estimated that the average annual earnings of an agricultural laborer was £30 in 1835, assuming that laborers were employed 52 weeks of the year. However, data from the 1832 Rural Queries suggest that, for England as a whole, the typical agricultural laborer was employed for 48 or 49 weeks a year. Adjusting Williamson's estimate to account for unemployment, the average annual earnings of agricultural laborers declines to approximately £28.
[5] My choice of a 5% discount rate follows Williamson (1985b: 36–7). If the discount rate was 0%, the present value of the child allowance was £19.5. A discount rate of 10% yields a present value of £16.3.
[6] The present value of the allowance to a laborer with three children spaced two years apart was £26.5. If births were spaced three years apart, the present value of the child allowance was £20.8.
[7] If allowances were given to laborers with three children under age 10, a laborer who had four children spaced two and a half years apart would receive a total of £39 in child allowances. The present value of the allowance, measured at the time of birth of the third child, was £33.4, or 119% of the laborer's annual earnings.

The effect of child allowances on birth rates should have been significantly smaller in parishes where relief began with the birth of a fourth child than in parishes that began relief at three children. Not only did a laborer's family get no allowance upon the birth of a third child, but also the duration of allowance payments was shorter if it was necessary to have four children (rather than three) under the age of 10 or 12 in order to collect relief. If the weekly allowance was equal to 1.5s., the age limit was 10, and births were spaced two and a half years apart, a laborer would receive relief for two and a half years upon the birth of a fourth child. The present value of the child allowance was equal to £9.4, or 34% of annual earnings. To compare the benefits from allowances beginning at three and four children, one should calculate the present value of both allowances from the birth of the third child. Discounted back to the birth of the third child, the present value of the allowance beginning at four children was £8.0.

In parishes where child allowances were given only to laborers with five children under 10 or 12, a laborer with five children spaced two and a half years apart would not have been eligible for relief if the age limit was 10. If the age limit was 12, he would have received an allowance for two years; the present value of the allowance was £7.6. Discounted back to the birth of the third child, the present value of the allowance was £6.0. A laborer would receive an allowance for as many as four years only if he had five children spaced two years apart (or less) and the age limit was 12.

In sum, the effect of child allowances on birth rates should depend on the number of children at which allowances began. Child allowances should have had a strong positive effect on birth rates in parishes where relief began upon the birth of a third (or second) child, a smaller effect on birth rates in parishes where relief was not obtainable until the birth of a fourth child, and a weak effect in parishes that began relief at five or more children. In the next section, I estimate a cross-sectional regression in order to test these predictions.

3. An Analysis of the Determinants of Birth Rates

A model to determine the effect of child allowances on birth rates must control for other socioeconomic variables thought to be determinants of fertility. Malthusian models focus on changes in income as the major determinant of movements in both birth rates and death rates. Societies adjust birth rates to changes in income through changes in marital fertility and in the age of marriage. Malthusian models are especially useful for the study of preindustrial population movements. For example, Ronald Lee (1980: 539), in his study of English demographic trends from 1539 to 1839, found that "both marital fertility and nuptiality were strongly influenced by short-run variations in the real wage."

Malthusian models cannot explain the steady decline in fertility rates that occurred along with increasing real wages in late-nineteenth-century Europe. According to the "Princeton school" of historical demography, the decline in fertility rates that accompanied industrialization was a result of various social and cultural changes brought about by the process of modernization. The explanatory variables focused on in "transition" models include urbanization, changes in occupational structure, increases in literacy, declining infant mortality rates, and secularization (see, for example, Lesthaeghe 1977; Teitelbaum 1984).

Economic models of the demographic transition focus on increases in the opportunity cost of mothers' time and in the relative pecuniary costs of children, the decline in child labor, and the decline in infant (or child) mortality rates (Schultz 1969; Lindert 1980). Unfortunately, it is difficult to incorporate these hypotheses into an analysis of early-nineteenth-century birth rates. There are no good proxies for the opportunity cost of mothers' time. Data on female wage rates exist for only a few parishes, and there are no data on female educational attainment. The existence of cottage industry might be considered a proxy for mothers' opportunity cost, but the fact that cottage industry was done at home suggests that females' ability to work was not greatly affected by the presence of children.

Similarly, cross-sectional differences in the relative pecuniary costs of children are difficult to measure. Children are food and space intensive, so the demand for children should have been lower in parishes with relatively high food or housing prices, other things equal (Lindert 1980: 53–4). No parish-level price data are available, although the relative price of housing can be proxied by the ratio of families to inhabited houses.

The model developed in this chapter includes both Malthusian and demographic transition variables to explain variations in birth rates across parishes. My data set consists of a sample of 214 parishes from 12 counties located in southeastern England.[8] The sample is not random;

[8] The counties are Sussex, Kent, Surrey, Essex, Suffolk, Norfolk, Cambridge, Huntingdon, Hertford, Bedford, Buckingham, and Berkshire.

all parishes for which data could be obtained were included. I chose to focus on the southeast because per capita relief expenditures were higher there than in any other region in England throughout the early nineteenth century, and because the Royal Poor Law Commission and most critics of the Old Poor Law focused on the region. Moreover, birth rates were higher in the southeast in 1821 than in any other region except for the industrial counties of Lancashire, Stafford, and the West Riding of Yorkshire.

The data used in the regression analysis were obtained from three sources. Data on the number of births and infant deaths in each parish for the years 1826–30 were obtained from unpublished parish returns for the 1831 census located in the Public Record Office in London.[9] The published returns for the 1831 census supplied information on population density, the occupational structure of the labor force, and the number of inhabited houses in each parish. The returns to the Rural Queries supplied information on the administration of poor relief, the annual income of agricultural laborers, and the existence of cottage industry and land allotments.

Question 24 of the Rural Queries asked whether privately employed laborers received regular relief "on their own account, or on that of their families; and if on account of their families, at which number of children does it begin." Thus it is possible to determine not only whether parishes used child allowances but also what family size was necessary to receive allowances. In some cases it is even possible to determine, from question 25, the increase in benefits for each additional child. However, not enough parishes answered this question to enable me to include generosity of relief in the regression analysis.

Because the 1831 census does not contain data on age distribution, it was not possible to define the birth rate as the number of births per 1,000 women aged 15–49. Instead, the birth rate is defined as the number of births per 100 families residing in the parish. There are obvious problems with this measure of birth rates. Not all families contain women of childbearing age. One cause of variations across parishes in

---

[9] The census data are classified as P.R.O. Home Office (H.O.) 71. This is the same data source used by Huzel (1980). The forms on which the data were returned contain a question asking the clergy to estimate the "average number of baptisms, marriages, and burials unentered [per year] due to nonconformity and other factors" (Huzel 1969: 447). This information enables one to correct for the problem of possible underregistration of births.

the ratio of births to families could simply be differences in the age distribution of married females.

Differential rates of out-migration also might have caused cross-parish variations in the ratio of births to families. Most migrants were young adults (Williamson 1988: 302–7). If out-migration rates were higher from poor, "unpromising" parishes than from more prosperous parishes, then poor parishes should have contained a relatively small share of young married couples and young unmarried adults. Excess out-migration of young fecund couples would have lowered the ratio of births to families in poor parishes, other things equal. Thus, there might be a spurious positive relationship between birth rates and measures of parish prosperity, such as wage rates. In addition, if generous child allowances were associated with poor parishes, there might be a spurious negative relationship between birth rates and child allowances.[10] Unfortunately, data do not exist to test these hypotheses.

On the other hand, high out-migration from poor parishes of young *unmarried* adults who otherwise would have formed separate (solitaire) households would have reduced the share of childless households in poor parishes and, by definition, increased the birth rate. Thus, excess out-migration of young unmarried persons might create a spurious negative relationship between birth rates and measures of parish prosperity, and a spurious positive relationship between birth rates and child allowances. However, the effect of differential out-migration rates of unmarried adults on birth rates (as measured here) was probably trivial, because they seldom formed separate households. Peter Laslett (1972: 142) found that only 5.7% of the households in 100 English parishes contained one person, and many of these solitaire households consisted of widows or widowers. Young unmarried adults lived either at home or in the households of others as servants or lodgers (Smith 1981: 600–4).[11]

---

[10] Rosenzweig and Wolpin (1986: 470–80) showed that "studies exploiting the cross-sectional variations in centrally allocated program intensities to evaluate programs . . . will produce misleading conclusions about program effectiveness" if there is a "compensatory pattern of program placement." Child allowance policies were set by the parish rather than a central authority, but it is possible that the generosity of allowances was systematically related to parish prosperity. In fact, the generosity of child allowances was negatively related to the level of agricultural laborers' income (see Table 5.3). However, the direction of causality is not obvious. Farmers might have reduced laborers' wages in response to the existence of child allowances (see above, Chapter 4).

[11] According to Richard Wall (1984: 463), in the late eighteenth and early nineteenth centuries "marriage entail[ed] for most a new household and determine[d], together with service patterns . . . the number of children who remain[ed] with their parents into their twenties."

Table 5.1. *Definition of variables*

BIRTHRATE	=	number of births per 100 families in parish
INCOME	=	annual income of adult male agricultural laborers
DENSITY	=	density of population in parish (population/acres)
INFMORT	=	number of deaths of infants aged 0–4 per 100 live births
HOUSING	=	ratio of families to inhabited houses in parish
CHILD3	=	dummy variable equal to 1 if parish began child allowance payments at three children
CHILD4	=	dummy variable equal to 1 if parish began child allowance payments at four children
CHILD5	=	dummy variable equal to 1 if parish began child allowance payments at five or more children
ALLOTMENT	=	dummy variable equal to 1 if laborers have allotments of farm land
CINDUSTRY	=	dummy variable equal to 1 if cottage industry exists in the parish
PRCNTAG	=	percentage of adult males employed in agriculture
LONDON	=	distance from London

The specific model to be estimated is

$$\text{BIRTHRATE} = \beta_0 + \beta_1\text{INCOME} + \beta_2\text{DENSITY} + \beta_3\text{HOUSING} + \beta_4\text{CHILD3} + \beta_5\text{CHILD4} + \beta_6\text{CHILD5} + \beta_7\text{ALLOTMENT} + \beta_8\text{CINDUSTRY} + \beta_9\text{INFMORT} \tag{1}$$

The variables are defined in Table 5.1.

The expected impact of each explanatory variable should be briefly noted. Agricultural laborers' annual wage income is included to test the Malthusian hypothesis that, other things equal, an increase in income caused birth rates to increase. Density is a measure of "population pressure"; high population density implies a low land–labor ratio (Mokyr 1985a: 45–6). I expect density to have a negative effect on birth rates.[12]

The variables CHILD3 through CHILD5 test Malthus's hypothesis that child allowances had a positive effect on birth rates. The calcula-

[12] Studies of the demographic transition often have found birth rates to be negatively related to the proportion of the work force in agriculture. I have not included the proportion of the work force in agriculture as an explanatory variable because it is highly correlated with density.

tions in Section 2 suggest that the effect of allowances will be positive, but should decline in magnitude as the number of children at which relief began increases. It is not possible to determine whether child allowances increased birth rates by raising marital fertility or by lowering the age at marriage.[13] Malthus believed that the effect of child allowances on birth rates occurred mainly through changes in nuptiality (see Section 1, above). His hypothesis is supported by the recent work of the Cambridge Group for the History of Population and Social Structure, which found that "marital fertility . . . shows no evidence of significant fluctuation . . . from the sixteenth to the nineteenth centuries. Nuptiality, in contrast, varied substantially over time" (Wrigley 1983: 131).[14]

Malthus also believed that birth rates were affected by the availability of housing and allotments of land for rural laborers. He claimed that the "principal reason" why poor relief did not cause birth rates to increase "so much as might naturally be expected" was because "the difficulty of procuring habitations" acted as a check to early marriages (1807b: 39–40). As a test of this hypothesis, I included the ratio of families to inhabited houses as an explanatory variable. A negative coefficient for HOUSING would support Malthus's claim.

Malthus was opposed to the policy of granting allotments to poor able-bodied laborers, adopted by some parishes as a substitute for poor relief. In France and Ireland, the ready availability of small allotments resulted in an increase in population that was "the specific cause of the poverty and misery of the lower classes" (1807a: II, 374–5). Malthus concluded that a policy of guaranteed allotments "would be incomparably more powerful in encouraging a population beyond the demand for

[13] The published 1831 census returns contain no data on marriages. The unpublished (H.O. 71) returns contain parish-level data on the number of marriages per year, but not data on age at marriage.

[14] From 1775–99 to 1800–24, the average age at first marriage for females declined from 24.7 to 23.7 years (Wrigley 1981: 147). Levine (1984) presents data on age-specific marital fertility for 14 parishes from 1650 to 1799, which, in his opinion, suggest that the payment of allowances raised marital fertility. He compared age-specific marital fertility of women who married before age 25 with that of women who married after age 25 and found that from 1650–99 to 1750–99, "at the crucial later age-parities (35–39 and 40–44)" the fertility of early marriers "rises dramatically" relative to late marriers (1984: 23). Levine concluded that "these results lend comfort to the Malthusian equation of the Old Poor Law with declining prudence" (1984: 23). But the entire increase in fertility occurred from 1650–99 to 1700–49, a period when child allowances were extremely rare. From 1700–49 to 1750–99, the fertility of the later age-parities of early marriers relative to late marriers actually declined slightly. In any case, the effect of child allowances on marital fertility cannot be determined from Levine's data, because he says nothing about the administration of poor relief in the 14 parishes for which he has fertility data.

labour, than our present poor laws" (1807a: II, 376). The variable AL-LOTMENT is included in the regression to test this hypothesis.

The existence of employment opportunities in cottage industry should have had a positive effect on birth rates. By providing a source of income for females (and for males during slack seasons in agriculture), cottage industry made it easier to begin a household, and thus should have caused a reduction in the age of marriage.[15] Cottage industry also provided employment opportunities for children, increasing their economic value to their parents. It should be noted, however, that wage rates in cottage industry were significantly lower in the 1820s than during the eighteenth century, so that the effect of cottage industry on birth rates during 1826–30 might have been relatively small.[16]

The infant mortality rate should have a positive effect on the birth rate, because a decline in infant mortality reduced the number of births necessary to attain a desired number of surviving children. The infant mortality rate is defined as the number of deaths of children aged 0–4 per 100 births. Because the denominator of INFMORT is the numerator of the dependent variable, if the number of births is measured with error there will be a spurious negative relationship between the birth rate and the infant mortality rate.[17] The obvious way to correct the problem is to instrument infant mortality by some measure of female education or health conditions in the parish, but no suitable instruments could be obtained at the parish level of observation. However, if one is willing to assume that the measurement error in number of births is multiplicative, the estimating equation can be rewritten in such a way as to solve the problem. Rewrite equation (1) as

$$\log\left(\frac{\text{BIRTHS} \times \epsilon}{\text{FAM}}\right) = \beta_0 + \beta_1 \log\left(\frac{\text{IDEATHS}}{\text{BIRTHS} \times \epsilon}\right) + \beta_2 \log(X) + u$$

where ϵ is the measurement error associated with births, FAM is the number of families in the parish, IDEATHS is the number of infant deaths, and X refers to the other right-hand-side variables. I assume that

---

[15] Braun (1978) and Almquist (1979) found that cottage industry caused a reduction in females' age at marriage. However, Mokyr (1985a) concluded that the "female propensity to marry" in early-nineteenth-century Ireland was unaffected by cottage industry.

[16] For more information on the decline of cottage industry in the southeast, see Chapter 1, Section 3, and Pinchbeck (1930: 142–7, 156, 208, 221, 224–5).

[17] The remainder of the section develops an estimating procedure to correct for the possible spurious relationship between birth rates and infant mortality. The nonquantitative historian might want to skip this and go straight to the regression results in Section 4.

log(ϵ) has a mean of zero and that ϵ is uncorrelated with the other variables. This equation can in turn be rewritten

$$\log(\text{BIRTHS}) = \frac{\beta_0}{1+\beta_1} + \frac{1}{1+\beta_1} \log(\text{FAM}) + \frac{\beta_1}{1+\beta_1} \log(\text{IDEATHS})$$

$$+ \frac{\beta_2}{1+\beta_1} \log(X) + \{u - \log(\epsilon)\} \tag{2}$$

Equation (2) can be estimated using nonlinear least squares. One can thereby directly estimate β_1, which represents an unbiased estimate of the effect of infant mortality on the birth rate. Note that there is a testable overidentifying restriction in equation (2): The coefficients on log(FAM) and log(IDEATHS) are different functions of the same parameter, namely, β_1. The restriction can be tested with a standard F-test (Gallant 1987: 56).

It is possible that infant mortality was endogenous. Evidence that "probabilities of survival are poorer for births to older women and women of higher parities" suggests that the birth rate had a positive effect on the infant mortality rate (Brass and Barrett 1978: 210). If, in addition, infant mortality was negatively related to income and child allowances, as one might expect, then assuming that infant mortality was exogenous would lead to an underestimate of the effect of income and child allowances on birth rates. Unfortunately, the lack of instruments for infant mortality mentioned above precludes testing whether infant mortality was endogenous.

4. Regression Results

The results obtained from estimating equations (1) and (2) are given in Table 5.2. The value of the F-test statistic implies that the overidentifying restriction in equation (2) cannot be rejected at the 5% confidence level.[18] The major difference between the two regressions lies in the behavior of infant mortality. The coefficient of INFMORT is negative, although not significant, in equation (1), and positive and significantly different from zero in equation (2). This result suggests that there may be a spurious negative relationship between the birth rate and the infant mortality rate due to measurement error, as discussed in Section

[18] The value of the F-statistic is 3.625, while the 5% critical value for $F(1,200)$ is 3.89.

Table 5.2. *The determinants of birth rates*

	Ordinary least squares Double-log specification			Nonlinear least squares		
	β̂	*t* Statistic	Prob > |*t*|	β̂	*t* Statistic	Prob > |*t*|
CONSTANT	1.12	2.06	0.041	−2.81	4.28	0.0001
INCOME	0.45	2.95	0.004	0.44	2.40	0.017
DENSITY	−0.09	2.70	0.007	−0.10	2.52	0.013
INFMORT	−0.06	1.17	0.242	0.38	5.82	0.0001
CHILD3	0.13	2.24	0.026	0.25	3.67	0.0003
CHILD4	0.11	2.15	0.033	0.17	2.64	0.009
CHILD5	0.09	1.50	0.124	0.17	2.25	0.025
HOUSING	−0.19	1.62	0.106	−0.28	1.94	0.054
ALLOTMENT	0.001	0.03	0.981	0.01	0.21	0.838
CINDUSTRY	0.04	0.76	0.446	−0.06	0.91	0.364
R^2	0.124					
N	214			214		

3. The results for the other variables are qualitatively similar between the two regressions. Therefore I will focus on equation (2) in my discussion of the results.[19]

The provision of child allowances had a positive effect on birth rates, suggesting that parents did indeed take economic factors into account when making decisions concerning family size. The quantitative impact of child allowances is large. Parishes that began allowances at three children experienced birth rates 25% greater than those of parishes without allowances, other things equal. The effect of allowances was smaller in parishes that began relief at four or more children. Birth rates were 17% higher in parishes that began relief at four children than in parishes without child allowances. Surprisingly, the effect of child allowances was as large in parishes that began allowances at five (or more) children as in parishes that began allowances at four children.

The large effect of allowances that began at five or more children is difficult to reconcile with the analysis in Section 2. Two possible explanations for the result come to mind. First, the age of children at which

---

[19] The low R^2s in Tables 5.2 and 5.3 are typical for cross-sectional regressions (Pindyck and Rubinfeld 1976: 37). They simply show that there was much random variation across parishes in birth rates. For the purposes of this analysis it is the size of the *t*-statistics, not the R^2, that is important.

relief stopped might have been positively correlated with the number of children at which relief began. Parishes that began allowances at five children might have continued relief as long as the eldest child remained under age 13 or 14, rather than 10 or 12. Second, the average spacing of births could have been affected by the administration of child allowances. In order to obtain relief for longer periods, families might have reduced birth intervals, perhaps by a reduction in the length of time children were breast-fed.[20] Unfortunately, data do not exist to test either of these hypotheses.

Three other Malthusian hypotheses are supported by the data. First, agricultural laborers' annual income had a positive effect on fertility; birth rates increased by 4.4% in response to a 10% increase in income, other things equal. Second, birth rates were checked by the unavailability of housing. A 10% increase in the ratio of families to inhabited houses resulted in a 2.8% decline in the birth rate.[21] Third, density had a negative effect on birth rates. A 10% increase in density resulted in a 1.0% decline in the birth rate.

There is no support for Malthus's contention that birth rates increased in response to the availability of allotments. However, it should be pointed out that Malthus's comments concerning the effect of allotments were directed against Arthur Young's (1800: 77) plan to grant each rural laborer with three or more children "half an acre of land for potatoes; and grass enough to feed one or two cows." Responses from southeastern parishes to the Rural Queries suggest that the typical laborer's allotment was no larger than an eighth of an acre. Thus, one could argue that allotments were simply too small to have a significant effect on birth rates.

Cottage industry did not have a significant effect on birth rates. It was mentioned above that wage rates in cottage industry had been declining since the late eighteenth century. The insignificance of CINDUSTRY suggests that the employment opportunities in cottage industry available to children were too small by the late 1820s to affect parents' decisions concerning family size.

---

[20] Evidence from nineteenth-century Europe and currently developing countries shows that "the practice of nursing increases the length of [birth] intervals by an estimated 15–33 percent" (Van Ginneken 1974: 201). Suppose that allowances were given to families with five children under age 12. A reduction in birth intervals from 30 to 21 months would increase the present value of an allowance to a laborer with five children from £7.6 to £17.7.

[21] This result also can be interpreted as support for Lindert's hypothesis that the demand for children is negatively related to the price of housing, since children are a space-intensive commodity.

5. A Test of the Exogeneity of Child Allowances

Up to this point I have ignored an important question (as did Malthus): Why did some parishes adopt child allowance policies while others did not, and why did the generosity of relief differ across parishes granting allowances? In particular, was the adoption of child allowances an endogenous response to changing demographic patterns? It is possible that Malthus had the causation backward, that child allowances were a response to high birth rates.

The hypothesis that child allowances were not exogenous in the above regression model can be tested using a technique developed by Durbin and Wu (Nakamura and Nakamura 1981).[22] The test consists of two parts. First, a model is estimated to explain cross-parish variations in child allowance policies, using as right-hand-side variables all the other explanatory variables from the regression model in Section 3 plus one or more instruments. The model to explain birth rates is then reestimated with the predicted values for child allowances, CALLOWHAT (obtained from the previous regression), included as a right-hand-side variable along with the original child allowance variable. If the coefficient of CALLOWHAT is significantly different from zero, then the null hypothesis that child allowance policy is exogenous is rejected.

It is useful to combine the child allowance dummies into one variable in order to perform the Durbin–Wu test. The variable CALLOW is equal to 0 if the parish did not use child allowances, 1 if allowances began at five or more children, 2 if allowances began at four children, and 3 if allowances began at three children. I used the proportion of the work force in agriculture and the parish's distance from London as instruments. The demand for child allowances should be positively related to the proportion of the work force in agriculture because of the seasonality of demand for labor in grain production. Distance from London is a proxy for cost of migration. As distance from London increased, the cost to farmers of maintaining an adequate peak-season labor force declined. Thus parishes' willingness to supply child allowances should be negatively related to distance from London.

The results of the test are given in Table 5.3. Columns 1–3 contain the estimated equation to explain variations in child allowance policies

---

[22] Nonquantitative historians might want to skip over this section. The test results support Malthus's (and my) hypothesis that child allowances were exogenous (that is, they were not a response to high birth rates).

Table 5.3. *Test for exogeneity of child allowances*

	Dependent variable: Child allowance			Dependent variable: Birth rate			Dependent variable: Birth rate		
	α̂	t Statistic	Prob > |t|	β̂	t Statistic	Prob > |t|	β̂	t Statistic	Prob > |t|
CONSTANT	8.26	3.67	0.0003	1.19	2.22	0.028	0.99	1.33	0.187
INCOME	−1.09	1.88	0.062	0.43	2.87	0.005	0.47	2.64	0.009
DENSITY	−0.05	0.30	0.766	−0.09	2.75	0.007	−0.08	2.19	0.030
INFMORT	−0.58	3.48	0.001	−0.05	1.20	0.231	−0.04	0.62	0.534
HOUSING	0.53	1.16	0.248	−0.19	1.61	0.110	−0.20	1.64	0.103
ALLOTMENT	−0.19	1.26	0.208	−0.001	0.02	0.982	0.003	0.07	0.943
CINDUSTRY	0.06	0.30	0.767	0.04	0.79	0.430	0.04	0.78	0.438
PRCNTAG	0.86	3.05	0.003						
LONDON	−0.21	1.13	0.262						
CALLOW				0.04	2.20	0.029	0.04	2.06	0.041
CALLOWHAT							0.03	0.38	0.706
R^2	0.134			0.119			0.119		
N	214			214			214		

across parishes. The instruments behave as expected, although the coefficient of LONDON is not significantly different from zero. The original regression to explain variations in birth rates is given in columns 4–6, while the regression including the predicted values for child allowances is given in columns 7–9. The coefficient of CALLOWHAT is not significantly different from zero, and its inclusion in the model has no effect on the coefficient of CALLOW. Child allowance policy is exogenous, as Malthus, and I, assumed.[23]

6. Implications for the Long-Term Increase in Birth Rates

Fertility increased sharply in England during the early nineteenth century. The crude birth rate (CBR) for the years 1799–1803 to 1829–33 was 10.8% higher than in 1749–53 to 1789–93 (Wrigley and Schofield 1981: 529). The CBR peaked during 1804–8 to 1819–23, 14.7% above its late-eighteenth-century level. The fertility increase occurred despite the fact that real wages of blue-collar workers remained roughly stable during 1755–1819 (Lindert and Williamson 1983: 13). Moreover, employment opportunities in cottage industry and the availability of land allotments for rural laborers declined throughout the period 1760–1830.

What caused fertility to increase at a time when real family income was stable or declining? Wrigley and Schofield (1981: 438) contend that fertility responded to fluctuations in real wages "with a time lag of about 40 years." The lag existed because "the chief method of altering the general level of fertility was through the timing and incidence of marriage [which were altered] only when any one generation came to perceive its circumstances as significantly better or worse than those of its predecessor" (1981: 419). This hypothesis has recently been called into question by Lindert (1983: 142–4), who found that wages lagged 50 years did not have

---

[23] The Durbin–Wu test also was performed with the unemployment rate included as an additional instrument in the equation to explain cross-parish differences in child allowance policies. The demand for child allowances should be positively related to the unemployment rate. Unemployment data were obtained from question 6 of the 1832 Rural Queries. Unfortunately, data were available for only 165 of the 214 parishes included in the sample. The coefficient for unemployment is positive and significantly different from zero at the 2% level. However, the addition of the unemployment rate as an instrument does not improve the performance of CALLOWHAT in the equation to explain variations in birth rates. The coefficient of CALLOWHAT remains insignificant, and its inclusion has no effect on the coefficient of CALLOW.

a statistically significant effect on birth rates between 1661 and 1871.[24] Lindert (1983: 144–5) contends that the early-nineteenth-century increase in fertility was largely illusory, a result of the underestimation of seventeenth- and eighteenth-century births by Wrigley and Schofield.

The above results suggest that the early-nineteenth-century increase in fertility was partly a result of the increased generosity of poor relief and, in particular, the widespread adoption of child allowance policies. The overall effect of child allowances on birth rates can be estimated using the regression coefficients for CHILD3 through CHILD5 from Table 5.2 and data on the administration of child allowances from the 1832 Rural Queries. Specifically, the increase in the birth rate is given by

$$\Delta \text{BIRTHRATE} = \Sigma_i \alpha_i [p_{0i}(0) + p_{1i}(b_1) + p_{2i}(b_2) + p_{3i}(b_3)]$$

where i refers to region; α_i is the proportion of England's population contained in region i; p_1, p_2, and p_3 are the proportion of parishes beginning allowances at three, four, and five or more children; p_0 is the proportion of parishes without child allowances; and b_1, b_2, and b_3 give the percentage increase in the birth rate resulting from allowances beginning at three, four, and five or more children. Estimates of p_0 through p_3 for each region in England in 1832 are given in Table 5.4. Combining these with the estimates of b_1, b_2, and b_3 obtained from the regression analysis, and assuming that the values of b_1 through b_3 did not vary across regions, we can estimate the effect of child allowances on birth rates in 1832. I conclude that the birth rate in 1832 was 8.7% higher than it would have been without child allowances.

The only other source of data on the use of child allowances is an 1824 questionnaire drawn up by the Select Committee on Labourers' Wages. The extent of child allowances in 1824 is given in column 6 of Table 5.4. Child allowances were more widespread in 1824 than in 1832 in all regions, but especially in the north, northwest, and Midlands. Assuming that the values of b_1 through b_3 and the relative number of parishes beginning relief at three, four, and five or more children remained constant from 1824 to 1832, the existence of child allowances caused birth rates to increase by 14.2% in 1824, other things equal.

[24] Martha Olney (1983) also questioned Wrigley and Schofield's conclusion. She estimated that the average lag length between changes in real wages and changes in birth rates during the eighteenth century was between 12 and 16 years (1983: 75–6). However, Olney's results also cannot explain the sharp increase in birth rates in the early nineteenth century.

Table 5.4. *Extent of child allowances by region*

Region	Parishes not giving child allowances in 1832 (%)	Parishes giving child allowances in 1832, beginning at			% of population in 1831	Parishes not giving child allowances in 1824 (%)	% of population in 1821
		3 children (%)	4 children (%)	5 or more children (%)			
Southeast	20.2	28.7	34.7	16.4	22.9	8.2	23.4
South	23.7	28.8	39.1	8.4	5.4		5.7
Southwest	47.1	20.0	27.1	5.8	13.4	21.2	13.7
Midlands	66.8	8.3	15.6	9.3	21.6	24.0	21.6
Northwest	79.2	5.2	9.8	5.8	17.8	45.7	16.6
North	80.6	4.9	9.1	5.4	8.4	50.0	8.7
London[a]	80.0	7.2	8.7	4.1	10.5		10.2

[a]Data on the extent of child allowances in London are not available. I have assigned London conservative estimates of the percentage of parishes giving child allowances in 1824 and 1832.

Sources: Data on the administration of child allowances in 1832 were obtained from the answers to question 24 of the Rural Queries (Parl. Papers 1834: XXXI). Data on the administration of child allowances in 1824 were obtained from the answers to questions 2 and 3 of those distributed by the Select Committee on Labourers' Wages (Parl. Papers 1825: XIX). Data on the regional distribution of population were obtained from the 1831 and 1851 censuses.

What role did child allowances play in the fertility increase of the early nineteenth century? Elasticities obtained from the regression model can be used to estimate what would have happened to birth rates in the absence of child allowances. According to Wrigley and Schofield (1981: 529), the crude birth rate increased by 14.4% from 1779–83 to 1819–23. Lindert's (1983: 145) revision of the Wrigley–Schofield data suggests an increase in the CBR of 6.4% over this period. My model's estimate of the change in the CBR is obtained from the following equation:

$$\Delta \text{BIRTHRATE} = e_1(\Delta \text{INCOME}) + e_2(\Delta \text{DENSITY}) +$$
$$e_3(\Delta \text{HOUSING}) +$$
$$e_4(\Delta \text{CHILDALLOW}) +$$
$$e_5(\Delta \text{INFMORT})$$

where Δ represents the percentage change in a variable from 1781 to 1821, e_i is the elasticity of the birth rate with respect to variable i, and $e_4(\Delta \text{CHILDALLOW})$ represents the overall effect of child allowances on the birth rate. Real annual earnings for blue-collar workers increased by approximately 14%, density increased by 63%, and infant mortality declined by 9% during this period.[25] I assume that no child allowances existed in 1779–83, that the effect of child allowances on birth rates in 1819–23 was equal to its estimated effect in 1824, and that the ratio of families to inhabited houses increased by 10–20% from 1781 to 1821.[26] Given these assumptions, the model estimates that the CBR increased by 5.0–7.8% from 1779–83 to 1819–23. If child allowance policies had not been adopted, the model predicts that the CBR would have *declined* by 6.4–9.2%, other things equal.[27]

[25] Real earnings data are from Lindert and Williamson (1983: 7; 1985: 148). An estimate of the infant mortality rate in the 1780s was obtained from Wrigley (1977: 310). I assume that the infant mortality rate for 1819–23 was equal to the rate for 1839–42, the earliest years for which data are available from the Registrar General's office. The infant mortality data are taken from Mitchell and Deane (1962: 36).

[26] According to Ashton (1963: 41–9) there was a serious housing shortage in the years following the Napoleonic Wars. Rapid population growth and urbanization during the previous decades had resulted in a large increase in the demand for housing, while the rate of construction of new houses had been slowed down by "a quarter of a century of war" and by the inordinately high level of building costs in the 1820s. The evidence presented by Ashton suggests that the ratio of families to inhabited houses increased sharply from 1779–83 to 1819–23.

[27] The above estimates do not take account of another possible effect of child allowances on the labor market. Farmers might have responded to the existence of child allowances by reducing their wage payments to laborers to a level just high enough to support a family of two or three children. In Chapter 4, I determined that the existence of child allowances caused a reduction of £1.36 in agricultural laborers' annual income. Given

Thus, if the Wrigley–Schofield numbers are correct, the adoption of child allowance policies after 1795 accounts for 60.2–68.3% of the gap between the actual change in birth rates and the model's predicted change (assuming child allowances were not adopted). If Lindert's estimates are correct, child allowances account for 91.0–110.9% of the gap. The conclusion to be reached is clear: Whether one believes Wrigley and Schofield or Lindert, the early-nineteenth-century increase in birth rates cannot be understood without taking child allowance policies into account.

Changes in the administration of poor relief after 1824 also were reflected in fertility rates. In particular, the stability of fertility after 1829–33 cannot be explained without taking into account the effect of Parliament's 1834 decision to abolish outdoor relief and hence child allowances. From 1829–33 to 1849–53, the crude birth rate increased by only 0.4%, despite a 25% increase in real wage rates of blue-collar workers.[28] My model estimates that the CBR increased by 2.3% over the period. If the use of child allowances in 1849–53 had remained at its 1832 level, the model predicts that the CBR would have increased by 11.0%. In other words, the birth rate remained stable only because the positive effect on fertility of a 25% increase in laborers' income was largely offset by the negative effect resulting from the elimination of child allowances.[29]

In sum, the results suggest that movements in the birth rate during the first half of the nineteenth century cannot be understood without taking into account changes in the administration of poor relief. Changes in the use of child allowances largely explain the increase in fertility from 1749–93 to 1804–23 and its stability from 1829–33 to 1849–53.

my estimate that 73% of English parishes used child allowances in 1824, the typical laborer's income would have increased by £0.99 in the absence of child allowances. According to the model, the increase in income would have resulted in a 0.8% increase in the crude birth rate. With the inclusion of allowances' effect on income, the model predicts that the CBR would have declined by 5.6–8.4% from 1779–83 to 1819–23 in the absence of child allowances.

[28] Birth rate data are from Wrigley and Schofield (1981: 529). Earnings data are from Lindert and Williamson (1983: 7; 1985: 148). Infant mortality increased by 5.2%, density increased by 29.3%, and the ratio of families to inhabited houses declined by 3.5% during this period. Infant mortality data are from Mitchell and Deane (1962: 36). Data on density, number of families, and inhabited houses are from the 1831 and 1851 censuses.

[29] Following the reasoning in footnote 27, part of the increase in laborers' income from 1829–33 to 1849–53 might have been in response to the elimination of child allowances. If the use of allowances had remained at its 1832 level, the typical laborer's income would have been £0.60 lower in 1851. Including this adjustment, the model estimates that the crude birth rate would have increased by 10.4% from 1829–33 to 1849–53 if child allowances had remained in use.

7. Conclusion

There are two important conclusions to be drawn from this chapter. First, Malthus's hypothesis that the use of child allowances had a positive effect on birth rates is correct. This result runs strongly counter to Huzel's conclusion (1980: 380) that "the Malthusian proposition should . . . be turned on its head." Huzel based his conclusion on simple comparisons of birth rates and child allowance policies, without controlling for other determinants of fertility. But the regression analysis has shown that income, infant mortality, crowding, and density had a statistically significant impact on birth rates and thus that Huzel's empirical work does not yield an accurate measure of the effects of child allowances.

Second, the widespread adoption of child allowances after 1795 appears to have been a major cause of the increase in birth rates during the first two decades of the nineteenth century. The seeming anomaly of birth rates increasing during a period of stable or falling real income largely disappears when Poor Law policy is brought into the analysis.

6

THE POOR LAW, MIGRATION, AND ECONOMIC GROWTH

Historians have debated the microeconomic effects of the Old Poor Law for nearly two centuries. The analysis in Chapters 3 and 4, along with the earlier studies by Blaug (1963; 1964), Baugh (1975), and Digby (1978), has shown that the granting of outdoor relief to able-bodied laborers did not have the disastrous consequences for the rural parish economy that contemporary observers and many historians had claimed. However, revisionist historians have yet to confront a second criticism of the Old Poor Law: that at the macro level outdoor relief caused a reduction in the rate of economic growth by slowing the rate of migration from the agricultural south to London and the industrial northwest. Because the marginal product of labor was significantly higher in industrial cities than in agricultural areas, the Poor Law might have caused the early-nineteenth-century British economy to forgo a large free lunch by fostering an inefficient allocation of labor.

One explanation for the large rural–urban wage gaps that existed during the first half of the nineteenth century was that the payment of outdoor relief to unemployed or underemployed agricultural laborers reduced their incentive to migrate to industrial areas. According to Arthur Redford (1964: 93–4), "the mistaken and lax administration of poor relief in the southern counties" before 1834 was a major cause of "the immobility of the southern agricultural labourer."[1] Karl Polanyi (1944: 94) agreed that the Poor Law slowed rural–urban migration, but his

[1] Redford's conclusion has been echoed in several of the leading textbooks on British economic history. For instance, T. S. Ashton (1964: 77) maintained that the system of outdoor relief "reduced the pressure on the labourers to move [and therefore] led to an over-population of the agricultural villages." Phyllis Deane (1979: 153) concluded that "a lax parish-relief system . . . constituted a positive disincentive to migration on the part of responsible labourers and their families. . . . The consequence was that while agricultural unemployment and under-employment were acute in the stagnating areas of the south and east, there were recurrent scarcities of labour in the expanding industrial towns of the north and west."

173

story differed from that of Redford. By the beginning of the nineteenth century, Polanyi argued, "agriculture could not compete with town wages. . . . Methods had to be found which would . . . prevent the draining off of rural labor, and raise agricultural wages without overburdening the farmer. Such a device was the Speenhamland Law." Both Redford and Polanyi maintained that relief expenditures raised laborers' annual incomes above the marginal product of labor. Unlike Redford, however, Polanyi did not dismiss the system of outdoor relief as mistaken. Rather, he argued that farmers used outdoor relief to raise their workers' incomes above the marginal product of labor without increasing their own contributions to the "wages fund."

Neither Redford nor Polanyi offered any evidence that the use of outdoor relief by rural parishes significantly slowed migration to industrial areas. This chapter presents an empirical analysis of the effect of poor relief on rural–urban migration and economic growth. An estimate of the Poor Law's effect on labor mobility is obtained by determining the extent to which relief payments raised agricultural laborers' incomes above the marginal product of labor and comparing this increase to rural–urban wage gaps. Because the results obtained from this procedure depend critically on one's assumptions, three models of the economic role of poor relief are presented.

A worker's income is assumed to consist of wages and poor relief. I assume that workers made migration decisions based on their overall income, and that they were indifferent about the source of their income. The three models developed below all assume that in the absence of poor relief, farmers would have paid laborers a wage equal to the marginal product of labor. The models differ in their assumptions about the effect of poor relief on wage rates, and therefore about the relationship of the observed wage to the marginal product of labor. These different assumptions yield very different conclusions about the effect of poor relief on rural–urban migration. If poor relief had no effect on wages, any relief payments raised workers' income above the marginal product of labor, so that the effect of poor relief on laborers' income and therefore on the rate of rural–urban migration was relatively large. If, on the other hand, farmers reduced wages below the marginal product of labor in response to relief payments to able-bodied workers, the effect of poor relief on laborers' income and on migration was correspondingly smaller.

The first model assumes that wage rates were unaffected by poor relief, so that a worker's income was equal to the marginal product of labor plus whatever relief benefits he received. This model resembles the one implicitly used by Redford. It yields an upper-bound estimate of the effect of poor relief on mobility.

The second model assumes that wage rates and poor relief were partial substitutes. Farmers are assumed to reduce wage rates below the marginal product of labor by precisely the amount of their per-worker contribution to the poor rate. A laborer's income therefore was equal to the marginal product of labor plus the share of his relief benefits paid by non-labor-hiring taxpayers. This model resembles Polanyi's analysis in that poor relief increased laborers' income but did not affect farmers' labor costs. It yields a significantly smaller estimate of the effect of poor relief on migration than the first model.

The third model follows the analysis of the rural labor market developed in Chapter 3. Farmers are assumed to use the Poor Law to reduce their labor costs rather than to increase their workers' income. They offer workers an implicit contract consisting of wage payments and poor relief that yields an expected income equal to the marginal product of labor. However, farmers' expenditures per worker are less than the marginal product of labor, because part of the poor rate is paid by non-labor-hiring taxpayers. Farmers' profits increase as a result of the Poor Law, while laborers' income and thus migration are unaffected.

1. The Effect of Poor Relief on Migration: The Redford Model

The first model assumes that farmers paid their workers a wage rate equal to the marginal product of labor. Any relief payments to able-bodied laborers therefore raised their income above the marginal product of labor. Such a policy was clearly inefficient from the point of view of labor-hiring farmers, because a farmer's total payment to each worker would exceed the marginal product of labor by an amount eB, where B is equal to the worker's relief benefits, and e equals the farmer's share of the poor rate. Although it is difficult to believe that parishes dominated by labor-hiring farmers would adopt such a relief policy, Redford and others have argued that relief was administered in this manner from 1795 to 1834.

The effect of poor relief on laborers' income can be estimated by calculating the ratio of annual relief benefits per agricultural laborer to annual wage income. Because it is not possible to determine what share of a parish's expenditures on poor relief went to agricultural laborers and their families, I calculated the benefit to wage–income ratio in three ways, assuming that payments to agricultural laborers' families constituted 33%, 50%, and 67% of total relief expenditures.[2] The results of these calculations are given for 15 southeastern counties for the year 1831 in Table 6.1.[3] The estimated effect of poor relief on the annual income of agricultural laborers varied significantly across counties. In Sussex, the county with the highest per capita relief expenditures in England in 1831, poor relief raised workers' annual income 12.6–25.3% above the marginal product of labor, while, at the other end of the scale, laborers in Hertford experienced a 7.7–15.4% increase in income as a result of the Poor Law.

To judge the effect of poor relief on rural–urban migration, the results in Table 6.1 must be compared with some measure of rural–urban wage differentials. I focus on wage gaps between London and the rural south, because London was the destination of most of the southern agricultural laborers who chose to migrate.[4] E. H. Hunt (1973: 5) maintains that "building labourers' [wage] rates are a good guide to the relative level of all unskilled wages in any particular district." In 1831, builders' laborers in London earned between 21s. and 22.5s. per week (Bowley 1900a: 83). Assuming a 44-week year, this implies an annual income of about £47.5.[5] The average expected wage income for agricultural laborers in 15

[2] Despite the extensive literature on the Old Poor Law, very little is known about the composition of the "pauper host." The Poor Law acted as "a welfare state in miniature" (Blaug 1964: 229), relieving not only able-bodied laborers but also aged and infirm persons, widows, and orphans. Unfortunately, available data do not enable one to distinguish among types of recipients. Instead of trying to estimate the share of relief expenditures going to agricultural laborers' families, I chose three plausible values for it (33%, 50%, and 67%), and provide three estimates of each result in Tables 6.1 to 6.6. For the counties included in the analysis, the share of adult males employed as agricultural laborers in 1831 varied from 31% to 51%. For the southeast as a whole, the share of adult males employed as agricultural laborers was 41% in 1831. These data, along with the fact that able-bodied laborers were not the sole recipients of relief, suggest that the actual share of relief expenditures going to agricultural laborers and their families was somewhere between 33% and 50%. The Webbs (1929: 89) concluded that "the bulk of the paupers were not, as the Commission seems to have imagined, either able-bodied men, or even wives and children of such men, but persons actually incapacitated by old age or laid low by sickness, with [their] dependents."

[3] Poor relief data are available only for yearlong periods running from March 25 of one year to March 25 of the next. Thus, the 1831 data are actually for the year beginning March 25, 1831.

[4] According to Hunt (1973: 281–2), "a large part of the southern labour force appears to have operated in a particularly restricted market. They moved overwhelmingly in one direction – towards London."

[5] Henry Mayhew estimated in 1851 that 30% of workers in the London building trade were unemployed during slack seasons (cited in Gareth Stedman Jones 1971: 41). If the slack season was six months long, a laborer's expected number of weeks worked per year would be 26 + 0.7(26), or 44.2.

Table 6.1. *Effect of poor relief on agricultural laborers' income:*
Model 1

County	Expected annual wage income (in £)	Estimated relief expenditures per agricultural laborer (in £)			% increase in laborers' income as a result of poor relief		
		(a)	(b)	(c)	(a)	(b)	(c)
Bedford	25.50	2.22	3.33	4.44	8.7	13.1	17.4
Berkshire	27.30	2.73	4.09	5.46	10.0	15.0	20.0
Buckingham	26.95	2.88	4.32	5.76	10.7	16.0	21.4
Cambridge	26.18	2.21	3.31	4.42	8.4	12.6	16.9
Essex	26.48	2.42	3.63	4.84	9.1	13.7	18.3
Hertford	28.39	2.18	3.27	4.36	7.7	11.5	15.4
Huntingdon	29.36	2.30	3.45	4.60	7.8	11.7	15.7
Kent	32.26	3.36	5.04	6.72	10.4	15.6	20.8
Norfolk	28.27	2.83	4.25	5.66	10.0	15.0	20.0
Northampton	24.96	2.89	4.34	5.78	11.6	17.4	23.2
Oxford	25.03	2.85	4.27	5.70	11.4	17.1	22.8
Southampton	26.95	3.12	4.67	6.24	11.6	17.3	23.2
Suffolk	26.00	2.82	4.23	5.64	10.8	16.3	21.7
Sussex	28.73	3.63	5.45	7.26	12.6	19.0	25.3
Wiltshire	22.25	2.69	4.03	5.38	12.1	18.1	24.2

Note: Columns labeled (a) through (c) assume that 33%, 50%, and 67%, respectively, of relief expenditures were paid to agricultural laborers and their families.
Sources: Wage income data were obtained from Chapter 4, Table 4.1. Data on relief expenditures were obtained from Parl. Papers (1839: XLIV, 4–7).

southeastern counties (excluding the home counties of Middlesex and Surrey) was £27.1 in 1832. Adjusting for regional differences in the cost of living, the unskilled wage differential between London and the south for 1832 was 60.2%.[6] Similar wage gaps existed between the rural south and the industrial northwest.[7] The calculated wage gap between London and each southeastern county is given in column 1 of Table 6.2. Columns

[6] Cost-of-living data were obtained from N. F. R. Crafts (1982: 62). I used his "southern agricultural" index with rent weighted as 6.5% of total expenditures.
[7] Manchester builders' laborers earned 17s.–18s. per week in 1839 (Bowley 1900b: 310). The average weekly wage of southern agricultural laborers was 9.7s. in 1837 (Bowley 1900a: table at end of book). The real wage gap between Manchester and the rural south was about 66%.

Table 6.2. Effect of poor relief on rural–urban wage gaps: Model 1

County	% real wage gap vis-à-vis London	% of wage gap eliminated by poor relief			% real wage gap (assuming a 15% disamenities premium)	% of wage gap eliminated by poor relief		
		(a)	(b)	(c)		(a)	(b)	(c)
Bedford	73.6	11.8	17.8	23.6	47.6	18.3	27.5	36.6
Berkshire	62.2	16.1	24.1	32.2	37.8	26.5	39.7	52.9
Buckingham	64.3	16.6	24.9	33.3	39.6	27.0	40.4	54.0
Cambridge	64.1	13.1	19.7	26.4	39.6	21.2	31.8	42.7
Essex	62.3	14.6	22.0	29.4	38.0	23.9	36.1	48.2
Hertford	55.9	13.8	20.6	27.5	32.5	23.7	35.4	47.4
Huntingdon	46.4	16.8	25.2	33.8	24.4	32.0	48.0	64.3
Kent	32.8	31.7	47.6	63.4	12.9	80.6	120.9	161.2
Norfolk	52.0	18.1	26.9	38.5	29.2	34.2	51.4	68.5
Northampton	66.8	17.4	26.0	34.7	41.8	27.8	41.6	55.5
Oxford	76.9	14.8	22.2	29.6	50.3	22.7	34.0	45.3
Southampton	59.0	19.7	29.3	39.3	35.2	33.0	49.1	65.9
Suffolk	65.3	16.5	25.0	33.2	40.5	26.7	40.2	53.6
Sussex	49.1	25.7	38.7	51.5	26.8	47.0	70.9	94.4
Wiltshire	97.7	12.4	18.5	24.8	68.1	17.8	26.6	35.5

Note: Columns labeled (a) through (c) assume that 33%, 50%, and 67%, respectively, of relief expenditures were paid to agricultural laborers and their families.
Sources: See text and Table 6.1.

2 through 4 contain estimates of the share of the wage gap eliminated by the payment of poor relief to able-bodied laborers.

What can be concluded about the effect of poor relief on labor mobility? If the share of relief expenditures paid to agricultural laborers was between 33% and 50%, poor relief eliminated, on average, 16–25% of the rural–urban wage gap. Although these results offer some support for Redford's hypothesis that the payment of poor relief to agricultural laborers hindered migration, large wage gaps remain after accounting for relief expenditures, suggesting that migration to London continued to be an attractive option for rural workers.

The results in Tables 6.1 and 6.2 can be used to estimate the loss in national product that the Poor Law caused by slowing rural–urban migration. I begin by estimating the potential gain to national product from eliminating the misallocation of labor between London and the southeastern agricultural counties. The dead-weight loss caused by labor misallocation can be seen in Figure 6.1, which depicts the labor market

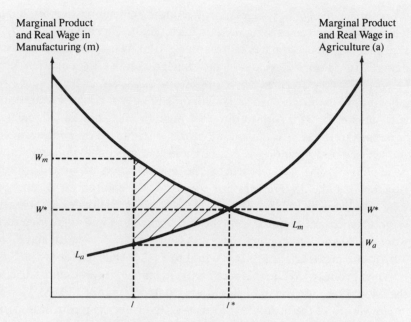

Figure 6.1. Rural–urban wage gaps and employment distribution.

in southern England in 1831. The demand curves for labor in urban unskilled occupations (manufacturing) and agriculture are represented by L_m and L_a. The optimal distribution of labor occurs at l^*, where $W_m = W_a = W^*$, that is, urban and rural wages are equal. Figure 6.1 shows, however, that the distribution of labor in southern England was suboptimal; there were $l - l^*$ too many (few) workers in agriculture (urban unskilled occupations), and there was a rural–urban wage gap equal to $W_m - W_a$. The size of the dead-weight loss caused by the labor misallocation is denoted by the shaded area in the figure.

To estimate the size of the dead-weight loss, suppose the demand for labor in agriculture and urban unskilled occupations can be written as

$$L_a = e^{\alpha_a} W_a^{\beta_a}$$

and

$$L_m = e^{\alpha_m} W_m^{\beta_m}$$

where L is the demand for labor, W is the wage rate, e is the exponential function, and a and m refer to agriculture and urban unskilled occupations, respectively. For simplicity, I assume that labor supply equals labor demand at the existing wage in each sector. Given data on L_a, L_m, W_a, and W_m, and estimates of β_a and β_m (the own-wage elasticities of demand for labor in agriculture and nonagriculture), the equations can be solved for e^{α_a} and e^{α_m}. The equilibrium wage rate in the absence of labor misallocation is then obtained by adding the equations together and solving for W^*. Substituting W^* into the original labor demand equations, one can determine the optimal distribution of labor between the two sectors, L_a^* and L_m^*. It is then a simple process to determine the dead-weight social loss caused by the misallocation of labor between London and the 15 southeastern counties. My choices for β_a and β_m follow Williamson (1987: 659), whose "best guess" estimates of the own-wage elasticity of demand for labor in agriculture and nonagriculture were -1.10 and -0.75, respectively. Assuming that $\beta_a = -1.0$ and $\beta_m = -0.75$, the dead-weight loss was equal to £462,000 in 1831, or 0.14% of national product.[8] While this is a small percentage, it represents 5.6% of the annual rate of growth of commodity output for 1821 to 1831.[9]

How much of the dead-weight loss resulted from the payment of poor relief to agricultural laborers? If poor relief eliminated 16–25% of the rural–urban wage gap, one could argue that no more than 25% of the dead-weight loss can be attributed to the Poor Law. In other words, the decline in migration caused by poor relief reduced national income by at most £115,500 in 1831.[10]

---

[8] Data on national product were obtained from Deane and Cole (1967: 166). Williamson provided a range of estimates for the labor demand elasticities: $\beta_a = -0.68$ and -1.10; $\beta_m = -0.25$, -0.75, and -3.0. I also estimated the loss in national product for other values of the labor demand elasticities. For $\beta_a = -0.5$ and $\beta_m = -0.75$, the estimated dead-weight loss was £335,000. For $\beta_a = -0.5$ and $\beta_m = -1.0$, the estimated dead-weight loss was £377,000. For $\beta_a = -1.0$ and $\beta_m = -1.0$, the estimated dead-weight loss equaled £546,000. For $\beta_a = -0.5$ and $\beta_m = -1.5$, the estimated dead-weight loss was £430,000. Obviously, the choice of own-wage elasticities does not have a large effect on the estimated loss in national product.

[9] Commodity output grew at an annual rate of 2.50% from 1821 to 1831 (Crafts 1985: 47).

[10] The above calculations assume that the rural–urban wage gap that remained after poor relief benefits are taken into account reflects a disequilibrium in the labor market. A similar assumption is made by Williamson (1987: 671–2), who concludes that the English labor market "failed" in the early nineteenth century. Part of the wage gap, however, might reflect migration costs, rural–urban differences in labor quality, "greater job uncertainty or the [high] cost of job search" in urban areas, or a compensating wage differential needed to attract rural migrants "to locations of poorer environmental quality" (Williamson 1987: 657, 653). If so, then the above calculations overstate the total dead-weight loss caused by rural–urban wage gaps and understate the share of the dead-weight loss attributable to the Poor Law. The possibility that part of the rural–urban wage gap represented an "urban disamenities premium" is addressed later in this section.

For those who consider the above estimate to be too small, a second method for determining the dead-weight loss is offered. Given estimates of the elasticity of migration with respect to rural income and data on the actual number of migrants out of the southern agricultural counties, the number of migrants in the absence of poor relief can be estimated. Greenwood and Thomas (1973: 102) and Vedder and Cooper (1974: 134) estimated the income elasticity of migration in mid-nineteenth-century England using birthplace data from the 1851 and 1861 censuses; they found that a 10% increase in rural income reduced rural out-migration by 2.92–4.98%. Combining these estimates with the estimates in Table 6.1 that poor relief increased laborers' income, on average, by 10.2–20.4%, I conclude that the rate of out-migration from the rural south declined by 3.0–10.2% as a result of the Poor Law.

Deane and Cole (1967: 118) estimate that 515,000 persons migrated out of the southern counties between 1801 and 1831, mostly to London. To get an upper-bound estimate of the impact of poor relief, suppose that 600,000 persons migrated during the period, or 20,000 a year. It follows that the payment of poor relief to rural laborers caused an an-nual reduction in migration of 619 to 2,272 persons from the rural south. Given an average real wage gap of £16.3 in 1831, the annual dead-weight loss attributable to poor relief was between £10,090 and £37,034. Even if the income elasticity of migration is assumed to be as high as -1.24 (the highest estimate cited in a survey article on migration in developing countries), the best-guess estimate of the annual dead-weight loss is only £76,300, or 0.02% of national product.[11]

Up to this point I have ignored the issue of urban disamenities. If part of the urban wage represented a "disamenities premium," the true rural–urban wage gap was smaller than 60.2%, and the percentage of the wage gap eliminated by poor relief was correspondingly larger. Sup-pose that 15% of the wage paid to unskilled London laborers was in fact a compensating wage differential necessary to induce workers to live in London.[12] Column 5 of Table 6.2 contains estimates of the real wage gap between London and each southeastern county in 1831, as perceived by rural workers, and columns 6 to 8 contain estimates of the share of the wage gap eliminated by poor relief. If 33–50% of relief payments went

---

[11] The income elasticity of migration estimate was obtained from Todaro (1980: 380). The best-guess estimate assumes that 50% of relief expenditures went to agricultural laborers.
[12] Williamson (1987: 654) estimated that the urban disamenities premium was between 8% and 20% in the south of England in the 1830s.

to agricultural laborers, then the Poor Law eliminated 30–40% of the wage gap. However, with a 15% disamenities premium the total dead-weight loss caused by the misallocation of labor in the southeast was equal to only £182,800 in 1831. If 40% of the dead-weight loss can be attributed to the payment of poor relief to agricultural laborers, the decline in national income caused by the Poor Law was about £73,100 in 1831, or 0.02% of national income.

The above results all lead to the same conclusion. Even if all relief payments to agricultural laborers were in excess of their marginal product, there is no evidence that the Poor Law kept the English economy from enjoying a large free lunch associated with transferring workers from low-productivity agricultural jobs to high-productivity urban employment. Moreover, there are two reasons to believe that the above results significantly overestimate the effect of poor relief on migration and national product. First, I have assumed, for simplicity, that relief expenditures were distributed evenly among agricultural laborers. However, married men with large families received larger relief payments than single males or young married men, and young adults dominated the flow of migrants to English cities.[13] The most mobile group of rural laborers, therefore, was the group least affected by poor relief.

Second, the assumption that all relief payments were in excess of laborers' marginal product is almost certainly incorrect. Labor-hiring farmers dominated parish politics. They would not have adopted a system of poor relief that increased their expenditures per worker above the marginal product of labor. The second and third models assume that wage income and poor relief were substitutes. Farmers used the system of outdoor relief to reduce wage rates below the marginal product of labor. Rather than increase farmers' labor costs, the Poor Law either had no effect on farmers' costs or reduced them.

2. The Effect of Poor Relief on Migration: The Polanyi Model

The second model assumes that the total compensation package paid by farmers to their employees (consisting of wages and farmers' contribution to relief benefits) was equal to labor's marginal product; that is

$$W + eB = MP_\ell$$

---

[13] Williamson (1988: 304–5) estimated that 53.3% of the migrants into British cities in the 1840s were aged 15–29, while only 7.4% were aged 30 or older.

In other words, the system of outdoor relief enabled farmers to reduce their wage payments by an amount eB, equal to their contribution to the poor rate. Farmers' total expenditure on labor was not affected by the Poor Law, and the difference between laborers' income and their marginal product was determined solely by the contribution of non-labor-hiring taxpayers to the poor rate. A laborer's annual income is thus

$$W + B = MP_\ell + (1 - e)B$$

where $(1 - e)B$ is the relief payment per worker made by non-labor-hiring taxpayers. The percentage increase in workers' income above the marginal product of labor brought about by the Poor Law is given by

$$(1 - e)B/MP_\ell \equiv (1 - e)B/(W + eB)$$

Notice that this is precisely the solution to the problem of rising urban wage rates suggested by Polanyi; farmers used the Poor Law to raise their laborers' annual incomes without increasing their own payments to labor.

The effect of such a policy on rural–urban migration depends on the value of $(1 - e)$, the share of poor relief expenditures paid by local taxpayers other than labor-hiring farmers. I assume that non-labor-hiring taxpayers and landlords paid 20–33% of the poor rate in the typical agricultural parish.[14] Tables 6.3 and 6.4 contain estimates of the percentage increase in agricultural laborers' annual incomes caused by the Poor Law, and the percentage of the rural–urban wage gap eliminated by relief payments, for the same counties as before.[15] Table 6.3 assumes that taxpayers who did not hire labor paid 20% of the poor rate, while Table 6.4 assumes that non-labor-hiring taxpayers paid 33% of the poor rate.

The conclusion to be reached from the results is clear. Farmers may have attempted to use the Poor Law as a dam to "prevent the draining off of rural labor," as Polanyi contended, but such a policy could not

[14] These represent lower- and upper-bound estimates for the value of $(1 - e)$, obtained from Section 3 of Chapter 3.

[15] The differences in the size of rural–urban wage gaps between Tables 6.2, 6.3, and 6.4 follow from my assumption that the proper measure of the rural wage to be used in calculating wage gaps is the marginal product of labor in agriculture, because that is the wage that would have existed in the absence of poor relief. Table 6.2 assumes that the marginal product of labor was equal to the observed wage. Tables 6.3 and 6.4 assume that the marginal product of labor equaled $W + eB$, the observed wage plus the farmer's contribution to the worker's relief benefit. Thus, the marginal product of labor is larger in Tables 6.3 and 6.4 than in Table 6.2, and therefore the estimated rural–urban wage gaps are smaller in Tables 6.3 and 6.4 than in Table 6.2. The wage gaps differ between Tables 6.3 and 6.4 because I assume that $e = 0.80$ in Table 6.3 and that $e = 0.67$ in Table 6.4.

Table 6.3. *Effect of poor relief on agricultural laborers' income: Model 2*

County	Estimated increase in laborers' income as a result of poor relief (%)			% real wage gap vis-à-vis London[d]	% of wage gap eliminated by poor relief[d]
	(a)	(b)	(c)		
Bedford	1.6	2.4	3.1	57.2	4.2
Berkshire	1.9	2.7	3.4	44.8	6.0
Buckingham	2.0	2.8	3.6	45.6	6.1
Cambridge	1.6	2.3	3.0	49.1	4.7
Essex	1.7	2.5	3.2	46.3	5.4
Hertford	1.5	2.1	2.7	42.8	4.9
Huntingdon	1.5	2.1	2.8	33.8	6.2
Kent	1.9	2.8	3.6	18.1	15.5
Norfolk	1.7	2.5	3.4	28.9	8.7
Northampton	2.1	3.1	3.9	46.5	6.7
Oxford	2.1	3.0	3.9	55.6	5.4
Southampton	2.1	3.0	3.9	39.6	7.6
Suffolk	2.0	2.9	3.7	46.3	6.3
Sussex	2.3	3.3	4.2	29.5	11.2
Wiltshire	2.2	3.2	4.1	72.8	4.4

[d]The calculations in these columns are based on the assumption that 50% of relief expenditures were paid to agricultural laborers.
Note: All calculations in this table are based on the assumption that non-labor-hiring taxpayers paid 20% of the poor rate. Columns labeled (a) through (c) assume that 33%, 50%, and 67%, respectively, of relief expenditures were paid to agricultural laborers and their families.
Sources: See text and Table 6.1.

have been successful. On average, poor relief raised workers' incomes 1.9–5.9% above their marginal product. Even in generous Sussex, poor relief raised laborers' incomes only 2.3–7.1% above their marginal product. The effect of the Poor Law on national income was correspondingly small. If 50% of relief expenditures were paid to agricultural laborers, and non-labor-hiring taxpayers paid 20% of the poor rate, the marginal product of agricultural labor $(W + eB)$ in the southeast in 1831 was, on average, £30.4, and the total dead-weight loss caused by labor misallocation was equal to £279,000. The payment of poor relief to agricultural laborers eliminated about 7% of the rural–urban wage gap. Assuming

Table 6.4. *Effect of poor relief on agricultural laborers' income:*
Model 2

County	Estimated increase in laborers' income as a result of poor relief (%)			% real wage gap vis-à-vis London[d]	% of wage gap eliminated by poor relief[d]
	(a)	(b)	(c)		
Bedford	2.7	4.0	5.1	59.6	6.7
Berkshire	3.1	4.5	5.8	47.4	9.5
Buckingham	3.3	4.8	6.2	48.4	9.9
Cambridge	2.6	3.8	5.0	51.4	7.4
Essex	2.8	4.1	5.4	48.7	8.4
Hertford	2.4	3.5	4.6	44.8	7.8
Huntingdon	2.5	3.6	4.7	35.7	10.1
Kent	3.2	4.7	6.0	20.2	23.3
Norfolk	3.1	4.5	5.8	38.1	11.8
Northampton	3.5	5.1	6.6	49.5	10.3
Oxford	3.5	5.1	6.5	58.7	8.7
Southampton	3.5	5.1	6.6	42.5	12.0
Suffolk	3.3	4.8	6.3	49.1	9.8
Sussex	3.8	5.6	7.1	32.3	17.3
Wiltshire	3.7	5.3	6.9	76.4	6.9

[d]The calculations in these columns are based on the assumption that 50% of relief expenditures were paid to agricultural laborers.
Note: All calculations in this table are based on the assumption that non-labor-hiring taxpayers paid 33% of the poor rate. Columns labeled (a) through (c) assume that 33%, 50%, and 67%, respectively, of relief expenditures were paid to agricultural laborers and their families.
Sources: See text and Table 6.1.

that 7% of the dead-weight loss is attributable to poor relief, the decline in national income caused by the Poor Law was about £19,500 in 1831. If non-labor-hiring taxpayers paid 33% of the poor rate, the dead-weight loss attributable to the Poor Law was about £33,400 in 1831.

The impact of the Poor Law was even smaller if part of the London wage represented an urban disamenities premium. Columns 1 and 2 of Table 6.5 contain estimates of the wage gap between London and each southeastern county, as perceived by rural workers, assuming a 15% disamenities premium, and columns 3 and 4 contain estimates of the share of the wage gap eliminated by poor relief. If 50% of relief expen-

Table 6.5. *Effect of poor relief on rural–urban wage gaps: Model 2*

County	% real wage gap (assuming a 15% disamenities premium)		% of wage gap eliminated by poor relief	
	(a)	(b)	(a)	(b)
Bedford	33.6	35.7	7.1	11.2
Berkshire	23.1	25.3	11.7	17.8
Buckingham	23.7	26.1	11.8	18.4
Cambridge	26.7	28.7	8.6	13.2
Essex	24.4	26.4	10.2	15.5
Hertford	21.3	23.0	9.9	15.2
Huntingdon	13.8	15.4	16.0	23.4
Kent	0.4	2.2	700.0	213.6
Norfolk	15.4	17.4	16.2	25.9
Northampton	24.6	27.1	12.6	18.8
Oxford	32.3	34.9	9.3	14.6
Southampton	18.7	21.1	16.0	24.2
Suffolk	24.4	26.7	11.9	18.0
Sussex	10.1	12.5	32.7	44.8
Wiltshire	46.9	49.9	6.8	10.6

(a) assumes that non-labor-hiring taxpayers paid 20% of the poor rate.
(b) assumes that non-labor-hiring taxpayers paid 33% of the poor rate.
Note: All calculations in this table are based on the assumption that 50% of relief expenditures were paid to agricultural laborers.
Sources: See text and Table 6.1.

ditures were paid to agricultural laborers, and non-labor-hiring taxpayers paid 20% of the poor rate, then the payment of poor relief to agricultural laborers eliminated, on average, about 13% of the rural–urban wage gap.[16] The total dead-weight loss caused by labor misallocation was equal to £76,200. By eliminating 13% of the wage gap, the Poor Law caused national income to decline by about £9,900 in 1831.

[16] The result that poor relief eliminated more than 100% of the Kent–London wage gap suggests that agricultural workers in Kent were better off than unskilled London workers. And yet Kent experienced a net loss of population due to migration from 1801 to 1831 (Deane and Cole 1967: 109, 115). The probable explanation for this result is that the correct urban disamenities premium was smaller than 15%. If the disamenities premium was equal to 10%, the Poor Law eliminated 45.2% to 57.3% of the Kent–London wage gap.

3. The Effect of Poor Relief on Migration: Model Three

The results obtained in Section 2 show that the payment of poor relief to agricultural laborers had a trivial negative impact on labor mobility and national income. I contend that these estimates represent an upper-bound measure of the loss in national income caused by the Poor Law. The Polanyi model assumes that farmers' labor costs were unaffected by the Poor Law. Because wage income and poor relief were substitutes, farmers were able to reduce wage rates by an amount equal to their contribution to the poor rate. The model assumes that farmers' expenditures per worker equaled labor's marginal product. However, if labor-hiring farmers dominated parish politics, they could have used the Poor Law to reduce their expenditures per worker below the marginal product of labor. The third model assumes that the system of outdoor relief enabled farmers to reduce their labor costs and therefore caused farmers' profits to increase. The resulting increase in capital accumulation had a positive effect on economic growth.

The model is similar to the implicit contracts model developed in Chapter 3, except that income is substituted for utility in the farmer's constraint. To retain an adequate peak-season labor force, farmers had to offer workers an implicit contract consisting of wage payments and poor relief that yielded an income equal to workers' reservation income R, determined by wage rates and disamenities in London, and the cost of migration. That is,

$$R = W + B = W + eB + (1 - e)B$$

Farmers' labor costs are equal to

$$W + eB = R - (1 - e)B$$

Farmers' expenditures per worker are reduced by an amount $(1 - e)B$ below workers' reservation income, where $(1 - e)B$ is the per-worker relief contribution of non-labor-hiring taxpayers. Note that if workers' reservation income equals the marginal product of labor plus the contribution of non-labor-hiring taxpayers to the relief fund (that is, if $R = R' \equiv MP_\ell + (1 - e)B$), then $W + eB = MP_\ell$ and this model is the same as the Polanyi model developed in Section 2. But this is a special case. If workers' reservation income is less than $MP_\ell + (1-e)B$ then

$$R - (1-e)B = W + eB < MP_\ell$$

So long as $R < MP_\ell + (1 - e)B$, farmers' expenditures per worker were less than the marginal product of labor, and the Poor Law increased farmers' profits.[17]

Suppose that workers' reservation income was equal to the marginal product of labor.[18] Then farmers' payments to workers were below the marginal product of labor by precisely the contribution to the poor rate of taxpayers who did not hire labor; that is,

$$W + eB = MP_\ell - (1 - e)B$$

If R was equal to the marginal product of labor, the system of poor relief had no effect on migration; relief replaced laborers' wage income one-for-one. On the other hand, the transfer of income from taxpayers who did not hire labor to labor-hiring farmers should have had a positive effect on economic growth. Non-labor-hiring taxpayers consisted mainly of artisans, shopkeepers, and family farmers, whose incomes were significantly below those of labor-hiring farmers. The Poor Law (ironically) transferred income from low- to high-income individuals and therefore might have increased savings. The reduction in farmers' labor costs should have increased the demand for land, causing rents to increase. Thus some of the gain to farmers was passed on to (wealthier) landlords.[19] The income transfer should have led to increased capital formation in agriculture or increased investment outside of agriculture.

Three estimates of the size of the income transfer are given in Table

---

[17] Profit-maximizing farmers would never offer workers a contract that yielded an income greater than $R' \equiv MP_\ell + (1 - e)B$, because under such a contract their expenditures per worker would be greater than the marginal product of labor. If workers' reservation income was greater than R', there would be out-migration, which would increase the marginal product of labor in the parish and thus increase R'. Out-migration would continue until $R' = R$. If the value of a worker's implicit contract never exceeded R', the Polanyi model gives an upper-bound measure of the effect of poor relief on labor mobility.

[18] This amounts to assuming that migration costs, rural–urban differences in labor quality, the employment uncertainty in urban areas, and the urban disamenities premium were large enough to account for the entire rural–urban wage gap, so that the regional labor market was in equilibrium.

[19] The suggestion that landlords might have benefited from the Poor Law runs sharply counter to the traditional hypothesis that farmers shifted part of their poor relief expenditures to landlords. However, the assumption that landlords lowered rents in response to high poor rates makes sense only if the payment of poor rates reduced farmers' profits below "normal" levels. If the Poor Law had no effect on farmers' profits, as in the Polanyi model, it should have had no effect on the rental price of land. If the Poor Law caused profits to increase, the rental price of land also should have increased. On the other hand, farmers might have been able to convince absentee landlords that production costs were positively correlated with relief expenditures even if they were not.

Table 6.6. *Income transfer to labor-hiring farmers or landlords: Model 3*

County	Estimated income transfer per agricultural laborer (in £s)			Estimated total income transfer to labor-hiring farmers or landlords (in £s)		
	(a)	(b)	(c)	(a)	(b)	(c)
Bedford	0.44	0.67	0.89	5,099	7,764	10,313
Berkshire	0.55	0.82	1.09	8,141	12,138	16,134
Buckingham	0.58	0.86	1.15	9,711	14,399	19,254
Cambridge	0.44	0.66	0.88	6,907	10,361	13,814
Essex	0.48	0.73	0.97	18,352	27,911	37,087
Hertford	0.44	0.65	0.87	6,468	9,555	12,789
Huntingdon	0.46	0.69	0.92	2,745	4,117	5,490
Kent	0.67	1.01	1.34	24,196	36,474	48,391
Norfolk	0.57	0.85	1.13	21,356	31,846	42,337
Northampton	0.58	0.87	1.16	10,310	15,464	20,619
Oxford	0.57	0.85	1.14	9,119	13,598	18,238
Southampton	0.62	0.93	1.25	15,299	22,948	30,844
Suffolk	0.56	0.85	1.13	18,502	28,084	37,335
Sussex	0.73	1.09	1.45	19,071	28,476	37,881
Wiltshire	0.54	0.81	1.08	13,342	20,014	26,685
Total				188,618	283,149	377,208

Note: Columns labeled (a) through (c) assume that 33%, 50%, and 67%, respectively, of relief expenditures were paid to agricultural laborers and their families.
Sources: See text and Table 6.1.

6.6. I assume that non-labor-hiring taxpayers paid 20% of the poor rate.[20] As to the magnitude of the transfer, total fixed capital formation in agriculture for all of Great Britain was £3.4 million per annum during the years 1830 to 1835 (Feinstein 1978: 75). Assuming that one-third of the capital formation took place in the counties listed in Table 6.6, the annual transfer of income to labor-hiring farmers or landlords represented 16.7–33.3% of fixed capital formation in agriculture in the south-

---

[20] It was determined in Section 3 of Chapter 3 that non-labor-hiring taxpayers other than landlords paid 17–25% of the poor rate. It is this transfer from low to high savers that would have caused an increase in capital formation.

east of England.[21] Of course, the actual increase in investment depends on the difference in savings rates among non-labor-hiring taxpayers, labor-hiring farmers, and landlords. Although it is not possible to measure precisely group-specific savings rates, what data are available suggest there were large differences in savings rates across income classes. Crafts (1985: 124–5) conjectures that the "savings rate from agricultural rent and profits" was as high as 30% in the 1820s. The savings rate of non-labor-hiring taxpayers (i.e., family farmers, artisans, and shopkeepers) was much lower, perhaps 5%.[22] Assuming these are reasonable estimates of the group-specific savings rates, the income transfer from non-labor-hiring taxpayers to labor-hiring farmers and landlords led to an annual increase in savings (and investment) of £47,200–£94,300, or 4.2–8.4% of fixed capital formation in agriculture. If the average savings rate of non-labor-hiring taxpayers was 10%, the income transfer to labor-hiring farmers and landlords led to an annual increase in savings of £37,700–£75,400. Thus, the Poor Law might have played a role (albeit a small one) in funding the agricultural improvements of the first third of the nineteenth century.

The results in Table 6.6 hold if workers' reservation income was equal to the marginal product of labor. If $MP_\ell < R < MP_\ell + (1 - e)B$, the Poor Law both slowed migration and increased farmers' profits. Migration declined because rural workers' income was greater than the marginal product of labor, and farmers' profits increased because their expenditures per worker were less than the marginal product of labor. In effect, farmers and workers shared the contribution of non-labor-hiring taxpayers to the poor rate. Part of it went to farmers, raising profits above "normal" levels, and part went to workers, raising wages above the marginal product of labor. The effect of poor relief on rural–urban wage gaps (and hence on migration) was smaller than that given in Tables 6.3–6.5, because those tables assume that $R = MP_\ell + (1 - e)B$.

[21] In 1831, the 15 southeastern counties included in Table 6.6 contained about 27% of the adult male agricultural laborers in Great Britain. My assumption that 33% of capital formation in agriculture took place in these counties is meant to yield a lower-bound estimate for the ratio of the income subsidy received by farmers to the amount of fixed capital formation.

[22] My conjecture of a 5% savings rate is based on the assumption that the average income of family farmers, artisans, and shopkeepers was too small to enable much saving. Evidence to support this assumption can be obtained from Appendix D of the 1834 Poor Law Report (on labor rates), which contains large numbers of complaints from non-labor-hiring taxpayers that they cannot afford to pay the extra taxes associated with the use of labor rates (Parl. Papers 1834: XXXVIII).

Similarly, the effect on farmers' profits or landlords' rental income (and hence on savings) was smaller than that given in Table 6.6, which assumes that $R = MP_\ell$.[23]

The above bounds on the value of R were set for the following reasons: Farmers would never offer workers a contract yielding an income larger than $MP_\ell + (1 - e)B$ because that would mean their expenditures per worker $(W + eB)$ were larger than the marginal product of labor. Similarly, workers would never set their reservation wage below the marginal product of labor because the marginal product represented their opportunity income in neighboring agricultural parishes.

The value of R was determined by wage rates in London, workers' valuation of urban disamenities, and the cost of migration. Real wages of London builders' laborers increased by 30% from 1800–14 to 1826–34 (Schwarz 1986: 40–1). The increase in London wages increased farm workers' reservation income, both absolutely and relative to the marginal product of labor in agriculture.[24] Therefore, the effect of poor relief on migration (farmers' profits) was likely to have increased (decreased) over time. Perhaps the results in Table 6.6 represent an accurate measure of the effect of poor relief in 1800–14 and the results in Tables 6.3, 6.4, and 6.5 are an accurate measure of the effect of poor relief in 1826–34. If so, the average annual effect of poor relief on migration from 1795 to 1834 was trivial.

4. Conclusion

The analysis presented in this chapter has reached some surprising conclusions, which suggest that the traditional interpretation of the Poor Law's effect on economic growth needs to be revised. The hypothesis that the payment of poor relief to able-bodied agricultural laborers significantly slowed rural–urban migration (and hence economic growth) is not supported by the evidence. Even if all relief benefits paid to able-bodied workers were in excess of the marginal product of labor (model one), the loss in national income caused by the Poor Law was small. However, the results obtained from the first model overstate the impact of poor relief

---

[23] If $R = MP_\ell$, the entire contribution of non-labor-hiring taxpayers went to farmers, while if $R = MP_\ell + (1 - e)B$ the entire contribution went to workers.

[24] There is no evidence of a comparable increase in the marginal product of agricultural labor. Wheat yields increased by 7% from 1815–19 to 1826–34 (Healy and Jones 1962: 578). No data on wheat yields exist for 1800–14. The price of wheat declined by 35% from 1800–14 to 1826–34 (Mitchell and Deane 1962: 488).

because they assume that farmers' expenditures per worker exceeded the marginal product of labor. If profit-maximizing farmers used poor relief to raise workers' income without increasing their labor costs (model two), or to reduce their labor costs below the marginal product of labor (model three), the Poor Law at worst had little effect on the economy and at best stimulated growth by increasing the profit rates of labor-hiring farmers or the rental income of landlords.[25]

---

[25] The idea that the Poor Law "may have had some overall positive effects on the Industrial Revolution" was recently suggested by Joel Mokyr (1985b: 14). The results of this chapter and Chapter 8 support some of Mokyr's hypotheses.

7

THE NEW POOR LAW AND THE AGRICULTURAL LABOR MARKET, 1834–1850

The debate over the economic impact of the Old Poor Law on the agricultural labor market has been paralleled by a debate over the economic consequences of the Poor Law Amendment Act. However, although the issues to be explained are similar, the number of participants in the latter debate has been surprisingly small. The purpose of this chapter is to determine how farmers and laborers responded to the abolition of outdoor relief in 1834.

The traditional literature maintained that the system of outdoor relief reduced laborers' wages and farmers' profits in the long run, and that its abolition raised laborers' living standards. According to the 1834 Report of the Royal Poor Law Commission, the system of outdoor relief enabled farmers "to reduce wages to the minimum, or even below the minimum of what would support an unmarried man," but it also reduced labor's productivity by so much that "the farmer finds that pauper labour is dear, whatever be its price" (Royal Commission 1834: 59, 71). The report predicted that the abolition of outdoor relief would eliminate unemployment, increase labor productivity, increase "the return to the farmers' capital[, and thus] induce the capitalist to give better wages" (1834: 329).

My conclusion that outdoor relief did not have a negative effect on farmers' profits or laborers' living standards implies that the traditional analysis of the economic impact of the Poor Law Amendment Act needs to be revised. The abolition of outdoor relief did not have a positive effect on living standards. The question that remains to be answered is whether it had a negative effect on living standards, or whether implicit labor contracts were altered in such a way that agricultural laborers' annual income was unaffected by the change in relief administration. K. D. M. Snell (1985) has recently argued that southern agricultural laborers experienced a large decline in income as a result of the New Poor Law. His

193

conclusion is based on the assumption that labor was immobile and therefore forced to accept any implicit contract offered by farmers. If labor was mobile, and evidence shows that it was, the New Poor Law should not have affected workers' income. On the other hand, the form in which labor was compensated should have changed, since the new law disallowed the dominant implicit labor contract in grain-producing areas.

The chapter proceeds as follows: Section 1 discusses the reasons why the Poor Law was reformed in 1834. Historians' conclusions concerning the effect of the New Poor Law on the agricultural labor market are summarized in Section 2. Section 3 considers the effect of Poor Law reform on the dominant form of implicit labor contracts in grain-producing areas. In Section 4, I offer estimates of the change in real income of southern agricultural laborers from 1832 to 1850. Rural–urban migration and changes in the earnings gaps between London and southern agricultural counties from 1834 to 1850 are discussed in Section 5.

1. The Revision of the Poor Law

The process of revising the Poor Law was set in motion in February 1832 when the Royal Commission to Investigate the Poor Laws was formed by the government. Its purpose was "to make a diligent and full inquiry into the practical operation of the laws for the relief of the poor . . . and into the manner in which those laws are administered; and to report whether any and what alterations, amendments, or improvements may be beneficially made in the said laws, or in the manner of administering them, and how the same may be best carried into effect" (Royal Commission 1834: 1). The commission published a 360-page report in March 1834, followed by several volumes of evidence. A bill for the amendment of the Poor Law was introduced in the House of Commons in April, and the Poor Law Amendment Act became law on August 14, 1834. The bill encountered little opposition in Parliament. The Webbs (1929: 94) maintained that "there can scarcely have been, during the past hundred years, a measure of first-class social importance, gravely affecting the immediate interests of so large a number of people, that aroused, in its passage through both Houses of Parliament, so little effective opposition, and even so little competent discussion, as the Poor Law Amendment Bill."

Before turning to the effect of the New Poor Law on the agricultural labor market, we need to confront two related issues: Why was the Royal Commission formed in 1832, and why was the Poor Law amended? After all, the analysis of the previous chapters suggests that the politically dominant groups in many agricultural parishes found outdoor relief to be part of a cost-minimizing labor contract. There were changes in the economic environment between 1815 and 1832, but none important enough to alter the general form of the optimal labor contract.

In fact, there is plenty of evidence in the reports of the assistant Poor Law commissioners that grain-producing farmers did not support the abolition of outdoor relief. For instance, Assistant Commissioner Pringle wrote that farmers were "averse to any measures that would render the labourer independent of parish assistance, which, by keeping him to its confines, retains him always at their command when wanted for urgent work," and Assistant Commissioner Cowell concluded that "farmers find that labour is cheaper to them when the labourers are paid partly by the rates and partly by wages, and therefore they will not permit the allowance system to be superceded" (Parl. Papers 1834: XXVIII, 297, 595–6).[1] Even the Royal Commission's Report (1834: 59) admitted that "employers of paupers are attached to a system which enables them to dismiss and resume their labourers according to their daily or even hourly want of them, to reduce wages . . . , and to throw upon others the payment of a part . . . of the wages actually received by their labourers." Polanyi (1944: 298–9) concluded that "by 1833 the farming community was stolidly in favor of retaining Speenhamland."

The key to understanding the amendment of the Poor Law is the makeup of Parliament. The major beneficiaries from the system of outdoor relief, labor-hiring farmers, were not well represented in Parliament, which was dominated by large landowners, whose knowledge of the administration of poor relief at the parish level was limited. Landowners had a personal interest in relief administration only to the extent that it affected their rental income.

Historians have given two major reasons for the formation of the Royal Poor Law Commission: fear of rising poor rates, and the agricultural laborers' revolt of 1830–1.[2] The hypothesis that the system of

---

[1] Other evidence in the assistant commissioners' reports that labor-hiring farmers supported continuing the system of outdoor relief can be found in Parl. Papers (1834: XXVIII, 208, 209, 232, 300, 307, 335, 344, 594).

[2] The reform of the Poor Law was not brought about by a change in the composition of Parliament. The Royal Poor Law Commission was formed four months before the passage of the Reform Act in June 1832. The Poor Law Amendment Act was adopted by the

outdoor relief caused poor relief expenditures to increase over time became popular after the Napoleonic Wars. The 1817 House of Commons Select Committee on the Poor Laws concluded that "unless some efficacious check be interposed, there is every reason to think that the amount of the [poor rate] assessment will continue as it has done, to increase, till . . . it shall have absorbed the profits of the property on which the rate may have been assessed, producing thereby the neglect and ruin of the land" (Parl. Papers 1817: VI, 8). Similarly, David Ricardo (1821: 106) concluded that "whilst the present laws are in force, it is quite in the natural order of things that the fund for the maintenance of the poor should progressively increase, till it has absorbed all the net revenue of the country."

The trend in relief expenditures from 1817 through 1832, the year the Royal Commission was appointed, is given in Table 7.1. Three time series are presented: nominal expenditures, real expenditures, and per capita real expenditures. The trend in expenditures differs across the three series. Nominal relief expenditures were 14% lower in 1832 than in 1817, whereas per capita real expenditures were virtually the same in 1817 and 1832. One could argue, however, that landowners concerned about falling profit and rental rates were most interested in the trend in real relief expenditures, and this was upward.[3] Real expenditures increased by 23% from 1817 to 1832. Landowners might have interpreted the trend in real relief expenditures as support for the 1817 committee's hypothesis, and therefore put pressure on the government to come up with a plan to amend the Poor Law in order to reduce expenditures.

The fear of continuously increasing poor rates probably was not strong enough by itself to cause the government to take action in 1832. The catalyst for Poor Law reform was the agricultural laborers' uprising of 1830–1, the so-called Captain Swing riots. The disturbances consisted mainly of threshing-machine breaking, arson, and wage riots (Hobs-

reformed Parliament, but Parliament continued to be dominated by large landowners for several decades after 1832. According to Evans (1983: 41), "between 70 and 80 per cent [of the MPs elected in December 1832] represented the landed interest. . . . Not more than one hundred members [out of 658] were bankers, merchants or manufacturers. Many pre-1832 parliaments had returned similar numbers of the professional and industrial middle classes." Clearly, the Poor Law Amendment Act would not have been adopted without the support of the landed interest.

[3] The amount of land that was taxed remained roughly constant from 1817 to 1832, so that any increase in real expenditures meant an increase in the real tax rate. Landowners concerned about rental income should have been indifferent between an increase in the poor rate caused by rising per capita expenditures (with population constant) and an equal increase caused by population growth (with per capita expenditures constant).

Table 7.1. *Trends in relief expenditures, 1817–32 (1817 = 100)*

Year	Nominal expenditures	Real expenditures	Per capita real expenditures
1817	100.0	100.0	100.0
1818	95.5	99.5	98.1
1819	92.9	104.2	101.2
1820	88.2	109.0	104.8
1821	80.6	108.9	102.7
1822	73.2	108.2	100.2
1823	72.7	101.2	92.3
1824	73.3	100.1	90.2
1825	75.1	92.9	82.2
1826	81.6	112.1	97.5
1827	79.8	113.1	97.5
1828	80.3	110.7	93.8
1829	86.6	116.5	97.9
1830	86.2	118.9	98.2
1831	89.2	121.8	99.3
1832	86.1	123.3	99.5

Note: Poor relief expenditure data are for a year beginning on March 25. Thus, the 1817 data are actually for the year beginning on March 25, 1817.
Sources: Data on relief expenditures were obtained from Blaug (1963: 180). Cost-of-living data were obtained from Lindert and Williamson (1985: 148). Population data were obtained from Wrigley and Schofield (1981: 534).

bawm and Rudé 1968: 304–5).[4] They were concentrated in the south, in counties with high per capita poor relief expenditures. For this reason, the uprising caused an increase in the demand for Poor Law reform (Webb and Webb 1929: 45; Bowley 1937: 282). The Webbs (1929: 45) maintained that the revolt "put the fear of revolution into the hearts of the English governing class."

Hobsbawm and Rudé (1968: 16) concluded that "the almost universal demand [of the laborers] was for higher wages, for better employment and/or for improvements in the system of social security (i.e., the Poor

[4] Of the 1,475 disturbances documented by Hobsbawm and Rudé (1968: 304–5), 390 (26%) consisted of threshing-machine breaking, 316 (21%) of arson, and 225 (15%) of wage or tithe riots. Other types of disturbances included 219 cases of "robbery," 100 "riots" and assaults, and 99 "Swing" letters.

Law)."[5] The sparks that set off the riots in the southeast were threshing machines, Irish harvest laborers, and, in some cases, attempts to cut relief generosity (Hobsbawm and Rudé 1968: 91).[6]

Two aspects of the riots were particularly disturbing to landowners. First, they offered further evidence that workers had come to believe that "they possessed a 'right' to full maintenance" (Webb and Webb 1929: 46). Second, there was evidence that farmers had acted as "passive, if not active, allies in the labourers' cause." Laborers' demands for higher wages were "frequently accompanied . . . by approaches to landlords and parsons to reduce rents and tithes in order to make it possible for the farmers to raise their wages" (Hobsbawm and Rudé 1968: 231–2, 196). In some parishes farmers were the instigators of wage riots.[7] The farmers' behavior is understandable: So long as any increase in wages was accompanied by a decline in rents or tithes of similar magnitude, their profit rates would be unaffected.[8]

Landowners viewed the riots as a strong signal that the local administration of poor relief was badly mismanaged. The increase in real relief expenditures after 1817 had increased rather than reduced the discontent of agricultural laborers. The laborers' demands and the response of tenant farmers suggested that relief expenditures (or wage rates) were

[5] Question 53 of the Poor Law Commission's Rural Queries asked parish authorities to give the causes of the agricultural riots of 1830 and 1831. Overall, 59% of the respondents listed low wages or unemployment as the cause of the disturbances. The Poor Law was listed as a cause of disturbances by 8% of the respondents (Hobsbawm and Rudé 1968: 82).

[6] Laborers' fear of threshing machines and Irish harvest laborers is understandable. The adoption of threshing machines greatly reduced the demand for labor during the fall, while the use of Irish harvest laborers reduced the demand for parish labor at harvest. The effect of Irish migrant workers on implicit labor contracts is discussed in Section 5 of Chapter 3.

[7] Farmers apparently were particularly active in instigating disturbances in East Anglia. A Norfolk newspaper reported that "in the great majority of instances the labourers were as much the instrument of proffering the complaints of the farmers as of their own" (quoted in Hobsbawm and Rudé 1968: 233).

[8] In terms of the model of the labor market developed in Chapter 3, farmers' behavior can be viewed as a rational response to rising urban wage rates, which raised the reservation utility of their workers, V^*. Real wages of London builders' laborers increased by 24% from 1800–14 to 1826–30 (Schwarz 1986: 40–1). In order to retain their labor force, farmers had to respond to the increase in V^* by increasing the expected utility of the contracts they offered workers, $E(V)$. A reduction in rents or tithes enabled farmers to increase the value of their contracts, and thus retain their labor force, at little or no cost to themselves. Hobsbawm and Rudé (1968: 158–60, 231–4) cite several instances where farmers agreed to increase wages if landlords or clergy would reduce rents or tithes. For example, in Wallop, Hampshire, "the farmers offered to increase wages from 8s. to 10s. provided that rents, tithes and taxes should be lowered in proportion; at Stoke Holy Cross [Norfolk] they agreed to raise wages by one-fifth provided that tithes were reduced by one-quarter and rents by one-sixth."

about to increase even more, and that the landowners would be expected to bear much of the increase in the form of reduced rents. It was time for the government to intervene to reduce relief expenditures and to increase the power of landowners in parish vestries.

In response to this pressure, the government appointed the seven-member Royal Poor Law Commission early in 1832. The Bishop of London was chosen to preside over the commission, but the investigation into the administration of poor relief was supervised by Nassau Senior (Checkland and Checkland 1974: 29). Senior was a known opponent of the system of outdoor relief. In the preface to the second edition of his *Three Lectures on the Rate of Wages* (1831), Senior wrote that the Captain Swing riots were caused by "the disturbance which the poorlaws, as at present administered in the south of England, have created in the . . . relation between the employer and the labourer" (1831: v–vi). He labeled as absurd the laborers' demands that rents and tithes should be reduced to enable farmers to raise wages. Senior concluded that agreement to the laborers' demands would produce disastrous results.

If the farmer . . . is to employ a certain proportion of the labourers, however numerous, in his parish, he is, in fact, to pay rent and tithes as before, with this difference only, that they are to be paid to paupers, instead of to the landlord and the parson; and that the payment is not a fixed but an indefinite sum, and a sum which must every year increase in an accelerated ratio, as the increase of population rushes to fill up this new vacuum, till rent, tithes, profit, and capital are all eaten up, and pauperism produces what may be called its natural effects . . . famine, pestilence, and civil war. (1831: xiii)

It is no wonder that the Webbs and other historians have concluded that the commission's investigation "was far from being impartially or judicially directed and carried out. . . . The then existing practice of poor relief . . . stood condemned in their mind in advance; with the result that such useful and meritorious features as it possessed were almost entirely ignored" (Webb and Webb 1929: 84, 86).[9]

[9] The contemporary economist J. R. McCulloch wrote that "the Commissioners, with very few exceptions, appear to have set out with a determination to find nothing but abuses in the Old Poor Law, and to make the most of them" (quoted in Webb and Webb 1929: 84). The most famous criticism of the Poor Law Report is R. H. Tawney's (1926: 269) description of it as "wildly unhistorical." According to Tawney, "the Commissioners of 1832–4 were right in thinking the existing methods of relief administration extremely bad; they were wrong in supposing distress to be due mainly to lax administration, instead of realizing, as was the fact, that lax administration had arisen as an attempt to meet the increase of distress. Their discussion of the causes of pauperism is, therefore, extremely superficial" (1926: 322).

The analysis of outdoor relief contained in the 1834 Report of the Royal Poor Law Commission was discussed in Chapter 2, but it is useful to review the report's conclusions concerning the effect of outdoor relief on landowners. The report presented evidence in support of the hypothesis that poor rates tended to increase perpetually, at the expense of profits and rents. In Cholesbury, Buckingham, rapidly increasing poor rates had caused the "abandonment" of farming in 1832, "the landlords having given up their rents, the farmers their tenancies, and the clergyman his glebe and his tithes" (Royal Commission 1834: 64). Although Cholesbury was an extreme case, in many other parishes "the pressure of the poor-rate has reduced the rent to half, or to less than half, of what it would have been if the land had been situated in an unpauperized district, and [in] some . . . it has been impossible for the owner to find a tenant" (1834: 64). The report concluded that "any parish in which the pressure of the poor-rates has compelled the abandonment of a single farm is in imminent danger of undergoing the ruin which has already befallen Cholesbury. . . . [T]he abandonment of property, when it has once begun, is likely to proceed in a constantly accelerated ratio" (1834: 67).

The report put much of the blame for the increase in poor rates on the tenant farmers. The system of outdoor relief enabled farmers "to throw upon others the payment of a part, . . . and sometimes almost the whole of the wages actually received by their labourers" (1834: 59). The farmer therefore "has strong motives to introduce abuses; he can reap the immediate benefit of the fall of wages, and when that fall has ceased to be beneficial, when the apparently cheap labour has become really dear, he can either quit [the farm] at the expiration of his lease, or demand on its renewal a diminution of rent" (1834: 73).

The solution to the problem of increasing poor rates, therefore, was either to reduce the power of tenant farmers over the administration of relief or to reduce (or eliminate) the benefits farmers obtained from having seasonally unneeded laborers collect relief. Farmers' power over relief administration could be reduced by increasing the power of landlords in the local administration of relief, or by creating a central authority to administer relief. The Poor Law Amendment Act did both of these things.

The act increased the power of landowners in two ways.[10] First, it

---

[10] For a detailed analysis of the effect of the Poor Law Amendment Act on the political power of landowners, see Brundage (1972; 1974; 1978: Chapters 3 and 5). Brundage's conclusion that the act substantially increased the power of landowners over the administration of relief is challenged by Dunkley (1973).

provided that any county magistrate who resided in a Poor Law union would be an ex officio member of the union's board of guardians. Second, the act adopted a system for electing members of the board of guardians that was radically different from the voting system that existed before 1834. Voting was restricted to parish ratepayers before 1834; landowners who rented their land to tenant farmers were not eligible to vote. The Poor Law Amendment Act not only gave landowners the right to vote for guardians, it adopted a system of plural voting that gave landowners up to six votes, depending on the value of their property (Brundage 1972: 29). Ratepayers, on the other hand, were given a maximum of three votes.[11] A landowner who was also a ratepayer (that is, a landowner who farmed his land rather than renting it) could have as many as nine votes in local elections.[12] In addition, landowners, but not ratepayers, were allowed to vote by proxy.

Historians do not agree as to the actual effect of the Poor Law Amendment Act on the power of landowners. Anthony Brundage (1972: 29) maintained that, as a result of the act, large landowners achieved dominance over rural Poor Law unions. However, Peter Dunkley (1973: 841) argued that "no convincing case can be made for a marked or general enhancement of the grip of the large landed proprietors on rural relief administration . . . under the New Poor Law." Anne Digby (1976) concluded that large landowners played an important role in the formation of unions but not in the actual administration of relief. She wrote that "continuity in rural relief administration, pre- and post-1834, was very strong; . . . the farmers [were] ascendant in the guardians' boardroom as they had been before 1834 in the parish vestry" (1976: 153).

To reduce the power of local farmers further, the Poor Law Commission recommended the creation of a central board to direct the administration of poor relief. Local authorities could not be trusted to cooperate with parliamentary attempts to reduce able-bodied pauperism, because "interests adverse to a correct administration prevail amongst those who are entrusted with the duties of distributing the fund for relief. . . . Wherever the allowance system is now retained, we may be sure that statutory provisions for its abolition will be met by every

[11] In 1844 the voting scale for landowners was adopted for ratepayers (Brundage 1972: 30). As a result, the political power of ratepayers relative to landowners increased.
[12] After 1844, a landowner who also farmed a property valued at £175 or more had 12 votes in local elections. Still, the 1844 law must have reduced the power of landowners relative to ratepayers in most southeastern Poor Law unions.

possible evasion" (Royal Commission 1834: 287). The central board was to be given "the same powers of making rules and regulations that are now exercised by upwards of 15,000 unskilled and (practically) irresponsible [parish] authorities" (Royal Commission 1834: 301). The Poor Law Commission predicted that a central board empowered by Parliament to undertake measures to reduce able-bodied pauperism would be able to reduce relief expenditures "by more than one-third . . . in a very short period" (1834: 331).

The Poor Law Amendment Act provided for the appointment of a three-member commission to "make and issue all such rules, orders, and regulations for the management of the poor, . . . and for the guidance and control of all guardians, vestries, and parish officers, so far as relates to the management of the poor, . . . as they shall think proper" (Nicholls 1898: II, 273). The commission specifically was empowered to group parishes into Poor Law unions; to regulate (and, presumably, to eventually eliminate) the payment of outdoor relief to able-bodied paupers; and, with the consent of a majority of a union's guardians, to order the construction of workhouses. However, despite the act's attempt to centralize the administration of relief, local boards of guardians retained "substantial autonomy over relief policies," as will be seen later in this chapter.

The Poor Law Report also proposed a method for reducing the benefits farmers obtained from having their seasonally redundant laborers collect poor relief. It recommended that the payment of outdoor relief to able-bodied persons or their families be abolished. Able-bodied workers were to be relieved only in "well-regulated" workhouses (Royal Commission 1834: 262). The Poor Law Amendment Act left the abolition of outdoor relief to the newly appointed commissioners. By 1842 most of the rural unions in southern England had received orders prohibiting the payment of outdoor relief to able-bodied laborers (Digby 1976: 157).

The substitution of indoor relief (that is, relief in the workhouse) for outdoor relief altered the form of farmers' cost-minimizing labor contracts for two reasons. First, indoor relief was more expensive than outdoor relief. MacKinnon (1987: 608) estimates that "expenditure per indoor pauper was at least 50 percent higher than outdoor relief per pauper. . . . When expenditure on salaries and on workhouse repairs and furniture is included, the gap between the total cost of maintaining paupers in the workhouse and granting them outdoor relief increases."

In the southeastern counties, the marginal cost of workhouse relief was nearly double the cost of outdoor relief.[13] Second, under the workhouse system unemployed laborers derived no utility from "leisure." The workhouse was to be "an uninviting place," where laborers were forced to work, prevented from using beer or tobacco, and from "going out or receiving visitors" (Webb and Webb 1929: 67). The workhouse system therefore made the use of seasonal layoffs both more expensive to farmers and less palatable to their laborers.

The problem of social disintegration also would be solved by the workhouse system and the increased power of landowners in relief administration. The Poor Law Report maintained that the use of outdoor relief reduced workers' skill, diligence, and honesty, and made them "positively hostile" to their employers (Royal Commission 1834: 67–8). This decline in workers' "moral condition" was a major cause of the agrarian riots of 1830–1, as well as of a long-term decline in labor productivity, which in turn caused farmers' profits and landlords' rents to decline (1834: 512, 69). The report included numerous examples of how laborers' behavior had changed as a result of local Poor Law reform (1834: 228–61). It concluded that "in every instance in which the able-bodied labourers have been rendered independent of . . . relief otherwise than in a well-regulated workhouse . . . their industry has been restored and improved . . . frugal habits have been created or strengthened . . . their discontent has been abated, and their moral and social condition in every way improved" (1834: 261).

In sum, it is not difficult to explain why the Poor Law Amendment Act encountered little opposition in Parliament. It "was devised by and for the leaders of the landed interest," who dominated both houses of Parliament (Brundage 1974: 406). The landowners were anxious to reduce relief expenditures and to "restore the social fabric of the countryside." The Poor Law Amendment Act was designed to do both these things. Relief expenditures would decline because farmers no longer had

---

[13] MacKinnon (1987: 618–19) estimated relief expenditure per indoor and outdoor pauper for 1868–9 by dividing indoor (outdoor) relief expenditures for the year ended Lady Day 1869 by the number of indoor (outdoor) paupers on July 1, 1868, and January 1, 1869. In the southeastern, south Midlands, and eastern regions, expenditure per indoor pauper was 102%, 89%, and 80% greater than expenditure per outdoor pauper. One can estimate the relative cost of indoor relief in 1840–8 by dividing indoor (outdoor) relief expenditures by the number of persons receiving indoor (outdoor) relief during the first quarter of the year. For England and Wales as a whole, expenditure per indoor pauper was 52% greater than expenditure per outdoor pauper. Data for 1840–8 were obtained from Williams (1981: 158, 169).

either the power or the desire to use the Poor Law as an unemployment insurance system. The problem of voluntary unemployment would be eliminated by the workhouse system, because laborers would not refuse employment in order to obtain indoor relief. Finally, the elimination of outdoor relief would reduce worker discontent and raise labor productivity, which would increase farmers' profits and therefore landlords' rents.

The New Poor Law did cause relief expenditures to decline. From 1830–3 to 1840–50, real per capita expenditures declined by 28%.[14] The available relief statistics do not enable one to determine how successful the Poor Law Commission was in eliminating the payment of outdoor relief to able-bodied workers. There are no statistics on the number of unemployed workers relieved in workhouses, and the available statistics on the number of unemployed or underemployed workers receiving outdoor relief are suspect because many parishes listed unemployed workers as being sick in order to take advantage of the sickness exception clause to the Outdoor Relief Prohibitory Order (Digby 1976: 158). What data are available suggest that few unemployed or underemployed workers were relieved indoors. From 1840 to 1846, 21.4% of adult able-bodied paupers (male and female) in England were relieved in workhouses.[15] In 1865, only 12.8% of able-bodied male paupers in the south of England received indoor relief (MacKinnon 1986: 304). The data do not reveal whether the number of able-bodied males relieved in workhouses was small because (1) laborers refused to enter workhouses, (2) parishes continued to grant outdoor relief to unemployed workers, or (3) farmers responded to the abolition of outdoor relief by offering workers yearlong employment contracts. These issues are discussed in Sections 2 and 3.

2. Historians' Analyses of the New Poor Law

There is considerable disagreement among historians as to the impact of the New Poor Law on the agricultural labor market. Few have accepted the Royal Poor Law Commission's conclusion that the adoption of the New Poor Law caused laborers' income to increase. Rather, the debate

---

[14] Relief expenditure data are from Williams (1981: 148, 169). Nominal expenditures were deflated using the revised Lindert–Williamson cost-of-living index (Lindert and Williamson 1985: 148). Population data are from Wrigley and Schofield (1981: 534–5).

[15] Data on the number of adult able-bodied paupers are from the printed returns in the seventh through the thirteenth annual reports of the Poor Law Commissioners.

concerns whether living standards declined or were largely unaffected by the abolition of outdoor relief.

Wilhelm Hasbach devoted much attention to the impact of the New Poor Law in his *History of the English Agricultural Labourer* (1908). He maintained that the change in relief administration marked "the beginning of a period of slow recovery in the labourer's standard of life, both moral and material. . . . [W]ith the removal of the allowance system went the removal, or at least the weakening, of the hindrances to a rise in money wages by means of free contract" (1908: 217, 223). However, Hasbach believed that the abolition of outdoor relief adversely affected laborers in the short run. By fostering high birth rates and slowing migration, generous outdoor relief had created an excess supply of labor in agricultural parishes (1908: 219–20). The New Poor Law was not well suited for dealing with surplus labor. Parishes attempted to raise laborers' income through the employment of their wives and children, and the increased use of allotments (1908: 224–41). The former policy was only partially successful, because "where . . . women's and children's labor was employed to excess, it threw both married and unmarried men out of employment" (1908: 229). Allotments were more successful in increasing income, but although they were "everywhere to be found" in the agricultural counties, they did "not become universal in any of them" (1908: 237).[16] In sum, Hasbach maintained that the income of laboring

---

[16] Hasbach's evidence for the increase in the employment of women and children and in allotments comes mainly from two 1843 parliamentary reports: the *Report . . . on the Employment of Women and Children in Agriculture* and the *Report from the Select Committee on the Labouring Poor (Allotments of Land)*. I argue in Section 5 that the increased use of allotments resulted in at most a £1–£1.5 per annum increase in rural families' income. It is much more difficult to estimate the change in earnings of women and children after 1834. Although both the 1832 Rural Queries and the 1843 report on women and children's employment contain wage data for women and children, the irregular nature of employment makes it difficult if not impossible to estimate annual earnings for either year. Historians since Hasbach have disagreed as to the movement in women and children's earnings after 1834. Pinchbeck (1930: 84–6) maintained that the employment of women and children increased as a result of the New Poor Law. Lindert and Williamson (1983: 18) conclude that wage rates for women and children were similar in 1832 and 1843. Snell (1981: 426–9) contends that the "evidence presented in the . . . Poor Law Report of 1834, in the subsequent Poor Law Reports, and in the 1843, 1867–8, and 1868–9 Reports on the Employment of Women and Children in Agriculture, provide numerous indications of the increasingly insignificant role of female agricultural labour" in grain-producing regions. He rejects Pinchbeck's (1930: 86) conclusion that "the increase in women workers was especially noticeable in the Eastern Counties as a result of the particular organisation which developed there, known as the Gang System." Snell (1981: 429) maintains that the gang system existed in few parishes, and therefore that "the controversy it aroused appears to have been significantly disproportionate to its extent, particularly in the 1830s and 1840s."

families declined somewhat after 1834, but the long-run impact of the New Poor Law was positive.

The Webbs (1929) concluded that the New Poor Law did not reduce laborers' living standards even in the short run. The reason was simple: the new law abolished the system of allowances-in-aid-of-wages but did not eliminate the payment of outdoor relief to laborers who were temporarily sick or unemployed. There were "so many exceptions and loopholes" to the orders prohibiting outdoor relief "as to leave in every Union a larger or smaller number of cases in which the Guardians were free to take their own line" (1929: 146–8). As a result, "outdoor relief was not in fact generally refused to those incapacitated for work, and often indeed not even to the able-bodied man in temporary distress" (1929: 156). Laborers' incomes did not decline even in parishes that strictly enforced the prohibition against outdoor relief. When outdoor relief was abolished, "the agricultural labourers' wages were in fact raised, if not very considerably; employment became somewhat more continuous; and, to say the least, little or no increase in human misery was manifest" (1929: 155).

Anne Digby (1975; 1976; 1978) maintained that grain-producing parishes continued to grant outdoor relief to able-bodied laborers after the passage of the Poor Law Amendment Act. The continuity in policy was "more striking than any differences which the 1834 Act had made" (1976: 170). Farmers continued to dominate the administration of relief, and they confronted "the same economic problems. The crucial difficulty in many rural areas of southern England continued to be that of [seasonal] surplus labour" (1976: 153; 1975: 70–4). Parishes evaded the Poor Law Commission's prohibition of outdoor relief because indoor relief was more expensive than outdoor relief. Unemployed workers were given outdoor relief "on the ostensible grounds of sickness or accident, which were exceptions to the prohibitory order" (1975: 73). Although she does not directly address the issue, Digby's analysis implies that agricultural laborers' living standards were not affected by the adoption of the New Poor Law.

The hypothesis that seasonally unemployed farm laborers continued to receive outdoor relief after 1834 has recently been challenged by Karel Williams (1981), K. D. M. Snell (1985), and William Apfel and Peter Dunkley (1985). Williams (1981: 83) maintains that "the exclusion of unemployed men from the classes obtaining relief and the wholesale construction of new union workhouses were the two most conspicuous discontinuities in the poor law of the mid-nineteenth century." There was a significant decline in the number of unemployed laborers receiving outdoor relief in the 1840s, and by the early 1850s "the number of such men was negligible" (1981: 71). Nor was there a corresponding increase in indoor relief. Parishes reduced the number of able-bodied male relief recipients through the threat of the workhouse. The widespread construction of workhouses in agricultural unions between 1834 and 1839 equipped relief administrators with "new technical instruments for a policy of repression" (1981: 87).[17] Thus, by the early 1850s, "relief to unemployed and underemployed men was effectively abolished and this abolition was not a temporary or local phenomenon" (1981: 75). Williams does not discuss whether the reduction in relief expenditures was followed by an increase in wage rates or employment rates, so his opinion of the effect of the New Poor Law on workers' living standards cannot be determined.

Snell (1985) maintains that parishes used the threat of the workhouse to reduce wage rates as well as relief expenditures. The New Poor Law increased the political power of farmers over the administration of relief; they used the law "to increase submissiveness of labour to employers" (1985: 116, 121). He contends that "the refusal of out-relief to the able-bodied, coupled with . . . widespread fear of the workhouse, created conditions of dependence in which precarious employment at low wages had to be accepted" (1985: 124). The passage of the New Poor Law therefore led not only to the elimination of the allowance system but also to a reduction in wage income. In support of this hypothesis, Snell presents evidence that nominal wages for southern agricultural laborers declined by approximately 13% from 1833 (actually 1832) to 1837, and by 22% from 1833 to 1850 (1985: 130).[18] He does not adjust the data for movements in the cost of living, because "prices in and around 1850 were only marginally lower than in" 1833 (1985: 129). Moreover, he claims that these results understate the true decline in wage income, because "the 1833 figures were probably atypically low" (1985: 129). The conclusion is obvious: Laborers' living

[17] Williams (1981: 79) calculated that 62% of rural unions had constructed new workhouses by 1839.
[18] Snell obtained his wage data from Bowley (1898: 704–6), who constructed his wage series for 1833 from the returns to the Rural Queries. However, the Rural Queries were mailed out in the summer of 1832 and returned to the Poor Law Commission by January 1833 (Royal Commission 1834: 2). The wage data obtained from the returns relate to 1832, not 1833.

standards declined sharply after the passage of the Poor Law Amendment Act.

Apfel and Dunkley (1985) reach a similar conclusion from their analysis of the impact of the New Poor Law in rural Bedfordshire. They reject the hypothesis that outdoor relief continued to be granted to able-bodied laborers (either overtly or in the form of medical relief) after 1834 (1985: 41–6). The new boards of guardians emphasized "the use of workhouses to deter and restrain the labouring poor" (1985: 50). Like Snell, Apfel and Dunkley maintain that the "greater degrees of deterrence and economy in the administration of public aid [under the New Poor Law] sent ripples through the agricultural labour market and left their marks on wages and employment" (1985: 58). Specifically, the New Poor Law "enhanced downward pressure on wages" toward subsistence and "increased the availability and regularity of agricultural employment" during slack seasons (1985: 62–3). Wage rates declined because the elimination of relief to able-bodied laborers led to an increase in labor supply "at times of low demand" (1985: 61). Apfel and Dunkley (1985: 62–3) maintain that large farmers interested "in preserving adequate supplies of labour for the busy seasons . . . had little choice but to take the lead in reacting to the reports of labourers threatening to leave the county if they were not given more regular work." And yet they reject the hypothesis that farmers increased slack season employment in order to avoid the high cost of indoor relief. They contend that the increase in employment was caused by the decline in wage rates. Overall, the New Poor Law strengthened "a buyers' market in labour." The typical laborer worked more hours for less money and became more dependent "on the goodwill of those who directly controlled access to work and wages" (1985: 66).

The work of Snell, and Apfel and Dunkley, suggests that a major reevaluation of the impact of the New Poor Law is needed. However, their analyses contain several errors, the correction of which significantly alters their results. Because Snell's conclusions are stronger and more controversial, I shall direct my criticisms to his analysis, although most of the comments apply to both works.

I begin with Snell's theoretical analysis of how the rural labor market worked. He admits that the problem faced by labor-hiring farmers in the grain-producing southeast was to determine the least-cost method "to hold labour in the parish during the winter, ready for the short arable season" (1985: 122–3). His conclusion that "the New Poor Law was a means of doing this at minimum cost" hinges on the crucial assumption that labor was immobile. If labor was immobile, and if laborers would do anything to avoid entering the workhouse, it follows that farmers could reduce wages to subsistence without fear of a reduction in the supply of labor. In effect, farmers faced a vertical labor supply curve. If, however, labor was mobile, then farmers' ability to reduce laborers' income was constrained by having to offer laborers a contract that yielded an expected utility equal to their reservation utility, determined by wage rates in London and migration costs. Any attempt by farmers to reduce laborers' expected utility below their reservation level would have resulted in out-migration. The New Poor Law did not alter the utility constraint faced by farmers and therefore did not enable them to reduce their labor costs.

Snell's conclusion that the workhouse system enabled farmers to minimize their labor costs raises another issue that he does not address. Why didn't parishes use indoor relief as part of a cost-minimizing implicit labor contract before 1834? The 1796 Act of Parliament that sanctioned the granting of outdoor relief to "any industrious poor person . . . in case of temporary illness or distress" did not make the use of indoor relief illegal. Parishes such as Southwell and Bingham substituted the workhouse system for outdoor relief more than a decade before the passage of the New Poor Law (Nicholls 1898: II, 227–33). If the threat of the workhouse reduced farmers' labor costs after 1834, it should have done the same before 1834. The fact that the great majority of southern agricultural parishes continued to grant outdoor relief to able-bodied laborers until the passage of the New Poor Law suggests that farmers believed that implicit labor contracts that included outdoor relief for seasonally unemployed laborers were better suited to their needs than contracts including indoor relief.

In fact, the unpopularity of indoor relief among labor-hiring farmers is readily explained. Implicit labor contracts including indoor relief were cost-minimizing only if labor was immobile. Although Snell *assumes* that labor was immobile, recent estimates of rural out-migration rates by Williamson (1987) reveal a relatively high rate of labor mobility. From 1816 to 1851, the rate of rural out-migration ranged from 0.87% to 1.73% per annum, compared to "between 0.97 and 1.21 percent per annum in the Third World in the 1960s and 1970s" (Williamson 1987: 646). During our period of interest, 1831 to 1851, slightly more than 2 million persons migrated out of rural England and

Wales, an annual rate of 1.38% (Williamson 1987: 646). These estimates are for all of rural England and Wales, whereas we are interested in migration from the rural south of England. Williamson (1985c:
18) calculated that from 1841 to 1851 the rural out-migration rate in
southern England was 1.24% per annum.[19] Thus, labor was *very* mobile, and farmers anxious to secure an adequate peak-season labor
force had to take this mobility into account when determining their
least-cost labor contract.[20]

Finally, Snell's estimates of the change in real wages of southern farm
laborers are incorrect because he assumes that prices in 1850 were "only
marginally lower than in" 1832.[21] According to the revised Lindert–
Williamson index, the cost of living declined by 22% from 1832 to 1850
(Lindert and Williamson 1985: 148–9).[22] Table 7.2 contains estimates of
the movement in real wages from 1832 to 1850 for each southeastern
county. If nominal wages are deflated using the Lindert–Williamson
cost-of-living index, one finds that real wages declined in only 3 of the 17
counties. The largest decline was in Suffolk, where wages fell by 9.0%.
Real wages increased by more than 10% in 6 counties. On average, real
wages increased by 5.4%. Because wages are determined by many
forces besides poor relief, it is not possible to determine the effect of the
New Poor Law on real wages. However, neither supply forces (e.g.,
changes in the rural labor force) nor demand forces (e.g., changes in the
output of grain) appear to have moved in such a way as to cause wages

[19] Labor also was mobile before the amendment of the Poor Law. From 1816 to 1831, the
rural out-migration rate was 1.07% per annum, very similar to out-migration rates in
developing countries in the 1960s and 1970s (Williamson 1987: 646).

[20] I am not claiming that all rural workers were equally mobile. Williamson (1988: 304)
estimates that the majority of migrants to English cities in the 1840s were aged 15–29,
and that only a small share were aged 30 or older. The age distribution of migrants can
be explained by human capital considerations. The older a migrant was, the less time he
or she had to reap the benefits of high urban wages, and thus the lower the potential
returns from migration. Moreover, older workers might have faced higher migration
costs than young workers, because they had "bigger accumulated rural commitments"
(Williamson 1988: 302). Older workers therefore were potentially less mobile than
young workers. The New Poor Law might have enabled farmers to reduce the expected
income of relatively immobile older workers. Unfortunately, the available wage and
relief expenditure data do not enable one to test whether the income (wage earnings +
relief benefits) of older workers declined relative to that of young workers from 1832 to
1850.

[21] Apfel and Dunkley (1985: 61–2) also ignore movements in the cost of living in their
discussion of changes in Bedfordshire laborers' wages from 1833 to 1850. Their conclusion that wages declined during this period does not hold when the decline in living costs
is taken into account, as can be seen in Table 7.2.

[22] For comparison, Phelps Brown and Hopkins (1956: 314) estimate that the cost of living
declined by 17% from 1832 to 1850. Crafts (1985: 101) estimates that the cost of living
declined by 17% from 1830 to 1850.

Table 7.2. *Agricultural wages in southeastern England, 1832–1850/1*

County	Nominal wage 1832		Nominal wage 1850/1		% change in real wage 1832–1850/1
Bedford	10s.	0d.	9s.	0d.	16.0
Berkshire	10	5	7	6	−7.2
Buckingham	10	2	8	6	7.7
Cambridge	10	6	7	6	−8.0
Essex	10	3	8	0	0.5
Hertford	11	0	9	0	5.4
Huntingdon	10	5	8	6	5.2
Kent	13	1	–		12.0[a]
Norfolk	10	9	8	6	1.9
Northampton	10	3	9	0	13.1
Oxford	10	1	9	0	15.1
Southampton	10	2	9	0	14.0
Suffolk	9	11	7	0	−9.0
Sussex	12	1	10	6	12.0
Wiltshire	9	1	7	3	2.8

[a]Real wages for Kent were assumed to increase at the same rate as wages for Sussex.
Sources: Nominal wage data were obtained from Bowley (1900: table at end of book). Cost-of-living data were obtained from Lindert and Williamson (1985: 148–9).

to increase. In other words, the results in Table 7.2 suggest that the New Poor Law did not have a negative effect on wage rates.[23]

[23] If Snell is correct in asserting that the 1832 wage data are "untypically low," then real wages may in fact have declined from 1832 to 1850. Snell's assertion is based on the hypothesis that parishes whose labor force was "more highly pauperised and lowly paid" would be "more likely to reply" to the questionnaire sent to rural parishes in 1832 by the Royal Poor Law Commission (1985: 128). However, although the assertion is plausible, it is not supported by other evidence concerning wages. Wage data for each southern county also exist for 1824. A comparison of the 1824 and 1832 data suggests that real wages increased by at least 21% (and at most 41%) in every southeastern county during this eight-year period. No available evidence concerning the agricultural labor market would lead one to expect such a rapid increase in wages. It is difficult to reconcile this result with the hypothesis that the available 1832 wage data are untypically low. If anything, the rapid increase in real wages suggests that either the 1832 wage figures are untypically high or the 1824 wage figures are untypically low. My own hunch is that the parishioners responding to the 1832 questionnaire would be more likely to overstate wage rates than to understate them. However, the size of any possible overstatement at the county level of aggregation is probably quite small. Indeed, the large number of responses to the questionnaire suggest that the 1832 wage data are the most reliable source of information on county-level agricultural wages that is available for the first half of the nineteenth century.

Of course, what we are really interested in is not the movement in laborers' weekly wage rates after 1834, but rather the change in annual family income. The fact that real wages increased slightly from 1832 to 1850 does not by itself disprove Snell's hypothesis that agricultural laborers' standard of living declined sharply after the passage of the Poor Law Amendment Act. The increase in wages might not have been large enough to offset the decline in relief benefits. In Section 4, I estimate the change in family income from 1832 to 1850.

3. An Economic Model of the Impact of Poor Law Reform

a. Introduction

What effect did the New Poor Law have on farmers' profit-maximizing implicit labor contracts? The abolition of outdoor relief for able-bodied workers altered the solution to the farmer's problem described in Chapter 3 by simultaneously increasing the cost of relieving unemployed laborers and reducing the utility of being unemployed. The cost of relieving a pauper in the workhouse was at least 50%, perhaps as much as 100%, higher than the cost of relieving him at home (MacKinnon 1987: 608, 618–19). However, the increased cost of indoor relief did not increase the consumption of persons on relief, and any utility obtained from the increase in leisure associated with unemployment was eliminated by the workhouse. Digby (1976: 162) contends that indoor relief was "psychologically repugnant" to workers, which suggests that the "leisure" associated with unemployment yielded negative utility to workers.

The nature of the farmer's problem was the same before and after 1834, to secure an adequate peak-season labor force for the least cost. In terms of the model developed in Chapter 3, the farmer's objective was to choose a profit-maximizing labor contract subject to the constraint that the contract had to yield an expected utility large enough to keep his workers from leaving the parish. The farmer's alternatives to a contract containing seasonal layoffs and indoor relief were as follows:

1. Increased employment of labor during slack seasons (at the extreme, yearlong labor contracts).
2. Increased wage rates during peak seasons, high enough to sustain a laborer's family for the entire year.

3. Increased use of allotments, large enough to make up for the loss of poor relief during periods of seasonal unemployment.
4. Continued use of the system of outdoor relief, perhaps in a new guise designed to evade the legislation of 1834.

A model of the farmer's problem is developed and solved in Section 3(b). Nonquantitative historians might want to skip this section and go directly to Section 3(c), which summarizes the results obtained from the model.

b. The Model

The economic model of the rural labor market developed in Chapter 3 can be used to determine whether contracts containing layoffs and unemployment insurance, in the form of indoor relief, dominated the alternative labor contracts. I assume that use of the workhouse increased the cost to the parish of relieving an unemployed laborer from d to $d + r$, where r equals the excess costs above outdoor relief of relieving an unemployed laborer in the workhouse, and that laborers' utility when unemployed was not affected by the substitution of indoor for outdoor relief.[24] The farmer's profit in season t, π_t, is now

$$\pi_t(x_t) = f[n_t(x_t)h_t(x_t), x_t] - n_t(x_t)c_t(x_t)$$
$$- [N - n_t(x_t)][d_t(x_t) + er_t(x_t) - s] \qquad (1)$$

where $f[\cdot]$ is the production function in agriculture, x is the stochastic seasonal factor, n_t is the number of workers employed in season t, h is hours per worker, c is the consumption (income) of an employed worker, d is the consumption (income) of an unemployed worker, N is the total number of workers under contract, e is the share of the poor rate paid by the farmer, and s is the contribution of non-labor-hiring taxpayers to the poor rate (the poor relief subsidy). Note that the only difference between this equation and equation (4) in Chapter 3 is the term $er_t(x_t)$, which represents the increased cost to the farmer of laying off a worker under the workhouse system.

The solution to the farmer's problem follows that given in the Appendix to Chapter 3. The effect of the workhouse on the number of layoffs

---

[24] The assumption that workers' utility when unemployed was not affected by the change in relief administration is made to simplify the mathematics of the model. I discuss later in this section the effect on the form of the profit-maximizing contract of dropping this assumption.

can be seen in inequality (2). Layoffs will occur during season t if, for some $n_t(x_t) < N$

$$f_1[n_t(x_t)h_t(x_t), x_t]h_t(x_t) < c_t(x_t)$$
$$- d_t(x_t) - er_t(x_t) + s - z_t(x_t) \qquad (2)$$

The left-hand side of the inequality is the output of the marginal worker, while the right-hand side represents the cost to the farmer of employing the marginal worker $(c_t - d_t - er_t + s)$ minus the amount the worker would pay not to be laid off, z_t. The substitution of the workhouse for outdoor relief reduced the cost of employing the marginal worker by er_t, and therefore reduced the probability of layoffs occurring, and the optimal number of layoffs, for any value of x_t.

It was shown in Chapter 3 that layoffs would never occur if the poor relief subsidy $s \equiv (1 - e)g$ was equal to zero, where g is the poor relief benefit paid to unemployed workers. In other words, full-employment contracts were dominant in parishes where labor-hiring farmers paid the entire poor rate ($e = 1$). If $s = 0$, for any contract containing layoffs there was a full-employment contract that yielded equal profits. Farmers therefore were indifferent between the two contracts, but risk-averse workers preferred the full-employment contract. A similar result is obtained when indoor relief is substituted for outdoor relief. Under the workhouse system, if $s = 0$, farmers always could find a full-employment contract that yielded higher profits than any contract containing layoffs. Farmers were indifferent between full-employment contracts and contracts with layoffs when $s = er_t$, that is, when the poor relief subsidy the farmer received equaled the extra cost to him of relieving unemployed laborers in the workhouse. Layoffs will occur only when

$$(1 - e)g > er \qquad (3)$$

This can be rewritten as

$$e < g/(g + r) \qquad (4)$$

Recall that g represents the benefit paid to an unemployed laborer under the outdoor relief system, which I assume was equal to the consumption value of the poor relief given to an unemployed laborer in the workhouse. Inequality (4) shows that layoffs will occur only if the farmer's share of the poor rate is less than the ratio of the cost of relieving an unemployed worker with outdoor relief to the cost of relieving him in the workhouse, $g + r$.

Indoor relief was 50–100% more expensive than outdoor relief; that is, $0.5g \leq r \leq g$. If $r = 0.5g$, then inequality (4) shows that farmers will not lay off workers unless $e < 0.67$; that is, layoffs will occur only in parishes where labor-hiring farmers paid less than 67% of the poor rate. If $r = g$, layoffs will not occur unless $e < 0.5$. I concluded in Chapter 3 that the typical share of the poor rate paid by labor-hiring farmers was 67–75%. Thus, the model suggests that the implementation of the workhouse system altered the form of farmers' profit-maximizing implicit labor contracts in most southeastern parishes, from one including seasonal layoffs and poor relief for unemployed laborers to one of yearlong employment contracts. Crop mix was no longer a major determining factor in the form of labor contracts. The high cost of indoor relief meant that even most grain-producing farmers found it in their interest never to lay off seasonally redundant laborers. Full-employment contracts were dominant in all parishes except those in which farmers' share of the poor rate was relatively low.

The above result was obtained assuming that laborers' utility when unemployed was not affected by the form of poor relief. If the workhouse was indeed "psychologically repugnant" to laborers, farmers who used layoffs would have had to raise peak-season wage rates as compensation for the positive probability of having to enter a workhouse. This increased the cost of layoffs still further, and therefore increased the attractiveness of full-employment contracts.

c. Summary

The model developed in this section shows that because of the high cost of indoor relief, even in grain-producing areas most farmers preferred full-employment contracts to contracts containing seasonal layoffs and indoor relief for unemployed laborers. Contracts including layoffs and indoor relief were cost-minimizing for grain-producing farmers only in parishes where they paid a relatively small share of the poor rate. (If indoor relief was 50% more expensive than outdoor relief, the model shows that under the workhouse system labor-hiring farmers would choose to lay off workers during slack seasons only if they paid less than 67% of the poor rate.)

The model predicts that in parishes where the payment of outdoor relief to able-bodied laborers was abolished, grain-producing farmers reduced or eliminated seasonal layoffs and instead hired laborers to yearlong contracts. On the other hand, the model's results support Digby's conclusion that it was in the interest of grain-producing farmers to ignore the Poor Law Commission's directives and continue to offer laborers contracts including seasonal layoffs and outdoor relief after 1834. The effect of the New Poor Law on the form of labor contracts in the grain-producing southeast therefore depended on the Poor Law Commission's enforcement of its orders prohibiting outdoor relief.

The model also shows why parishes did not decide on their own to substitute indoor relief for outdoor relief. Farmers dominated parish politics before 1834, so they were able to tailor the poor relief system to fit their needs. The high costs associated with relieving the unemployed in workhouses made implicit contracts containing seasonal layoffs and indoor relief unattractive to profit-maximizing farmers. The workhouse was well suited for the problem of voluntary unemployment envisioned by the Poor Law Commission, but it was not well suited for the farmers' problem of how to secure an adequate peak-season labor force for the least cost.

It is time to turn to the empirical evidence concerning the effect of the Poor Law Amendment Act on the agricultural labor market. The remainder of the chapter addresses two related questions: How did implicit labor contracts change in response to the New Poor Law? What happened to the standard of living of agricultural laborers in the south of England from 1834 to 1850? There is no systematic evidence that can be used to answer the first question. The major sources of information are the testimony before the 1838 Select Committee on the Poor Law Amendment Act, the annual reports of the Poor Law Commission, and two 1843 reports on the employment of women and children in agriculture and the use of allotments. An approximate answer to the second question can be obtained at the county level of aggregation from data on wage rates and relief expenditures.

4. Movements in Real Income, 1832–50

In order to determine the change in real family income for southern agricultural laborers from 1832 to 1850, it is necessary to have data on changes in: real poor relief expenditures, real wage rates, seasonal unemployment rates, prevalence and size of allotments, and earnings of wives and children. I begin by focusing on changes in relief expenditures and real wages, assuming that the unemployment rate, use of allotments, and earnings of women and children remained constant. One is forced to proceed in this manner because of the lack of systematic evidence concerning the latter three variables. However, anecdotal evidence suggests that each of these three variables changed in such a way as to increase laborers' earnings, so that focusing the analysis on poor relief and real wages should yield a pessimistic estimate of the change in family income.

The passage of the Poor Law Amendment Act caused a sharp reduction in per capita relief expenditures. Column 1 of Table 7.3 shows that real per capita poor relief expenditures in southeastern counties declined, on average, by 34% from 1831–2 to 1850–1. The reduction in relief expenditures per agricultural laborer must have been even larger, since one of the major goals of the New Poor Law was to reduce expenditures on able-bodied laborers. Columns 2 through 4 present estimates of relief expenditures per agricultural laborer in 1831–2 and 1850–1, in 1832 pounds. The absolute decline in expenditures per worker is given in columns 5 and 6. These estimates should be considered rough approximations, since it is not possible to determine what share of a county's relief expenditures went to agricultural laborers and their families. To take account of the probable decline in the share of relief expenditures going to able-bodied adult males after 1834, I have assumed that payments to agricultural laborers and their families constituted 33% of relief expenditures in 1831–2, and between 20% and 25% of expenditures in 1850–1. Given these assumptions, relief expenditures per agricultural laborer declined, on average, by 46–57% from 1831–2 to 1850–1. In absolute terms, laborers' annual income from poor relief declined by an average of £1.3–£1.6.

Given the objectives of the New Poor Law, it might be expected that relief expenditures per agricultural laborer declined by more than 50% after 1834. However, profit-maximizing farmers should have attempted to evade the Poor Law Commission's orders prohibiting outdoor relief. Contracts containing seasonal layoffs and outdoor relief were shown in Section 3 to be cheaper than either full-employment contracts or contracts containing layoffs and indoor relief. There is evidence that rural Poor Law unions continued to grant outdoor relief to able-bodied laborers after 1834. Digby (1978: 109–14) has shown that East Anglian farmers anxious to reduce labor costs returned to the outdoor relief system in the early 1840s. They evaded the prohibitory order by granting outdoor "relief ostensibly in aid of sickness" to seasonally unemployed labor-

Table 7.3. Changes in poor relief expenditures, 1831/2–1850/1

County	% decline in real per capita relief expenditures 1831/2–1850/1	Relief expenditures per agricultural laborer (1832 £s)			Decline in expenditures per laborer (1832 £s)	
		1831/2[a]	1850/1[b]	1850/1[c]	1831/2–1850/1[a,b]	1831/2–1850/1[a,c]
Bedford	50.1	2.22	0.80	1.01	1.42	1.21
Berkshire	27.0	2.73	1.06	1.32	1.67	1.41
Buckingham	38.2	2.88	1.36	1.70	1.52	1.18
Cambridge	21.6	2.21	1.05	1.31	1.16	0.90
Essex	34.6	2.42	1.19	1.49	1.23	0.93
Hertford	26.3	2.18	0.95	1.18	1.23	1.00
Huntingdon	31.1	2.30	1.03	1.29	1.27	1.01
Kent	44.2	3.36	1.42	1.78	1.94	1.58
Norfolk	30.1	2.83	1.26	1.58	1.57	1.25
Northampton	37.6	2.89	1.18	1.47	1.71	1.42
Oxford	33.6	2.85	1.19	1.48	1.66	1.37
Southampton	30.0	3.12	1.50	1.88	1.62	1.24
Suffolk	43.5	2.82	1.02	1.27	1.80	1.55
Sussex	45.4	3.63	1.30	1.63	2.30	2.00
Wiltshire	23.4	2.69	1.41	1.77	1.28	0.92

[a]Assumes that 33% of relief expenditures in 1831/2 were paid to agricultural laborers and their families.
[b]Assumes that 20% of relief expenditures in 1850/1 were paid to agricultural laborers and their families.
[c]Assumes that 25% of relief expenditures in 1850/1 were paid to agricultural laborers and their families.

Sources: Relief expenditure data for 1831/2 were obtained from Blaug (1963: 178–9) and Table 6.1. Relief expenditure data for 1850/1 were obtained from Parl. Papers (1852: XXIII). Cost-of-living data were obtained from Lindert and Williamson (1985: 148–9).

ers.[25] James Caird (1852: 515) concluded from his tour of the rural southeast that "the same system" of poor relief as that adopted in 1795 "is, in effect, still in existence." Even Edwin Chadwick, the coauthor of the 1834 Poor Law Report, wrote in 1847 that "in Norfolk and Suffolk . . . the apparently small exception of allowing relief to a poor family, on the occurrence of sickness to one of them . . . was made the means of flooding the unions or parishes with the allowance system" (quoted in Digby 1978: 113).

In addition, available evidence concerning the relief of non-able-bodied paupers suggests that the elderly and widows also experienced a reduction in real relief benefits after 1834, of as much as 40% (Snell 1985: 131–5). If overall expenditures per capita declined by 34%, and the generosity of relief for non-able-bodied paupers was reduced by, say, 25%, then relief expenditures for able-bodied paupers could not have declined by much more than 50%.

Estimates of changes in wage income from 1832 to 1850–1 for agricultural laborers in southeastern counties are presented in Table 7.4. Column 2 gives the expected annual earnings of an agricultural laborer in 1850–1, in 1832 pounds, assuming that the unemployment rate remained unchanged from 1832 to 1850. The absolute change in income from 1832 to 1850–1 is given in column 5. The data display a pronounced regional pattern. Earnings declined in two of the four East Anglian counties – Cambridge and Suffolk – and increased by only £0.5 in Norfolk and £0.1 in Essex. Outside East Anglia, laborers' earnings increased in ten of eleven counties, declining only in Berkshire. I shall have more to say about East Anglia in Section 5.

To determine what happened to the "total" income (wage income + poor relief benefits) of agricultural laborers from 1832 to 1850, the numbers in column 5 must be added to the previous estimates of the decline in relief benefits per laborer, given in columns 5 and 6 of Table

[25] Digby's (1975: 72) study of relief administration in six grain-producing eastern counties revealed that two-thirds of the "adult able-bodied paupers receiving outdoor allowances between 1842 and 1846 were described as receiving it because of sickness or accident, compared with fewer than one out of two in England and Wales." In 1848–59, 50.7% "of the adult able-bodied outdoor poor in this area were men relieved because of their own sickness, accident, or infirmity" or that of their wives and families (1975: 73). Digby concluded that rural boards of guardians systematically used "medical relief to give outdoor relief to the able-bodied poor" (1975: 73). On the other hand, Williams (1981: 74) maintained that most adult males relieved on account of sickness "were genuinely sick," and therefore that "negligible numbers of unemployed men [were relieved] under the exception clauses."

Table 7.4. *Movements in wage income of agricultural laborers,*
1832–1850/1

| County | Expected annual wage income (1832 £s) | | | | Change in income 1832–1850/1 (1832 £s) | | |
	1832	1850/1 (a)	1850/1 (b)	1850/1 (c)	(a)	(b)	(c)
Bedford	25.50	29.58	30.31	32.28	4.08	4.81	6.78
Berkshire	27.30	25.33	25.64	26.46	−1.97	−1.66	−0.84
Buckingham	26.95	29.03	29.55	31.00	2.08	2.60	4.05
Cambridge	26.18	24.09	24.48	25.59	−2.09	−1.70	−0.59
Essex	26.48	26.61	26.98	27.98	0.13	0.50	1.50
Hertford	28.39	29.92	30.22	31.05	1.53	1.83	2.66
Huntingdon	29.36	30.89	31.19	32.03	1.53	1.83	2.67
Kent	32.26	36.13	36.65	38.10	3.87	4.39	5.84
Norfolk	28.27	28.81	29.38	30.95	0.54	1.11	2.68
Northampton	24.96	28.23	28.95	30.93	3.27	3.99	5.97
Oxford	25.03	28.81	29.44	31.16	3.78	4.41	6.13
Southampton	26.95	30.72	31.20	32.51	3.77	4.25	5.56
Suffolk	26.00	23.66	24.21	25.70	−2.34	−1.79	−0.30
Sussex	28.73	32.18	32.86	34.74	3.45	4.13	6.01
Wiltshire	22.25	22.87	23.41	24.89	0.62	1.16	2.64

(a) assumes that the unemployment rate did not change from 1832 to 1850/1.
(b) assumes that the unemployment rate declined by 20% from 1832 to 1850/1.
(c) assumes that the unemployment rate declined by 75% from 1832 to 1850/1.
Sources: Data on expected income and the unemployment rate in 1832 were obtained from Chapter 4, Table 4.1. Data on the change in wage rates 1832–1850/1 come from Table 7.2.

7.3. The results obtained from this calculation are given in Table 7.5, columns 2 and 3, and Table 7.6, columns 1 and 2. The first, and most important, conclusion to be drawn from these results is that, in contrast to Snell's conclusion, agricultural laborers' income did not decline throughout southern England after 1834. Laborers' total income increased from 1831–2 to 1850–1 in 9 of the 15 counties. Second, the change in laborers' income was generally small, in percentage terms. Workers experienced a decline in income of over 10% in only 3 of the 15 counties, and an increase of over 10% only in Bedford. The largest change was in Suffolk, where laborers' income declined by 13.5–14.4%.

Table 7.5. *Movements in "total" income of agricultural laborers,*
1832–1850/1

County	Estimated total income 1831/2 (in £)	Change in total income 1831/2–1850/1 (1832 £s)				
		(a)	(b)	(c)	(d)	(e)
Bedford	27.72	2.66	2.87	3.39	3.60	4.56
Berkshire	30.03	−3.64	−3.38	−3.33	−3.07	−3.57
Buckingham	29.83	0.56	0.90	1.08	1.42	1.17
Cambridge	28.39	−3.25	−2.99	−2.86	−2.60	−2.80
Essex	28.90	−1.10	−0.80	−0.73	−0.43	−0.92
Hertford	30.57	0.30	0.53	0.60	0.83	0.48
Huntingdon	31.66	0.26	0.52	0.56	0.82	0.37
Kent	35.62	1.93	2.29	2.45	2.81	2.48
Norfolk	31.10	−1.03	−0.71	−0.46	−0.14	−0.15
Northampton	27.85	1.56	1.85	2.28	2.57	3.08
Oxford	27.88	2.12	2.41	2.75	3.04	3.28
Southampton	30.07	2.15	2.53	2.63	3.01	2.44
Suffolk	28.82	−4.14	−3.89	−3.59	−3.34	−3.12
Sussex	32.36	1.12	1.45	1.80	2.13	2.38
Wiltshire	24.94	−0.66	−0.30	−0.12	0.24	−0.05

(a) assumes that 20% of relief expenditures in 1850/1 were paid to agricultural laborers and their families.
(b) assumes that 25% of relief expenditures in 1850/1 were paid to agricultural laborers and their families.
(c) assumes that 20% of relief expenditures in 1850/1 were paid to agricultural laborers and that the unemployment rate declined by 20% from 1832 to 1850/1.
(d) assumes that 25% of relief expenditures in 1850/1 were paid to agricultural laborers and that the unemployment rate declined by 20% from 1832 to 1850/1.
(e) assumes that no relief expenditures in 1850/1 were paid to agricultural laborers and that the unemployment rate declined by 75% from 1832 to 1850/1.
Sources: Calculated from Tables 7.3 and 7.4.

Third, laborers' income declined by more than 3% in each East Anglian county. Outside East Anglia, income declined in only 2 of 11 counties, and declined by more than 3% in only one county, Berkshire. The average decline in income from 1831–2 to 1850–1 in East Anglia was 7.3–8.4%. In the rest of the southeast, laborers' income increased by 2.5–3.5%, on average.

Up to this point I have assumed that the unemployment rate in agricul-

Table 7.6. *Percentage change in "total" income of agricultural laborers,*
1831/2–1850/1

County	(a)	(b)	(c)	(d)	(e)
Bedford	9.6	10.4	12.2	13.0	16.5
Berkshire	−12.1	−11.3	−11.1	−10.2	−11.9
Buckingham	1.9	3.0	3.6	4.8	3.9
Cambridge	−11.5	−10.5	−10.1	−9.2	−9.9
Essex	−3.8	−2.8	−2.5	−1.5	−3.2
Hertford	1.0	1.7	2.0	2.7	1.6
Huntingdon	0.8	1.6	1.8	2.6	1.2
Kent	5.4	6.4	6.9	7.9	7.0
Norfolk	−3.3	−2.3	−1.5	−0.5	−0.5
Northampton	5.6	6.6	8.2	9.2	11.1
Oxford	7.6	8.6	9.9	10.9	11.8
Southampton	7.2	8.4	8.8	10.0	8.1
Suffolk	−14.4	−13.5	−12.5	−11.6	−10.8
Sussex	3.5	4.5	5.6	6.6	7.4
Wiltshire	−2.7	−1.2	−0.5	1.0	−0.2

Note: Assumptions (a) through (e) are the same as in Table 7.5.
Sources: Calculated from Table 7.5.

ture remained constant from 1832 to 1850. However, there is reason to believe that the unemployment rate declined after 1834. The substitution of the workhouse for outdoor relief reduced the attractiveness of seasonal layoffs to both farmers and laborers. The model developed in Section 3 showed that, in Poor Law unions that adopted the workhouse system, profit-maximizing farmers should have responded by increasing their employment of labor during slack seasons. Indeed, full-employment contracts should have become widespread in unions unable (or unwilling) to evade the outdoor relief prohibitory order.

The testimony given by local officials before the 1838 Select Committee on the Poor Law Amendment Act suggests that farmers increased their slack-season employment of labor in response to the adoption of indoor relief. J. P. Kay, the assistant Poor Law commissioner for Norfolk and Suffolk, stated that the workhouse system "places on the part of the occupier the strongest possible motive . . . to provide employment for the labourers in the parish." The reason for this was simple: The alternative to providing the laborer "with sufficient employment and sufficient wages [was] the maintenance of the labourer at double the cost in the workhouse" (Parl. Papers 1837–8: XVIII, Part I, 482, 487). Kay's opinion was echoed by several others. For instance, the chairman of the Loddon and Clavering Union in Norfolk wrote that "the refusal of out-relief to the able-bodied labourers has caused the owners and occupiers of land to give employment to a much greater extent than ever was known," and the vice-chairman of the board of guardians in Ampthill Union, Bedford, testified that, since the passage of the Poor Law Amendment Act, "the condition and comforts of the labouring poor [were] much improved, they being much more in work" (Parl. Papers 1837–8: XVIII, Part I, 520; Part II, 526).

The effect of a decline in the unemployment rate after 1834 on income can be seen in Table 7.4. Columns 6 and 7 present estimates of the change in agricultural laborers' earnings from 1832 to 1850–1, assuming that the unemployment rate declined by 20% and 75%, respectively. The upper-bound estimate is admittedly very high, but, according to the testimony given before the Poor Law Commission, it represents a reasonable measure of what happened to unemployment rates in parishes that abolished outdoor relief for able-bodied laborers. The estimated change in "total" income from 1831–2 to 1850–1, given a decline in the unemployment rate of 20–75%, is presented in Table 7.5, columns 4–6, and Table 7.6, columns 3–5. Obviously, the assumption that unemployment declined in response to the passage of the New Poor Law makes the estimated change in income more "optimistic." If the unemployment rate declined by 20%, the total income of agricultural laborers outside East Anglia increased by 4.3–5.3%, while in East Anglia income declined by 5.7–6.6%. Income declined by more than 4% in only three counties: Berkshire, Cambridge, and Suffolk. The estimates contained in column 6 of Table 7.5 (column 5 of Table 7.6) assume that the unemployment rate declined by 75% and that *no* relief expenditures were paid to agricultural laborers and their families after 1834. These estimates are an attempt to determine what happened to laborers' income in parishes that abolished outdoor relief. A comparison of column 5 with columns 3 and 4 of Table 7.6 shows that the estimated change in laborers' income is not greatly affected by one's assumptions concerning the change in unemployment rates and the administration of poor relief after 1834. This result supports the hypothesis that in order to retain an adequate peak-season labor force, farmers had to offer their laborers an implicit contract with an expected utility equal to some reservation level.

In parishes where outdoor relief remained an option after 1834, farmers continued to use seasonal layoffs in order to minimize labor costs. Where outdoor relief was replaced by the workhouse, farmers responded by reducing seasonal layoffs and retaining their laborers in employment for most, if not all, of the slack season. Farmers' profit rates varied across contracts, but laborers' income did not.

5. The Regional Labor Market, 1832–50

The real earnings gap between London and the agricultural southeast increased sharply after 1834. The results in Table 7.6 show that, from 1831–2 to 1850–1, the income of southeastern farm laborers outside of East Anglia increased by 2.5–5.3%, on average, while the income of farm laborers in East Anglia declined by 5.7–8.4%. Over the same period, the income of London builders' laborers increased by 30%.[26] This section analyzes the causes of the increase in the rural–urban earnings gap, and its implications concerning the integration of the regional labor market.

Before discussing why the earnings gap increased, it is important to note that the data in Tables 7.5 and 7.6 might underestimate the increase in agricultural laborers' income from 1831–2 to 1850–1 because they do not take account of increases in income from sources other than wage labor and poor relief. In particular, the data in Tables 7.5 and 7.6 do not include estimates of the increase in income resulting from the increased availability of allotments for agricultural laborers. It will be recalled that Hasbach (1908: 235–41) maintained that allotments became more widespread after 1834, as did Clapham (1930: 472–4). The 1843 *Report . . . on the Employment of Women and Children in Agriculture* (Parl. Papers 1843: XII, 220, 15) concluded that allotments were "becoming general" in Norfolk, Suffolk, and Lincoln, and were "rapidly on the increase of late years" in Wiltshire, Dorset, and Devon. In the same year, the *Report from the Select Committee on the Labouring Poor (Allotments of Land)* (Parl. Papers 1843: VII, iii) concluded that although allotments were rare before 1830, they were now "to be met with in all the agricultural counties, but have not become universal in any one of them."

[26] Nominal wage data for London bricklayers' laborers were obtained from Schwarz (1986: 38). Nominal wages remained constant from 1819 to 1852, so that the entire increase in real wages was caused by a fall in the cost of living. Schwarz estimates that real wages increased by 21–37% from 1832 to 1851 (1986: 41). My estimate was obtained by deflating nominal wages by the revised Lindert–Williamson cost-of-living index (1985: 148–9).

Persons who testified before the latter committee estimated that the typical allotment was a quarter acre in size, and yielded £4–£5 profit per year (Parl. Papers 1843: VII, 1, 21, 84, 92–3).

To determine the increase in the typical laborer's income from allotments from 1831–2 to 1850–1 we need to know the increase in the share of agricultural laborers with allotments and the increase in the average size of allotments. Such data are not available, but what information exists suggests that the typical agricultural laborer's annual income from allotments increased by perhaps £1.5 in the East Anglian counties of Essex, Suffolk, Norfolk, and Cambridge, and by no more than £1 in the remaining southeastern counties.[27] Column 1 of Table 7.7 presents estimates of the percentage change in agricultural laborers' income from 1831–2 to 1850–1 when the increased income from allotments is taken into account.[28] On average, laborers' income declined by 1.5% in East Anglia and increased by 7.7% in the other southeastern counties.[29]

A sharp increase in the rural–urban earnings gap from 1831–2 to 1850–1 remains after the increased use of allotments is taken into account. The increase in the earnings gap suggests that the southeastern labor market became less efficient after the adoption of the New Poor Law. But the results obtained from comparing rural–urban earnings gaps in 1831–2 and 1850–1 are very misleading. The years 1849–53 were

[27] Question 20 of the Rural Queries contains information on the prevalence of allotments in 1832. Of the 446 southeastern parishes that responded to the question, 195 (43.7%) mentioned the existence of allotments, although in some parishes allotments were rented to only a small share of the laborers. The typical allotment was about one-eighth acre in size, which, by the estimates cited above, should have yielded a profit of £2–£2.5 per year. If 15% of southeastern laborers rented allotments averaging one-eighth acre in size in 1832, the typical laborer's annual income from an allotment was £0.3–£0.38. The available data suggest that both the prevalence and average size of allotments increased from 1832 to 1850. If one-third of southeastern laborers rented allotments of a quarter acre in 1850, the typical laborer's annual income from an allotment was £1.33–£1.67. That is, the increased use of allotments increased the average laborer's annual income by £1–£1.3 from 1832 to 1850. Allotments were less prevalent in East Anglia than in other southeastern counties in 1832, but by 1843 the extent of allotments appears to have been as great (or perhaps greater) in East Anglia as in the rest of the southeast. This suggests that from 1832 to 1850 income from allotments increased by more for East Anglian laborers than for other southeastern laborers.

[28] The estimates in column 1 of Table 7.7 were obtained by adding the estimated increase in income from allotments (£1.5 for East Anglian counties and £1 for other counties) to the estimates of the change in income from 1831–2 to 1850–1 given in column (c) of Table 7.5, and dividing the result by the total income in 1831–2. I chose column (c) of Table 7.5 because I believe it represents the best-guess estimate of the change in laborers' income from 1831–2 to 1850–1.

[29] The average increase in laborers' earnings was 9.2% in the 10 southeastern counties other than East Anglia and Berkshire.

Table 7.7. *Movements in income of agricultural laborers, 1831/2–1869/70*

| | % change in income | | |
County	1831/2–1850/1[a]	1831/2–1846[b]	1850/1–1869/70
Bedford	15.8	13.0	15.6
Berkshire	−7.8	−10.0	15.2
Buckingham	7.0	4.4	24.9
Cambridge	−4.8	−4.8	24.6
Essex	2.7	2.7	21.3
Hertford	5.2	2.6	18.8
Huntingdon	4.9	2.3	19.9
Kent	9.7	7.0	5.7
Norfolk	3.3	3.3	13.3
Northampton	11.8	9.1	11.7
Oxford	13.5	10.7	15.6
Southampton	12.1	9.4	2.2
Suffolk	−7.3	−7.3	31.4
Sussex	8.7	6.0	−4.3
Wiltshire	3.5	1.0	24.0

[a]These numbers were obtained by adding the estimated increase in income from allotments to the estimates of the change in income from 1831/2 to 1850/1 given in column (c) of Table 7.5, and dividing the result by the total income in 1831/2.
[b]These numbers were calculated from the numbers in column 1, assuming that from 1846 to 1851 workers' real income remained constant in Cambridge, Essex, Norfolk, and Suffolk, and increased by 2.5% elsewhere.
Sources: See text.

"a time of great agricultural depression" (Fox 1903: 280). The depression was especially severe in grain-producing areas. Hasbach (1908: 245) maintained that, in the corn districts, "the crisis of 1849 to 1853 . . . was among the worst of the century." In 1849–51 the price of wheat averaged 41.0s. per quarter, 35% below the price in 1830–2 and 21% below the price in 1843–6 (Mitchell and Deane 1962: 488). The price decline was not caused by a series of good harvests. Fairlie (1969: 114) estimates that domestic wheat output declined by 17.8% from 1843–6 to 1849–51.[30] The total revenue (output times price) of grain farmers declined by 34.6% from 1843–6 to 1849–51.

[30] Imports of wheat and wheat meal and flour increased by 238% from 1843–6 to 1849–51 (Mitchell and Deane 1962: 98).

Southeastern farmers responded to the decline in revenue by cutting nominal wages. The *Second Report on the Wages, Earnings, and Conditions of Employment of Agricultural Labourers* (Parl. Papers 1905: XCVII) contains time series of wages for 12 southeastern farms from 1846 to 1851.[31] The time series show that nominal wages of East Anglian farm laborers declined by 17.1% from 1846 to 1851; elsewhere in the southeast wages declined by 15.0%. The cost of living fell by 17.1% over the period (Lindert and Williamson 1985: 148), so real wages of East Anglian laborers remained constant from 1846 to 1851, while real wages of laborers elsewhere in the southeast increased by 2.5%. Nominal wages of London builders' laborers remained constant from 1846 to 1851 (Schwarz 1986: 38); the decline in living costs caused real wages to increase by 20.7%. The rural–urban earnings gap therefore increased sharply from 1846 to 1851.

From 1832 to 1846, real wages of London builders' laborers increased by only 8%. The increase in farm laborers' income during this period can be estimated by assuming that from 1846 to 1851 real income remained constant in East Anglia and increased by 2.5% elsewhere. The estimates obtained from this procedure are given in column 2 of Table 7.7. Apart from East Anglia and Berkshire, farm laborers' earnings increased by 6.6% from 1832 to 1846, roughly the same as the increase in London laborers' earnings. Farm laborers' income increased by more than 8% in 4 counties; the earnings gap between London and these counties declined. On the other hand, East Anglian laborers' earnings declined, on average, by 1.5% from 1832 to 1846.

It is not surprising that the earnings gap between London and East Anglia increased by more than the earnings gap between London and the rest of the southeast, because East Anglia was the major wheat-producing region in England. In 1836, 19.2% of the farmland in East Anglia was devoted to wheat, as compared to 15.6% in the rest of the southeast and 10.8% in England and Wales.[32] From 1842 to 1851 wheat prices were on average 20% below their level in 1830–2 (Mitchell and Deane 1962: 488).

---

[31] The report presents time series for 133 English farms of "weekly cash wages . . . to ordinary farm labourers in receipt of full men's wages, exclusive of payments for piecework, or extra payments during hay and corn harvest, or for overtime, or the value of any allowances in kind" (Parl. Papers 1905: XCVII, 65). Although most of the series begin in 1850 or later, the series for 12 southeastern farms (5 in East Anglia) begin at or before 1846.

[32] The estimates are based on land use and crop data from the tithe surveys compiled at the county level by Kain (1986). I calculated the share of farmland devoted to wheat by dividing each region's estimated acreage in wheat by its estimated acreage in arable and grass.

The precarious situation of East Anglian farmers in 1850–1 was noted by Caird, who wrote (1852: 146) that "the position of the Suffolk farmer has been gradually reduced; and . . . a continuation of low prices will bring ruin on those who have been farming with borrowed capital." Concerning Cambridge, Caird wrote that "in any district of England in which we have yet been, we have not heard the farmers speak in a tone of greater discouragement than here" (1852: 467–8).

The agricultural depression ended in 1853, and as a result the earnings gap between London and the rural southeast declined. From 1851 to 1855 nominal wages of agricultural laborers on 12 farms in the "chief corn-growing counties" of Essex, Suffolk, Norfolk, Cambridge, Lincoln, and Huntingdon increased by 38.3%, while the nominal wage of London builders' laborers increased by 16.7%.[33] From 1855 to the early 1870s the earnings gap between London and the rural southeast remained roughly constant. Column 3 of Table 7.7 contains estimates of the change in real wages of southeastern agricultural laborers from 1850–1 to 1869–70. During this period real wages of London builders' laborers increased by 5.4%.[34] The wage gap between London and 13 of the 15 southeastern counties declined from 1850–1 to 1869–70. Agricultural laborers' wages increased most rapidly, and therefore the wage gap declined most sharply, in East Anglia, the region that had experienced the largest relative decline in earnings from 1832 to 1850–1.

The above results show that the earnings gap between London and the rural southeast reached a maximum from 1849 to 1852.[35] An accurate measure of the long-term trend in labor market integration after 1834 therefore cannot be obtained by comparing rural–urban earnings gaps in 1831–2 and 1850–1. From 1832 to 1846 the earnings gap between London and most southeastern counties remained roughly constant. The earnings gap increased sharply from 1846 to 1851, as a result of the severe agricultural depression that began in 1849. The return of agricultural prosperity after 1853 brought a sharp increase in rural laborers'

---

[33] Data on nominal wages of farm laborers are from the *Second Report on the Wages, Earnings, and Conditions of Employment of Agricultural Labourers* (Parl. Papers 1905: XCVII, 68). Wage data for London builders' laborers are from Schwarz (1986: 38).

[34] Wage data for London builders' laborers in 1850–1 are from Schwarz (1986: 38). Data for 1869–70 are from Bowley (1901: 104). Both sources present data for bricklayers' laborers.

[35] Williamson (1982: 17) found that the "wage gap between farm and nonfarm unskilled workers" for England as a whole reached a maximum in 1851, then declined sharply from 1851 to 1871.

Table 7.8. *Migration rates and changes in labor supply in the southeast,*
1841–51

County	Net number of migrants 1841–51[a]	Migrants per 1,000 population[a]	% change in agricultural labor force 1841–51
Bedford	717	5.9	16.2
Berkshire	−10,250	−52.6	6.7
Buckingham	−10,705	−75.9	3.4
Cambridge	−267	−1.5	10.0
Essex	−13,446	−40.4	4.2
Hertford	−8,823	−52.5	12.3
Huntingdon	−3,266	−56.4	23.4
Kent	−12,927	−27.7	6.8
Norfolk	−13,332	−31.8	13.8
Northampton	−10,810	−52.3	2.6
Oxford	−9,702	−58.2	10.8
Southampton	12,106	32.1	6.7
Suffolk	−18,423	−56.6	11.4
Sussex	464	1.4	9.3
Wiltshire	−24,969	−103.2	12.6

[a] A negative number represents net out-migration. A positive number
represents net in-migration.
Sources: All data were obtained from the 1841 and 1851 censuses.

wages, and from 1850–1 to 1869–70 the earnings gap between London
and most southeastern counties declined. In sum, the available evidence
suggests that the adoption of the New Poor Law had little effect on the
size of rural–urban earnings gaps.

One issue remains to be considered, namely, the effect of the relative
decline in agricultural laborers' wages during the 1840s on rural–urban
migration and on the supply of agricultural labor. The net loss (or gain)
of migrants and the net migration rate for the period 1841–51 for each
southeastern county are given in columns 1 and 2 of Table 7.8.[36] The

[36] A county's net number of migrants from 1841 to 1851 can be calculated from the
following equation:
$NETMIGRATION(1841–51) = POPULATION(1851) − [POPULATION(1841) +$
$BIRTHS(1841–51) − DEATHS(1841–51)]$
A positive value for NETMIGRATION signifies that the county experienced net in-
migration during the decade, a negative value signifies net out-migration. The calculation cannot be done for earlier decades because data on the number of births and deaths
are not available before 1837.

total net out-migration from the southeast was 123,366 persons, or 3.3% of the average population of the southeastern counties during the decade.[37] The out-migration rate was related to the rate of growth of farm laborers' income. The six counties in which laborers' income either declined or increased by less than 4% (Essex, Suffolk, Norfolk, Cambridge, Berkshire, and Wiltshire) had a net out-migration of 47.7 persons per 1,000 population. The nine counties in which laborers' income increased by more than 4% had a net out-migration of 21.1 persons per 1,000 population. The main destination of these migrants was London (Hunt 1973: 281–4).[38]

What effect did out-migration have on the supply of agricultural labor? The percentage change from 1841 to 1851 in the number of adult male agricultural laborers in each county is given in column 3 of Table 7.8.[39] The southeast as a whole experienced a 9.1% increase in its agricultural labor force from 1841 to 1851. Available price and output data for wheat suggest that the demand for farm labor declined during the 1840s.[40] It is therefore no wonder that farm laborers' earnings grew slowly or declined during the decade. Assuming that the rural labor market was at or near equilibrium in 1841, the decline in the demand for

---

[37] The net out-migration rates in Table 7.8 are not comparable with Williamson's (1987) estimates of gross out-migration rates presented above. Net out-migration equals gross out-migration minus gross in-migration. The extent to which a county's net out-migration rate understates its gross out-migration rate therefore depends on the extent of gross in-migration to the county.

[38] The importance of London as a destination for migrants from the rural south can be seen by comparing data on the birthplaces of persons living in London in 1851 with birthplace data for the major industrial region of England, the counties of Lancashire, Cheshire, and the West Riding. Norfolk was not much farther from the West Riding than from London, and yet there were only 2,008 Norfolk-born inhabitants of the West Riding in 1851 compared to 31,866 Norfolk-born Londoners. There were 2,627 Northampton-born and 1,175 Oxford-born inhabitants of Lancashire, Cheshire, and the West Riding compared to 10,511 and 16,092 inhabitants of London. According to E. H. Hunt (1981: 157), "London's attraction was probably due partly to accessibility – road and rail links focused on the capital – and must have owed something also to the combination of London's dominance in pre-industrial Britain and the tendency of migration streams to perpetuate themselves. . . . Southern farm labourers and their offspring were in any case unlikely to be particularly attracted by factory employment."

[39] Occupational data in the 1841 census are given for ancient counties. In the 1851 census data are given for registration counties. To adjust for differences in county boundaries, I divided the number of agricultural laborers in 1851 by the ratio of the area of the registration county to the area of the ancient county.

[40] The price of wheat declined by 22.7% from 1838–42 to 1843–51 (Mitchell and Deane 1962: 488). Fairlie's (1969: 114) estimates of domestic wheat production suggest that output was roughly constant from 1838 to 1844, increased in 1845 to a level 25% above its 1838–44 level, then declined sharply after the repeal of the Corn Laws in 1846. Annual wheat output in 1847–51 was 9% below output in 1838–44.

labor, combined with the increase in labor supply, resulted in a labor surplus in rural parishes.

It was in the interest of farmers (and other parish taxpayers) to keep the number of surplus laborers as small as possible. In terms of the model developed in Chapter 3, farmers could encourage the out-migration of surplus labor by setting the expected utility of the implicit contract offered to workers, $E(V)$, below workers' reservation level of utility, V^*, which was determined by wage rates in London. One could argue that southeastern farmers deliberately chose not to increase the value of their workers' contracts by enough to match the rapid increase in London wage rates from 1846 to 1851, in order to encourage surplus labor to migrate to London.[41] Of course, farmers would not have encouraged out-migration if they considered the sharp decline in grain prices in 1849–52 to be a temporary phenomenon. But many grain farmers must have viewed the agricultural depression as the beginning of a long-term decline in the profitability of grain farming caused by the repeal of the Corn Laws in 1846. Such farmers would have been anxious to reduce the number of farm laborers in their parishes. The fact that the supply of farm labor increased by 9.1% in the 1840s suggests that, from the standpoint of southeastern farmers, the rate of out-migration was too low, which implies that the utility value of the contracts that farmers offered their laborers in the late 1840s was too high. Rather than use the threat of the workhouse to reduce wages to subsistence, it appears that southeastern farmers offered their laborers contracts that were more generous than necessary to retain an adequate labor force.

6. Conclusion

The New Poor Law altered the cost-minimizing form of grain-producing farmers' implicit labor contracts, from one including seasonal layoffs and poor relief for unemployed laborers to one of yearlong employment. The form of labor contracts changed because the substitution of relief in workhouses for outdoor relief significantly increased the cost to

---

[41] Sometimes parishes helped surplus laborers to migrate. From 1835 to 1837, East Anglia sent 2,999 persons to the manufacturing districts of the northwest and 4,518 persons overseas under the auspices of the Poor Law Commission's migration programs (Redford 1964: 105–9). The 7,517 migrants from East Anglia represented 70% of the total number of migrants relocated by the Poor Law Commission. Redford claimed that "the local authorities in the agricultural counties" regarded these migration schemes "as an outlet for the disposal of their most troublesome paupers" (1964: 115–6).

farmers of laying off unneeded workers in slack seasons. It is therefore no wonder that many southeastern parishes ignored the Poor Law Commission's directives and continued granting outdoor relief to seasonally unemployed farm workers after 1834. The extent of this practice cannot be measured, but Digby (1975: 71–4; 1978: 110–14) presents evidence that it was widespread in East Anglia, especially after the number of Poor Law inspectors was reduced from 21 to 9 in the mid-1840s.

Although the New Poor Law affected the form of rural labor contracts, the model developed in this chapter suggests that it should not have affected farm laborers' living standards. Farmers anxious to retain an adequate peak-season labor force had to offer laborers a contract that yielded an expected utility equal to their reservation utility, which was determined by wage rates in London and migration costs and therefore was not affected by the New Poor Law. This conclusion runs strongly counter to Snell's (1985: 124) conclusion that the New Poor Law reduced farm laborers' living standards by creating "conditions of dependence in which precarious employment at low wages had to be accepted." Snell's conclusion holds only if labor was immobile and therefore forced to accept any contract that farmers offered. The available estimates of migration rates show, however, that labor was very mobile from 1831 to 1851.

This chapter has presented several estimates of the change in farm laborers' income from 1831–2 to 1850–1 in 15 southeastern counties. The estimates differ in their assumptions concerning the changes in unemployment rates and poor relief administration after 1834, but they all yield the same conclusion: Farm laborers' income increased in the majority of southeastern counties (9 to 12 out of 15, depending on the assumptions), and nowhere declined by as much as 15%. The best-guess estimates in Table 7.7 suggest that laborers' income declined on average by 1.5% in the 4 East Anglian counties and increased by 7.7% in the other 11 counties. The earnings gap between London and most southeastern counties remained roughly constant from 1832 until the agricultural depression of the late 1840s. In sum, the data support the model's conclusion that farm laborers' income was not affected by the New Poor Law.

8

THE ECONOMICS OF POOR
RELIEF IN INDUSTRIAL CITIES

The Royal Poor Law Commission viewed outdoor relief as a rural institution, and most historians, myself included, have focused their analyses on poor relief in agricultural parishes. But outdoor relief also played an important role in the manufacturing cities of northwest England.[1] Along with industrialization came business cycles and the problem of how to deal with cyclical fluctuations in the demand for industrial workers. Manufacturers used the Poor Law as an unemployment insurance system: Workers not needed during downturns were laid off or put on short time, and collected outdoor relief. Because a large share of the poor rate was paid by non-labor-hiring taxpayers, by laying off workers manufacturers were able to pass some of their labor costs on to others during downturns.

However, there was a problem with using the Poor Law as an unemployment insurance system. Parishes were obliged to relieve only those paupers who had their legal settlement in the parish. In the first half of the nineteenth century, 50% or more of the work force in most industrial cities had been born, and were legally settled, elsewhere. Industrial cities not only were under no obligation to relieve nonsettled workers, they had the right to send any nonsettled applicants for relief back to their parish of settlement. A city's policy concerning whether to remove or relieve nonsettled able-bodied applicants depended in part on the political power of its manufacturers. Manufacturers supported granting relief to nonsettled workers during downturns, to ensure that an adequate work force would be available upon the return of prosperity. Non-

[1] The major works on the economic role of poor relief in the industrial northwest during the first half of the nineteenth century are by Michael Rose (1965; 1966; 1970; 1976) and David Ashforth (1976; 1979; 1985). Rose's (1965) unpublished dissertation on poor relief in the West Riding is especially valuable. See also Midwinter (1969), Redford (1964), and Edsall (1971).

233

labor-hiring taxpayers were more anxious to remove nonsettled applicants in order to reduce their relief expenditures. All urban taxpayers agreed, however, that the power of removal was an important weapon that should not be surrendered, because it enabled cities to reduce their expenditures on persons, such as widows or handloom weavers, likely to be long-term recipients of relief.

The purpose of this chapter is to outline the economic role played by outdoor relief in the textile-producing cities of Lancashire and the West Riding of Yorkshire. I focus on manufacturers' use of the Poor Law as an unemployment insurance system, and on cities' selective use of the power of removal to manipulate the size and structure of the urban labor force. No distinction is made between pre-1834 and post-1834 relief administration because most historians agree that industrial cities continued using outdoor relief for at least two decades after 1834.[2] I conclude that in the absence of outdoor relief and the power of removal, manufacturers' profit rates would have been significantly lower. The existence of unemployment insurance, in the form of outdoor relief, enabled manufacturers to use layoffs to shift some of their labor costs to non-labor-hiring taxpayers, while the power of removal enabled urban taxpayers in general to pass some of the cost of relieving nonsettled paupers to their (generally rural) parishes of settlement and to the paupers themselves.

1. The Economic Role of Poor Relief in Industrial Areas

Industrial cities did not face large seasonal fluctuations in labor requirements, but they did have to contend with fluctuations in demand caused by the trade cycle.[3] The early-nineteenth-century trade cycle was to a large extent driven by fluctuations in the demand for exports and therefore was especially pronounced in the textile-producing cities of the northwest. The cyclical behavior of the Lancashire cotton industry and the Yorkshire woollen industry were similar (Matthews 1954: 152). During the period from 1819 to 1850, major downturns in trade occurred in 1826, 1839, 1841–2, and 1847–8, while minor downturns occurred in

---

[2] See, for example, Rose (1966; 1970), Ashforth (1976), and Hunt (1981: 136–7).
[3] This is not to say that seasonality did not exist in industrial cities. The demand for labor in the building trades was seasonal, as was the demand for dressmakers, shirtmakers, and other female-dominated occupations (Jones 1971: 33–51; Treble 1979: 72–80). But seasonality was more of a problem in London and in port cities than in the textile-producing cities in the northwest (Jones 1971: 34).

Table 8.1. *Unemployment and short time in Manchester cotton mills,*
1848

Month	Number of workers	% fully employed	% working short time	% unemployed
January	28,193	79.0	3.0	18.0
February	28,278	76.9	4.4	18.7
March	28,145	71.1	8.7	20.2
April	28,262	63.7	16.8	19.5
May	28,316	69.0	12.8	18.2
June	28,163	71.6	11.1	17.3
Average	28,226	71.9	9.5	18.6

Source: The Economist, weekly issues from January 8, 1848, through July 1,
1848.

1829, 1832, and 1837 (Gayer, Rostow, and Schwartz 1953: 688, 692;
Matthews 1954: 127–44).

Although information concerning unemployment during this period is
scarce, what data are available suggest that unemployment rates were
quite high in the industrial cities during the downturns of 1841–2 and
1847–8. Data reported by Lancashire factory inspectors suggest an unemployment rate of 15% for Lancashire cotton mills during the last
quarter of 1841 (Matthews 1954: 143). Unemployment rates in the
woollen industry were somewhat higher during this period (Matthews
1954: 154).[4] These unemployment rates do not tell the whole story,
however, since many factory workers were put on short time rather than
dismissed. Table 8.1 presents data on unemployment and underemployment in Manchester cotton mills in the first six months of 1848. On
average, 18.6% of the work force was unemployed, while another 9.5%
was on short time. Data on 382 cotton mills in "cotton towns around
Manchester" show that, while 14.3% of the factory workers were unemployed in 1847, another 37.3% were on short time (Pollard 1978: 127).

A major function of the Poor Law in the textile-manufacturing cities
was to provide relief to industrial workers who either had been temporar-

[4] Hobsbawm (1975: 69–71) and Pollard (1978: 126–7) cite unemployment rates of up to
50% for several industrial cities in 1841–2. However, Lindert and Williamson (1983: 13–
16) maintain that these numbers are gross exaggerations of the actual unemployment
rates.

Table 8.2. *Number of adult able-bodied men relieved in Lancashire and the West Riding, 1839–45*

Quarter ended Lady Day	Number relieved on account of		Total
	Want of work	Insufficiency of earnings	
Lancashire			
1839	304	1,461	1,765
1840	883	2,632	3,515
1841	978	2,904	3,882
1842	3,841	4,597	8,438
1843	5,213	5,058	10,271
1844	2,031	3,416	5,447
1845	1,041	2,402	3,443
West Riding			
1839	230	539	769
1840	2,967	838	3,805
1841	2,528	1,118	3,646
1842	4,090	1,993	6,083
1843	7,674	2,222	9,896
1844	1,943	979	2,922
1845	810	717	1,527

Source: Sixth through twelfth annual reports of the Poor Law Commissioners.

ily dismissed or had their hours reduced during downturns in trade. Expenditures on poor relief and the number of able-bodied adults relieved increased sharply during recessions. Between prosperous 1836 and the depression year 1842, real per capita relief expenditures increased by 85% in Bradford and by 209% in Stockport.[5] Most of the increase went to able-bodied workers. Detailed data on the number of persons granted poor relief exist at the county level of aggregation for the years 1839–45. Data on the relief of able-bodied men in Lancashire and the West Riding are given in Table 8.2. Between the first quarter of 1839 and the first quarter of 1843, the number of able-bodied adults relieved because of "want of work" or "insufficient earnings" increased by 482% in Lancashire and by 1187% in the West Riding.[6] The return of

[5] Data on relief expenditures in 1836 and 1842 were obtained from appendixes to the third and tenth annual reports of the Poor Law Commissioners.
[6] The number of non-able-bodied persons relieved in the West Riding increased by 73% during the same period.

prosperity in 1845 brought a sharp reduction in the number of able-bodied workers on relief. From the first quarter of 1843 to the first quarter of 1845, the number of adult able-bodied males relieved declined by 67% in Lancashire and by 85% in the West Riding.

The downturn of 1847–8 brought another sharp increase in relief expenditures and recipients. Table 8.3 presents data on movements in nominal and real relief expenditures from 1844–5 to 1850–1 for five textile-producing cities. Real expenditures roughly doubled from 1844–5 to 1848–9 in Bradford, Leeds, Manchester, and Salford, then declined by between 25% and 63% from 1848–9 to 1850–1.[7] On July 1, 1848, 9,529 and 3,456 adult male workers received poor relief because of "want of work" in Lancashire and the West Riding.[8] Two years later, the number of unemployed and underemployed workers on relief had fallen to 2,070 in Lancashire and 546 in the West Riding, a decline of 78% and 84%, respectively.

The system of poor relief clearly played an important role in aiding workers who suffered declines in income during downturns in trade. The relief policies developed by industrial areas to deal with cyclical unemployment were similar to the policies for dealing with seasonal unemployment in the rural south. The use of the Poor Law as an unemployment insurance system proved so successful, in the eyes of manufacturers and labor, that the industrial cities of the northwest almost uniformly continued to grant outdoor relief to able-bodied workers into the 1860s, in defiance of the Poor Law Amendment Act.[9] Workers saw the right to "a customary minimum standard of comfort, regardless of unemployment and other hazards" as part of an "unwritten social contract" with employers (Hunt 1981: 215). Relief administrators agreed. They argued that "it

[7] Real relief expenditures increased by only 12.9% from 1844–5 to 1848–9 in Stockport. I have no explanation for the small rate of increase in expenditures relative to that of other textile-producing cities.

[8] Data on the number of adult males relieved because of "want of work" were obtained from Parl. Papers (1849: XLVIIb). As of July 1, 1848, able-bodied adult males and their families constituted approximately 50% of the persons relieved in Manchester, Salford, Stockport, and Bradford.

[9] This is the conclusion reached by each of the studies of relief administration in the industrial northwest. It has been challenged by Karel Williams (1981: 81–90). Williams dismisses much of the evidence presented by Rose and Ashforth as being anecdotal and concludes that they "are so committed to received ideas that they end up misrepresenting relief practices" (1981: 89). However, Williams offers no evidence that cyclically unemployed workers were denied outdoor relief after 1834. Rather, he infers the result from the fact that many urban unions built new workhouses in the 1830s and 1840s and that "from 1850 onwards, the number of unions without any workhouse was insignificant" (1981: 78–9).

Table 8.3. Expenditures on poor relief in five manufacturing cities, 1844/5–1850/1

	1844/5	1845/6	1846/7	1847/8	1848/9	1849/50	1850/1
Nominal Expenditures (in £)							
Bradford	17,821	17,999	23,680	39,708	35,564	13,881	11,808
Leeds	20,797	21,104	25,626	37,555	39,087	32,918	25,941
Manchester	47,266	67,333	66,414	125,004	96,174	74,408	60,477
Salford	9,348	9,970	13,771	22,078	18,985	13,261	8,954
Stockport	12,326	9,602	10,710	18,675	13,625	11,436	9,145
Real Expenditures (1844/5 = 100)							
Bradford	100.0	103.3	129.7	185.7	203.9	87.5	76.3
Leeds	100.0	103.7	120.3	150.5	191.8	177.7	143.6
Manchester	100.0	145.7	137.2	220.5	207.8	176.9	147.4
Salford	100.0	109.0	143.8	196.8	207.3	159.3	110.3
Stockport	100.0	76.0	84.8	126.3	112.9	104.2	85.5

Sources: Data on nominal relief expenditures were obtained from the annual reports of the Poor Law Commission (1845–47) and the Poor Law Board (1848–51). Cost-of-living data obtained from Lindert and Williamson (1985: 148–9).

was wrong to force deserving paupers in genuine need of relief to enter a workhouse or to perform task work in the company of idle and shiftless characters" (Rose 1966: 612). Outdoor relief also was cheaper than indoor relief (Rose 1966: 613; MacKinnon 1987: 608). The question I want to address, however, is not why unemployed workers received outdoor relief instead of indoor relief, but rather why an "unwritten social contract" containing cyclical layoffs and poor relief dominated full-employment contracts.

I contend that outdoor relief was adopted in manufacturing cities for the same reason it was adopted in agricultural parishes: It represented the cheapest method for manufacturers to maintain their work force during downturns in trade. The power of manufacturers over the administration of poor relief is difficult to ascertain. Redford (1964: 92) argued that "in most of the large towns the manufacturers were the ruling party, and were willing to spend the public funds . . . in order to keep a plentiful supply of labour in the parish." In Lancashire, "manufacturers and other employers were the largest single element, often a majority, on the Boards" of urban Poor Law unions (Edsall 1971: 66). Rose (1970: 124, 136) maintained that in the West Riding the members of urban boards of guardians were "usually local manufacturers or tradesmen" but that "few of the elected Guardians were men of any considerable wealth." However, even where large manufacturers did not serve on the board of guardians, they still had an influence on the administration of relief. Numerous relief administrators commented to parliamentary committees that manufacturers pressured them to grant relief to unemployed or underemployed factory workers.[10]

The cost-minimizing form of manufacturers' implicit labor contracts can be determined using a model similar to the one developed in Chapter 3. The major difference between the problems faced by manufacturers and those of farmers is that manufacturers faced cyclical fluctuations in demand instead of seasonal fluctuations. Manufacturers anxious to reduce labor turnover caused by cyclical demand fluctuations offered workers an implicit contract promising an amount of employment, hours per employed worker, wages while employed, and relief benefits while unemployed as a function of the realized state of the economy. The manufacturer's objective was to maximize profits subject to the constraint that the contract he offered workers had to yield an expected

[10] See, for instance, the comments of the Manchester and Stockport relief officers cited in Section 2 of this chapter.

utility large enough to keep them from leaving the firm.[11] The model is outlined and the conditions under which the manufacturer will choose to lay off workers are given in footnote 12.[12] There it is shown that layoffs will occur during a cyclical downturn if the output of the marginal worker (which is affected by the level of demand) is less than the cost to the manufacturer of employing him minus the amount the worker is willing to pay to avoid layoffs. The number of layoffs is determined by the extent of the downturn and by the size of the contribution of taxpayers other than manufacturers to the poor rate (the poor relief subsidy). The worse the state of the economy, the lower the marginal product of labor for any given-sized labor force, and hence the more layoffs that occur. Similarly, the larger the poor relief subsidy, the lower the cost to an employer of laying off workers and therefore the more layoffs that will occur in any given downturn.

The result just described corresponds to the situation in which workers had to be unemployed to collect relief. In many cities factory work-

[11] Huberman (1987: 179) writes that "in urban Lancashire spinners had the opportunity of moving quite readily from factory to factory, and to reduce turnover firms had to meet workers' demands."

[12] The model is essentially the same as the model developed in Chapter 3. I therefore will only sketch the manufacturer's problem. The manufacturer's production function is $y = g(\ell, x)$, where ℓ is labor input and x is a random variable denoting the state of the economy. I assume that $g_{1x} > 0$ and $g_x > 0$, that is, high values of x signify boom periods and low values of x signify recessions. Note that the only difference between the manufacturer's production function and the farmer's production function in Chapter 3 is the interpretation of the random variable x. Workers' utility is defined exactly as in Chapter 3. The manufacturer's objective is to maximize profits subject to the constraint that the expected utility of the contract offered workers must be at least as large as their reservation utility V^*.

The method used to solve the manufacturer's problem is detailed in the Appendix to Chapter 3. The conditions under which layoffs occur are obtained from the first-order conditions of the Lagrangian. The manufacturer will choose to lay off workers in year t if, for some number of workers $n_t(x_t) < N$

$$g_1[n_t(x_t)h_t(x_t), x_t]h_t(x_t) < c_t(x_t) - d_t(x_t) + s - z_t(x_t)$$

where $n(x)$ is the number of workers employed in state x, N is the total number of workers under contract, h is the hours per worker, c is the consumption of an employed worker, d is the consumption of an unemployed worker, s is the contribution of taxpayers other than manufacturers to the poor rate (the poor relief subsidy), and z is the marginal benefit of being employed rather than unemployed. The above inequality says that the manufacturer should lay off workers if the output from the marginal worker, given x_t, is less than the cost of employing him ($c_t - d_t + s$) minus the amount the worker would be willing to pay not to be laid off, z_t. For any given value of $s \geq s^*$, the lower the value of x_t (that is, the worse the state of the economy), the more layoffs that will occur. Also, for any given state of the economy, the larger the poor relief subsidy, the lower the cost to manufacturers of laying off workers. For any value of x, there exists a critical value of s, s^*, so that if $s \geq s^*$, manufacturers will choose to lay off workers. Given s is greater than s^*, the larger the value of s, the more layoffs that will occur.

ers put on short time were eligible for relief. Allowing workers on short time to collect relief changes the solution to the manufacturer's problem. Profit-maximizing firms will respond to minor downturns by reducing hours per worker rather than by laying off workers. There is, however, a minimum hours per worker, h^*, below which the length of the workday will not fall. If the state of the economy is sufficiently bad that hours are reduced to h^*, firms begin to lay off workers and there are no further reductions in hours per worker.[13] That is, the model predicts that layoffs will occur only during major downturns.[14] Apparently the minimum hours constraint was reached during the recessions of 1841–2 and 1847–8, because large numbers of textile mills laid off workers and many completely stopped production.[15]

As mentioned above, manufacturers' layoff strategies were affected by the size of the poor relief subsidy, $s \equiv (1 - e)g$, where e is the share of the poor rate paid by manufacturers and g is the relief benefit paid to unemployed workers. It was determined in Chapter 3 that layoffs would not occur if $s = 0$. In particular, manufacturers would maintain full-employment contracts during recessions if they paid the full cost of the relief benefits received by their employees, that is, if $e = 1$. But the cost to manufacturers of laying off workers was typically much less than the benefits received by their employees. In most industrial cities, the poor rate was assessed as a property tax on "land, houses, and buildings of every description," but not on firms' profits or stock in trade. Machinery generally was not taken into account in estimating the value of factory buildings (Parl. Papers 1818: V, 163; Rose 1965: 348–59). As a result of this system of assessments, a large share of the poor rate was paid by the occupiers of dwelling houses. Some details concerning the distribution of tax assessments in Lancashire cities for 1848–9 are presented in Table

[13] The value of h^* was determined by several factors, including the substitutability of capital and labor, and of persons and hours, in production, and the existence of "nonconvexities [of preferences such] as set-up costs of going to work" (Azariadis 1981: 230; Rosen 1985: 1162–3). The minimum length of the workday therefore varied across firms. For a given state of the economy, x_t, and poor relief subsidy, s, some firms found it optimal to lay off workers while others did not. For an analysis of the issue of layoffs versus worksharing in implicit contracts models, see Rosen (1985: 1162–5).

[14] Huberman (1986) offers a somewhat different explanation for firms' use of short time and layoffs. He ignores the role of poor relief as unemployment insurance and focuses instead on the "initial set-up costs [to employment] paid by workers and firms" and on the heterogeneity of labor. His analysis closely follows that of Okun (1981: 49–62).

[15] Factory inspectors reported that 131 Lancashire cotton mills were "not at work" in the last quarter of 1841 (Matthews 1954: 143). In 1847, 44 of 382 cotton mills in the vicinity of Manchester had stopped production (Pollard 1978: 127).

Table 8.4. *Distribution of poor rate assessments in Lancashire cities*

City	Total number of assessments	% of collected assessments valued at less than £20	Estimated % of poor rate collected from assessments under £20
Ashton-under-Lyne	11,346	91.9	39.3
Manchester	38,199	81.0	30.7
Oldham	10,414	88.4	37.1
Preston	11,980	85.6	42.6
Salford	12,668	91.5	49.1

Source: Parl. Papers (1849: XLVIIa, 10–15).

8.4, which clearly demonstrates the importance of small assessments to urban poor rates. In each city, more than 80% of the assessments actually collected were valued at less than £20. The estimated contribution of these assessments varied from 31% to 49% of the total poor rate. Unfortunately, it is not possible to determine how much of the remaining 50–70% of the poor rate was paid by factories. According to an 1834 assessment, factories paid only 16.6% of the poor rate in Sheffield (Rose 1965: 349). While factories' contribution to the poor rate was higher in more industrialized cities such as Manchester or Leeds, even if factories in these cities contributed three times as much as Sheffield factories, they would have accounted for only half of the city's poor rate.

The implications of such a tax policy are clear. Firms that regularly laid off workers were subsidized by firms that did not and by other urban ratepayers. The subsidy was a strong inducement to manufacturers to lay off workers during downturns. Indeed, the exceptionally high unemployment rates experienced by industrial cities during 1841–2 and 1847–8 must have been, in part, a result of the way in which the poor rate was financed.

The total subsidy received by manufacturers varied significantly from year to year, being small during periods of prosperity and large during recessions. The size of the subsidy in year t, S_t, can be estimated using the following formula

$$S_t = (1 - e)p_t R_t$$

where R_t is total relief expenditures in year t and p_t is the percentage of relief expenditures going to able-bodied workers in year t.

Table 8.5. *Estimated income transfer to manufacturers in Lancashire,*
Cheshire, and the West Riding: 1848 (in £)

	e = 0.25	e = 0.35	e = 0.5
p = 0.5			
Bradford	14,891	12,905	9,927
Leeds	14,083	12,205	9,389
Manchester	46,877	40,626	31,251
Salford	8,279	7,175	5,520
Sheffield	9,821	8,511	6,547
Stockport	7,003	6,069	4,670
Other	95,815	83,041	63,880
All industrial unions	196,769	170,532	131,184
p = 0.4			
Bradford	11,912	10,324	7,942
Leeds	11,267	9,764	7,511
Manchester	37,501	32,501	25,001
Salford	6,623	5,704	4,416
Sheffield	7,857	6,809	5,238
Stockport	5,603	4,856	3,735
Other	76,652	66,432	51,102
All industrial unions	157,415	136,390	104,945

Source: Poor relief expenditure data were obtained from the first annual report
of the Poor Law Board (Parl. Papers 1849: XXV, 38–53).

Table 8.5 presents estimates of the size of S for several industrial cities
for the recession year ending March 25, 1848. Available data suggest
that the value of p was approximately equal to 0.5 during recessions.[16] In
order to be sure not to overstate the size of the subsidy, I have also
calculated S using $p = 0.4$. Since it is not possible to determine the share
of the poor rate paid by manufacturers, I have included three estimates
of e, so as to yield upper and lower bounds for S.

According to Table 8.5, the subsidy received by manufacturers in 19
industrial cities in Lancashire, Cheshire, and the West Riding was equal
to somewhere between £105,000 and £197,000 in 1847. The best-guess
estimate, in my opinion, is that obtained from $e = 0.35$ and $p = 0.5$,
namely £170,500. The magnitude of the subsidy was similar in 1826,
1839, 1841, 1842, and 1848, smaller in 1829, 1832, and 1837, and, pre-

[16] See above, footnote 8.

sumably, very small during the rest of the period 1825–50. Averaged over the entire period, the annual subsidy associated with the unemployment insurance function of the Poor Law was probably about £50,000 to £60,000, which was quite small compared to the textile industry's annual wage bill. Still, during prolonged downturns manufacturers must have welcomed the ability to pass some of their labor costs on to others.

2. The Economic Role of the Settlement Law in Industrial Areas

By the 1840s, migrants made up a majority of the population, and the work force, in most industrial cities. In 1851, the earliest year for which data are available, 70% of the adult population of Manchester, Salford, and Bradford, and 60% of the population of Stockport and Huddersfield, were born outside their city of residence. It will be recalled that individuals had a right to poor relief only in their parish of settlement. As amended in 1795, the Settlement Law gave parishes the power to order the removal back to their parish of settlement of any nonsettled applicants for relief. Because urban areas were not anxious to grant settlements to migrants, most persons who migrated to cities in search of employment during the first half of the nineteenth century retained their birthplace as their parish of settlement and hence were faced with the possibility of removal during economic downturns.

In Chapter 6 it was determined that the large rural–urban wage gaps of the first half of the nineteenth century were not caused by rural parishes' use of outdoor relief. Many contemporaries and historians maintained that urban parishes helped create the wage gaps through their liberal use of the power of removal. William Cobbett claimed that urban areas were quick to use their power of removal. "When there was any cessation of employment in a manufacturing town," he wrote, "the labourers were [removed by the coach-load and] scattered all over England" (quoted in Redford 1964: 90). Contemporaries maintained that such removal policies significantly slowed the rate of migration from the south to the industrial northwest because southern agricultural laborers were "unwilling to leave a secure settlement for the prospect of high but uncertain wages in industry" (Redford 1964: 89).[17]

---

[17] Even Adam Smith blamed the Settlement Law for the regional wage gaps that existed in the 1770s. Smith (1776: 140–1) wrote that "the very unequal price of labour which we frequently find in England in places at no great distance from one another, is probably owing to the obstruction which the law of settlements gives to a poor man who would

In addition, by reducing the available labor supply during downturns industrial cities ensured that a labor scarcity would occur when trade revived, and by slowing migration they ensured that the scarcity would be eliminated slowly.

The Settlement Law was left unchanged by the 1834 Poor Law Amendment Act. Any effect that it had on migration therefore continued until at least 1846, when the law was amended so as to render "persons continuously resident for five years in a parish" irremovable, even if they applied for relief. By reducing the uncertainty involved in migrating to industrial cities, the 1846 act increased labor mobility, although the magnitude of its effect cannot be measured.

Just because urban areas had the right to remove nonsettled persons who applied for relief, however, does not mean that they always were anxious to do so. If labor was generally scarce in the industrial cities, one would expect manufacturers to want to grant relief to unemployed nonsettled workers during temporary downturns in trade, in order to ensure that an adequate labor force would be on hand when trade recovered. The liberal use of removals reduced cities' relief expenditures in the short run but increased manufacturers' wage bills in the long run. Statements by urban relief officers suggest that manufacturers were well aware of the detrimental long-run effects of a wholesale removal policy. For instance, Manchester relief officers testified that they were pressured by manufacturers to relieve nonsettled persons during the 1841 downturn, in order for the city to retain a stock of "cheap labour" (Parl. Papers 1846: XXXVIb, 48–52). A member of the Stockport Board of Guardians commented in 1847 that "if you remove or disperse the working population [during downturns] you very much injure the manufacturers. . . . Therefore the wise course would be to deal with the cause of pauperism where it arose, and . . . let it remain there until trade revives" (Parl. Papers 1847: XI, 520).

carry his industry from one parish to another without a certificate. . . . There is scarce a poor man in England of forty years of age . . . who has not in some part of his life felt himself most cruelly oppressed by this ill-contrived law of settlements." Not all contemporaries agreed with Cobbett and Smith. John Howlett wrote in 1796 that the effect of the Settlement Law "has been very trifling indeed. . . . Were it otherwise, how has it happened, that Sheffield, Birmingham, and Manchester, have increased, from almost mere villages, to populous towns, that rival, or even surpass, in magnitude, our largest cities?" (quoted in Eden 1797: I, 297–8). Eden agreed with Howlett, and wrote that although "instances of vexatious removals . . . did, now and then, occur, . . . I am far from agreeing . . . that these oppressions were very generally practiced" (1797: I, 297–9). Eden went so far as to write that "I believe there is no country in Europe in which [a worker] changes his residence so often as in England" (1797: I, 298).

It is true that a certain number of removals from urban industrial areas occurred each year, and that the number of removals increased substantially during recessions. Moreover, industrial areas opposed all attempts to make it easier for nonsettled laborers to obtain a settlement in the parish where they resided. But evidence that industrial areas used the power of removal and desired to continue to use it is not incompatible with the hypothesis that manufacturers were willing to grant relief to nonsettled laborers in order to retain an adequate labor force.

It was in the interest of even labor-scarce industrial areas to remove "all paupers not belonging to the Union, who are likely to be a permanent charge" on the relief rolls (Bradford Board of Guardians Minute Book 1842). The category of persons "likely to be a permanent charge" included non-able-bodied laborers (e.g., aged or infirm), single women (especially those with young children), and persons employed in declining industries (handloom weavers, woolcombers, etc.).[18] Although the removal of able-bodied laborers employed in declining industries might seem odd in light of the general shortage of urban labor, manufacturers apparently were not anxious to hire such persons to work in factories, because of their age (manufacturers preferred hiring younger workers) and "the working habits [they had previously] acquired" (Pollard 1968: 190; Lyons 1987: 41–3). Moreover, Assistant Poor Law Commissioner J. P. Kay maintained that "the unwillingness of hand-loom weavers to enter the mills and manufactories, is known to the whole trade. . . . They are unwilling to surrender their imaginary independence, and prefer being enslaved by poverty, to the confinement and unvarying routine of factory employment" (quoted in Pollard 1978: 111).[19] The removal of all such categories of persons was in the interest of industrial areas, because it led to a decline in the poor rates without causing a depletion of the supply of factory workers.

There were even circumstances in which it was in the interest of manufacturing cities to remove able-bodied laborers. For instance, during re-

[18] Ashforth (1985: 71) maintains that "[wool]combers could be removed with impunity because their continued poverty was assured and there was no danger of creating a labour shortage."
[19] The plight of handloom weavers and woolcombers during periods of relative prosperity can be seen in the 1834 report of Assistant Poor Law Commissioner Alfred Power and in the answers given by Lancashire and West Riding parishes to question 30 of the Town Queries (an 1832 questionnaire circulated by the Royal Poor Law Commission), which asked for the occupations of able-bodied persons who received outdoor relief, and to question 37, which asked for the classes of workmen "most subject to distress" (Parl. Papers 1834: XXXV–XXXVI).

cessions cities should have been willing to remove laborers who were likely to rejoin the urban labor force quickly upon the return of better economic conditions. Thus it was in their interest to remove laborers whose parish of settlement was close to the city. Such removals eliminated the cost to the urban parish of relieving these persons without removing them from the industrial reserve army available to the manufacturers.

Industrial cities were sometimes forced by special circumstances to remove able-bodied laborers. In the 1840s, a "locust-like swarm of destitute and disease-stricken" Irish peasants poured into the industrial cities of Lancashire, spurred by famine and the lack of poor relief in Ireland. The influx of close to 500,000 Irish migrants occurred during a decade that experienced two serious downturns in trade (Redford 1964: 158). The depression of 1837–43 was especially severe in Lancashire, and the cotton-manufacturing cities were unable to cope with the wave of Irish migrants. It became necessary to remove able-bodied workers simply because the cities could not afford to grant them relief. In such circumstances, the first to be removed were generally those resident in the city for the shortest period. Many recently arrived Irish workers therefore were sent back to Ireland by the depressed industrial cities during the 1840s. Even so, the great majority of Irish laborers were not removed, and manufacturers anxious to maintain an adequate labor force sometimes contributed to public relief subscriptions during depression years to relieve Irish paupers (Ashforth 1976: 145).[20]

The only available detailed data on removals are for manufacturing towns in Lancashire, Cheshire, and the West Riding of Yorkshire for the period from Lady Day 1840 to Lady Day 1843 (Parl. Papers 1846: XXXVIa). The data set contains information on "the number of families and persons removed, their occupations prior to removal, the length of their residence in the manufacturing districts, and the parishes to which they were removed."[21] Unfortunately, it does not contain information on the demographic and occupational characteristics of nonsettled applicants who were granted relief rather than removed, so it is not possible to determine whether certain attributes were associated with high re-

---

[20] From 1841 through 1843, 2,647 Irish were removed from 19 manufacturing towns in Lancashire, Cheshire, and the West Riding. The 1841 census estimated the Irish population of these three counties to be 133,000.

[21] Unfortunately, information on the length of residence of removed persons was not reported in most instances. Leeds was the only city consistently to report length of residence. Also, it proved to be difficult to locate the parishes to which persons were removed. I therefore did not use these data.

moval rates. However, an analysis of the characteristics of those persons removed does offer some insight into industrial areas' removal policies.

A tabulation of the occupations of persons removed from six north-western cities during the period from Lady Day 1840 to Lady Day 1843 is presented in Table 8.6. The occupations have been classified into seven groups: general unskilled laborers, skilled laborers in declining industries, skilled laborers in nondeclining textile occupations, female-headed households and orphans, workers in building trades, domestic workers, and all other occupations. A listing of the occupations contained in each classification is given in the Appendix to this chapter. Because of the length and depth of the 1837–43 depression, and because of the large influx of Irish workers at this time, the results should represent an upper-bound estimate of the share of able-bodied factory workers among the persons removed.

A simple measure of the percentage of persons removed from industrial areas who could be considered a permanent burden on the relief rolls can be obtained by looking at the number of persons removed who were either female heads-of-household or employed in declining industries. Combining the two classifications yields a lower-bound estimate of the percentage of persons removed who did not detract from the urban labor supply, as viewed by an industrial area's manufacturers. The percentage of persons removed over the three-year period who were either female heads-of-household or employed in declining industries was 46.4% in the West Riding and 31.8% in Lancashire–Cheshire.[22] It varied from 28.4% for non-Irish removals from Stockport to 88.6% for Bradford.[23] Moreover, most persons classified as domestic servants were probably single women, and should therefore be classified with the other female heads-of-household.

It is also not clear how the removal of laborers in the building trades or of laborers classified under "other occupations" affected the labor supply in the factories. It could be argued that these persons, who in

[22] There is no reason to assume that such persons were removed only during years of depressed economic activity, since they were as likely to be a burden on the parish during times of normal economic conditions as during recessions. Especially in the case of single women with young children, parish officials were anxious to remove them as soon as they applied for relief. This classification of persons therefore must have made up a significantly larger share of the families removed during times other than the depression years 1840–3.

[23] Every Irish person removed from Stockport over the period was listed as a laborer. The occupational distribution of the Irish in the nearby cities of Manchester and Salford suggests that the Stockport returns are of questionable validity.

Table 8.6. *Occupations of persons removed: Lady Day 1840 to Lady Day 1843*

	Unskilled laborers	Skilled in declining industries	Female heads & orphans	Skilled in textiles	Domestic workers	Building trades	Other	Number of observations
Bradford								
1840/1	5.6%	47.9%	33.8%	5.6%	0.0%	4.2%	2.8%	71
1841/2	6.6	56.6	30.3	0.0	0.0	2.6	3.9	76
1842/3	2.7	65.8	31.5	0.0	0.0	0.0	0.0	73
Leeds								
1840/1	26.7	8.4	38.9	9.9	1.5	1.5	13.0	131
1841/2	32.4	9.3	25.0	12.7	0.0	2.9	17.6	204
1842/3	27.5	9.7	18.9	14.6	0.7	4.5	24.1	403
Huddersfield								
1840/1	27.8	5.6	27.8	16.7	0.0	0.0	22.2	18
1841/2	13.8	13.8	24.1	27.6	0.0	0.0	20.7	29
1842/3	16.2	29.7	35.1	10.8	0.0	0.0	8.1	37
Manchester								
1840/1[a]								
1841/2 total	18.8	17.2	18.5	12.8	10.4	1.6	20.8	384
English	24.4	12.2	16.3	17.9	11.4	2.4	15.4	123
Irish	16.1	19.5	19.5	10.3	10.0	1.1	23.4	261
1842/3 total	16.3	19.6	16.1	13.2	9.3	2.9	22.7	547
English	20.3	18.2	15.2	15.6	6.5	4.3	19.9	231
Irish	13.3	20.6	16.8	11.4	11.4	1.9	24.7	316

249

Table 8.6. (cont.)

	Unskilled laborers	Skilled in declining industries	Female heads & orphans	Skilled in textiles	Domestic workers	Building trades	Other	Number of observations
Salford								
1840/1 total	10.1	13.8	29.0	16.7	5.1	5.1	20.3	138
English	12.2	7.3	31.7	14.6	4.9	8.5	20.7	82
Irish	7.1	23.2	25.0	19.6	5.4	0.0	19.6	56
1841/2 total	5.7	7.5	30.2	23.3	9.4	1.3	22.6	159
English	4.7	5.7	32.1	24.5	7.5	1.9	23.6	106
Irish	7.5	11.3	26.4	20.8	13.2	0.0	20.8	53
1842/3 total	3.4	13.5	21.3	28.5	4.3	1.9	27.1	207
English	2.7	9.3	21.3	30.7	4.0	2.7	29.3	150
Irish	5.3	24.6	21.1	22.8	5.3	0.0	21.1	57
Stockport								
1840/1 total	77.6	3.1	5.1	5.1	1.0	2.0	6.1	98
English	35.3	8.8	14.7	14.7	2.9	5.9	17.6	34
Irish	100.0	0.0	0.0	0.0	0.0	0.0	0.0	64
1841/2 total	48.5	4.6	16.3	16.3	1.3	0.4	12.6	239
English	32.8	6.0	21.3	21.3	1.6	0.5	16.4	183
Irish	100.0	0.0	0.0	0.0	0.0	0.0	0.0	56
1842/3 total	41.5	7.5	17.0	18.2	0.8	2.4	12.6	253
English	27.8	9.3	21.0	22.4	1.0	2.9	15.6	205
Irish	100.0	0.0	0.0	0.0	0.0	0.0	0.0	48

Weighted average for regions

West Riding								
1840/1	20.0	20.9	36.4	9.1	0.9	2.3	10.5	223
1841/2	24.3	21.4	26.2	11.0	0.0	2.6	14.6	309
1842/3	23.2	19.1	21.8	12.3	0.6	3.5	19.5	513
Lancashire								
1840/1 total	38.1	9.3	19.1	11.9	3.4	3.8	14.4	236
English	19.0	7.8	26.7	14.7	4.3	7.8	19.8	116
Irish	56.7	10.8	11.7	9.2	2.5	0.0	9.2	120
1841/2 total	25.2	11.4	20.2	16.0	7.4	1.2	18.7	782
English	23.1	7.8	22.6	21.1	6.1	1.5	18.0	412
Irish	27.6	15.4	17.6	10.3	8.9	0.8	19.5	370
1842/3 total	20.0	15.3	17.4	17.6	6.3	2.6	21.1	1,007
English	18.4	12.8	18.8	21.8	3.9	3.4	20.8	586
Irish	22.1	18.8	15.4	11.6	9.3	1.4	21.4	421

[a]No returns.
Source: Parl. Papers (1846: XXXVIa).

251

general were skilled workers, were in an altogether different labor market from textile workers, and that their removal did not reduce the supply of labor available to work in the textile mills upon the return of "normal" economic conditions. These skilled workers tended to be employed in trades affected by the economic climate of the city. Shoemakers or masons applied for relief because the economic conditions created by a downturn in the textile trade reduced the demand for their services. A return to good times in the textile trade also meant an increase in the demand for their services. The only condition under which skilled workers from other trades would enter the textile labor market would be if there was an excess supply of, say, masons even during normal economic conditions. A board of guardians dominated by textile manufacturers would be interested in relieving nonsettled skilled workers from other trades only if the workers were in trades that were in some way important to the textile manufacturers and that were in general plagued by a shortage of labor.

The two groups of workers that the textile manufacturers were anxious to retain were the skilled workers in textiles and, to a lesser degree, general unskilled laborers, who were often employed in textile mills. The share of persons removed over the three-year period who were listed as skilled workers in nondeclining textile trades was 11.2% for the West Riding and 16.3% for Lancashire–Cheshire. The share of persons removed who were listed either as skilled textile workers or unskilled laborers was 34.1% in the West Riding and 40.4% in Lancashire–Cheshire. In other words, between one-third and two-fifths of the removals from industrial areas during the 1840–3 depression caused a reduction in the industrial labor force.[24]

There are reasons to suspect that Table 8.6 overstates the number of *able-bodied* skilled textile workers and unskilled laborers removed. In Leeds, the only city consistently to report the length of residence of persons removed, 36.7% of the unskilled laborers removed during the three-year period had resided in the city for at least 20 years. There is some evidence, therefore, to support a Manchester magistrate's statement in 1817 that workers who had resided in the city for a number of

---

[24] This assumes that all unskilled workers who were removed were considered by relief officers to be potentially a part of the factory labor force. But some of the persons listed as laborers must have been employed in the building trades or in other nontextile occupations. If only half of those removed were viewed as potential textile workers, the share of removals that caused a reduction in the industrial labor force was 23% in the West Riding and 28% in Lancashire.

years were often removed when they became old and infirm (Parl. Papers 1818: V, 160). From the standpoint of local manufacturers, it obviously made sense to remove workers who were old and sick, even if their occupation was in short supply. Given that local relief administrators could remove whomever they desired, one would suspect that a substantial share of the skilled textile workers and unskilled laborers removed were not able-bodied.

Lack of data on the occupations of nonsettled persons who were relieved (rather than removed) during 1840–3 makes it impossible to determine the rate of removal of nonsettled persons by occupation. It is possible, however, to estimate the overall rate of removal of nonsettled persons applying for relief. Data on the number of nonsettled persons relieved exist only for Bradford. From 1840 to 1842, approximately 25% of the persons relieved in the Bradford Poor Law union were nonsettled.[25] Ashforth (1979: 298) maintains that the share of nonsettled paupers in other West Riding towns was similar to that of Bradford. I therefore assumed that 25% of the persons relieved in the other two West Riding cities (Leeds and Huddersfield) were nonsettled. Birthplace data for residents of the industrial cities suggest that the share of nonsettled paupers was larger in Lancashire and Cheshire cities than in West Riding cities. In 1851, 54% of the population of Manchester, Salford, and Stockport were born outside their city of residence, compared to 41% of the population of Bradford, Leeds, and Huddersfield.[26] This difference was largely owing to the relatively large number of Irish immigrants in Lancashire and Cheshire cities. In 1851, 13% of the population of Manchester, Salford, and Stockport had been born in Ireland, compared to 6% of the population of Bradford, Leeds, and Huddersfield. To take account of the larger share of migrants in Lancashire and Cheshire cities, I assumed that one-third of the paupers relieved in these cities were nonsettled.

The number of persons relieved and the estimated share of nonsettled

---

[25] This percentage was obtained by dividing the number of nonsettled paupers relieved during the quarter ended December 25 in 1840, 1841, and 1842 by the total number of paupers relieved during the quarter ended March 25 in 1841, 1842, and 1843. Data are from Ashforth (1985: 70). The share of nonsettled paupers was significantly larger in the four Bradford borough townships than in the other sixteen townships in the union. For example, "during the quarter ended 25 December 1841, 23.5 per cent of the union's paupers were non-settled, but in Bradford township the figure was 39.7 per cent" (Ashforth 1985: 64).

[26] Birthplace data are from the census of 1851 (Parl. Papers 1852–3: LXXXVIII, part 2, 664, 737).

Table 8.7. *Statistics on number of removals*

Poor Law Union	1841	1842	1843	Average
Number of paupers relieved: quarter ended Lady Day				
Bradford	7,340	9,514	9,572	
Huddersfield	6,880	9,431	13,092	
Manchester	12,978	15,994	20,449	
Salford	2,388	3,463	4,291	
Stockport	3,918	8,153	6,895	
Estimated % of nonresident paupers removed: year ended Lady Day				
Bradford	18.1	9.7	8.3	11.0
Huddersfield	1.6	2.1	1.8	1.8
Manchester	No returns	8.0	10.2	9.3
Salford	19.1	15.8	16.2	16.9
Stockport	11.9	12.6	15.8	13.7

Sources: Data on number of paupers relieved were obtained from Parl. Papers (1844: XL, 5, 12, 25). Data on number of nonresident paupers removed were obtained from Parl. Papers (1846: XXXVIa).

paupers who were removed from each industrial city over the three-year period is given in Table 8.7. The removal rate was estimated by dividing the number of persons removed during any one year by the estimated number of nonsettled persons applying for poor relief. Data on the number of persons relieved are available only for the first quarter of the year, while the data on removals are for the entire year. I assumed that the annual number of persons relieved was twice that of the number of persons relieved during the first quarter.[27] The estimates in Table 8.7 show that, over the three-year period, between 10% and 15% of the nonsettled persons who applied for relief were removed to their parish of settlement.[28]

A nonsettled person applying for relief faced a probability of removal of 10–15%, *on average.* Assuming that a city's propensity to remove persons who were expected to be a permanent charge on the relief rolls was well above 15%, the probability of removal faced by an unemployed

[27] My assumption that the annual number of persons relieved was twice the number relieved in the first quarter of the year follows Ashforth (1985: 70). This assumption provides a lower-bound estimate of the number of persons relieved, and therefore an upper-bound estimate of the share of nonsettled relief applicants who were removed.
[28] The probable explanation for the low removal rate from Huddersfield is that it was less industrial than the other cities included in Table 8.7.

skilled textile worker must have been well below 10%. This suggests that
the effect of the Settlement Law on the rural–urban migration of workers not in declining industries was small. On the other hand, the higher
removal rate of persons with characteristics considered undesirable by
urban manufacturers should have reduced their propensity to migrate to
industrial areas. Cities' use of the power of removal therefore might
have affected the average characteristics of the stream of migrants to
industrial areas. Certainly urban relief administrators believed that a
policy of selective removals affected individuals' decisions to migrate.
When a bill to "prohibit poor removal" was put before Parliament in
1822, they argued that "the effect of the Bill would be to send every idler
from the country parishes into the towns" (quoted in Redford 1964: 90).

Without the ability to remove persons likely to be a permanent charge
on the parish, industrial areas' annual relief expenditures would have
significantly increased. The Settlement Law protected cities from large
influxes of economically undesirable migrants that sometimes accompanied agricultural depressions or other disturbances to regional labor
markets. For instance, the collapse of the Irish cotton industry in the
early decades of the nineteenth century precipitated a large migration of
handloom weavers to Manchester and other Lancashire cities. Given the
already depressed market for handloom weavers, it clearly was not in
the interests of these cities to grant poor relief to Irish weavers. Similarly, thousands of economically undesirable (in the view of manufacturers) migrants must have been included in the enormous migration from
Ireland to the industrial northwest during the "hungry forties" (Redford
1964: 156–8).

The testimony of urban relief officials before the 1847 and 1855
Select Committees on Poor Removal reveals that the mere threat of
removal was enough to keep large numbers of unwanted migrants from
applying for relief. Most poor persons believed that their economic
opportunities were better in the industrial cities than in their parishes
of settlement, and they were willing to forgo relief and shift for themselves until the return of better times in order to avoid removal. For
instance, only 23% of the 5,011 Irish paupers ordered to be removed
from Manchester during 1852–4 were actually removed. The rest "took
themselves off the relief lists [and] became self-supporting" (Parl. Papers 1854–5: XIII, 261). Similarly, only 30% of the paupers ordered
removed from Stockport during 1840–6 were in fact removed (Parl.
Papers 1847: XI, 514).

Relief officers were selective in their use of the threat of removal. Unemployed factory workers generally were not threatened with removal. According to a Leeds official, "if a man had come to Leeds and got work and if he fell out of work even at the end of a month, he would be relieved the same as if he had belonged to Leeds" (Parl. Papers 1847: XI, 520). The clerk of the Bradford Union testified that the guardians distinguished among Irish relief applicants according to "whether there is any prospect of a man getting into employment soon" (Parl. Papers 1854–5: XIII, 92). He went on to state that most of the Irish in Bradford were unemployed or underemployed woolcombers, who existed without poor relief because they "refuse to be removed."

Overall, the power of removal saved industrial cities thousands of pounds in relief expenditures each year, by enabling them to pass some of the costs of maintaining economically undesirable migrants to rural parishes and to the migrants themselves. Much of the expenditure that was saved would have been borne by manufacturing firms. By reducing urban poor rates, the Settlement Law raised manufacturers' profits. It is therefore no wonder that a Manchester magistrate who was asked his opinion in 1818 of a proposal that settlement should be obtained by residing in a parish for three years replied that "the idea of such a proposal has excited the very greatest alarm in Manchester and other manufacturing districts" (Parl. Papers 1818: V, 159).

The Settlement Law was amended in 1846 to make irremovable persons who had continuously resided in a parish for five years, widows whose husbands had been dead for less than a year, and persons "who applied for temporary relief on account of sickness or accident" (Rose 1976: 29). Predictably, the passage of the Poor Removal Act caused an increase in the relief expenditures of industrial cities. For example, Bradford's relief expenditures increased by "perhaps £5,000 annually" as a result of the act (Ashforth 1985: 79), while Leeds's annual relief expenditures increased by £3,000–£4,000 (Rose 1976: 41). To help ease the financial burden on industrial parishes caused by the Poor Removal Act, Parliament passed laws in 1847 and 1848 that shifted the cost of relieving irremovable paupers from their parish of residence to the common fund of the Poor Law Union. The Poor Removal Act reduced the subsidization of manufacturers by rural parishes and nonsettled urban migrants, and therefore probably caused an increase in urban parishes' removal of nonsettled paupers. Available evidence suggests, however, that the magnitude of the increase was small. Rose (1965: 300) concluded that "despite the disturbance caused by the 1846 Act, removal in the West Riding seems, in general, to have been kept as a reserve weapon."[29]

3. The System of Nonresident Relief

The Settlement Law, and in particular the power of removal, led to the development of another institution that enabled industrial cities to pass some of their relief costs on to nonindustrial unions, namely, the system of nonresident relief. When a nonsettled person applied for relief, industrial areas often contacted the person's parish of settlement and asked to be reimbursed for any relief payments granted. If the parish of settlement agreed to pay the nonresident relief, the urban parish did not remove the person who applied for relief. At first glance, the system of nonresident relief does not appear to fit in with my hypothesis that there was not an oversupply of labor in rural areas. Why would rural parishes have been willing to pay relief to persons residing in industrial areas rather than allow them to be removed, unless the rural areas were already plagued with an overabundance of labor? The key to understanding the system of nonresident relief is the same as the key to understanding urban parishes' removal policies. It concerns the demographic and occupational characteristics of those persons receiving nonresident relief. The persons that urban parishes were most anxious to remove, such as widows or handloom weavers, were also the persons that rural parishes least wanted returned, for they were bound to be a permanent charge whatever their parish of residence. Moreover, it was probably cheaper for a rural parish to pay for the relief of a widow and her children or a handloom weaver in an urban area than to have them removed back to the rural parish, because the job opportunities for women, children, and workers in declining industries were better in urban areas. The chairman of the London Committee for the Relief of the Manufacturing Districts remarked in 1827 that not only were the employment opportunities for handloom weavers better in urban than in rural areas, there was also some chance that displaced handloom weavers in urban areas could become powerloom weavers (Parl. Papers 1826–

---

[29] The Settlement Law was further amended in 1861 and 1865. The 1861 act reduced the time of continuous residence necessary to become irremovable to three years. The 1865 Union Chargeability Act made nonsettled persons irremovable after one year's continuous residence and "took all powers over settlement and rating out of the hands of the parish and made them the responsibility of the union and its board of guardians" (Rose 1976: 30–1).

7: V, 238). Another category of persons who often received nonresident relief was "old or infirm people who had gone to live with younger or fitter relatives in the industrial towns" (Rose 1965: 281). Such persons required less relief if they were living in an urban area with relatives than if they were returned to a rural parish.

I suspect that the share of persons receiving nonresident relief who were unemployed workers in nondeclining industries was small. There were situations, however, where it made sense for rural parishes to grant nonresident relief to able-bodied workers. If the urban workers were only temporarily unemployed, it would cost the rural parish less in the long run to pay part of the workers' relief for a short time than to allow them to be returned. This was especially true if the workers were put on short time rather than laid off. Only if a rural parish experienced a scarcity of labor during peak seasons did it make sense to allow its nonresident workers to be removed.

The discussion in the preceding paragraph assumed that unemployed nonsettled workers would be removed from urban areas if they did not receive nonresident relief. I argued above, however, that industrial areas were usually willing to relieve nonsettled workers in order to retain an adequate supply of labor. They often attempted to bluff unions into granting nonresident relief to able-bodied workers by threatening to remove persons that they in fact had no intention of removing (Ashforth 1979: 314). There is evidence that threatened unions were often willing to call the industrial cities' bluffs by refusing to pay for temporarily unemployed workers. For instance, the Leicester Union decided in 1844 "only [to] repay relief administered to its non-resident paupers in cases of sickness, infirmity, or old age" (Ashforth 1979: 315). In other words, Leicester refused to pay nonresident relief to able-bodied workers. Wycombe Union agreed to pay nonresident relief only for persons "maintained in the workhouse," which, of course, excluded unemployed or underemployed workers (Ashforth 1979: 315). In sum, the parishes of settlement agreed to pay nonresident relief only for those paupers whom they thought the industrial cities would in fact remove.

The effect of the system of nonresident relief on urban relief expenditures probably was small because in most cases nonresident relief was not a substitute for relief paid by industrial parishes. Persons who received nonresident relief typically would have been removed in its absence, rather than relieved. The major savings to industrial cities, therefore, was the cost of removing recipients of nonresident relief. If nonresident relief had not existed, the number of removals from industrial areas would have increased, and the share of persons removed who were likely to be a permanent charge on the parish would have been significantly larger than the numbers obtained from Table 8.6.

4. Urban Attitudes Toward the Poor Law Amendment Act

It was mentioned earlier in this chapter that Poor Law officials in most industrial cities refused to follow the recommendation of the Poor Law Commission in 1834 that no outdoor relief be granted to adult able-bodied males. The same persons who bitterly opposed the implementation of the New Poor Law in their cities, however, supported its implementation in the agricultural south and east of England. In their opinion, the policy of "less eligibility enforced through the workhouse system could not be sensibly applied to the North, however beneficial it might prove to be in the South" (Edsall 1971: 48). Some members of Parliament from the industrial northwest went so far as to argue during the debate over the Poor Law Amendment Act that the north should be excluded from the act's provisions.[30]

There is no doubt, however, that industrial areas were eager for the workhouse test to be enforced in the south and east. Before 1834, manufacturers had complained that the lax administration of the Poor Law in agricultural regions hindered the migration of labor to the industrial cities. Edmund Ashworth, a Lancashire manufacturer, wrote in 1834 that "under the present law, . . . [s]o highly do the poor value their parish allowance, which from long habit they consider their lawful inheritance, and so thoroughly do they understand the laws regarding their settlements, that scarcely any prospects of bettering their condition will induce them to remove" (Parl. Papers 1835: XXXV, 212). Similarly, manufacturer Robert Greg blamed "the operation of the poor laws in binding down the labourers to their respective parishes" for the "difficulty in obtaining labourers at extravagant wages in these northern counties" (Parl. Papers 1835: XXXV, 213).

Ironically, trade was booming in the northern textile cities in the summer of 1834 when the Poor Law Amendment Act was being debated. Not only was there a serious shortage of labor in the textile-

---

[30] For instance, Edward Baines, MP from Leeds, stated that "at Manchester and other places, there was no necessity for the exercise of that power, the parishes being well administered" (quoted in Brundage 1978: 66–7).

producing areas at this time, there was also an "outbreak of trades unionism," spurred by the strong position of labor (Redford 1964: 113).[31] The labor shortage was exacerbated by the Factory Acts of 1833, which curtailed the use of child labor in the factories (Redford 1964: 101). Several textile manufacturers, notably Edmund Ashworth and Robert Greg, responded to the labor scarcity by writing members of the Royal Poor Law Commission and asking them to encourage the migration of surplus rural laborers to the industrial north. Ashworth wrote to Edwin Chadwick that he was "most anxious that every facility be given to the removal of labourers from one county to another according to the demand for labour; this would have a tendency to equalize wages as well as prevent in degree some of the turn-outs [that is, strikes] which have been of late so prevalent." Greg wrote that "we are now in want of labour," and that unless labor could be obtained from the low-wage south, "any farther demand for labour would still further increase the unions, drunkenness, and high wages" (Parl. Papers 1835: XXXV, 213).

Assistant Commissioner James Kay, in an 1835 report to the Poor Law Commissioners, estimated that an additional 45,000 "mill hands" would be required in the Lancashire cotton district in the next two years. Because the neighboring counties could supply no more labor, the only available sources were the rural south and Ireland (Parl. Papers 1835: XXXV, 186–8). Kay recommended that the commissioners appoint an agent in Manchester to "form a medium of communication between the mill-owners, seeking a supply of labour, and the Commissioners, who, by means of their Assistant Commissioners in the south, may make a proper selection of the workmen, and transmit them directly to the mills for which they are required" (Parl. Papers 1835: XXXV, 189).

In response to the manufacturers' suggestions, the Poor Law Commissioners sent a circular letter in March 1835 to manufacturers in districts where "there existed the greatest demand for labourers," offering "to those who had a demand for labourers to make the circumstance known

---

[31] Unionism experienced an "exceptional and short-lived [burst] of expansion" from 1829 to 1834 (Hunt 1981: 193). The cotton spinners were particularly successful in organizing during this period. The expansion culminated in the formation of the Grand National Consolidated Trades Union in 1833. The GNCTU collapsed in midsummer 1834, but it claimed to have 800,000 members during its short life (Hunt 1981: 202–3). As can be seen from the quotes later in the paragraph, manufacturers were hopeful that the unions could be broken by an influx of labor from the south, although, ironically, the union movement had collapsed by the time the first migrants were sent to the northwest.

in parishes containing families willing to migrate, from whom such a selection could be made as might meet the wishes of the employer" (Parl. Papers 1835: XXXV, 22). Migration offices were opened in Manchester and Leeds in the summer of 1835. From then until May 1837, when a recession ended the demand for labor, approximately 4,700 laborers were aided in their migration from the rural south to northern industrial cities.[32] The majority of migrants came from East Anglia, in particular Suffolk, and 84% of them went to Lancashire, Cheshire, and the West Riding (Redford 1964: 107–8).

One of the themes of this book is that farmers and manufacturers used their local political power to institute a system of poor relief which involved a transfer of income from other local taxpayers to themselves. The information in this section suggests that the use of political power to reduce costs of production occurred at the national as well as the local level. The northwest's support of the Poor Law Amendment Act was based on the belief that rural–urban wage gaps were caused by the lax administration of poor relief in the south, which discouraged surplus labor from migrating to the labor-scarce northwest. The elimination of outdoor relief in the south would lead to an increase in migration to industrial areas. Northern manufacturers did not institute the call for Poor Law reform, but they quickly recognized reform as a method to attract labor and hence to lower wages and reduce the power of labor unions. Although northern MPs supported the implementation of the workhouse test in the rural south, they refused to implement it in their own parishes, arguing that it was not suited to the problem of cyclical unemployment.

Their strategy proved only partly successful. Most industrial unions continued to grant outdoor relief to able-bodied workers at least into the 1850s, despite attempts by the Poor Law Commission to stop the practice. But the expected large increase in migration from the rural south was not forthcoming. Manufacturers, like the Poor Law Commissioners, had significantly overestimated the effect of rural parishes' use of outdoor relief on labor mobility, and therefore overestimated the extent of

---

[32] During the same period, 6,400 individuals from the rural south left England for overseas destinations as part of a Poor Law emigration scheme (Redford 1964: 108–9). Why did the Poor Law Commission sponsor an emigration scheme, given the scarcity of labor in the northwest? According to Redford (1964: 110), "the Commissioners themselves preferred the home migration scheme," but the sending parishes "favored emigration, because this made it more difficult for the paupers to return or to be brought back to their place of settlement."

surplus labor in the agricultural south. Moreover, those persons who migrated out of the rural south after 1834 generally went either to London or overseas. London was more accessible than the northwest, and southern farm workers "preferred to seek work with which they were at least partly familiar. Outdoor work . . . and domestic service met their needs far better than the factories, and there was ample employment of this kind in London" (Hunt 1981: 157).[33] The major sources of migrants to the industrial northwest both before and after 1834 were the rural areas within Lancashire, Yorkshire, and Cheshire, and, in the case of Lancashire cities, Ireland (Redford 1964: 183–4).

5. Conclusion

The payment of poor relief to temporarily unemployed workers occurred in urban as well as agricultural parishes. Indeed, urban relief administrators continued granting outdoor relief to able-bodied workers for at least two decades after the passage of the Poor Law Amendment Act. The use of the Poor Law as an unemployment insurance system enabled manufacturers, who dominated local politics in most industrial cities, to pass some of the costs of maintaining factory workers not required during cyclical downturns to non-labor-hiring taxpayers. I estimated in Section 1 that this income transfer to manufacturers averaged £50,000 to £60,000 per year.

In addition, the Settlement Law and in particular the power of removal enabled cities to pass most of the cost of maintaining nonsettled migrants who were likely to be a permanent charge on the relief rolls to their parishes of settlement and to the migrants themselves (by keeping them from applying for relief). The importance of the Settlement Law to urban parishes is shown by the effect on relief expenditures of the Poor Removal Act of 1846, which made any nonsettled person who lived in the same parish for five years irremovable. "By destroying the deterrent effect of the threat of removal and . . . by undermining the system of non-resident relief," the 1846 act caused a sharp increase in urban

---

[33] Southern farm workers' preference for London over the industrial northwest was not because of differences in wages between the two regions. In 1839 and 1849 nominal wages of bricklayers' laborers were equal in London and Manchester, 18s. per week. London data are from Schwarz (1986: 38); Manchester data are from Bowley (1900b: 310). Crafts (1982: 62) and Williamson (1987: 652) agree that in the 1840s the cost of living was slightly higher in London than in the industrial northwest. Real wages of low-skilled workers therefore were slightly higher in the industrial northwest than in London.

unions' relief expenditures (Ashforth 1985: 78–9, 81). For the five years ended Lady Day 1861, irremovable paupers accounted for 62.2% of relief expenditures in Bradford, 60.8% of expenditures in Manchester, and 39.6% of expenditures in Sheffield (Ashforth 1985: 81).

The Settlement Law and the power of removal saved urban industrial unions in Lancashire, Cheshire, and the West Riding perhaps £50,000 to £80,000 per year. If manufacturers paid 35% of the poor rate, as was assumed above, then the Settlement Law saved them £17,500 to £28,000 per year. The total income transfer from rural taxpayers, non-labor-hiring urban taxpayers, and nonsettled urban workers to manufacturers therefore was on the order of £67,500 to £88,000 per year.[34] Given that savings rates varied across income classes, the income transfer caused capital accumulation to increase by perhaps £15,000 to £20,000 per year.[35]

However, the Settlement Law also might have had a negative effect on industrialization. If migration from the agricultural south to the north-west was slowed by rural workers' fear of removal, then the Settlement Law fostered a misallocation of labor and slowed the rate of economic growth. It was determined in Section 2, however, that the selective use of the power of removal by textile manufacturing cities should not have deterred able-bodied young adults from migrating to urban areas. More-over, urban Poor Law unions often granted relief to temporarily unem-ployed nonsettled workers, which reduced the risk associated with migra-tion and therefore should have increased the number of migrants. In sum, urban poor relief had a positive (but small) impact on the English economy during the first half of the nineteenth century.

[34] This estimate was obtained by adding the estimated annual transfer from non-labor-hiring urban taxpayers to manufacturers resulting from the use of the Poor Law as an unemployment insurance system (£50,000–£60,000) and the estimated annual transfer from rural taxpayers and nonsettled urban workers to manufacturers resulting from the Settlement Law (£17,500–£28,000).

[35] I assume that the savings rate of manufacturers, farmers, and landlords was 30%, that the savings rate of non-labor-hiring taxpayers was 5–10%, and that workers did not save. Crafts (1985: 124–5) estimated that the savings rate of farmers and landlords was 30% and that the savings rate out of nonagricultural nonlabor income was "not . . . less than 23 per cent." I assume that textile manufacturers' savings rate was the same as that of farmers and landlords. Von Tunzelmann (1985: 215) and Crafts (1985: 124) conclude that "saving out of wages was zero." See also Fishlow (1961: 36). Feinstein (1978: 76, 93) estimated that fixed capital formation averaged £50.5 million per annum in the 1840s, and that 25% of total investment (£12.6 million) was devoted to industrial buildings and machinery. If one-third of industrial investment took place in Lancashire, Cheshire, and the West Riding, then the Poor Law caused capital formation in manufacturing to increase by 0.4–0.5%.

Appendix
Occupations Contained in Each Classification of Worker in
Table 8.6

General unskilled laborer

Laborer   Factory worker

Skilled worker in declining industry

Handloom weaver   Calico printer
Woolcomber   Fustian cutter

Female and child head of household

Widow   Seamstress
Charwoman   Washerwoman
Housewife   Orphan
Single woman with children

Skilled worker in textiles (nondeclining)

Fuller   Reeler
Dyer   Silk weaver
Spinner   Sizer
Bleacher   Cloth dresser, flax dresser
Block printer   Power-loom weaver
Piecer   Silk winder, cotton winder
Slubber   Cotton picker
Stretcher   Jobber in cotton mill

Worker in building trades

Carpenter   Tiler
Joiner   Slater
Brickmaker, bricklayer   Painter
Mason   Glazier

Domestic worker

Servant   Porter
Gardener

Worker in other occupations

Machinist   Winder, cordwinder
Millwright   Collier
Fitter   Fruit dealer
Turner   Cutler
Typecutter   Cooper
Watchmaker   Warehouseman
Smith   Jobber
Shoemaker   Ostler
Baker   Heckler
Tailor   Hawker
Confectioner   Bookkeeper

CONCLUSION

1. Summary of the Argument

The aim of this book has been to provide an explanation for the development and persistence of policies providing outdoor relief for able-bodied workers, and to examine the effect of such policies on certain aspects of the rural economy. The book is an extension of the revisionist analysis of the Old Poor Law begun by Mark Blaug in 1963. As such, it builds on the pioneering work of Blaug (1963; 1964), Daniel Baugh (1975), and Anne Digby (1975; 1978). These authors rejected the traditional literature's conclusion that outdoor relief policies had disastrous consequences on the rural labor market. Their arguments concerning the effects of the Poor Law on labor are convincing, and leave little else to be addressed. The revisionists' explanation for the adoption and persistence of outdoor relief, however, is not as well developed. To date, no study has appeared that adequately explains the economic role of outdoor relief and the reason why it developed in the last third of the eighteenth century.

Three issues must be resolved in order to determine the economic role of outdoor relief. The first concerns the system's origins. Was outdoor relief an emergency response to the high food prices of 1795, as the traditional literature claimed, or was it a response to long-term changes in the economic environment? Evidence from local studies and available data on relief expenditures suggest that outdoor relief became widespread during the period from 1760 to 1795. The year 1795 was not a watershed in the administration of poor relief. I contend that parishes adopted outdoor relief policies in response to two major changes in the economic environment in the south and east of England: the decline in allotments of land for agricultural laborers, and the decline in cottage industry. Before the late eighteenth century, the typical agricultural la-

265

borer's family had three sources of income: a small plot of land for growing food; wage labor in agriculture during peak seasons; and slack-season employment (yearlong for women and children) in cottage industry. The income earned from two of these sources declined sharply after 1760. Parishes responded to the loss in income by guaranteeing seasonally unemployed laborers a minimum weekly income in the form of poor relief.

This raises the second issue: Why was outdoor relief adopted over other methods for dealing with the decline in income, especially in grain-producing areas? To answer this question an economic model was developed that yielded the conditions under which implicit labor contracts including seasonal layoffs and outdoor relief were an efficient method for securing an adequate peak-season labor force. The two key determinants of the form of farmers' cost-minimizing labor contracts were the extent of seasonal fluctuations in the demand for labor (a function of crop mix), and the size of the contribution of non-labor-hiring taxpayers to the poor rate. Contracts containing seasonal layoffs and outdoor relief were cost-minimizing in the grain-producing southeast, while full-employment contracts were cost-minimizing in the pasture-farming west and north.

Even in grain-producing areas, however, the importance of outdoor relief was a function of the share of the poor rate paid by taxpayers who did not hire labor, such as family farmers, artisans, and shopkeepers. The smaller the share of the poor rate paid by labor-hiring farmers, the larger the number of layoffs during slack seasons, other things equal. If labor-hiring farmers paid the entire cost of relieving unemployed workers (that is, if they were perfectly experience-rated), full-employment contracts were cost-minimizing even in grain-producing areas. This is a very important result. Seasonality by itself would not have caused the development of outdoor relief. What was required was a combination of seasonality and a tax system that allowed farmers to be subsidized by other parish taxpayers. A further implication of the fact that some ratepayers subsidized others under the Poor Law is that the administration of relief must have been affected by the political makeup of the parish. The widespread use of outdoor relief suggests that most rural parishes were dominated by labor-hiring farmers, and available evidence supports this conclusion.

The hypotheses advanced in Chapters 1 and 3 concerning the adoption and persistence of outdoor relief were tested using data for 311 rural southern parishes obtained from the 1832 Rural Queries. The results of the regression analysis support several hypotheses of the implicit contracts model. Crop mix, the political power of labor-hiring farmers, the existence of cottage industry, and distance from London were all important determinants of parishes' per capita relief expenditures. The results are consistent with the hypothesis that farmers adopted outdoor relief policies because they were part of a cost-minimizing labor contract.

The last issue that needs to be considered in order to determine the role of outdoor relief is the amendment of the Poor Law in 1834. The abolition of outdoor relief fits nicely into the traditional literature's conclusion that generous poor relief had disastrous consequences for the rural parish economy, but it would appear to pose a problem for the hypotheses advanced in this book. Why would Parliament abolish an institution that farmers considered part of the lowest-cost solution to the problem of seasonality? I contend that the key to understanding the abolition of outdoor relief is the makeup of Parliament. The demand for Poor Law reform did not come from labor-hiring farmers. Indeed, the reports of the assistant Poor Law commissioners who visited parishes in 1832 suggest that "the farming community was stolidly in favor of retaining Speenhamland" (Polanyi 1944: 298–9). However, Parliament was dominated by large landowners, who by 1832 were convinced that outdoor relief represented a threat to their rental income. This fear had existed since at least 1817, but it was heightened by the Captain Swing riots of 1830–1. Landowners supported the Poor Law Amendment Act because it promised to sharply reduce relief expenditures and "restore the social fabric of the countryside," which they believed would increase the value of agricultural land. Unfortunately, the landowners' fears were based to a large extent on hypotheses of the long-run effect of outdoor relief on labor supply and productivity that have since been discredited.

In sum, I conclude that the system of outdoor relief was consciously developed by grain farmers as an inexpensive method to provide income for seasonally unemployed laborers. The system was successful: Regression results for 1832 and available qualitative evidence show that farmers were still using outdoor relief in grain-producing areas when the Royal Commission was formed, and wanted to continue using it. Outdoor relief was abolished not because it had disastrous consequences on the rural economy but rather because the landowners who controlled Parliament feared that such consequences would occur in the future.

2. The Old Poor Law in Perspective

Agricultural production is a long, discontinuous operation with periodic bouts of hectic activities and intervals of relative idleness. Weather dependence not merely makes the timing of each individual operation somewhat unpredictable, it also means that when the time comes the job has to be done very quickly and there are various risks and costs of delay. This implies that the employer is usually keen on entering into some explicit or implicit contract with workers about a dependable supply of labor at the right time. (Bardhan 1980: 92)

The problems created by seasonal fluctuations in the demand for agricultural labor were not confined to early-nineteenth-century England. Seasonality is an inherent characteristic of arable agriculture that continues to pose problems for farmers, particularly in developing countries. However, the solution to seasonality that was adopted in early-nineteenth-century England is unique: the systematic use of poor relief to provide income for seasonally unemployed laborers.[1] One key to understanding why English farmers chose to use outdoor relief is the nature of the local tax system. Because taxpayers who did not hire labor contributed to the poor rate, it was cheaper for farmers to lay off part of their work force in slack seasons than to offer yearlong contracts to all their workers or to provide workers with allotments of land or low-interest consumption credit to get through slack seasons, alternatives that Indian farmers provide today (Bardhan 1979: 488; Bardhan and Rudra 1981: 96–111).

This does not mean, of course, that outdoor relief solved the problem of seasonality. Grain-producing parishes still were plagued by a pool of unemployed laborers each winter. It was in the interest of the parish to find year-round employment for these seasonally unemployed workers. There are two ways to reduce the seasonal underemployment of labor: (1) to reduce the demand for agricultural labor during peak seasons, and (2) to provide nonagricultural employment for seasonally unemployed agricultural laborers. Before we can conclude that outdoor relief represented a cost-minimizing method for dealing with seasonality, we need to consider whether its use slowed the adoption of policies to reduce seasonality.

---

[1] Joan Hannon (1984: 1030–1) found evidence of the payment of poor relief to seasonally unemployed laborers in western New York during the 1850s. Additional research on labor markets in grain-producing areas may reveal that the English solution to seasonality was not unique.

A reduction in the peak season demand for agricultural labor would have reduced the number of workers to whom farmers offered implicit contracts, and, assuming that workers who were not offered contracts left the parish, would have reduced the number of seasonally underemployed workers. Peak-season demand can be reduced by substituting either machinery or migrant workers for parish labor. Did the system of outdoor relief affect farmers' decisions concerning the use of migrant labor or machinery? It was determined in Chapter 3 that farms using the four-course Norfolk system were not amenable to the use of migrant labor at harvest time, because they required as many laborers in March as at harvest. The Poor Law had no effect on farmers' decisions in this case. Farms using the three-course system required many more laborers at harvest than at any other time, and therefore were amenable to the use of migrant labor. However, the use of migrant harvest workers reduced rural underemployment (and farmers' labor costs) only if parish laborers who were made redundant left the parish. Because settled workers were guaranteed poor relief, they might have chosen to remain in the parish on relief rather than leave in search of work. Farmers afraid of this possibility would have chosen not to employ migrant labor. Thus the Poor Law might have helped to perpetuate the underemployment of labor in areas where the three-course system of agriculture predominated.[2] However, parishes anxious to reduce their labor force could have made the conditions for obtaining relief onerous enough to convince redundant workers to leave. The effect of poor relief on the use of migrant labor therefore was small.[3]

Similarly, outdoor relief had little if any effect on harvest technology. The major labor-saving innovations available during the early nineteenth century were the scythe and the heavy hook, which reduced the demand for labor in the harvesting of wheat by 25–45% compared with the traditional hand-reaping tools (Collins 1969a: 82). The adoption of scythes and heavy hooks proceeded rapidly from 1790 to 1815, then slowed down or even declined from 1815 to 1835, the years when relief expenditures were at their peak. However, the trend occurred in France,

[2] By the early nineteenth century, the three-course system was the dominant form of crop rotation only on "the wet and cold clays [of] the midland clay triangle and other districts of similar soils." These soils "remained too wet for the Norfolk system"; they continued to use the three-course system "until cheap under-drainage came in towards the middle of the nineteenth century" (Chambers and Mingay 1966: 58).

[3] The "vast influx" of Irish harvesters into the southeast in the late 1820s is evidence that outdoor relief did not eliminate the demand for migrant labor.

Germany, and northern England as well as in the southeast, which suggests that outdoor relief was not the cause of the slowdown.[4]

The alternative to reducing the peak-season demand for labor was to increase the demand for labor during slack seasons. One way to do this was to promote the seasonal migration of unemployed agricultural workers to the industrial cities. Rural–urban seasonal migration occurred in nineteenth-century France and Russia and in twentieth-century Asia (Redford 1964: 5; Oshima 1958: 261). There is little evidence of seasonal migration from southeastern England either before or after 1834. The fact that seasonal migration from agriculture to urban areas did not occur even after the abolition of outdoor relief suggests that the Poor Law was not the major cause of laborers' winter immobility.

A more widespread solution to the problem of seasonality was the development of nonagricultural employment opportunities within agricultural parishes. Cottage industry developed throughout much of western Europe during the early modern period as an endogenous response to the existence of seasonal surplus labor. In the words of Franklin Mendels (1972: 242), "the role of rural industry consisted of improving the time pattern of rural employment, not so much increasing the productivity of labor as increasing the productivity of workers." Daniel Defoe (1724–6) found cottage industry to be flourishing in large parts of southeast England in the early eighteenth century. However, employment opportunities and wage rates in cottage industry began to decline during the third quarter of the century and had almost disappeared from some southeastern counties by 1832.[5] Eric Jones (1974: 131, 138) attributed the decline in cottage industry to an "improvement of agricultural techniques between 1650 and 1750," which led southern parishes to shift resources from cottage industry to farming. But the new techniques did not eliminate seasonality, so cottage industry still had a role to play in southern parishes after 1750.[6] Moreover, Snell (1981: 413, 421–2) found that the southeast's increased specialization in grain in the second half of

---

[4] One reason for the slow adoption of the scythe and heavy hook was the seasonal labor requirements of the four-course Norfolk system. The high demand for labor in March reduced the benefits to be obtained from the adoption of labor-saving harvesting innovations.

[5] For evidence of the decline in cottage industry, see Chapter 1, Section 3.

[6] According to Timmer (1969: 392–4), the adoption of the four-course rotation increased the annual labor requirements of a typical farm by 45% but did not increase the demand for harvest labor. However, seasonality remained a problem under the four-course system: A 500-acre farm required approximately 65 workers in March and August but fewer than 30 workers during seven months of the year.

the eighteenth century reduced the demand for female labor in agriculture. The decline in female agricultural employment increased the available labor supply for cottage industry. Indeed, Snell (1981: 435–6) and Berg (1985: 124–5) have suggested that the development of lacemaking and straw plaiting in the southeast was caused in part by the decline in agricultural employment for women. The agricultural innovations therefore cannot explain the decline in cottage industry.

It has been suggested that the decline in cottage industry was an endogenous response to the development of outdoor relief. Workers who were guaranteed outdoor relief during slack seasons found it unnecessary to engage in cottage industry, and therefore chose not to work. There are two major problems with this hypothesis. First, parish overseers would not have granted relief to able-bodied workers during slack seasons unless workers were unable to earn a subsistence income from private employment. Cottage industry represented a costless method to the parish for maintaining seasonally redundant agricultural laborers. It therefore was in the parish's interest to promote cottage industry and to use discretion in granting relief. The second problem is one of timing. Cottage industry began to decline in the southeast in the 1750s and 1760s, whereas the widespread adoption of outdoor relief began during the 1770s. In addition, southeastern parishes that responded to the 1824 parliamentary inquiries and the 1832 Rural Queries reported that the decline in cottage industry caused relief expenditures to increase, and not vice versa.[7]

In my opinion, the decline of cottage industry in the southeast was caused by a decline in demand for the goods produced there, as a result of either the drying up of foreign markets or competition from cottage (or modern) industry in the north. It was not an endogenous response to the adoption of outdoor relief. Indeed, many parishes responded to the decline of cottage industry by setting up "houses of industry" intended to profitably employ the poor, including seasonally unemployed workers, in the production of textiles (Webb and Webb 1927: 221–7). Such parish-sponsored cottage industry schemes invariably failed to yield a profit, and were largely abandoned by the early nineteenth century (Webb and Webb 1927: 233–7).

The decline of cottage industry forced grain farmers to find a new solution to the problem of seasonality. They responded by adopting

[7] See Chapter 1, Section 3.

outdoor relief policies. Given the economic environment of the rural southeast, implicit contracts including seasonal layoffs and outdoor relief for unemployed workers represented the lowest-cost method available to grain farmers for securing an adequate peak-season labor force. The fact that labor-hiring farmers dominated parish politics and therefore the administration of relief suggests that outdoor relief policies were consciously designed for the express purpose of reducing labor costs.

REFERENCES

Manuscript Sources

Public Record Office, London

Home Office Papers: H. O. 71.

Bedfordshire County Record Office, Bedford

Ampthill (P. 30/12/10–12), Harrold (P. 33/12/1).

Cambridgeshire County Record Office, Cambridge

Benwick (P 12/12/2), Bourn (P 14/11/1), Cherryhinton (P 39/8/1), Dry Draton (P 58/11/3), Fowlmere (P 72/11/1), Kirtling (P 101/11/2), Little Abington (P 2/11/1), Swaffham Bulbeck (P 149/11/1), Wentworth (P 165/11/1), Wicken (P 172/11/2), Witchford (P 183/11/3).

Essex County Record Offices, Chelmsford and Colchester

Aldham (D/P 208/11/1), Ardleigh (D/P 263/11/5), Ashdon (D/P 18/11/5), Birchanger (D/P 25/8/2), Bobbingsworth (D/P 127/11/3), Boreham (D/P 29/11/1), Broomfield (D/P 248/11/3), Castle Hedingham (D/P 48/12/3), Copford (D/P 186/11), Fingringhoe (D/P 369/11), Great Coggeshall (D/P 36/8/3–5), Great Easton (D/P 232/11/8), Great Leighs (D/P 137/11/4), Great Oakley (D/P 47/11/6), Great Saling (D/P 311/12/2), Great Warley (D/P 195/11/10), Great Yeldham (D/P 275/11), High Roothing (D/P 226/8/1A), Hutton (D/P 143/12/1), Layer Breton (D/P 190/11/1), Little Baddow (D/P 35/11/3), Little Bentley (D/P 359/8), Little Burstead (D/P 100/11), Little Coggeshall (D/P 276/11/1), Little Horksely (D/P 307/12/1), Little Tey (D/P 38/12/3), Messing (D/P 188/12/3), Pebmarsh (D/P 207/11/6–7), Stanford Rivers (D/P 140/8/1–4), Stansted Mountfitchet (D/P 109/8/4–5), Stapleford Tawney (D/P 141/8/1), Steeple Bumstead (D/P 21/8), Stondon Massey (D/P 98/11/2), Terling (D/P 299/8/5), Thaxted (D/P 16/11/3), Tillingham (D/P 237/11/3), Wakes Colne (D/P 88/11/2), White Notley (D/P 39/12/1), Wormingford (D/P 185/11/2).

Suffolk County Record Office, Ipswich

Benhall (FC 131/G16/2), Blaxhall (FC 133/G1/3), Boxford (FB 77/G5/6), Bredfield (FC 27/G1/1), Brome (FB 127/G1/3), Chattisham (FB 63/G1/1), Cransford (FC 128/G1/3), Earl Stonham (FB 23/G7/3), Great Bealings (FC 31/G1/1), Kenton (FB 44/G2/1), Kersey (FB 70/G6/1), Peasenhall (FC 67/G1/2), Polstead (FB 78/G3/11), Redgrave (FB 132/G2/3), Saxtead (FC 102/G3/1), Sibton (FC 61/G2/1), Snape (FC 123/G1/1), Thornham Parva (FB 164/G2/1), Thwaite (FB 153/G4/7), Tunstall (FC 164/G1/3).

Bradford City Library

Bradford Township (Minute Book of Board of Guardians).

Parliamentary Papers

Parl. Papers (1817: VI). *Report from the Select Committee on the Poor Laws.*
Parl. Papers (1818: V). *Report from the Select Committee of the House of Lords on the Poor Laws.*
Parl. Papers (1821: IX). *Report from Committee on the Agriculture of the United Kingdom.*
Parl. Papers (1824: VIa). *Report from the Select Committee on Poor Rate Returns.*
Parl. Papers (1824: VIb). *Report from the Select Committee on Labourers' Wages.*
Parl. Papers (1825: XIX). *Abstract of Returns prepared by order of the Select Committee on Labourers' Wages.*
Parl. Papers (1826–7: V). *Third Report from the Select Committee on Emigration from the United Kingdom.*
Parl. Papers (1830–1: XI). *Local Taxation: Poor Rates, County Rates, Highway Rates, and Church Rates . . . of the several Counties in England and Wales.*
Parl. Papers (1831: VIII). *Report from the Select Committee of the House of Lords Appointed to Consider the Poor Laws.*
Parl. Papers (1831: XVIII). *Comparative Account of the Population of Great Britain . . . With Annual Value of Real Property, 1815.*
Parl. Papers (1833: V). *Report from the Select Committee on the Present State of Agriculture.*
Parl. Papers (1833: XXVI–XXVII). *Census of Great Britain, 1831: Enumeration Abstract.*
Parl. Papers (1834: XXVIII). *Report from His Majesty's Commissioners for Inquiry into the Administration and Practical Operation of the Poor Laws. Appendix A, Part I: Assistant Commissioners' Reports.*
Parl. Papers (1834: XXX–XXXIV). *Report from His Majesty's Commissioners for Inquiry into the Administration and Practical Operation of the Poor Laws. Appendix B1: Answers to Rural Questions.*
Parl. Papers (1834: XXXV–XXXVI). *Report from His Majesty's Commissioners*

for Inquiry into the Administration and Practical Operation of the Poor Laws. Appendix B2: Answers to Town Queries.

Parl. Papers (1834: XXXVIII). *Report from His Majesty's Commissioners for Inquiry into the Administration and Practical Operation of the Poor Laws. Appendix D: Labour Rate.*

Parl. Papers (1835: XXXV). *First Annual Report of the Poor Law Commissioners for England and Wales.*

Parl. Papers (1836: XXIX). *Second Annual Report of the Poor Law Commissioners for England and Wales.*

Parl. Papers (1837: XXXI). *Third Annual Report of the Poor Law Commissioners for England and Wales.*

Parl. Papers (1837–8: XVIII). *Reports from the Select Committee on the Poor Law Amendment Act.*

Parl. Papers (1837–8: XXVIII). *Fourth Annual Report of the Poor Law Commissioners for England and Wales.*

Parl. Papers (1839: XX). *Fifth Annual Report of the Poor Law Commissioners for England and Wales.*

Parl. Papers (1839: XLIV). *Poor Rate Assessment and Expenditure on the Poor in each County of England and Wales, 1748 to 1839.*

Parl. Papers (1840: XVIIa). *Sixth Annual Report of the Poor Law Commissioners for England and Wales.*

Parl. Papers (1840: XVIIb). *Fifth Annual Report of the Poor Law Commissioners for England and Wales. Appendix E.*

Parl. Papers (1840: XVIII). *Fourth Annual Report of the Poor Law Commissioners for England and Wales. Appendix D.*

Parl. Papers (1841: XI). *Seventh Annual Report of the Poor Law Commissioners for England and Wales.*

Parl. Papers (1842: XIX). *Eighth Annual Report of the Poor Law Commissioners for England and Wales.*

Parl. Papers (1843: VII). *Report from the Select Committee on the Labouring Poor (Allotments of Land).*

Parl. Papers (1843: XII). *Report of Special Assistant Poor Law Commissioners on the Employment of Women and Children in Agriculture.*

Parl. Papers (1843: XXI). *Ninth Annual Report of the Poor Law Commissioners for England and Wales.*

Parl. Papers (1844: XIX). *Tenth Annual Report of the Poor Law Commissioners for England and Wales.*

Parl. Papers (1844: XXVII). *Census of Great Britain, 1841. Occupational Abstract.*

Parl. Papers (1844: XL). *A Return of the Average Annual Expenditure of the Parishes comprised in each of the Unions in England and Wales . . . also the Number of In-door and Out-door Paupers relieved during each of the Quarters ended Lady-day 1841, 1842, and 1843.*

Parl. Papers (1845: XXVII). *Eleventh Annual Report of the Poor Law Commissioners for England and Wales.*

Parl. Papers (1846: XIX). *Twelfth Annual Report of the Poor Law Commissioners for England and Wales.*

Parl. Papers (1846: XXXVIa). *Poor Removals from Nineteen Towns in Lancashire, Cheshire, and Yorkshire, 1841–43.*

Parl. Papers (1846: XXXVIb). *A Copy of Reports received by the Poor-Law Commissioners in 1841, on the state of the Macclesfield and Bolton Unions.*

Parl. Papers (1847: XI). *Reports from the Select Committee on Settlement and Poor Removal.*

Parl. Papers (1847: XXVIII). *Thirteenth Annual Report of the Poor Law Commissioners for England and Wales.*

Parl. Papers (1847–8: XXXIII). *Fourteenth Annual Report of the Poor Law Commissioners for England and Wales.*

Parl. Papers (1847–8: LIII). *Returns Relative to Poor Rates, County Rates, Population, etc.*

Parl. Papers (1849: XXV). *First Annual Report of the Poor Law Board.*

Parl. Papers (1849: XLVIIa). *Returns Relating to Rating of Tenements in Lancashire, Suffolk, Hampshire, and Gloucestershire.*

Parl. Papers (1849: XLVIIb). *A Return of the Number of Paupers in the Receipt of Relief in the Several Unions of England and Wales on the 1st day of July 1848.*

Parl. Papers (1850: XXVII). *Second Annual Report of the Poor Law Board.*

Parl. Papers (1851: XXVI). *Third Annual Report of the Poor Law Board.*

Parl. Papers (1851: XLIX). *Return of the Annual Value of Property Assessed to the Poor Rates.*

Parl. Papers (1852: XXIII). *Fourth Annual Report of the Poor Law Board.*

Parl. Papers (1852–3: LXXXVIII). *Census of Great Britain, 1851. Population Tables. II. Ages, Civil Condition, Occupations, and Birth-Place of the People.*

Parl. Papers (1854–5: XIII). *Report from the Select Committee on Poor Removal.*

Parl. Papers (1905: XCVII). *Second Report on the Wages, Earnings, and Conditions of Employment of Agricultural Labourers.*

Books, Pamphlets, Articles, and Papers

Almquist, E. L. (1979). "Pre-Famine Ireland and the Theory of European Proto-Industrialization: Evidence from the 1841 Census." *Journal of Economic History* 39: 699–718.

Apfel, William, and Peter Dunkley (1985). "English Rural Society and the New Poor Law: Bedfordshire, 1834–47." *Social History* 10: 37–68.

Ashby, A. W. (1912). "One Hundred Years of Poor Law Administration in a Warwickshire Village." In P. Vinogradoff (Ed.), *Oxford Studies in Social and Legal History.* Volume 3. Oxford: Oxford University Press.

Ashforth, David (1976). "The Urban Poor Law." In Derek Fraser (Ed.), *The New Poor Law in the Nineteenth Century.* London: Macmillan.

Ashforth, David (1979). "The Poor Law in Bradford c. 1834–1871." Ph.D. dissertation, University of Bradford.

Ashforth, David (1985). "Settlement and Removal in Urban Areas: Bradford,

1834–71." In M. E. Rose (Ed.), *The Poor and the City: The English Poor Law in its Urban Context, 1834–1914.* New York: St. Martin's.

Ashton, T. S. (1955). *An Economic History of England: The Eighteenth Century.* London: Methuen.

Ashton, T. S. (1963). "The Treatment of Capitalism by Historians." In F. A. Hayek (Ed.), *Capitalism and the Historians.* Chicago: University of Chicago Press.

Ashton, T. S. (1964). *The Industrial Revolution 1760–1830.* Oxford: Oxford University Press.

Azariadis, Costas (1975). "Implicit Contracts and Underemployment Equilibria." *Journal of Political Economy* 83: 1183–1202.

Azariadis, Costas (1981). "Implicit Contracts and Related Topics: A Survey." In Zmira Hornstein (Ed.), *The Economics of the Labour Market.* London: HMSO.

Baack, B. D., and R. P. Thomas (1974). "The Enclosure Movement and the Supply of Labour During the Industrial Revolution." *Journal of European Economic History* 3: 401–23.

Baily, Martin N. (1974). "Wages and Employment Under Uncertain Demand." *Review of Economic Studies* 41: 37–50.

Bardhan, Kalpana (1977). "Rural Employment, Wages and Labour Markets in India: A Survey of Research–III." *Economic and Political Weekly* 12: 1101–18.

Bardhan, P. K. (1979). "Wages and Unemployment in a Poor Agrarian Economy: A Theoretical and Empirical Analysis." *Journal of Political Economy* 87: 479–99.

Bardhan, P. K. (1980). "Interlocking Factor Markets and Agrarian Development." *Oxford Economic Papers* 32: 82–98.

Bardhan, P. K., and A. Rudra (1981). "Terms and Conditions of Labour Contracts in Agriculture: Results of a Survey in West Bengal 1979." *Oxford Bulletin of Economics and Statistics* 43: 89–111.

Barnett, D. C. (1968). "Allotments and the Problem of Rural Poverty, 1780–1840." In E. L. Jones and G. E. Mingay (Eds.), *Land, Labour and Population in the Industrial Revolution.* New York: Barnes and Noble.

Bauer, Peter, and Basil Yamey (1957). *The Economics of Underdeveloped Countries.* Chicago: University of Chicago Press.

Baugh, Daniel A. (1975). "The Cost of Poor Relief in South-East England, 1790–1834." *Economic History Review,* 2nd Series, 28: 50–68.

Berg, Maxine (1985). *The Age of Manufactures.* London: Fontana.

Blackmore, J. S., and F. C. Mellonie (1927–8). "Family Endowment and the Birth-Rate in the Early Nineteenth Century." *Economic History* 1: 205–13, 412–18.

Blaug, Mark (1963). "The Myth of the Old Poor Law and the Making of the New." *Journal of Economic History* 23: 151–84.

Blaug, Mark (1964). "The Poor Law Report Reexamined." *Journal of Economic History* 24: 229–45.

Bowley, A. L. (1898). "The Statistics of Wages in the United Kingdom During the Last Hundred Years. Part I. Agricultural Wages." *Journal of the Royal Statistical Society* 61: 702–22.

Bowley, A. L. (1900a). *Wages in the United Kingdom in the Nineteenth Century.* Cambridge: Cambridge University Press.

Bowley, A. L. (1900b). "The Statistics of Wages in the United Kingdom During the Last Hundred Years. Part VI. Wages in the Building Trades – English Towns." *Journal of the Royal Statistical Society* 63: 297–314.

Bowley, A. L. (1901). "The Statistics of Wages in the United Kingdom During the Last Hundred Years. Part VIII. Wages in the Building Trades – Concluded." *Journal of the Royal Statistical Society* 64: 102–12.

Bowley, Marian (1937). *Nassau Senior and Classical Economics.* London: Allen and Unwin.

Boyer, George R. (1982). "The Economic Role of the English Poor Law c. 1780–1834." Ph.D. dissertation, University of Wisconsin–Madison.

Boyer, George R. (1985). "An Economic Model of the English Poor Law circa 1780–1834." *Explorations in Economic History* 22: 129–67.

Boyer, George R. (1986a). "The Old Poor Law and the Agricultural Labor Market in Southern England: An Empirical Analysis." *Journal of Economic History* 46: 113–35.

Boyer, George R. (1986b). "The Poor Law, Migration, and Economic Growth." *Journal of Economic History* 46: 419–30.

Boyer, George R. (1989). "Malthus Was Right After All: Poor Relief and Birth Rates in Southeastern England." *Journal of Political Economy* 97: 93–114.

Boys, John (1796). *General View of the Agriculture of the County of Kent.* London.

Brass, W., and J. C. Barrett (1978). "Measurement Problems in the Analysis of Linkages Between Fertility and Child Mortality." In Samuel H. Preston (Ed.), *The Effects of Infant and Child Mortality on Fertility.* New York: Academic Press.

Braun, R. (1978). "Early Industrialization and Demographic Change in the Canton of Zurich." In C. Tilly (Ed.), *Historical Studies of Changing Fertility.* Princeton, N.J.: Princeton University Press.

Brown, A. F. J. (1969). *Essex at Work 1700–1815.* Chelmsford: Essex Record Office.

Brundage, Anthony (1972). "The Landed Interest and the New Poor Law: A Reappraisal of the Revolution in Government." *English Historical Review* 87: 27–48.

Brundage, Anthony (1974). "The English Poor Law of 1834 and the Cohesion of Agricultural Society." *Agricultural History* 48: 405–17.

Brundage, Anthony (1978). *The Making of the New Poor Law.* New Brunswick, N.J.: Rutgers University Press.

Burdett, Kenneth, and Randall Wright (1989a). "Unemployment Insurance and Short-Time Compensation: The Effect on Layoffs, Hours per Worker, and Wages." *Journal of Political Economy* 97: 1479–96.

Burdett, Kenneth, and Randall Wright (1989b). "Optimal Firm Size, Taxes, and Unemployment." *Journal of Public Economics* 39: 275–88.

Caird, James (1852). *English Agriculture in 1850–51*. London: Longman, Brown, Green, and Longmans.

Cannan, Edwin (1912). *The History of Local Rates in England*. 2nd edition. London: P. S. King.

Chambers, J. D. (1953). "Enclosure and Labour Supply in the Industrial Revolution." *Economic History Review*, 2nd Series, 5: 319–43.

Chambers, J. D., and G. Mingay (1966). *The Agricultural Revolution 1750–1880*. London: B. T. Batsford.

Checkland, S. G., and E. O. A. Checkland (1974). "Introduction." In S. G. and E. O. A. Checkland (Eds.), *The Poor Law Report of 1834*. Harmondsworth: Penguin.

Clapham, J. H. (1930). *An Economic History of Britain: The Early Railway Age*. 2nd edition. Cambridge: Cambridge University Press.

Coats, A. W. (1960). "Economic Thought and Poor Law Policy in the Eighteenth Century." *Economic History Review*, 2nd Series, 13: 39–51.

Collins, E. J. T. (1969a). "Labour Supply and Demand in European Agriculture 1800–1880." In E. L. Jones and S. J. Woolf (Eds.), *Agrarian Change and Economic Development*. London: Methuen.

Collins, E. J. T. (1969b). "Harvest Technology and Labour Supply in Britain." *Economic History Review*, 2nd Series, 22: 45–73.

Collins, E. J. T. (1976). "Migrant Labour in British Agriculture in the Nineteenth Century." *Economic History Review*, 2nd Series, 29: 38–59.

Cowherd, Raymond (1977). *Political Economists and the English Poor Laws*. Athens: Ohio University Press.

Crafts, N. F. R. (1978). "Enclosure and Labor Supply Revisited." *Explorations in Economic History* 15: 172–83.

Crafts, N. F. R. (1982). "Regional Price Variations in England in 1843: An Aspect of the Standard-of-Living Debate." *Explorations in Economic History* 19: 51–70.

Crafts, N. F. R. (1985). *British Economic Growth During the Industrial Revolution*. Oxford: Oxford University Press.

Darby, H. C. (1976). "The Age of the Improver: 1600–1800." In H. C. Darby (Ed.), *A New Historical Geography of England Since 1600*. Cambridge: Cambridge University Press.

Davies, David (1795). *The Case of Labourers in Husbandry*. Bath, England.

Day, R. H., and I. Singh (1977). *Economic Development as an Adaptive Process: The Green Revolution in the Indian Punjab*. Cambridge: Cambridge University Press.

Deane, Phyllis (1979). *The First Industrial Revolution*. 2nd edition. Cambridge: Cambridge University Press.

Deane, Phyllis, and W. A. Cole (1967). *British Economic Growth, 1688–1959*. 2nd edition. Cambridge: Cambridge University Press.

Defoe, Daniel (1724–6). *A Tour Through the Whole Island of Great Britain*. 2 volumes. Reprinted 1962. London: Dent.

Digby, Anne (1975). "The Labour Market and the Continuity of Social Policy after 1834: The Case of the Eastern Counties." *Economic History Review*, 2nd Series, 28: 69–83.

Digby, Anne (1976). "The Rural Poor Law." In Derek Fraser (Ed.), *The New Poor Law in the Nineteenth Century.* London: Macmillan.

Digby, Anne (1978). *Pauper Palaces.* London: Routledge and Kegan Paul.

Dunkley, Peter (1973). "The Landed Interest and the New Poor Law: A Critical Note." *English Historical Review* 88: 836–41.

Eden, Frederic Morton (1797). *The State of the Poor.* 3 volumes. Reprinted 1966. London: Frank Cass.

Edsall, Nicholas C. (1971). *The Anti-Poor Law Movement 1834–44.* Manchester: Manchester University Press.

Ehrenberg, Ronald, and Robert Smith (1982). *Modern Labor Economics.* Glenview, Ill.: Scott, Foresman.

Emmison, F. G. (1933). "The Relief of the Poor at Eaton Socon, 1706–1834." *Bedfordshire Historical Record Society Publications* 15: 1–98.

Ernle, Lord (R. E. Prothero) (1912). *English Farming Past and Present.* London: Longmans, Green.

Evans, Eric J. (1983). *The Great Reform Act of 1832.* London: Methuen.

Fairlie, Susan (1969). "The Corn Laws and British Wheat Production, 1829–1876." *Economic History Review,* 2nd Series, 22: 88–116.

Feinstein, C. H. (1978). "Capital Formation in Great Britain." In Peter Mathias and M. M. Postan (Eds.), *Cambridge Economic History of Europe.* Vol. 7, part 1. Cambridge: Cambridge University Press.

Feldstein, Martin (1978). "The Effect of Unemployment Insurance on Temporary Layoff Unemployment." *American Economic Review* 68: 834–46.

Fishlow, Albert (1961). "The Trustee Savings Banks, 1817–1861." *Journal of Economic History* 21: 26–40.

Fox, A. Wilson (1903). "Agricultural Wages in England and Wales During the Last Fifty Years." *Journal of the Royal Statistical Society* 66: 273–348.

Fussell, G., and M. Compton (1939). "Agricultural Adjustments After the Napoleonic Wars." *Economic History* 3: 184–204.

Gallant, A. Ronald (1987). *Nonlinear Statistical Models.* New York: Wiley.

Gayer, A. D., W. W. Rostow, and A. Schwartz (1953). *The Growth and Fluctuation of the British Economy 1790–1850.* 2 volumes. Oxford: Oxford University Press.

Gilboy, Elizabeth W. (1934). *Wages in Eighteenth Century England.* Cambridge, Mass.: Harvard University Press.

Gonner, E. C. K. (1912). *Common Land and Inclosure.* Reprinted 1966. London: Frank Cass.

Gordon, Donald F. (1974). "A Neo-Classical Theory of Keynesian Unemployment." *Economic Inquiry* 12: 431–59.

Greenwood, M. J., and L. Thomas (1973). "Geographic Labor Mobility in Nineteenth Century England and Wales." *Annals of Regional Science* 7: 90–105.

Griffith, G. T. (1926). *Population Problems in the Age of Malthus.* Cambridge: Cambridge University Press.

Hammond, John, and Barbara Hammond (1913). *The Village Labourer 1760–1832.* 2nd edition. London: Longmans, Green.

Hampson, E. M. (1934). *The Treatment of Poverty in Cambridgeshire, 1597–1834.* Cambridge: Cambridge University Press.

Hannon, Joan (1984). "Poverty in the Antebellum Northeast: The View from New York State's Poor Relief Roles." *Journal of Economic History* 44: 1007–32.

Hasbach, W. (1908). *A History of the English Agricultural Labourer.* London: P. S. King.

Healy, M. J. R., and E. L. Jones (1962). "Wheat Yields in England, 1815–59." *Journal of the Royal Statistical Society* 125: 574–9.

Hirashima, S., and M. Muqtada (Eds.) (1986). *Hired Labour and Rural Labour Markets in Asia.* New Delhi: ILO.

Hobsbawm, Eric (1968). *Industry and Empire.* Harmondsworth: Penguin.

Hobsbawm, Eric (1975). "The British Standard of Living, 1790–1850." In A. J. Taylor (Ed.), *The Standard of Living in Britain in the Industrial Revolution.* London: Methuen.

Hobsbawm, Eric, and George Rudé (1968). *Captain Swing.* New York: Pantheon.

Howlett, John (1792). "The Different Quantity, and Expence of Agricultural Labour, in Different Years." *Annals of Agriculture* 18: 566–72.

Huberman, Michael (1986). "Invisible Handshakes in Lancashire: Cotton Spinning in the First Half of the Nineteenth Century." *Journal of Economic History* 46: 987–98.

Huberman, Michael (1987). "The Economic Origins of Paternalism: Lancashire Cotton Spinning in the First Half of the Nineteenth Century." *Social History* 12: 177–92.

Hunt, E. H. (1973). *Regional Wage Variations in Britain 1850–1914.* Oxford: Oxford University Press.

Hunt, E. H. (1981). *British Labour History 1815–1914.* London: Weidenfeld and Nicolson.

Huzel, James P. (1969). "Malthus, the Poor Law, and Population in Early Nineteenth-Century England." *Economic History Review*, 2nd Series, 22: 430–52.

Huzel, James P. (1980). "The Demographic Impact of the Old Poor Law: More Reflexions on Malthus." *Economic History Review*, 2nd Series, 33: 367–81.

James, John (1857). *History of the Worsted Manufacture in England.* London.

Jones, E. L. (1964). *Seasons and Prices.* London: Allen and Unwin.

Jones, E. L. (1974). *Agriculture and the Industrial Revolution.* Oxford: Basil Blackwell.

Jones, Gareth Stedman (1971). *Outcast London.* Oxford: Oxford University Press.

Kain, Roger J. P. (1986). *An Atlas and Index of the Tithe Files of Mid-Nineteenth-Century England and Wales.* Cambridge: Cambridge University Press.

Kain, Roger J. P., and Hugh C. Prince (1985). *The Tithe Surveys of England and Wales.* Cambridge: Cambridge University Press.

Kerr, Barbara M. (1942–3). "Irish Seasonal Migration to Great Britain, 1800–38." *Irish Historical Studies* 3: 365–80.

Kidd, Alan J. (1987). "Historians or Polemicists? How the Webbs Wrote Their History of the English Poor Laws." *Economic History Review*, 2nd Series, 40: 400–17.

Krause, J. T. (1958). "Changes in English Fertility and Mortality, 1781–1850." *Economic History Review*, 2nd Series, 11: 52–70.

Laslett, Peter (1971). *The World We Have Lost*. 2nd edition. New York: Scribner.

Laslett, Peter (1972). "Mean Household Size in England Since the Sixteenth Century." In Peter Laslett and Richard Wall (Eds.), *Household and Family in Past Time*. Cambridge: Cambridge University Press.

Lee, Ronald D. (1980). "A Historical Perspective on Economic Aspects of the Population Explosion: The Case of Preindustrial England." In R. A. Easterlin (Ed.), *Population and Economic Change in Developing Countries*. Chicago: University of Chicago Press.

Lesthaeghe, R. J. (1977). *The Decline of Belgian Fertility, 1800–1970*. Princeton, N.J.: Princeton University Press.

Levine, David (1984). "Parson Malthus, Professor Huzel, and the Pelican Inn Protocol." *Historical Methods* 17: 21–4.

Lewis, W. Arthur (1954). "Economic Development with Unlimited Supplies of Labour." *Manchester School of Economic and Social Studies* 22: 139–91.

Lindert, Peter H. (1980). "Child Costs and Economic Development." In R. A. Easterlin (Ed.), *Population and Economic Change in Developing Countries*. Chicago: University of Chicago Press.

Lindert, Peter H. (1983). "English Living Standards, Population Growth, and Wrigley–Schofield." *Explorations in Economic History* 20: 131–55.

Lindert, Peter H., and Jeffrey G. Williamson (1983). "English Workers' Living Standards During the Industrial Revolution: A New Look." *Economic History Review*, 2nd Series, 36: 1–25.

Lindert, Peter H., and Jeffrey G. Williamson (1985). "English Workers' Real Wages: Reply to Crafts." *Journal of Economic History* 45: 145–53.

Lloyd-Prichard, M. F. (1949). "The Treatment of Poverty in Norfolk from 1700 to 1850." Ph.D. dissertation, Cambridge University.

Lloyd-Prichard, M. F. (1951). "The Decline of Norwich." *Economic History Review*, 2nd Series, 3: 371–7.

Lyons, John (1987). "Family Response to Economic Decline: Handloom Weavers in Early Nineteenth-Century Lancashire." Department of Economics, Miami University. Working Paper No. 87–05.

MacKinnon, Mary (1986). "Poor Law Policy, Unemployment, and Pauperism." *Explorations in Economic History* 23: 299–336.

MacKinnon, Mary (1987). "English Poor Law Policy and the Crusade Against Outrelief." *Journal of Economic History* 47: 603–25.

Malthus, Thomas (1798). *An Essay on the Principle of Population*. 1st edition. London: J. Johnson.

Malthus, Thomas (1807a). *An Essay on the Principle of Population*. 4th edition. 2 volumes. London: J. Johnson.

Malthus, Thomas (1807b). *A Letter to Samuel Whitbread . . . on His Proposed Bill for the Amendment of the Poor Laws*. 2nd edition. Reprinted in

The Pamphlets of Thomas Robert Malthus, 1970. New York: Augustus Kelley.

Malthus, Thomas (1817). *An Essay on the Principle of Population*. 5th edition. 3 volumes. London: John Murray.

Mantoux, Paul (1928). *The Industrial Revolution in the Eighteenth Century*. Reprinted 1952. London: Jonathan Cape.

Marshall, Dorothy (1926). *The English Poor in the Eighteenth Century*. Reprinted 1969. New York: Augustus Kelley.

Marshall, J. D. (1968). *The Old Poor Law 1795–1834*. London: Macmillan.

Matthews, R. C. O. (1954). *A Study in Trade-Cycle History: Economic Fluctuations in Great Britain, 1833–42*. Cambridge: Cambridge University Press.

McCloskey, Donald (1973). "New Perspectives on the Old Poor Law." *Explorations in Economic History* 10: 419–36.

Mendels, Franklin (1972). "Proto-Industrialization: The First Phase of the Industrialization Process." *Journal of Economic History* 32: 241–61.

Mendels, Franklin (1982). "Protoindustrialization: Theory and Reality." In *Eighth International Economic History Congress, Budapest, 1982: "A" Themes*. Budapest: Akadémiai Kiadó.

Midwinter, Eric C. (1969). *Social Administration in Lancashire, 1830–1860: Poor Law, Public Health and Police*. Manchester: Manchester University Press.

Mitchell, B. R., and Phyllis Deane (1962). *Abstract of British Historical Statistics*. Cambridge: Cambridge University Press.

Mokyr, Joel (1976). *Industrialization in the Low Countries, 1795–1850*. New Haven, Conn.: Yale University Press.

Mokyr, Joel (1985a). *Why Ireland Starved*. London: Allen and Unwin.

Mokyr, Joel (1985b). "The Industrial Revolution and the New Economic History." In Joel Mokyr (Ed.), *The Economics of the Industrial Revolution*. Totowa, N.J.: Rowman and Allanheld.

Mujumdar, N. A. (1961). *Some Problems of Underemployment*. Bombay: Popular Book Depot.

Nakamura, Alice, and Masao Nakamura (1981). "On the Relationships Among Several Specification Error Tests Presented by Durbin, Wu, and Hausman." *Econometrica* 49: 1583–8.

Neuman, Mark (1969). "A Suggestion Regarding the Origins of the Speenhamland Plan." *English Historical Review* 84: 317–22.

Neuman, Mark (1972). "Speenhamland in Berkshire." In E. W. Martin (Ed.), *Comparative Development in Social Welfare*. London: Allen and Unwin.

Nicholls, George (1898). *A History of the English Poor Law*. 2 volumes. London: P. S. King.

Okun, Arthur M. (1981). *Prices and Quantities: A Macroeconomic Analysis*. Washington, D.C.: Brookings Institution.

Olney, Martha L. (1983). "Fertility and the Standard of Living in Early Modern England: In Consideration of Wrigley and Schofield." *Journal of Economic History* 43: 71–7.

Oshima, Harry T. (1958). "Underemployment in Backward Economies – An Empirical Comment." *Journal of Political Economy* 66: 259–64.

Oxley, Geoffrey (1974). *Poor Relief in England and Wales, 1601–1834.* London: David and Charles.

Pepelasis, A. A., and P. A. Yotopoulos (1962). *Surplus Labor in Greek Agriculture, 1953–1960.* Athens: Center of Planning and Economic Research.

Phelps Brown, E. H., and S. V. Hopkins (1956). "Seven Centuries of the Prices of Consumables, Compared with Builders' Wage-Rates." *Economica* 23: 296–314.

Pinchbeck, Ivy (1930). *Women Workers and the Industrial Revolution, 1750–1850.* Reprinted 1981. London: Virago.

Pindyck, Robert S., and Daniel L. Rubinfeld (1976). *Econometric Models and Economic Forecasts.* New York: McGraw-Hill.

Polanyi, Karl (1944). *The Great Transformation.* New York: Farrar and Rinehart.

Pollard, Sidney (1968). *The Genesis of Modern Management.* Harmondsworth: Penguin.

Pollard, Sidney (1978). "Labour in Great Britain." In Peter Mathias and M. Postan (Eds.), *Cambridge Economic History of Europe,* Vol. 7, part 1. Cambridge: Cambridge University Press.

Poynter, Sidney (1969). *Society and Pauperism.* London: Routledge and Kegan Paul.

Prince, H. C. (1976). "England Circa 1800." In H. C. Darby (Ed.), *A New Historical Geography of England Since 1600.* Cambridge: Cambridge University Press.

Raup, Philip M. (1963). "The Contribution of Land Reforms to Agricultural Development: An Analytical Framework." *Economic Development and Cultural Change* 12: 1–21.

Redford, Arthur (1964). *Labour Migration in England, 1800–1850.* 2nd edition. Manchester: Manchester University Press.

Ricardo, David (1821). *On The Principles of Political Economy and Taxation.* 3rd edition. Reprinted 1951. Cambridge: Cambridge University Press.

Rodgers, G. B. (1975). "Nutritionally Based Wage Determination in the Low-Income Labour Market." *Oxford Economic Papers* 27: 61–81.

Rogerson, Richard, and Randall Wright (1988). "Involuntary Unemployment in Economies with Efficient Risk Sharing." *Journal of Monetary Economics* 22: 501–15.

Rose, M. E. (1965). "The Administration of Poor Relief in the West Riding of Yorkshire c. 1820–1855." Ph.D. dissertation, Oxford University.

Rose, M. E. (1966). "The Allowance System Under the New Poor Law." *Economic History Review,* 2nd Series, 19: 607–20.

Rose, M. E. (1970). "The New Poor Law in an Industrial Area." In R. M. Hartwell (Ed.), *The Industrial Revolution.* Oxford: Oxford University Press.

Rose, M. E. (1976). "Settlement, Removal and the New Poor Law." In Derek Fraser (Ed.), *The New Poor Law in the Nineteenth Century.* London: Macmillan.

Rosen, Sherwin (1985). "Implicit Contracts: A Survey." *Journal of Economic Literature* 23: 1144–75.

Rosenzweig, Mark R., and Kenneth I. Wolpin (1986). "Evaluating the Effects of

Optimally Distributed Public Programs: Child Health and Family Planning Interventions." *American Economic Review* 76: 470–82.

Royal Commission to Investigate the Poor Laws (1833). *Extracts from the Information Received as to the Administration and Operation of the Poor Laws.* London: B. Fellows.

Royal Commission to Investigate the Poor Laws (1834). *Report on the Administration and Practical Operation of the Poor Laws.* London: B. Fellows.

Rudra, A., and R. Biswas (1973). "Seasonality of Employment in Agriculture." *Economic and Political Weekly* 8: A91–100.

Schofield, Roger (1970). "Age-Specific Mobility in an Eighteenth Century Rural English Parish." *Annales de Démographie Historique*, 261–74.

Schultz, T. Paul (1969). "An Economic Model of Family Planning and Fertility." *Journal of Political Economy* 77: 153–80.

Schultz, Theodore W. (1964). *Transforming Traditional Agriculture.* New Haven, Conn.: Yale University Press.

Schultz, Theodore W. (1980). "Nobel Lecture: The Economics of Being Poor." *Journal of Political Economy* 88: 639–51.

Schwarz, L. D. (1986). "The Standard of Living in the Long Run: London, 1700–1860." *Economic History Review*, 2nd Series, 39: 24–41.

Sen, A. K. (1977). "Famines, Food Availability and Exchange Entitlements." *Cambridge Journal of Economics* 1: 33–59.

Sen, A. K. (1981). *Poverty and Famines.* Oxford: Oxford University Press.

Senior, Nassau (1831). *Three Lectures on the Rate of Wages.* 2nd edition. Reprinted 1966. New York: Augustus Kelley.

Smith, Adam (1776). *The Wealth of Nations.* Reprinted 1937. New York: Modern Library.

Smith, Richard M. (1981). "Fertility, Economy, and Household Formation in England over Three Centuries." *Population and Development Review* 7: 595–622.

Snell, K. D. M. (1981). "Agricultural Seasonal Unemployment, the Standard of Living, and Women's Work in the South and East, 1690–1860." *Economic History Review*, 2nd Series, 34: 407–37.

Snell, K. D. M. (1985). *Annals of the Labouring Poor.* Cambridge: Cambridge University Press.

Tawney, R. H. (1926). *Religion and the Rise of Capitalism.* Reprinted 1980. Harmondsworth: Penguin.

Taylor, J. S. (1969). "The Mythology of the Old Poor Law." *Journal of Economic History* 29: 292–7.

Taylor, J. S. (1972). "The Unreformed Workhouse, 1776–1834." In E. W. Martin (Ed.), *Comparative Development in Social Welfare.* London: Allen and Unwin.

Teitelbaum, M. S. (1984). *The British Fertility Decline.* Princeton, N.J.: Princeton University Press.

Thompson, E. P. (1966). *The Making of the English Working Class.* New York: Vintage.

Timmer, C. Peter (1969). "The Turnip, the New Husbandry, and the English Agricultural Revolution." *Quarterly Journal of Economics* 83: 375–95.

Todaro, Michael (1980). "Internal Migration in Developing Countries: A Survey." In Richard Easterlin (Ed.), *Population and Economic Change in Developing Countries*. Chicago: University of Chicago Press.

Townsend, Joseph (1786). *A Dissertation on the Poor Laws*. Reprinted 1971. Berkeley: University of California Press.

Treble, James (1979). *Urban Poverty in Britain 1830–1914*. New York: St. Martin's.

Tucker, G. S. L. (1975). "The Old Poor Law Revisited." *Explorations in Economic History* 12: 233–52.

Turner, Michael (1980). *English Parliamentary Enclosure*. Hamden, Conn.: Archon.

Van Ginneken, Jeroen K. (1974). "Prolonged Breastfeeding as a Birth Spacing Method." *Studies Family Planning* 5: 201–6.

Vancouver, Charles (1795). *General View of the Agriculture in the County of Essex*. London: W. Smith.

Vedder, R. K., and D. Cooper (1974). "Nineteenth Century English and Welsh Geographic Labor Mobility: Some Further Evidence." *Annals of Regional Science* 8: 131–9.

Von Tunzelmann, G. N. (1985). "The Standard of Living Debate and Optimal Economic Growth." In Joel Mokyr (Ed.), *The Economics of the Industrial Revolution*. Totowa, N.J.: Rowman and Allanheld.

Wall, Richard (1984). "Real Property, Marriage and Children: The Evidence from Four Pre-industrial Communities." In Richard M. Smith (Ed.), *Land, Kinship and Life-Cycle*. Cambridge: Cambridge University Press.

Webb, Sidney, and Beatrice Webb (1927). *English Local Government: English Poor Law History: The Old Poor Law*. London: Longmans, Green.

Webb, Sidney, and Beatrice Webb (1929). *English Local Government: English Poor Law History: The Last Hundred Years*. London: Longmans, Green.

Williams, Karel (1981). *From Pauperism to Poverty*. London: Routledge and Kegan Paul.

Williamson, Jeffrey G. (1982). "The Structure of Pay in Britain, 1710–1911." *Research in Economic History* 7: 1–54.

Williamson, Jeffrey G. (1985a). *Did British Capitalism Breed Inequality?* Boston: Allen and Unwin.

Williamson, Jeffrey G. (1985b). "Did Rising Emigration Cause Fertility to Decline in 19th Century Rural England?" Harvard Institute of Economic Research Discussion Paper No. 1172, Harvard University.

Williamson, Jeffrey G. (1985c). "The Urban Transition During the First Industrial Revolution: England 1776–1871." Harvard Institute of Economic Research Discussion Paper No. 1146, Harvard University.

Williamson, Jeffrey G. (1987). "Did English Factor Markets Fail During the Industrial Revolution?" *Oxford Economic Papers* 39: 641–78.

Williamson, Jeffrey G. (1988). "Migrant Selectivity, Urbanization, and Industrial Revolutions." *Population and Development Review* 14: 287–314.

Wrigley, E. A. (1967). "A Simple Model of London's Importance in Changing English Society and Economy, 1650–1750." *Past and Present*, no. 37: 44–70.

Wrigley, E. A. (1977). "Births and Baptisms: The Use of Anglican Baptism Registers as a Source of Information About the Numbers of Births in England Before the Beginning of Civil Registration." *Population Studies* 31: 281–312.

Wrigley, E. A. (1981). "Marriage, Fertility and Population Growth in Eighteenth-Century England." In R. B. Outhwaite (Ed.), *Marriage and Society: Studies in the Social History of Marriage.* New York: St. Martin's.

Wrigley, E. A. (1983). "The Growth of Population in Eighteenth-Century England: A Conundrum Resolved." *Past and Present,* no. 98: 121–50.

Wrigley, E. A., and R. S. Schofield (1981). *The Population History of England, 1541–1871: A Reconstruction.* Cambridge, Mass.: Harvard University Press.

Young, Arthur (1788). "On the Prices of Wool, and State of Spinning at Present in England." *Annals of Agriculture* 9: 266–78, 349–64.

Young, Arthur (1797). *General View of the Agriculture of the County of Suffolk.* London.

Young, Arthur (1800). *The Question of Scarcity Plainly Stated, and Remedies Considered.* London: Richardson.

Young, Arthur (1801). "An Inquiry into the Propriety of Applying Wastes to the Better Maintenance and Support of the Poor." *Annals of Agriculture* 36: 497–658.

Young, Arthur (1807). *General View of the Agriculture of the County of Essex.* London.

Young, Arthur (1808). *General Report on Enclosures.* Drawn up by order of The Board of Agriculture. Reprinted 1971. New York: Augustus Kelley.

INDEX

Abstract of Returns Relative to the State of the Poor, 22

administration of poor relief, 1, 4, 10–23, 57, 143, 151, 195, 200, 266; and birth rates, 167–71; central boards in 201–2; in cities, 239; data on, 122; discretion in, 3, 20–1, 23, 43, 80; labor-hiring farmers in, 81, 94–5, 200, 272; landowners in, 198–9, 200–1, 203; and migration of surplus labor, 261; under New Poor Law, 205–8; timing of changes in, 9, 23–30; variables affecting, 94–9; *see also* outdoor relief; poor relief

aged (the), 23, 219, 246, 253, 258

agrarian riots, *see* Captain Swing riots

agriculture: complementarity with cottage industry, 40–1; depression in, 28–9, 226–8, 231; seasonality in, 86–93; three/four-course rotation system, 88, 113–15, 116, 117, 269; *see also* labor market

Alconbury, Huntingdon, 33

allotment schemes, 4, 54, 55, 57, 58, 67, 68–9; in labor contracts, 100–1; private, 101n21

allotments, 32, 47, 63, 73, 124, 136, 213, 268; and birth rates, 160–1, 164, 167; cross-county variations in, 131, 132t; decline of, 32n28, 34–7, 35t, 42, 43; effects of, 138–40, 205, 224–5; outdoor relief in answer to decline in, 265–6; and poor relief, 117, 125, 126; and poor relief expenditures, 36–7, 38, 127, 138, 148; prevalence and size of, 216–17

allowances-in-aid-of-wages (allowance system), 10–14, 16, 19, 20, 25, 31n27, 43, 73–4, 82, 201–2; abolition of, 76, 206, 207; decline in 49; as dominant form of poor relief, 78–9; effect on birth rates, 152–3; effect on work–leisure decision, 19, 20f; effects of, 61, 67–8, 70, 77; farmers and, 62–3; inadequacy of, 80–1; and

increase in poor relief expenditures, 127, 137, 138, 142, 143, 146

Almquist, E. L., 161n15

Ampthill, Bedfordshire, 91–3, 92t; Poor Law Union, 223

Apfel, William, 206, 208, 210n21

Ashforth, David, 233n1, 237n9, 246n18, 253, 254n27

Ashton, T. S., 6, 170n26, 173n1

Ashworth, Edmund, 259, 260

Azariadis, Costas, 101

Badwell Ash, Suffolk, 42

Baily, Martin N., 101

Baines, Edward, 259n30

Bardhan, P. K., 86, 87

Baugh, Daniel, 2, 3, 12, 28, 79–80, 84, 173, 265

Bedfordshire, 11, 12n4, 24, 39, 40, 131, 156n8, 208, 210n21, 220

benefit–wage ratios, 2–3, 15n12, 77–8

Bentham, Jeremy, 60

Berg, Maxine, 38n37, 271

Berkshire, 12n4, 24–5, 39, 156n8, 221, 223, 227, 230; allowance scales, 10, 11, 54

Bingham, Nottinghamshire, 209

birth rates, 205; analysis of determinants of, 155–64; effect of child allowances on, 4–5, 15, 155–64, 172; effect of poor relief on, 1, 3, 7, 150–72; long-term increases in, 167–71; variations across parishes, 156–64

Blackmore, J. S., 151, 152

Blaug, Mark, 2, 3, 4, 11, 15n12, 20, 51, 80, 81, 82, 83–4, 90n6, 96n18, 110n33, 124, 128, 146, 151–2, 173, 265; analysis of Poor Law, 76–9

Bottisham, Cambridgeshire, 16n15

Bowley, Arthur L., 44, 123n1, 131n7

Boys, John, 37

288